# Health for Everyone

# Health for Everyone

## A Guide to Politically and Socially Progressive Healthcare

Edited by Zackary Berger

ROWMAN & LITTLEFIELD
*Lanham • Boulder • New York • London*

Published by Rowman & Littlefield
An imprint of The Rowman & Littlefield Publishing Group, Inc.
4501 Forbes Boulevard, Suite 200, Lanham, Maryland 20706
www.rowman.com

86-90 Paul Street, London EC2A 4NE

British Library Cataloguing in Publication Information Available

**Library of Congress Cataloging-in-Publication Data**

Names: Berger, Zackary, 1973- editor.
Title: Health for everyone : a guide to politically and socially
    progressive healthcare / edited by Zackary Berger.
Description: Lanham : Rowman & Littlefield, [2022] | Includes
    bibliographical references and index. | Summary: "Health for Everyone is
    a guide to making our health care system more progressive and features
    contributions from clinicians, researchers, and advocates for those that
    are disadvantaged, overlooked, and historically oppressed within the US
    healthcare system"— Provided by publisher.
Identifiers: LCCN 2021048903 (print) | LCCN 2021048904 (ebook) | ISBN
    9781538141854 (cloth) | ISBN 9781538141861 (epub)
Subjects: LCSH: Medical care, Cost of—United States. | Medical
    economics—United States.
Classification: LCC RA410.53 .H4485 2022  (print) | LCC RA410.53 (ebook) |
    DDC 338.4736210973—dc23/eng/20211116
LC record available at https://lccn.loc.gov/2021048903
LC ebook record available at https://lccn.loc.gov/2021048904

# Contents

# 1

## What Is Progressive Healthcare?

*Zackary Berger*

### INCREMENTALISM VERSUS FUNDAMENTAL CHANGE

Sometimes you need to make a revolution, and sometimes the best way to change things is little by little. You can criticize the ways in which the Affordable Care Act, for instance, cemented a system based on immoral and corrupt private insurance, and postponed the moment of reckoning in which the system is moved toward single payer or universal healthcare. Even so, the Affordable Care Act added millions of people to the insurance rolls and decreased the proportion of uninsured. Progressivism does not necessarily mean wholesale remaking of systems, but rather the moving of the needle toward good, even within imperfect systems.

But there is so much that can't be changed little by little. So often the injustices are baked into the system, and you need a revolution to fix things. Such injustices include the abandonment of the marginalized to the economic logic of the capitalist nation-state; the difference in care received by African Americans (and other marginalized groups) compared to others; the ways in which reproductive healthcare, care for trans people, and other types of care is stigmatized and sometimes not provided at all. To say that the problem of healthcare is merely inequality or disparities, while potentially laudable, can obscure the larger systemic issues that underlie injustice in health.[1] It is not just that people in certain groups, or certain individuals, do not receive the care due them, it's that different sorts of people need care tailored to their needs, which is not provided either.

There are different kinds of revolution, but we take as our model political theories of revolution, which have to do with upending an established order to achieve something new. Our revolution must answer three questions: what is the system we seek to change, what are the goals for which we aim, and how do we get there?

The system we seek to change is not just the healthcare system. The healthcare system is large, important, and capacious, but it does not include everything in our society that affects health. Health involves a sense of well-being in all domains of life. Thus, cultural and political sectors that determine, and control, patterns of life directly affect health, and a health revolution must change these as well.

If our view is broad—there are few areas of society that are not included in this broad definition—it stands to reason that our goals must be broad as well. Our goals are not derived from any belief in a utopian state of existence, or a completed revolution that will bring society to its desired end. We can't hope to reach perfection. But neither are they derived from a notion that all measures of control, all regulations and institutions are by their nature suspect. The former is the realm of the spiritual or the eschatological, not of health. The latter, complete mistrust of institutions, does not work either, because there is benefit in the advances of modern medicine.

Remaking healthcare with a progressive vision must be founded on two principles: (a) the equality of every individual and (b) the existence in past and present of groups that have been the subject of oppression, marginalization, and vulnerability. Even though the equality of individuals as human beings deserving of respectful treatment seems obvious, our healthcare system does not act this way, and we need to consider how to get there. Beyond individuals, however, is the issue of particular groups that have been the victim of historical and present-day processes. We cannot remake our system without having in mind those who suffer most at its hands.

These twin principles—the equality of every individual and the existence of socially, politically, and historically disadvantaged subgroups—cannot help but conflict. Each individual cannot at the same time both be treated equally but unequally depending on the subgroup. We cannot both treat everyone equally but differently. To figure out when we consider a patient's subgroup and when we do not—to understand how we redesign our healthcare system to treat both groups and individuals—requires having a specific end goal in mind. What would a progressive healthcare system look like, in terms of the goals it achieves?

One ethical priority is equality of access and outcomes. If we didn't know anything about the belonging or identification of two people, we would want them to have exactly the same spectrum of opportunities and ways to fulfill their goals, desires, and talents in life. Of the various health problems that could happen to a person during their time on this earth, we would want that person—whoever they are, wherever they are—to be treated the best way.

In order to make that attention to the individual equal for all, systematic change—revolution—needs to occur, but a particular kind of systematic change. Changing how existing systems see patients, how patients are put through the system, how the electronic medical record treats patients, these cannot possibly amount to a thoroughgoing change that ensures that each individual is treated according to their desires and concerns. Why not? Because healthcare systems are aimed at groups.

The tools of our current healthcare system are all meant to achieve population health goals: controlling blood pressure, for example, or getting blood sugar in the proper range in diabetes; screening for breast cancer; ensuring that blood tests are done only for good reasons.

Do our healthcare systems aim at groups in a progressive way? Does it even make sense to talk about morally "good" or "bad" healthcare systems? Can we relate to a system—a political unit, a sports team, a university, a church—the same way in which we relate to a person? If we are morally obligated to other people, we expect that in turn they will be obligated to us. That's the Golden Rule. But we do not expect love from institutions—only from other people. We do not expect love from our boss or our department.

Of course, there are beings and entities to which we express allegiance without expecting love or commitment in return (e.g., animals or human beings who might be unable to communicate or express love in a way which we are able to interpret). But we do that because they are living creatures.

If we believe that we have moral obligations to a system, we do that because the system represents a set of values to us, or a history, or a shared culture. The broken healthcare system does none of these things. On the contrary, it fails to inspire loyalty or commitment because the values it represents are not those most people consider ideal for human beings.

Thus, remaking our system—revolutionizing it—should have a goal placing individuals and disadvantaged groups at the center. The system should be obviously humane. Now it is frequently and clearly the opposite. One big reason this is the case: gatekeepers. The system puts walls in front of people getting care.

Care is not freely available; clinicians (mostly physicians) decide what care can be provided and denied. There is much vitriol currently aimed, deservedly so, at insurance companies and pharmacy benefit managers who act as gatekeepers in the way of needed care. The first decision, however, is usually made by the clinician. Not all gatekeeping on the part of clinicians is justified. Sometimes doctors and nurses make decisions that limit the care that people need.

On the basis of much published literature, we know that clinicians—doctors and to a lesser extent nurses—are still biased in the way that they understand what care people need.

Thus, the revolution in the system must enable individuals to direct their own care, to put them in the driver's seat; acknowledging the expertise they have and providing them the needed additional expertise to get them control of needed care.

We might think that we could get rid of clinicians' bias little by little—incrementally making them better gatekeepers, more conscious of the true situation of patients. Such clinicians would work with patients, not in service of an unattainable, supposedly  bias-free medicine that is actually biased toward the powerful.

But eliminating the bias of providers is an impossible goal, because the structure of the system itself encourages and incentivizes such bias. Moreover, the need for expert advice will not be eliminated. Even if patients are put in the driver's seat they will not be able to control or navigate the fiendishly complicated biomedical system, even if major parts of it are dismantled. There are portions of our current system that can bring benefit to patients, and patients will not be able to operate it by themselves. Thus, gatekeepers will still be required, even if their bias cannot be eliminated. This means hierarchies must be reconsidered, expertise must be held up to the light and disassembled, not to be put back together in the same way.

## HOW THINGS CURRENTLY WORK FOR INDIVIDUAL PATIENTS IN THE SYSTEM WE HAVE

If they are lucky to have healthcare access, they might go to an individual clinician for the treatment of their health problem. But the clinician, by the virtue of their participation in our broken system, is the primary gatekeeper to healthcare even if they might not consider themselves as such.

They do not provide, by and large, the care the individual would want for themselves (the system does not encourage them to do this) but provide, by their expert estimation, the care they think is appropriate to the patient in the system that we have. Physician culture involves listening to the patient. But the listening is only done in service of the physician's goals, not the patient's. If the latter were the case, doctors would start the encounter by asking patients what they want. This is not common practice and not even proposed as the ideal.

I am not speaking just to criticize doctors. I am one of them and know in my best moments I try to bring the patient closer to what they want. But much of the time in my role I am constricted. I am not supposed to do what the patient wants, but I am expected to conform to the dictates of what is called evidence-based medicine. Evidence is not, by definition, accessible to patients. Unless patients play a dual role as scientists or participants in academic medicine, they are not expected to contribute to evidence-based medicine—a realm available only to clinicians (physician or nurses, mostly) or researchers.

## IF PATIENTS ARE REALLY GOING TO BE AT THE CENTER OF THE SYSTEM, WE NEED TO REEXAMINE THE NOTION OF EXPERTISE

The problem of expertise is central to the question of how healthcare should be revolutionized.[2] If expertise exists as a separate domain accessible only to the elite, then patients have no hope of being on equal footing with clinicians.

How can someone who has not gone to medical or nursing school, or is not being paid to practice medicine, become initiated into the guild of evidence-based medicine? One way is to painstakingly sift through studies, making various assumptions, as much ideological as objective, that randomized control trials are the pinnacle of unbiased scientific knowledge. But—as evidenced by the recent controversy over the Cochrane Center and Paul Gotzsche[3]—there is a basic difference of opinion regarding how evidence-based medicine is to be understood. This matters to actual care, which should make people feel better.

This controversy had to do with the following question: who determines what evidence-based medicine is? Are subject matter experts, those who know the most about the clinical conditions under consideration, to be included in its deliberations, or is there a science of evidence-based medicine, apart from clinical expertise? That is, is the best, most reliable evidence about heart attacks, say, to be gleaned only from the opinions of cardiologists, or are "evidence scientists" ideally those just concerned with the quality of evidence itself, free from the bias of the specialty under consideration?

The latter position would militate not just against the inclusion of clinicians in the evidence-based medicine determination process, but all the more so against the inclusion of patients themselves. What do patients know about controlled trials (unless they have access to expertise in their professional lives or in their own time)? They only have access to their own experience.

There would be no way to truly partner with patients in the use of evidence-based medicine, because they would be irredeemably biased. They might, granted, assist in the development of research questions, even in the ways in which these questions are—or are not—applicable to their lives, but they are not allowed to engage with the machinery itself.

According to that view of evidence-based medicine, there is no way it can be made sensitive to or inclusive of patients, and the entire enterprise should be seen as insusceptible to any revolutionary ambitions.

But there is a more expansive view of evidence-based medicine that has taken root in recent years. That is a view that rejects the strict hierarchy of evidence-based medicine in which a randomized control trial is seen as the gold standard. In the real world, there are many factors that have to be considered in deciding whether a treatment works in people. Not everything can be randomized, not everything can be controlled. Imagine, for example, an intervention in Baltimore City that for the sake of health would redistribute budget away from police overtime and toward improved school facilities and increased hours for after-school recreation facilities. It stands to reason that this intervention could not be evaluated with a randomized control trial. Residents of a city cannot be assigned into random groups.

This broader approach to evidence-based medicine recognizes that the number of potential study designs must be as diverse as the kinds of problems that exist in society, as all of them—to greater or lesser degree—affect health. Thus, it should be possible to include patients in the research enterprise. While such attempts are being made now, they still restrict patients to sources of data—to inputs into the machine. They are accepted as sources of symptom reports that can be quantified, as generators of topics and priorities to which the research enterprise can bend its ear. But they are not, by and large, accepted as full research collaborators.

For a truly patient-centered evidence-based medicine, which is not afflicted by epistemic injustice regarding (i.e., refusing to fully believe) the claims and experiences of patients, there are a number of serious questions.[4] Why does one person get better and the other get worse? Why was my diagnosis missed? Why do medications cost so much? Why did this doctor not listen to me? These are some common questions that evidence-based medicine, as currently practiced, does not prioritize.

But even if patients are included wholly as full collaborators in this enterprise, evidence-based medicine is still riddled with problems. It does not include vast areas of life that impact health and well-being for most people.

This is where we have to talk about not just remaking healthcare so that it provides equal concern for each individual, but also so that it addresses historical and present-day unequal treatment of groups.

The patient by themselves does not have the wherewithal to act as an effective self-advocate in the system as it is. This is also true in a system that is undergoing radical and revolutionary change. In the debate over universal healthcare and single payer, the point has often been made that the marginalized and vulnerable, who theoretically are meant to be helped by many revolutionary schemes, are often ones to be harmed[5]—because they have come up with strategies, unstable and jerry-rigged though they may be, to survive in the status quo. Disrupting the status quo may lead to harm for those in the present even as it bids to help those in the future.

Thus, it is unreasonable, even cruel, to expect those in the present day—with their vulnerabilities and health needs—to be able to act as effective self-advocates throughout significant system change. But those with similar needs, acting together as groups, can fill that role.

If our current system is very good at ignoring inconvenient individuals, it is even better at ignoring groups that are seen as wanting the wrong things, or with the wrong problems. Ideally groups would come together by themselves, though every group's definition is partially determined by outsiders. However a group defines or constitutes itself, we should not depend on the current definitions of our healthcare system to define which disadvantaged groups should determine the current directions of healthcare. It is not enough to adopt the current language of diversity and health disparities to address the needs of previously disadvantaged groups—we need to adopt the language and practice of inclusion.

## HOW DO WE ADDRESS THE NEEDS OF THE GROUP AND HOW DOES THAT AFFECT MEETING THE NEEDS OF THE INDIVIDUAL?

The group must constitute itself, undergoing a process of self-definition. Community-based research has something to recommend it, after all. While the term "community" implies an in-group (the researchers) and an out-group (those who live near, or in relationship to, the research institutions but are not considered part of them), including those people, at least in theory, rather than considering them excluded and only approached after the research findings have been published is better than the alternative.

This definition of community is too limiting. Researchers, clinicians, and those who they treat should all be included in the same collaborative. Community is not the group of people just outside the walls of the academy or the medical center or clinic, but everyone around and in it: those who clean the corridors and operating rooms, those who clean the streets, and those who clean the homes. The people who run the hospital and the people whose kids are seen in the hospital should both be involved in decision making. Community is not an advisory board to the elite that runs healthcare institutions; it includes all of us.

But including all of us can't happen all at once. It needs to be done by assembling different groups with different ends. In what follows, we will consider—from the point of view of the groups themselves—how they should come together to revolutionize our healthcare system, each bearing the banner of its own particular needs.

# 2

## Shortness of Breath

### Not So Simple

*Zackary Berger*

Some health conditions are surprisingly simple. There is nothing political or social about them. At least, that's what it seems like at first glance. Someone begins coughing and feeling short of breath. This lasts a few days. Then the fevers start—nothing dramatic: no night sweats, but they are accompanied by malaise. The person afflicted can barely get up and go to work, but somehow, they do it. This doesn't feel like a flu. COVID testing is negative. The cough doesn't have anything come up with it (that might be easier, as they read that if you can just make the stuff come up with the cough, you have a chance of clearing the infection.) This lasts a week. Finally, the person can't take it anymore. They worry something is really wrong. They head to an urgent care center. "Cough and fever," says the nurse practitioner on duty, "sounds like a bronchitis. I'll prescribe an antibiotic. To be on the safe side, let's order an X-ray."

The nurse practitioner visit costs $20. The prescription costs another $10. The X-ray is free. After two weeks, the person starts feeling a bit better.

Then there's a phone call. The X-ray showed a pneumonia. They start feeling worse. They don't know what to do. The urgent care gives them more antibiotics. These are soon finished, after another thirty dollars.

Now a month has passed, and the person feels no better. There is no clear route about what to do. They haven't had a primary care provider before: it's just too hard to get to see one what with work and everything.

Finally, they put aside some time to find a primary care provider who is covered by their insurance. They had to get off work—they work for a cleaning services company that is under contract to a large academic medical center.

They find someone to take care of their kids, and they go see their primary care provider. They are still short of breath, perhaps because of their demanding work schedule and perhaps the infection—whatever it was they had—is still around. Or maybe, and this is something they don't tell the clinician who saw them, they are unable to catch their breath because their spouse is sick and their oldest child is incarcerated.

Understandably, the primary care clinician is concerned about the fact that their patient is still short of breath—it has been a month already, and after a course of antibiotics there has not been significant improvement. So she thinks about what she should do, and orders a computed tomography scan of the person's chest (their lungs).

As computed tomography scans are wont to do, this finds swollen lymph nodes at the hilum—the area where the bronchus, artery, and veins enter and exit the lung. The diagnosis of sarcoidosis is raised as a possibility, and additional tests are suggested. They are performed—blood tests and an appointment with a rheumatologist.

Meanwhile, the shortness of breath has gotten worse. The person is still showing up to work, their son is still incarcerated, and there is more and more desperation felt at every encounter between them and the clinician.

At the next visit, the clinician again asks about the person's shortness of breath, and again there has been no change. It is not clear what is going on. The person is not sure they will go and see the clinician again, because they don't feel better—in fact, they keep feeling worse.

You will have noticed that I have left certain details out of the story. I have not said what sort of clinician is taking care of the patient as their primary care provider. I have not described what sort of patient this is, where they live (what city or country), their sexual identity and orientation, their race.

It is important to talk about why such information is necessary, as so often it gets left out in these stories of patients who are ill-served by our system. Much that is imperfect in this encounter has been the topic of discussion in the world of healthcare practice and theory, the subject of approaches that are promising but assume an undifferentiated clinician and a patient without identity.

In this book, we will make the argument that a progressive approach to health goes hand in hand with a progressive approach to human beings. By progressive we mean nothing very innovative—merely the steady addition, step by step, of ways that recognize people (both healthcare workers and patients) as human beings. That also means dismantling systems, and removing barriers, that prevent that identification. There are many ways in which the renovation of these systems (additions and dismantlers) must happen, and we will detail them in what follows.

But there are ways in which these systemic changes should probably not happen, which we also need to detail. We will start discussing the potential tempting missteps based on the case already discussed.

A person with shortness of breath is not an undifferentiated protoplasmic mass. Each human being has an identity. Some of the individuality of patients can be usefully understood through the theory of intersectionality, in which membership in different vulnerable or victimized groups is not additive or multiplicative, but can place one in different risk categories that are not explicable a priori from individual identifies.

The theory of intersectionality comes from law, understanding that one can have standing according to one category (e.g., Black), or another (e.g., a woman), but not both (e.g., a Black woman).

In understanding injustice in healthcare, intersectionality might be quite helpful in certain cases, such as those mentioned in Wilson,[1] which attempts to provide a theory for the use of intersectionality in clinical medicine. Ways of being do not replace each other but multiply the barriers and difficulties to receiving equal care.

But there are many sorts of clinical cases in which intersectionality is perhaps not the most useful rubric, and the case we are talking about here is one of those. Certainly, it matters what sort of person is being discussed here. Is this an African American woman who lives in a dilapidated house, due to the under-supported and neglected housing stock to which many urban governments have consigned African Americans, and which is associated with worsened asthma? Her children might indeed be incarcerated—due to the victimization of Black people by the carceral state. Her shortness of breath might be due to the sub-standard housing and stress. Or it could be a Spanish-speaking undocumented immigrant. It could be a trans adolescent with multiple work exposures. Or a white male chronic smoker, or an immigrant with a long history of qat use.

The theory of intersectionality holds that the disadvantage associated with the statuses of each of these individuals is greater because of their membership in multiple disadvantaged groups. In this case, therefore, to cure, diagnose, or treat their shortness of breath—whatever it might be due to—one cannot apply one solution. The patient and the clinician together must consider the multiple intersecting sources of disadvantage in context.

But the difficulty is in how to use this approach to inform the care of the person when they are suffering. The systems that deal disadvantage to

African American women, for example, are thickly layered (or interwoven) and cannot be feasibly modified in the moment. We do obviously aim at systemic changes, which we will also consider in this book, but socially and politically progressive healthcare must be able to practice progressivism even in the context of our current systems, for the benefit of presently existing people with problems like the one we just described. We need to help in the context of our knowledge of systematic injustice, even if patients and clinicians together cannot fix systems in the moment when help is needed. How is this possible? How does progressive healthcare leap over the systemic barriers?

Both patients and clinicians need to do it on a case-by-case basis. In the case of the story where shortness of breath might be explained by microphysiologic causes (e.g., an infection, a blood clot in the lung, a blockage in the breathing tubes, a pneumonia) but seems on further examination not to be due to those most common causes—at least according to the tests that have already been done—the question is how best to proceed. Should one continue to delve deeper into biomedical causes of disease, even if the long duration of the symptoms and the possibility of outward effects caused by pressures of society and politics make it likely that neither physician nor patient will be able to bring about significant improvement by further diagnostic tests?

## SHORTNESS OF BREATH . . . CURED BY COMPASSION?

Perhaps compassion itself is the key to improving the ways that physicians and patients work together. In this case, the typical armamentarium of the physician has come up short, and we ask how best to proceed. We might say that the patient should rely on the physician's realization of the patient's basic human needs.

Compassion means relating to a patient as a fellow human being. This is difficult enough in a general way, though many doctors excel at compassion and many patients, in the midst of their lives with acute or chronic illness, perform acts of compassion; many advocate or agitate for a world that possesses more compassionate systems. The question is whether the exercise of compassion, either by the doctor or the patient, will assist in remedying a symptomatic burden such as the one described in the story. This is not chiefly an empirical question, though surely studies have been done that measure the progression of patients' symptoms in the case of doctors who do, or do not, demonstrate compassion. Rather, the question is whether compassion will motivate activities and interventions that might recognize the interplay of multiple factors contributing to symptoms like unremitting shortness of breath. In other words, what is the point of compassion as a route to improving the life of the person with symptoms?

Is compassion even relevant in a country where so much is defined (or is lacking) through the relations among races and classes? It is important to say just what question we are asking here. Compassion is of course a clear moral priority. But the role of compassion in medical care is still uneasily situated. Compassion is most commonly seen as a nonegalitarian act. We demonstrate compassion toward the one who is in most need of help.

Certainly, the person in this story is vulnerable. We don't want our approach to a progressive healthcare to be the myth that patient and physician should be equal. One of the patient and physician is suffering; one of them is exposed to multiple vulnerabilities at the hands of the healthcare system. One of them needs help more than the other. The person who is short of breath needs help because they are short of breath, not because they are engaged in a heart-to-heart discussion of equals in the exam room or hospital.

On the other hand, however, equality is necessary for the doctor to exercise such compassion. It is not enough to voice the need for equality, the doctor—who has the power and access from being a healthcare professional in the current system—must use their position in the hierarchy to act upon it, much as the patient, with the knowledge of their own body and situation, has the sole responsibility to their own self. The doctor can only think their way into the possibilities of treatment or cure with the person with shortness of breath if the doctor sees the patient not as a disadvantaged individual in need of sympathetic attention, but as a fellow human being who shares a simple characteristic—a human organism, embedded in society, which can suffer by virtue of its own physiology or in the context of its community. Were compassion the sole foundation of care, then minimal care might be enough to satisfy that need. If equality is the true foundation of good healthcare, then the patient should be cared for in the way that the physician would want themselves or their loved ones cared for.

That realization is necessary for the doctor to go those extra steps that make progressive healthcare, in political or social context, different from just go-along-get-along healthcare. The doctor will use that compassionate recognition embedded in equality to motivate themselves to supersede the barriers that will be in the way of the doctor, family, and patient. The doctor must ask the patient to participate in lowering those barriers not through asking them what they cannot do but by taking ownership of what should be rightfully theirs and participating, visit by visit, individual encounter by individual encounter, in an effort to set society on a footing that enables just processes and just outcomes in health. This should by no means be a foisting of responsibilities onto the patient, as society so often forces patients to do, but a recognition that patients know their own interests and should be empowered to act on them.

The necessity for the doctor to realize the patient's basic humanity, and the patient to take ownership of their human right to political participation and ownership of equal opportunity to healthcare, is not equally obvious across the spectrum of health conditions. It is partially for this reason that we begin this book with a discussion of a case featuring a symptom that is deceptively common and apolitical. Shortness of breath does not establish a stigmatized identity, at least at face value.

The point here is not that the patient take responsibility for their own care, for that is impossible, especially when individual people are victims of inequality and systemic brutality, of deliberate ignorance of people's chronic symptoms and needs. But the patient must be ready to advocate for themselves as best they can.

## THE LIVING ENVIRONMENT
## AND SHORTNESS OF BREATH

What is the living environment—architectural, urban, social, space-related— in which the patient is found? How does that affect the patient's breathing? Or asked another way: should we see the problem in this case as a patient possessing a pair of lungs (or perhaps even just one, or lungs not their own), a circulatory and pulmonary system, a system of blood bringing oxygen to the tissues, at the center of the story—and the social context of the patient's life and stressors, living environment and employment, as ancillary elements surrounding that center?

Or is shortness of breath a reflection of the fully inhabited life of the person affected by the symptom, who does not distinguish their shortness of breath as due to lungs, or airways, or heart, or infectious or metabolic causes, nor do they attribute it to social-political phenomena. They might notice when it is worse or when it is better, what stressors affect it and what things relieve it. At this point, they have had the shortness of breath for a number of months and do not know how to proceed, and the clinician might be at loose ends as well. Many are the cases of a chronic symptom, such as shortness of breath, in which a particular cause is not identified. Both parties might then throw up their hands, either identifying a tentative cause or arriving at a collection of pharmacologic measures that might or might not work.

If they work, wonderful. But if not, how can the clinician and the patient together use knowledge of the political and social environment, and their commitment to progressive values that we have detailed in the introduction as foundational to healthcare, to address this particular symptom?

## BARRIERS TO CARE

To work outward, that is from recognition of the microphysiology—perhaps the most inward realm of the patient, understood reductively—to broader spheres, we consider the possibility that there are ways to alter that physiology that social and political barriers are making impossible. Perhaps a pharmaceutical company (whose research might have even been sponsored by the employer of the physician who might be down the street from the patient) has developed a medication that might aid in the patient's shortness of breath (e.g., an inhaled narcotic). Perhaps you, as the patient, have researched a medication on the internet that some patient groups have found helpful, but for whatever reason you cannot manage to get your hands on it.

One way to confront this barrier as physician and patient together would be to identify routes such that a medication, or new treatment, could be made available to the patient. Not, I hasten to add, through one of the programs advertising itself as a compassionate route to access. I am thinking of direct lobbying of the company through bringing pressure by a coalition of patients and providers, or through collaborating with regulators (whether at the state or federal level) to convince them to take action. Surely, if there are effective medications available that might help treat shortness of breath (e.g., inhaled narcotics, various inhalers that are out of reach of many limited-income people, etc.), then the individual hypothetical patient described here, together with their provider, are not the only ones who are interested in widening availability of that medication or medications.

Another route to securing access to potentially helpful medications is to advocate for ending patents for medications that are monopolized by a given company.

Another barrier is not access to the medication, but inability to afford the medication, which works out to nearly the same thing. Few are the trials or guidelines that explicitly specify cost as a barrier to patient access to individual treatments—we will address this more specifically in later chapters. But if a given treatment is too expensive, apart from the options we discussed previously, there might not be a ready alternative to it—unless the institution where the clinician works can provide a program to support medications for those without much money.

This does happen in a number of institutions through a medication voucher program.[2] It is unclear how many institutions have such programs, how well they enable people to access needed treatments, and what encourages or makes it more difficult for institutions to pursue them. (That they exist does not mean they are systematic solution, or without slippery ethical features [e.g., promoting the medications that pharmaceutical companies see fit to incentivize].) In the case of this patient, the clinician might be able—through a program at their practice or institution—to provide vouchers for, for example, one of the more expensive inhalers.

The problem with voucher programs is that they are (as the euphemism goes) "compassionate." They are departures from the all-powerful profit motive, which individual institutions might quarrel with but do not act against because, practically speaking, they cannot. In our system, when institutions provide "charity" care, they do so not to undermine their predominant motivation—to make money from patients—but either to ensure their legal status, to attract the good-intentioned donations of philanthropists, or to salve the consciences and smooth the path of those who must work with the community (those affected by the hospital's actions) in its name. Helping patients goes hand in hand with these goals (intentions are good) but cannot be allowed to directly contradict them. Thus, even the compassionate programs under which medication vouchers are usually administered are not meant to supply medications for an indefinite time but are meant to be strictly controlled so that the risk (to the institution's bottom line) and benefit (to the reputation and philanthropic attractiveness) can be titrated.

In any given situation, however, neither you as the patient nor you as the clinician are bound to the institution's criteria regarding the limits on the use of medication vouchers. If there is an inhaler that might help you with your shortness of breath, or if your doctor has found something that might help you, both of you should together devise a plan to get as reliable and as long-term a supply of medication vouchers as possible. None of this is, of course, to sacrifice the moral and ethical requirement of truth-telling. I emphasize that vouchers are only useful if the medication for shortness of breath is useful. But, as a strategy, it might be worthwhile in your context.

If one option is to make the useful medications more available, another option is to address—in the short term, for the person we are talking about, and not just in the theoretical or political-social vein—the social factors that impact the shortness of breath. This too is policy, not just decisions made by government organs at the federal or state level.

It is important, in the biomedical vein, to explore the potential causes for the shortness of breath; such an approach is important and even basic in the way that patients and doctors usually do things. But there are many situations in which the specific cause is not to be identified, and attention must be turned to improving the symptom at issue—to making life more bearable. No matter what the potential specific cause, the elements of life that make the symptom worse should be identified.

We might concentrate less on what the potential cause is and more on how to make common cause in the moment—in the present tense, the actual state of affairs affecting current life—with patients and providers to alter the circumstances worsening that breathing. That means using legal avenues, for example, to bring pressure on those who own the housing at issue. (Often it is an owner of a rental property who supervises, but does not repair or improve, a "sick building" that worsens shortness of breath.)

What avenues are available for advocacy and agitation depend on the local setting, and on the individual experiences of the patient who is suffering the shortness of breath. Much will also depend on the ways in which the person with shortness of breath spends their time. Rare is the person with shortness of breath whose condition (whatever the microphysiologic cause may be) is not worsened at the workplace. People who work in cleaners and laundries are exposed to cleaning chemicals and high temperatures. Those who work as housekeepers in hotels or private homes also are exposed to cleaning chemicals; those with outdoor work, to extremes of temperatures.

Then there are those who work as hairdressers, in bakeries, and in food service jobs. So many people, with this one symptom, find it worsened at their workplace. But what can the patient or the clinician do to help break this connection between occupational exposure and worsening symptoms?

There is more room than frequently acknowledged for the clinician to try and intervene on behalf of the patient in their work environment. While the physician, for example, does not have the enforcement power to make the employer follow either moral or legal codes, or consider the health effects of the work environment on the lives of their employees, they do have a bully pulpit. They can demonstrate to the employer that someone is looking out for the employee.

Of course, the patient, in their work environment, has to be comfortable sticking their neck out, potentially placing their employment (or their standing in their work cohort) at risk. This is where we cross over the line, invisible in some ways—because not explicitly forbidden to cross—yet obvious in others (because everyone knows the line is there) separating the health and politics domains. How can workers look out for their own interests in an environment that can be detrimental to their health?

To use some evidence from my own clinical world: I see Spanish-speaking undocumented immigrants at the Esperanza Center in downtown Baltimore. Many of these immigrants do the jobs that other people don't want to do. They work as cleaners in hotels or private homes; they push heavy carts of clothing in dry cleaning establishments; they work as cooks or servers in restaurants. Each of these types of workplace has its own characteristics that might commonly worsen shortness of breath. This has not just to do with the individual substances workers might be exposed to, but the levels of stress and conflict in the workplace and the freedom given by workers to pursue their own health, either by taking time off, seeing a doctor, or simply in taking measures to address their stress—not to mention smoking, which affects most often the poorest and those with the least resources to pursue smoking cessation. And smoking can serve as a release valve in those with stressful jobs.

Employers are not likely to make an effort to improve these conditions, especially if they can get away with not doing so. Therefore, the final common pathway to improve the lot of those with respiratory conditions worse at their workplace, whether we are acting from the point of view of patient or clinician, is to restructure society. There are two potential steps to this restructuring, one more immediate and available to us and one farther off in the future and dependent on the general ideology one subscribes to. The nearer goal is to make it possible for workers to organize to meet their own needs in the workplace. If they have respiratory difficulty from workplace exposures, they should be able to negotiate a reduction in exposures, increased pay in order to pursue treatment (if smaller scale, microphysiologic treatment is available), different or lesser work responsibilities.

Whether current employers will have the wherewithal or interest to support workers in such a way is an open question. That's why the second step might be required. According to this, in a direction perhaps reminiscent of Plato's *Republic*, according to which each person is matched up to an employment fitting for them, no one would work at a job that would exacerbate their chronic symptoms. No one would need to.

Progressive care would not require people to work in a role that would exacerbate their bodily or mental symptoms. Thus there are a number of domains in which the clinician and the patient, working together, can act to improve shortness of breath outside of the microphysiologic domain predominantly addressed by the biomedical dogma. It might be possible to address all of them at once, if groups of patients and different kinds of healthcare workers, acting in a restructured society, can act together.

# 3

## Chronic Pain and the Movement Toward Progressive Healthcare

*Tamara A. Baker, Mary Janevic, and Staja Q. Booker*

"We cannot solve our problems with the same thinking we used when we created them."

—Albert Einstein

Society's approach to health and healthcare cannot be the same as it was in the past. We must change the message while acknowledging the historical embeddedness of healthcare institutions in discriminatory practices, social inequities, and explicit biases. This perpetuates a system premised on power and wealth and formal structures that disregard the needs of the poor and disenfranchised. To approach this issue, this fragmented and noninclusive system must be restructured toward liberation from capitalism. This movement, however, should not be the onus of one person, community, or institution, but rather a collective obligation of those willing to serve as change agents for the betterment of those who not only seek care, but for those also providing care. For example, advancing from the traditional disparities-focused paradigm to an enhancement model that promotes population health equity,"[1] the Institute of Medicine calls this movement a "cultural transformation" of pain care.[2]

Defined as a physiologic response to disease and tissue damage, pain is often classified into different categories based on its origin: nociceptive (tissue damage or inflammation), neuropathic (nerve damage), mixed, or unspecified (unknown causes or a combination of nociceptive and neuropathic).[3] Chronic pain, often assessed by duration that persists three to six months or longer,[4] impacts the well-being and quality of life of many individuals.

As a subjective experience, pain is contingent on several factors including the history of the illness, duration of the medical condition, type of pain (acute versus chronic), pain variability, physiological changes, cultural background, and sociodemographic factors such as gender and age.[5] The subjectivity of the pain experience is a dynamic and complex process interconnected with affective, cognitive, and behavioral patterns.[6] Although accepted as a symptom of a disease diagnosis or injury, pain can also be considered a disease in itself. Data suggest that while many patients are diagnosed with a primary pathology (e.g., arthritis, diabetes mellitus), secondary pathology may be evident (e.g., changes to the peripheral nervous system). An individual may then develop persistent pain as a disease, meeting diagnostic criteria with established symptomatology.[7] This secondary pathology may have implications in understanding the association of pain and other chronic medical conditions. This is all the more relevant when discussing the short- and long-term implications of a painful medical diagnosis, particularly among historically marginalized populations.

The putatively inclusive term "marginalized populations" does not capture the complexities and salient differences seen within and between cultural communities. This extends beyond one's physical characteristics (i.e., race) to identities bound up with the self such as age, gender, and other micro (and macro) determinants of health. These descriptors have often been misunderstood, particularly as relevant to the social, emotional, physical, and mental health needs of marginalized groups. What must be recognized, however, is that these identities contribute to the diverse characteristics that influence pain-related medical diagnoses, treatment, disease management, and access to resources.

To advance the field of pain care, we must make use of the science of progressive healthcare in general, while incorporating the work of scholars in pain care with similar ideals. The intersection of chronic pain and progressive healthcare requires understanding the underlying social, behavioral, and biological influences. This is all the more relevant when addressing the needs of chronic pain patients. Progressive healthcare for example, suggests change, reform, and continuous improvement, all of which define the future of pain care. Yet adapting this approach while elaborating  the historical context of chronic pain, particularly within and between marginalized populations, is key in restructuring how we define and accept the progressive healthcare model.

While not meant as a diagnostic explanation or clinical assessment, this chapter focuses  pain outcomes across specific areas, while  addressing both micro/macro social determinants and their influence in perpetuating disparities and inequities in pain care. Although there is a myriad of content areas that require attention in pain care, addressing the broader issues of race and age are of more immediate concern. Recognizing the involvedness of these issues allows for a more dynamic dialogue around racism, ageism, and other defined "-isms" (e.g., sexism, ableism, etc.) that do not allow for sustainable progression toward equality, equity, and systemic change.

## PROGRESSING TOWARD RACIAL PAIN EQUITY

People of color living with chronic pain face lack of access to health resources and adequate healthcare. Many African American pain patients, for example, are viewed through a lens of deviant and criminal behavior(s) (e.g., drug abusers/seekers, doctor-shopping) rather than as patients with legitimate pain pathology.[8] This has resulted in a deficient approach in treating those who are not the majority."

This disparagement of those with chronic pain, particularly the marginalized, suggests that the experiences, perceptions, and responses surrounding chronic pain must be credited to the same degree as the biological mechanisms of pain. The so-called experience*ome* is defined as the sum total of varieties of the felt impact of chronic pain, and the conditions that contribute to and/or exacerbate the pain experiences. This perspective allows for a more thorough assessment of pain through a social and cultural lens. Yet, while many factors contribute to disparities and inept pain care, the counternarratives (to those of mainstream healthcare) of those from diverse race and ethnic populations continue to be undermined or ignored despite numerous studies documenting the abhorrent mismanagement of pain.[9] The multidynamic constructions of these factors are defined by the underlying influences of social determinants of health (SDoH). The global reach of these determinants allows for a broader reasoning for not only how, but why these disparities continue to immobilize communities in receiving adequate pain care even in the most advanced healthcare settings.

## SOCIAL DETERMINANTS OF HEALTH
## AND THE IMPACT ON PAIN CARE

To improve health among the nation's most vulnerable communities, efforts are needed to better understand and interpret the root causes of health, well-being, and distributed inequalities, inequities, and disparities. These factors are termed as SDoH, which are multifaceted, integrated, and overlapping social and economic systems defined by five key areas (i.e., economic stability, education, health and healthcare, neighborhood and built environment, social and community context). These domains determine the ways in which people are born, grow up, live, work, and age.[10] They allow for a collective understanding of not only disease onset, but the circumstances (of the individual) that affect the occurrence of illnesses. Changes in multiple social determinants may have an additive effect. For example, neighborhood environments with quality housing, reduced exposure to crime and violence, and better environmental conditions (i.e., green space) may facilitate improved quality of and availability of specialized pain care.

Understanding the influence of SDoH allows for a conceptual framework to explaining disparities within and between communities.[11] Until these determinants are prioritized, generational disparities in health and pain care will continue to persist. This helps reconsider the national pain agenda and the next steps pursuant to equitable pain care.

## CURRENT PAIN AGENDA

There has been an increase in efforts addressing the nation's current chronic pain crisis. Currently, these initiatives have provided high-performing interdisciplinary care that incorporates a personalized, evidence- and outcomes-guided approach intended for all patients.[12] Despite these efforts, there remain inequities in patient care and pain-related disability, particularly for those from historically marginalized populations (e.g., African Americans), as well as those defined by structural circumstances such as income inequities, (un)employment, and residence in impoverished communities. Recognizing the continued mistreatment of these groups requires a systematic assessment of how oppressive economic boundaries stifle progress. This calls for research and policies that account for social conditions and environmental factors relevant to pain disparities, health equity, and social justice. It suggests that we should refocus our attention to understanding how macrosocial determinants (e.g., corporate practices, political ideologies, economic philosophies, industrialization, taxation) influence how we define pain outcomes, and access and availability to resources and specialty care, particularly among people of color.[13] For example, some predominantly African American communities report provider bias(es), high out-of-pocket healthcare costs, and pharmacies that are not adequately stocked with opioid analgesics.[14] While seen as a detriment to the African American community, there are those who interpret this as protective, in that the lack of access reduces the risk of misuse and/or addiction.

There are, however, two inherent problems with this argument. First, a lack of access to and availability of healthcare should never be considered equity in care, even if it unintentionally decreases the risk of certain harmful outcomes. Secondly, this argument assumes that the endpoint of unequal care can be fair, so a need to address the root cause(s) of differential access is not needed. These perspectives lack merit and emphasize the importance of addressing SDoH. As we emphasize, access to proper pain care has been dictated by racism. Despite the negative implications of racism and receipt of adequate pain care, we must also recognize that the intersection of multiple identities (e.g., being an older African American adult) further perpetuates an inadequate healthcare system that often disregards the well-being of not only persons of color, but older adults as well. More Westernized societies place higher value on youthfulness and vitality, whereby "aging" is described as a disease or affliction rather than a dynamic process that defines the life course.[15] The assumptions prevalent in caring for the aged are damaging and may have short- and long-term implications on one's health and well-being. Recognizing that pain is a primary reason why many older adults seek medical care, efforts are needed to ensure that resources are accessible, available, and equitable. This is important as persistent pain that is not adequately treated may lead to poor physical, psychological, cognitive, and social functioning,[16] an increased risk of falls, and mortality.[17]

Despite an increase in chronic pain among older adults over the past two decades, the reasoning behind this change remains unclear.[18] Thus we face another complicated issue: ageism, as we strive for a more inclusive healthcare system that treats all pain patients across the life course.

## THE INTERSECTION OF PAIN, THE LIFE COURSE, AND STRUCTURAL RACISM

As with other medical conditions, the burden of chronic pain ranks higher among older African American adults and those of lower socioeconomic status. Findings from a number of studies show that these individuals are more likely to report greater pain severity and pain-related disability compared to their white and higher socioeconomic status counterparts.[19] Older African Americans also have less access to effective pain treatment and are more likely to receive substandard care across the spectrum of pain treatment.[20]

To understand the structural factors that contribute to these findings, we reference the widely accepted biopsychosocial model. Accounting for the biological, social, and psychological influences of the pain experience among older adults allows for a recognition of the historical, cultural, and social contexts that shape the aging experience.[21] Experienced health inequities in older adulthood, for example, including those related to the treatment of pain and/or other health conditions, are often concomitant to systemic racism experienced across the life course.[22] Structural racism can be thought of as the unofficial rules of the game, whereby laws, policies, and practices yield inequitable and toxic conditions such as residential segregation, economic deprivation, and inferior medical care.[23] These conditions operate over time to form the biopsychosocial context in which African Americans, for example, experience and manage chronic pain in older adulthood. These dimensions of chronic pain are described as follows.

*Biological* factors are represented as increased allostatic load (a physiologic measure of "wear and tear" on the body) and accelerated aging, or "weathering."[24] This results in disproportionately high rates of multimorbidity in older African American adults, including health conditions and functional impairments that make pain more difficult to manage. A lifetime of inferior access to high-quality medical care and provider discrimination often leaves pain misdiagnosed, underreported, and undertreated, increasing the likelihood of the pain to persist over time, thus resulting in pain-related disability.

*Psychological* factors include distress and trauma—including historical trauma from racial oppression, passed down in families over generations.[25] These accumulated experiences (of racial discrimination) are associated with physical pain in older African American adults.[26]

*Social* factors include stressors of social networks (e.g., familial, friendships) that may also trigger pain reports and/or exacerbate the pain experience. African Americans experience a higher rate of bereavement at every stage of life due to the deaths of relatives and friends when compared to other groups.[27] This is often associated not only with emotional pain but felt physical pain among older adults as well.[28] In yet another example, the unjust mass incarceration of African Americans has a cumulative economic impact on families, thus producing familial stress, whereby the older family members are left with the responsibility of caring for younger members of the family (i.e., custodial grandparenting).[29] This level of responsibility, welcomed or not, can have lasting health implications, such as being diagnosed with a debilitating pain condition (e.g., diabetes, arthritis).

In acknowledging the impact of racial inequities and societal threats in the health and physical pain of older African Americans, we are reminded that despite these injustices, these individuals remain steadfast in coping with the mental and physical determinants across generations. Even when tackling the detrimental impact of pain, it is well documented that older African Americans in particular have learned to adjust to these experiences by sharing their pain with others and trusting God as a healer. Booker and colleagues[30] so poignantly described this type of pain self-management as a "cultured and social experience steeped in historical tradition, reflection and generativity . . . and resilience."

## A PROGRESSIVE PAIN AGENDA

The equitable treatment of pain is central to continued discussions to advance the field of progressive healthcare. This narrative change will no longer be tangential, but will rather bring about reassessment of the definition, treatment, and management of pain. These efforts should reflect the nation's changing demographics, while ensuring a healthcare system that is equitable and just.

Renowned pain scholars S. Q. Booker, T. A. Baker, and colleagues (under review)[31] propose five strategies aimed at transforming the pain disparities model through inclusive policies, while refocusing attention on the underlying influences of SDoH on pain and health outcomes.

1. Reshape the conceptualization of pain and pain theories including the types of questions we ask and whom we ask. This includes redefining and/or operationalizing pain in ways relevant to diverse populations.
2. Use innovation to remove structured and virulent systems of inequity through multilevel, multigenerational, and multidisciplinary interventions. This is a necessary approach for overcoming multilevel disparities evident in the population health of ethnic and racial minorities.
3. Foster health empowerment and emancipation from disproportionate morbidity and mortality through integrative, collaborative, and community-engaged models of care.
4. Devote efforts to exploring the mechanisms of behavior and precision lifestyle medicine that work against the imbalances created by societal stigmas, cultivating patients' resilience to implement and sustain positive behavior change in preventing and managing pain.
5. Integrate and translate research findings and evidence-based models of pain and pain disparities into the (re)education of clinicians, patients, and the public.

These strategies will continue to support the pain care renaissance that began with the Affordable Care Act of 2010 and the subsequent release of the Institute of Medicine's report *Relieving Pain in America* in 2011.[32]

## CONCLUSION

The timely and adequate treatment of pain is a moral obligation of all health-care professionals in preventing suffering for all patients.[33] Yet this ethical duty has yet to manifest significant changes in pain care or policy for people of color. Pain care reform will best be achieved under the standards of healthcare equity, while reinforced by emancipatory social action. From a broader analytic view, healthcare reform must investigate the direct effects of proximal and distal social and environmental determinants of health in the nation's war on pain. This illustrates the critical need to go beyond describing the issue to that of finding solutions. And, as so powerfully stated in the commanding words of Dr. Martin Luther King Jr., "Of all the forms of inequality, injustice in health is the most shocking and inhumane."

Whether you are old or young, rich or poor, Black or white, suffering from pain can no longer be overlooked.

# 4

# Progressive Healthcare for People with Substance Use Disorder

*Danielle S. Jackson, Stefanie Gillson, Shayla Partridge, Kimberly L. Sue, and Ayana Jordan*

The Centers for Disease Control and Prevention report that fatal overdoses exceeded seventy thousand in 2019. Exacerbated by the COVID-19 pandemic, it is estimated that overdoses in 2020 will have exceeded ninety thousand deaths. Many factors have contributed to the increased prevalence of overdose in the United States in recent years. In this chapter we will highlight existing barriers to progressive care for people with substance use disorders (SUDs), novel partnerships and treatment approaches that focus on community- versus system-centered care, and the importance of collaborations with partners outside of the healthcare system to approach progressive treatment in a trauma-informed manner and through a lens of social justice.

## THE PRICE OF HEALTHCARE: PROGRESS MUST BE AFFORDABLE

No matter on what side of the political aisle one sits, one must admit that there is a significant problem with the cost of healthcare in this country, and healthcare for people with SUDs is no exception. Recent estimates report that the annual cost of SUD in U.S. hospitals exceeds $13 billion.[1] This figure only comprises the hospital emergency department and inpatient hospital stays.

Among people who use substances, several factors are associated with not receiving treatment including not being ready to stop using, not knowing where to go for treatment, and lack of insurance coverage or affordable care.

One hallmark of progressive healthcare is affordability, and that measure varies depending on the population being discussed.

Progressive healthcare can impact barriers from the individual to the systems level of care. While the Affordable Care Act improved parity policies between mental and behavioral health and medical health coverage among those with healthcare insurance, large gaps remain, especially for care of SUDs. Often if someone finds themselves in a hospitalization for substance use, for example secondary to complicated alcohol withdrawal, the next level of care such as a partial hospital program or intensive outpatient treatment will not be covered by their insurance provider. Once the patient has recovered from the acute medical dangers of alcohol withdrawal, they may have limited support after discharge from the hospital. Furthermore, even if a prescription coverage plan is in place, harm reduction medications such as naltrexone may be too expensive for the individual. This previous example assumes the best situation: that the person is safely housed, has a support system to help navigate their healthcare needs, and experiences minimal financial vulnerabilities. This is simply not the case for many people with SUD. Therefore, affordability becomes a large barrier to healthcare among those experiencing homelessness, poverty, and social isolation.

## CULTURALLY INFORMED, TRAUMA-INFORMED, AND INCLUSIVE OF THE FULL SUBSTANCE USE DISORDER COMMUNITY

Cultural humility is "a lifelong commitment to self-evaluation and critique to redressing power imbalances in the patient/physician dynamic and to develop mutually beneficial and non-paternalistic partnerships with communities on behalf of individuals and defined populations."[2] As the community of people with SUDs is not a monolith, neither should be our approach to providing care. Approaching healthcare through cultural humility involves not only respect for individuals and the communities in which they reside, but a commitment to understanding domains such as ethnic/racial background in addition to gender, sexual identities, and spiritual belief systems. Healthcare is improved for all when we understand the historical contexts and experiences of marginalized communities seeking care in our system and the continued barriers that prohibit just and equitable care, including individual and systemic racism.

For example, although the prevalence of substance use is equal among Black and white Americans, consequences of drug use can vary widely. Systemically racist drug policies and practices that have been established over the last half-century continue to impact members of the Black community more severely. Black Americans are experiencing a rapidly rising rate of overdose deaths and continued barriers to accessing medications for opioid use disorder and harm reduction services.[3] The treatment gap and the disparities in nonfatal and fatal overdose events continued to widen during the COVID-19 pandemic. This further increases the urgency for culturally competent care to minoritized communities. Treatment options offered should be person-centered and incorporate a trauma-informed framework. The Substance Abuse and Mental Health Services Administration describes the components of a trauma-informed treatment for SUD using the four Rs: realization/acknowledgment that trauma occurred, recognizing signs of trauma within the population, responding to trauma, and avoiding re-traumatization.

Progressive healthcare should include participants from the full spectrum of the SUD community. This includes not only those in traditional caregiver roles such as physicians, nurses, and social workers, but also those with lived experience and in recovery. The integration of peer-delivered recovery support services has been shown, in a clinical review, to have a beneficial effect on patients.[4] Incorporation of peer recovery support within treatment teams and outside of the clinical team in community recovery organizations can be of benefit to those at all stages of recovery. Peer support enhances engagement with hard-to-reach, often underserved communities.[5] They have been shown to increase engagement among populations experiencing homelessness and involved with the carceral system. In addition, they improve harm reduction programs, such as syringe exchange, by providing additional education and outreach for already marginalized populations.[6]

## NON-WESTERNIZED APPROACHES TO TREATING SUBSTANCE USE DISORDERS

The rates of substance use in Indigenous people, as well as per capita abstinence rates, vary significantly by tribe and community.[7] The diversity of Indigenous people comprises 576 federally recognized tribes, each with unique cultures, traditions, and languages. When considering substance use in Indian Country, it is important to contextualize the history of colonization policies, and their roles in assimilation or extermination.

Colonization introduced substances as a tool for exploitation, and often traders and settlers promoted heavy use to exploit Indigenous people to cede land or resources. Policies that promoted forced relocation and starvation became the foundation of contemporary oppression now seen in inadequate healthcare funding, ongoing discrimination, and persistent erasure of native experience. For example, negative stereotypes of Indigenous people and alcohol use exemplify racism that continues to be perpetuated today.

Despite historic and present oppression, Indigenous people continue to thrive in the United States and develop community- and culturally focused substance use programs. Many Indigenous persons believe that struggles with alcohol are connected to historical trauma and disconnection from traditional culture.[8] Further, there is often a disconnect between Indigenous values and Western treatment modalities for substance use. Many Westernized treatments focus on the individual and isolation during treatment with reintegration after achieving wellness. In contrast, many Indigenous modalities instead focus on interconnectedness and emphasize the importance of culture, tradition, and spirituality. Evidence demonstrates that cultural identity and feeling connected to one's tribe are important for preventing substance abuse and that community-based/culturally grounded programs are effective strategies.[9]

Indigenous-led research teams, grassroots organizations, and communities have been using centuries of accumulated knowledge and cultural traditions to address substance use. Given the breadth of diversity of Indigenous people, it is important to consider how cultural interventions are intimately tied to each specific tribe or group who developed them. Broadly speaking, however, many programs focus on cultural symbols and specific traditions like the medicine wheel, building a canoe, drumming, or honoring a long coexistence with horses.

Drumming is recognized as a sacred symbol used for ceremonies, and in some communities represents Mother Earth's heartbeat. This core cultural value has been used in programs such as drum-assisted recovery therapy for treatment of SUDs.[10] Other successful programs are aimed at improving overall wellness, self-efficacy, and economic status.

One such example is the White Mountain Apache Tribe Youth Entrepreneurship program. This innovative program was developed with community members to provide culturally tailored training by partnering adolescent tribal members with mentors to develop business ideas, ultimately deciding on a café that is still being operated by youth today.[11] Decreased substance use was just one of the many positive outcomes of this program. An Indigenous paraprofessional program called the Family Spirit Program supports new mothers from pregnancy until their child is three years old. The paraprofessionals have been trained to provide education and support families around myriad of topics with cultural undertones.[12] Along with decreased substance use, the participants also have decreased depression and greater knowledge of parenting.[13]

Indigenous solutions to substance use incorporate traditional aspects of healing and connectedness that are driven by the values and participation of the community. Despite ongoing attempts of erasure and assimilation, Indigenous people in the United States are one of the fastest-growing populations and are employing centuries of traditional knowledge to help their people move toward recovery. Indigenous communities continue to adapt, thrive, and pass on knowledge and history to the next generations.

## PROGRESSIVE HEALTHCARE FOR PEOPLE WITH SUBSTANCE USE DISORDER: HARM REDUCTION

A key component of providing high-quality care to people who use drugs includes incorporating a harm reduction framework. Harm reduction is defined as "a set of practical strategies and ideas aimed at reducing negative consequences associated with drug use."[14] The philosophy of harm reduction can be extrapolated to a broader public health context including other examples of harm reduction such as encouraging patients to cut back on sugary beverages, promoting daily sunscreen use, and requiring car passengers to wear seatbelts. In the context of people who use drugs, where the harm reduction framework originated over thirty years ago during the early HIV epidemic in the 1980s, interventions focused on preventing transmission of blood-borne infections of diseases like HIV and hepatitis C (HCV), which can be contracted from sharing injection supplies, reducing the incidence of use-related injuries like oral burns from smoking or abscesses from needles, and reducing the fatality associated with substance overdose.

One of the most well-known and prevalent harm reduction interventions to reduce new infections of HIV and HCV include syringe services programs (SSPs), which have been in existence—both formally and informally—for many decades and have proven efficacious.[15] SSPs offer a sterile supply of injection equipment including needles, alcohol swabs, cookers, sterile water, condoms/lubricants, and connection to other health resources including formal treatment programs and counseling.[16]

Naloxone, an opioid antagonist medication that can be administered quickly and safely in order to reverse an opioid overdose, is another powerful harm reduction strategy. Naloxone distribution has become ubiquitous in many cities and is now carried by many first responders as well as given directly to people who use drugs and their families via harm reduction programs. In many states, naloxone is available to the general public through a standing order at any pharmacy via naloxone access laws, and these states have noticed an average 10 percent decrease in opioid overdose–related deaths.[17]

Overdose prevention centers (OPCs), also sometimes called supervised consumption spaces, are perhaps one of the most comprehensive and holistic harm reduction models that exist. These centers offer a safe facility for people who use drugs to access clean supplies, prepare preobtained substances, and consume those substances with peer or professional supervision who monitor them for signs of overdose or other adverse effects. One of the most well-known OPCs is called Insite, which opened in 2003 in downtown Vancouver. This accomplishment was led by people who use drugs and other activists. Since its opening, Insite has been regularly evaluated and found to be effective in reducing infectious disease transmission, overdose, and general "public disorder."[18] Insite has also proven that the model of OPCs can be cost-effective. One study identified three major opportunities for cost savings at Insite: decreased needle sharing, the health effects of safer injection, and increased referral to methadone maintenance treatment. Altogether, projects showed that these opportunities could result in a net savings of more than $18 million and 1,175 gained life-years. These models also predict that Insite could reduce new infections of HIV and HCV significantly.[19] In a study specifically examining HCV rates among the population that access Insite's OPC, research showed that given the already high rates of HCV in the community, Insite's services offered an opportunity for "containment" of the spread due to reduced syringe lending and referrals to HCV treatment as well as other health education opportunities.[20] Importantly, no evidence has shown that the existence of OPCs encourages drug injection initiation, which is often used as an argument against implementing harm reduction measures of all kinds, but particularly these facilities that serve as safe spaces for substance use.[21]

Though SSPs, OPCs, and naloxone access are some of the most commonly known and researched forms of harm reduction, it is important to remember that one of the hallmarks of harm reduction in practice is to increase access to medications that treat opioid use disorder (MOUD) like methadone and buprenorphine in a low threshold, nonpunitive manner. These medications, even in cases of low adherence, can reduce risk of overdose and encourage individuals to cut back on other forms and types of substance use.[22] Other important ways to reduce harm to individuals who use drugs is to create a safer supply of drugs (i.e., prescription hydromorphone or diacetylmorphine) and to decriminalize substance use such that people who use drugs are not further impacted by the harms of incarceration.

Lastly, it is crucial that in all forms and contexts of harm reduction services, linkage to other health resources including primary care, substance use treatment, and social services, including housing, are consistently offered. Harm reduction is a framework that offers individuals resources and opportunities to make healthier decisions and involves meeting individuals where they are in their substance use while also working to address the broader context of their substance use, including interventions on structural violence, trauma, and stigma toward people who use drugs.

## STIGMA AS SOCIAL DEATH: THE IMPORTANCE OF REFRAMING ADDICTION AND ADDICTION TREATMENT

Addiction, more specifically SUD, is one of the most stigmatized conditions,[23] resulting in shame, isolation, fear, and death. Stigma, defined as a mark of disgrace associated with a particular circumstance, quality, or person,[24] when applied to having a SUD, can be redefined as social death, given how difficult it can be for one to assimilate into society. In contrast to other health conditions, where empathy is more readily provided, there are deeply entrenched views associated with SUDs. People with an SUD can be seen as criminal, unscrupulous, or not worthy of respect.[25] Beyond the lack of humanity, re-framing stigma as social death underscores the serious treatment implications, whereby people avoid or delay SUD treatment for fear of being "found out" or being classified as an "addict." In certain professions, there are harsh consequences or risk for loss of licensure, if there is a self-disclosure of having a SUD or being in recovery from one.[26] As such, this chapter focuses on the types of stigma associated with addiction and the importance of reframing, to affirm the humanity of those with SUDs, as a means to promote treatment initiation and ongoing recovery.

Stigma and its consequences can be understood in terms of the types of stigma and the different ways it can manifest on individual, sociocultural, and structural levels. The National Alliance of Mental Illness provides working definition of seven types of stigma.[27] Please see Table 4.1, which provides definitions about the seven types of stigma, including (1) public, (2) self, (3) perceived, (4) label avoidance, (5) stigma by association, (6) structural, and (7) health practitioner.

There is fluidity in these characterizations; however, stigma at the individual level (self, perceived, label avoidance, and stigma by association) is a subjective process that is "characterized by negative feelings about one's self, maladaptive behavior, identity transformation or stereotype endorsement resulting from an individual's experiences, perceptions or anticipation of negative social reac-

**Table 4.1. Seven Types of Stigma**

| Type of Stigma | Definition |
| --- | --- |
| *Individual Level* | |
| Self | Internalizes negative messages about having mental illness or substance use disorders |
| Perceived | Belief others have negative cognitions about people with mental illness/substance use disorders |
| Label Avoidance | Decision not to seek mental health/substance use disorder treatment to avoid being assigned a stigmatized label |
| Stigma by Association | Effects of stigma are extended to someone linked to a person with mental health difficulties |
| *Sociocultural Level* | |
| Public | Public endorses negative stereotypes and prejudices → discrimination against people with mental illness/substance use disorders |
| Health Practitioner | Health professional allows stereotypes and prejudices to negatively affect a patient's care |
| *Structural Level* | |
| Structural | Institutional polices or other social structures → decreases opportunities for people with mental illness/substance use disorders |

tions on the basis of a stigmatized social status or health condition."[28] At the sociocultural level (public and health practitioner), stigma is operationalized when social groups endorse stereotypes about and acting against a marginalized group.[29] Finally, structural stigma describes how institutions restrict the rights and opportunities of others in minoritized, heavily stigmatized groups via policies and procedures.[30]

Given the harm associated with stigma or social death in addiction, providing concrete examples of stigma at each level and then reframing the way SUD is discussed at each of these levels offers practical tools for those committed to destigmatizing addiction.

At the individual level, using patient-centered language is key. Because many people with an SUD have been socialized to think their lives don't matter because they are an "addict," countering internalized negative messages are essential. When people refer to themselves as "addict" or "criminal," inferring past or ongoing substance use, or having a carceral history, a crucial reframing includes offering the following sample language: "you are someone who uses drugs and is committed to being healthier," or "you were involved in the carceral system, but that doesn't define who you are." Another commonly used word that devalues people with an SUD is "clean," that is, if there are no substances present in the urine toxicology report. Similarly, one can use other language such as having a positive or negative urine, instead of being "clean." Please see Table 4.2 for other examples of how language on an individual letter can be reframed to combat individual stigma.[31]

At the sociocultural level, representation of addiction in the mainstream media, knowledge of how the war on drugs has heavily criminalized the iden-

**Table 4.2.  Patient-Centered Language in Addiction Medicine**

| Avoid | Prefer |
|---|---|
| Abuse | Use; low-risk/unhealthy/harmful use |
| Addicted baby | Baby experiencing substance withdrawal |
| Addict, drug user, alcoholic, crackhead | Person with substance use disorder |
| Medical marijuana | Medical cannabis |
| Fix, binge, relapse | Dose, use, heaving drinking episode, return to use |
| Smoking cessation | Tobacco use disorder treatment |
| Detoxification | Withdrawal management |

tity of people with SUDs, and increasing general knowledge about the many medications for addiction treatment and psychotherapeutic interventions available to people with SUDs, beyond Alcoholics Anonymous or Narcotics Anonymous, is essential. For instance, as a way to limit and provide alternatives to stigmatizing images of people who use drugs in the media, often featuring unkempt people, or images of syringes, dirty needles, and so on, the Health in Justice Action Lab from Northeastern University[32] attempts to "change the narrative," by providing access to culturally humane images of people with an SUD, along with how anyone can be involved with deliberate initiatives to affirm the humanity of those who use drugs.

Equally important to representation is an understanding of how damaging the war on drugs has been in effectively sending people with an SUD to prison instead of providing medical treatment.[33] There continues to be a rise in the number of drug overdoses related to ongoing substance use, despite these punitive laws. Education of the public, healthcare organizations, and policy makers as to how the United States perpetuates stigma by making it difficult to access treatment remains paramount in countering stigma.

## THE IMPORTANCE OF COLLABORATION: CARING FOR THOSE INVOLVED IN THE CARCERAL SYSTEM

An integral part of progress in our healthcare system includes not just acknowledging the history and current-day impact of drug policies and practices, but to work as advocates to dismantle these policies as they continue to perpetuate harm, increase disparities, and serve as barriers to care. Between 1970 and 2010, the rate of incarceration in the United States quintupled, mostly secondary to changes in federal drug laws that produced lengthier sentences associated with the harsh criminalization of drug use.[34] Individuals who are incarcerated with SUDs require our collaboration at multiple points of care during the process of reintegration, including access to MOUD, treatment programs, housing, and general medical and mental healthcare. Barriers to use of MOUD occur at both the patient-provider and systems levels.[35] Access to medication during community reentry can vary widely and depend upon factors like housing access and model of recovery program, with some programs/housing requiring people with SUD to be "drug free" in order to access services.[36] Individuals referred by community corrections agents are less likely to receive MOUD than those referred by other pathways, and when they are referred to treatment are more likely to be referred to methadone versus buprenorphine due to bias.[37] Partnering with reentry programs decreases stigma by improving education among those referring individuals with SUDs to services, but systems levels barriers (such as insurance coverage) remain.[38] Among states who participate in Medicaid expansion, individuals referred by criminal justice were more likely to receive MOUD than those living in states who do not participate.[39] A progressive approach to healthcare involves coordination of stakeholders including physicians, multidisciplinary care team members, policy makers, and other entities outside of the healthcare system if we are to truly impact health outcomes for the SUD community.

# 5

# Child and Adolescent Mental Health

*Hal Kronsberg*

By the third time I had to jostle Reggie Brown awake, I decided to become a child psychiatrist. As his seventh-grade math teacher in the tiny (and heavily segregated) town of Indianola, Mississippi, I often felt overwhelmed trying to help Reggie manage his volcanic rage, set off by any manner of perceived injustices, but it was easier to teach a kid with his eyes open than one passed out on his desk. Today was his first day back at school after being psychiatrically hospitalized two hours away for violent outbursts in his home, and he couldn't keep his eyes open.

"It's the pills," he told me when I asked what he needed to do to stay awake.

The longer I taught, the more interested I became in understanding why and how so many of my students struggled with their feelings in school and at home. I had thought I would most likely end up training to become a therapist. "But what's the point of therapy," I wondered, "if some faraway doctor is going to 'solve' my kids' problems by just putting them to sleep?"

Admittedly, my understanding of therapy and psychiatry at the time was more than a little naive, but I knew that as a psychiatrist I had the capacity to use every tool, medication included, to help the kids with whom I would work. Seeing the treatment received by Reggie and other young Black boys in Mississippi, I wanted to make sure that the ability to prescribe medications included the ability *not* to prescribe medications as well.

After medical school, I completed my adult psychiatry training (which all child psychiatrists need to finish first) at New York Presbyterian Hospital and my child psychiatry fellowship at Massachusetts General Hospital. My

37

training was phenomenal, and the reputation of these institutions is richly deserved. Both programs deeply emphasized therapy training as well as medication treatment. My supervisors were brilliant and demanding, and nearly all of them were in private practice themselves, seeing children and adults with significant challenges but also with the financial resources to afford to see psychiatrists who do not participate in any insurance plans.

While my training programs ensured that I worked tirelessly to learn to make use of everything at my disposal to help kids and adults be their best selves, they also covertly implied that the ideal form of psychiatric practice involved acting as therapist and prescriber concurrently. Practicing psychiatry in this way often forces doctors into a difficult choice: either accept dramatically lower reimbursements from insurers compared with other specialties or opt out of the insurance system altogether.[1] This reality helps explain why fewer than 60 percent of psychiatrists accept any insurance, whether or not they practice therapy, and fewer than 45 percent of psychiatrists see individuals with Medicaid.[2] As a trainee, it was easy to see the appeal of being a psychiatrist who is also a therapist; I could have more time to understand and feel closer to those I treated and with both tools at my disposal I felt like I could be a more effective doctor. By encouraging psychiatrists to be therapists, and by extension opt out of accepting insurance, many psychiatric training programs further reinforce the two-tiered system of mental healthcare that exists in our country. If you can afford hundreds of dollars per session or have uniquely generous out-of-network insurance benefits, you can access the sort of holistic approach prized at elite training programs. If you can't, you face months-long waiting lists.

I went to medical school to work with kids similar to those I taught in Mississippi, living under socioeconomic strain and poorly served by the existing mental health infrastructure. Even if I chose to practice therapy and prescribe for kids with Medicaid, seeing kids for weekly hour-long sessions would dramatically limit how many I could treat, especially compared to partnering with therapists and focusing on prescribing. In 2000, of the 324 counties nationwide where more than 30 percent of kids lived in poverty, only 31 had even a single child psychiatrist[3] and more kids, regardless of socioeconomic status, are treated for mental conditions by pediatricians than psychiatrists.[4] A more equitable system of healthcare would ensure that the expertise of child psychiatrists be harnessed to care for as many kids as possible that are most in need of specialty care. Meeting with kids for an hour at a time in a nice office carefully curated with toys and other objects meant to facilitate the therapeutic process is an enjoyable and effective way to practice, but when two-thirds of adolescents with psychiatric disorders receive no treatment of any kind,[5] this model of care is neither scalable nor financially accessible to be considered even remotely equitable. A more far-reaching approach would have the psychiatrist as a complementary, but still critical, part of a treatment team that leverages the skills and expertise of multiple people and professions, including therapists and individuals who can help families navigate Byzantine systems and institutions. When I finally finished my training, I was fortunate to join a team that does exactly that.

When my child psychiatry training ended, I returned to my hometown and took a position with Johns Hopkins' Child Mobile Treatment Team. Our team treats kids in Baltimore at especially high risk for being psychiatrically hospitalized multiple times or being removed from the home and placed into foster or institutional care. Children cared for by the Child Mobile Treatment Team have faced incredible stressors, both economic and interpersonal, witnessing shootings in their neighborhoods and wondering if there will be food at home for dinner. True to its name, we see our kids wherever they may be: in their homes, at school, at a bus stop, in front of a courthouse. That sort of flexibility has enabled us to continue to provide treatment for kids who have struggled through homelessness and extreme poverty, when they might otherwise fall out of treatment altogether.

Expanding mental health treatment that is flexible in its delivery and available outside of the traditional clinic is essential to building a system of treatment that reaches all children who need help. A study of children accessing mental healthcare at a large public agency showed that only one-third of children remained in treatment for more than eight sessions.[6] In cities like Baltimore, where children from the most challenged neighborhoods may need to take multiple buses to reach a clinic (if the bus routes connect them at all), therapists and psychiatrists must be empowered to go directly to the community and treat kids where they are. In Baltimore, the public school system has partnered with a number of organizations, including Johns Hopkins, to create an immense and audacious school-based mental health program, where therapists and psychiatrists provide care directly within the public school system. The program has been hugely successful in reaching kids that typically would not be able to access care and stay in treatment,[7] but, for it to be successful, cash-strapped schools need to contribute financially and districts need an ample supply of therapists and psychiatrists willing to work outside the comfortable confines of an office.

When you work with children in the community who struggle with psychiatric illness while also living in severe poverty, the day-to-day challenges they face become much more apparent. In the office, it's always tempting to hear patient stories and shape them into problems I was taught to solve: the inattentive kid has attention deficit/hyperactivity disorder that I can treat with a stimulant; the avoidant kid has an anxiety disorder that I can treat with an antidepressant (which is actually our first-line treatment for anxiety). When I see the same kid in his or her home or school, it's so much harder to over-look years of unmet educational need from an overtaxed and underfunded school system or the neighborhoods where violence necessitates constant and exhausting vigilance. Almost as soon as I began to practice in the community, it became clear just how inadequate diagnosing and prescribing, primary tools of my training, were to address the myriad of social stressors and challenges that generate, exacerbate, and obfuscate child mental health challenges. My experience with Child Mobile Treatment and the school-based program has highlighted the need for child psychiatry training to dramatically broaden its scope and teach doctors about how to coordinate and work with the myriad of supports and services that are critical for healthy development. I still pre-scribe medications and enter diagnoses into the medical record, but I also go to Individualized Education Plan meetings, help kids find employment, make sure there is food in the refrigerator, and write letters to utility companies and housing authorities.

Working with kids and families living in extreme poverty can also feel over-whelming to child psychiatrists, and it can be easy to retreat into a defensive position and say that anything not related to medication is "someone else's problem." However, expanding the scope of medical training to include a broader understanding of how institutions, neighborhood conditions, policies, and history can impact mental health can go a long way toward empowering physicians to provide more holistic and effective care. The act of recogniz-ing how social, economic, and political conditions produce health inequali-ties and contribute to mental illness is increasingly referred to as "structural competency."[8] Teaching this skill set, which builds on the idea of "cultural competency," requires that physicians also work to address these underlying social conditions both inside and outside of the traditional clinic setting.[8] To train child psychiatrists capable of providing more equitable mental healthcare to all children, structural competency will need to be a central part of train-ing. However, while training directors consider social and structural issues an essential area for child psychiatry education, at least one-fifth of all programs don't allot even a single hour to it.[9]

Yet while improving child psychiatry education and expanding treatment to better reach the most vulnerable kids would go some ways toward achiev-ing justice in our mental healthcare system, we must also strive to address the unique stressors, traumas, and dearth of opportunities disproportionately faced by children living in poverty. Psychiatrists must loudly and humbly admit that fluoxetine, amphetamine/dextroamphetamine, and therapy have limits to what they can alleviate. The tragedy and triumph of DeShawn Jones illustrates this idea.

I met DeShawn through our school-based program. He was finishing his junior year in high school and his typically solid grades had dropped precipitously, as had his attendance. His teachers had noticed that he'd seemed more withdrawn in class, and he was eventually referred to treatment for the first time. A football player who was well respected by teachers and popular with peers, as I got to know DeShawn, whose name and other identifying information have been altered to protect his anonymity, during our initial meeting it was clear to me that he had many strengths. However, for reasons that puzzled both him and his grandmother, he had been struggling over the last few months with symptoms of depression, including feeling sad on most days for most of the day, losing his motivation in school, struggling to focus, and (in quieter moments) wishing he might go to sleep and never wake up. In digging a little more to learn about his early life experiences, DeShawn described for me the event from when he was five years old that would profoundly impact him and his family.

DeShawn had never had a relationship with his father. While his mother had a large and inclusive family, he and his mother were the only members of his household. One Saturday afternoon at his home, DeShawn heard a loud knock on the front door and a voice that he thought belonged to a friend of his mother. The moment he turned the knob, the door flew open and knocked DeShawn to the ground and a man ran into the house and shot DeShawn's mother in the chest three times. Both DeShawn's and his grandmother's eyes welled with tears as DeShawn described watching his mother die.

I asked DeShawn why, after experiencing an unimaginable trauma, he didn't come into treatment until eleven years later. "I felt like I just had to be okay," he said. DeShawn's grandmother knew that he had taken the loss hard, but DeShawn had the remarkable ability to disguise his pain. "The whole family was falling apart," she said. "I was actually grateful because DeShawn seemed to be doing the best of any of us, and I felt like I didn't have to worry about him."

In a way, DeShawn's grandmother was right. Despite experiencing this profound trauma, DeShawn never failed a class, had a good collection of friends, was a popular student and excellent athlete, and never got in trouble in school or with the law. But finally given the chance to speak about his internal world, DeShawn shared that for years he would ruminate on his mother's murder and how he blamed himself for opening the door to her assailant. However,

DeShawn was able to use his remarkable fortitude to push thoughts and feelings of his mother away.

As shocking as DeShawn's story may seem, it's entirely too common among African American youth in Baltimore. Among a sample of high school students seeking mental health treatment in Baltimore City, 93 percent knew at least one person who had been the victim of a violent act and 77 percent reported having witnessed a violent act.[10] One might think that children exposed to trauma will go on to develop post-traumatic stress disorder (PTSD). However, PTSD is a constellation of symptoms that better describes the experiences of adults and may be considered a relatively rare condition in children, whose brains and minds are still developing. In fact, in a large survey of kids exposed to trauma, only about 16 percent of those who witnessed a traumatic event happen to a loved one go on to develop PTSD.[11] Children who experience significant trauma are at high risk of developing an assortment of difficulties, including challenges with managing their emotional intensity, diminished attention and academic performance, and difficulty forming and maintaining relationships, and they are much more likely to develop other mood or anxiety disorders.[12] In particular, children and adolescents who do not get any treatment in the wake of a major trauma are especially at risk for eventually developing a major depressive disorder,[13] which certainly fit the description for DeShawn. Furthermore, depressive disorders that emerge in individuals with a history of childhood trauma can be more severe, may be more likely to be associated with suicide attempts or deliberate self-harm, and may respond less favorably to antidepressant medications.[14]

In recent years, numerous news stories and best-selling books have been written about resilience and "grit" as the secret ingredient for children to overcome poverty and hardship. In her TED talk, psychologist Angela Duckworth described how her research into the characteristics that predict perseverance through difficulty was inspired, like my own path to medicine, by her experiences as a seventh-grade math teacher in a high-poverty school whose students were predominantly children of color.[15] Many schools have raced to try to include resilience and character building in their curricula with the aim of helping students overcome hardship and disadvantages that our society actively generates.

It's hard to imagine a student more resilient than DeShawn. Raised in the Perkins Homes, East Baltimore's notoriously dangerous and poorly maintained public housing development, DeShawn faced terrible housing conditions and neighborhood violence, and witnessed the murder of his mother. Despite these challenges, DeShawn built a vibrant social life and grew into a good athlete, student, and friend. Yet some of those same traits that some might classify as "resilience," the capacity to push through distress, made him less likely to be identified as someone who might benefit from treatment and facilitated the development of an avoidant coping style that contributed to ultimately developing a depressive episode.

Black children are nearly twice as likely as white children to experience the sort of childhood trauma that is most likely to impact them as adults.[16] Imagine if a boy in a wealthy suburban private school suffered the same trauma as DeShawn did. It's easy to picture that child's entire school and community coming to his aid, ensuring that his mental health needs are looked after and even making sure that his classmates weren't negatively impacted by it as well. For DeShawn, his "reward" for his remarkable resilience was to suffer quietly for years and only come to treatment fully in the midst of a depressive episode, when his ability to graduate on time was jeopardized.

Efforts to emphasize character building and "grit" in public schools in high-poverty areas may be well intended, but they also risk communicating to children who are disproportionately exposed to trauma that their difficulties stem from character flaws or a lack of toughness. Even more troubling, over-hyping these sorts of unproven interventions can blunt the urgency to address systemic inequality by offering the promise that with specialized teaching, kids can overcome the ways that poverty and white supremacy impact child development. The truth is, the most effective way to help kids like DeShawn recover from the sequelae of trauma is to make sure that they don't experience it in the first place. It's tempting to think that if environmental factors put low-income kids of color at greater risk for developing mental health problems, a simple solution might be simply changing the environment. In the 1990s, the federal government ran an experiment to do just that, and the results were wholly unexpected.

In 1992, Congress authorized $70 million to help families living in particularly distressed public housing developments find new neighborhoods in which to live. Unlike other social programs, this undertaking was part of a broader effort to find out how much families can benefit from moving from a high-poverty neighborhood to a low-poverty neighborhood. Called "Moving to Opportunity," over four thousand participating families in five cities were randomized to three groups: a group that was given a housing voucher that could only be used in low-poverty neighborhoods, a group that was given a housing voucher that could be used anywhere, and a group that did not receive any voucher. The children in these families were closely followed ten to fifteen years after they were randomized to those groups, with particular attention to the development of mental health problems. The lower-poverty neighborhoods were indeed safer than the public housing developments where most families started the experiment, and so it was expected that outcomes would be better as well.[17] Years later, when girls in the low-poverty voucher group were compared with those who did not receive a voucher, those given the voucher were less likely to have behavior problems, but the rates of mental health problems were largely the same.[18] However, boys given vouchers for low-poverty neighborhoods did substantially worse than those who received no vouchers and were more than twice as likely to develop a depressive disorder and more than three times as likely to develop PTSD and have conduct problems. Rather than dramatically improve the trajectory of children living in poverty opportunities to uproot families and move them to low-poverty neighborhoods marginally benefited girls and actually made outcomes for boys significantly worse. Interviews with the kids who moved to low-poverty neighborhoods indicated that challenges forming social connections and feeling accepted in their new neighborhoods, as well as severing social supports in their old ones, may help explain why boys struggled so much after they moved.[19]

To imagine a system that more equitably addresses mental health problems in children, it may help to revisit DeShawn. After enrolling in treatment, which consisted of therapy and a somewhat brief trial of antidepressant medication, DeShawn improved considerably. He would graduate from high school with his grades mostly recovered and ended up at a four-year college. As his depressive symptoms lifted, DeShawn was able to work through his grief while also confronting the worries that he had about leaving home and not being able to look after his grandmother from college. DeShawn got better with treatment that he might never have accessed had it not been located within his school, but it wasn't treatment alone by any means that led to his success.

Though DeShawn lost his mother at a young age, thanks to his talents and charisma, he had an easy time connecting to other support figures and structures. DeShawn had always been a strong student who drew the attention and affection of his teachers, and it was his teachers that first noticed his change in mood and behavior and led him to treatment. In Baltimore, where nearly 40 percent of high schoolers miss twenty or more school days per year,[20] it can be easy for struggling students to slip through the cracks. Had DeShawn been only an average student, or if he was often out of school, his teachers might never have noticed his emerging depressive symptoms. The track team also played a central role in DeShawn's life. Practices after school each day kept him busy and away from the dangerous courtyards of his housing complex, and he described his coach as a critically important male role model in his life. But not every kid can be a popular student and a varsity athlete.

To create a just mental healthcare system, we must not only treat mental illness, we also need to ensure that children live in the sort of conditions that promote healthy development. Identity formation is the crucial developmental task of adolescence.[21] The act of determining who we are, what we like, who we affiliate with, and what we aspire to be depends fully on opportunities to try different things and meet different people and see what fits us best. Schools with higher percentages of students of color or those who qualify for free lunch have fewer media, academic, sports, and service activities.[22] DeShawn was fortunate that high school track team may be only modestly impacted by budget cuts and inner-city fiscal crises, but Black kids in Baltimore whose talents lie elsewhere may never have the opportunity to see them realized and build bonds with others who share those interests. Track connected DeShawn with caring mentors and close friends, structured his time, and gave him a sense of mastery, all of which were critical for his identity formation.

Simply transplanting kids to safer suburbs and giving them access to better-funded schools will not solve the gap in opportunities. Instead, we need to fund inner city schools to the level where they can provide the same sort of critical and protective developmental opportunities and activities that kids in wealthy suburbs can access, ignoring useless metrics like dollars allotted per student and focusing instead on ensuring that children in Baltimore City and its wealthy suburbs can enjoy the same opportunities to grow and explore.

These sorts of inequality of opportunities have only been exacerbated by the COVID-19 crisis. Not only has the disease itself disproportionately impacted racial and ethnic minorities, in Baltimore we can see how children of color have also had their developmental opportunities impacted unequally. As wealthy parents with access to physical space and means to hire private teachers are able to form "pandemic pods" that afford their children in-person learning (or send their children to private schools, which are free to reopen in person), lower-income children in Baltimore had no option but virtual learning for the start of the 2020/2021 school year. This is made worse by huge disparities in access to high-speed internet between white households (nearly 75 percent) compared with African American and Latinx (around 50 percent).[23] The "summer slide," the phenomenon in which academic achievement scores regress during summer vacation, has been shown to be significantly more pronounced for lower-income students.[24] Due to the impact of COVID-19, lower-income Baltimore students, who are predominantly students of color, are at much greater risk for falling behind.

DeShawn was also fortunate in the way that a social support system coalesced around him after his mother was murdered. Extended family members, teachers, and coaches all became central figures in his life. We know forming stable emotional attachments to adult figures is essential for children to learn how to regulate their own emotions.[25] At the same time, state and federal government policies and practices have specifically targeted African American young men for prolonged incarceration for drug-related offenses.[26] Notably, African Americans and whites use drugs at similar rates, but African Americans are six times more likely to be imprisoned for drug offenses.[27] As a result, by 1990 over a quarter of all African American children would see their fathers go to prison, seven times the rate for white children.[28] Among Baltimore City children in particular, a 2015 survey found that 15 percent had a parent that was either currently incarcerated or on parole or probation.[29]

While protecting children from fathers who commit acts of domestic violence and violent crime certainly is necessary, mass incarceration has ensnared thousands of parents who have committed nonviolent drug offenses. When researchers control for a host of factors, including socioeconomic status, race, and parental alcohol use, kids whose fathers were ever incarcerated were between 40 percent and 70 percent more likely to develop a depressive disorder, anxiety disorder, or PTSD.[30] Ending mass incarceration, which vastly disproportionately impacts African American families and children in places like Baltimore, not only would stop needless disruptions of critical parental attachment but would also likely directly reduce rates of childhood mental illness.

Nearly half of all children are at risk for developing a psychiatric illness during the course of their childhood,[31] and it's easy to see how much recovering from disorders depends on access to care and community resources. My training in psychiatry showed me how the process of educating child psychiatrists can exacerbate inequalities in accessing psychiatric care, pushing many child psychiatrists to participate in a two-tiered system that offers top-notch treatment only to those who can afford it. Even if we devised a system in which care from a child psychiatrist was more broadly available to all children, such as by emphasizing the need for treatment availability in community settings, it is critical that child psychiatrists and other mental health professionals are trained to more effectively address the social conditions that drive and shape child mental illness. Fundamentally, a system designed to more equitably provide mental healthcare to all children cannot exist without a more just educational system, criminal justice system, and neighborhoods and communities that afford all children the opportunity to safely discover who they are and hope to be. We cannot focus solely on treating mental illness, but we must train our eyes on eradicating the conditions that promote it.

# 6

# Cancer

*Inas Abuali, Don S. Dizon, and Narjust Duma*

## THE CURRENT STATE OF CANCER CARE
## IN THE UNITED STATES

"The time has come in America when the same kind of concentrated effort that split the atom and took a man to the moon should be turned toward conquering this dread disease [cancer]. Let us make a total national commitment to achieve this goal."

—State of the Union address, January 1971, President Nixon

In the 1970s, cancer became, and has since remained, the second leading cause of death in the United States, prompting President Nixon to declare "war on cancer" and sign the National Cancer Act into law.[1]

Each year, almost five thousand people are newly diagnosed with cancer and more than 1,600 die each day in the United States as a result. The lifetime probability of being diagnosed with cancer in America is approximately 40 percent, which means that one in every two or three individuals will develop cancer during their lifetime, subject to individual variability according to genetic and environmental risk factors—issues we are still trying to fully understand.

There has been significant progress against cancer since Nixon's declaration, reflecting improvements due to reduction in tobacco use, early detection through screening initiatives, and effective treatment options. The death rate has declined by 1.5 percent per year for cancer in the 2010s, mainly due to advances in lung, breast, prostate, and colorectal cancers.[2] Estimates are that 2.6 million cancer deaths were averted in the United States in the past two decades and that two out of three people with cancer live for at least five years after diagnosis, with the highest number of cancer survivors in U.S. history.[3]

Despite these gains, significant challenges remain in the fair and appropriate allocation of resources toward the approach to cancer care in the United States, with persistent and glaring disparities that continue to require attention and action.

## Healthcare Costs, Financial Toxicity, and Medical Tourism.

"America's healthcare system is neither healthy, caring, nor a system."

—Walter Conkrite

The proportion of the gross domestic product spent toward healthcare spending has increased from 6.9 percent in 1970 to 17.7 percent by 2019.[4] The U.S. Centers for Medicare and Medicaid Services estimates that healthcare spending will increase from $3.6 trillion in 2018 to nearly $6 trillion by 2027. The leading contributor to this increase is the cost of drugs, including cancer drugs.[5] There have been ongoing price increases in cancer drugs that exceed increases due to inflation, which persist even when later studies demonstrate that a drug is less effective than what was initially believed or at the time of the U.S. Food Drug Administration approval.[6] Furthermore, many drugs may be efficacious at lower doses, but further studies are not performed to investigate this or the long-term consequences of receiving a higher than necessary dose of the medication.

With the rising healthcare costs and the gaps in insurance coverage, one-third of cancer survivors between the ages of eighteen and sixty-four in the United States incur debt because of their treatment. In one report from 2017, 55 percent of them owed more than $10,000 and 3 percent had declared bankruptcy.[7]

The current state of the healthcare system has given rise to the phenomenon of "medical tourism." Americans seek medical care abroad, attracted by lower costs, easier access to subspecialists, and reduced wait time.[8] This raises a host of challenges in terms of variability of quality and standard of care, ethical dilemmas, and health equity concerns.[9] Once patients return to the United States, establishing appropriate follow-up and transitioning care can be particularly challenging and provide added risks to the procedures or treatment decisions taken at the medical center outside of the U.S. territory.

## Bias in Cancer Care

The National Cancer Institute (NCI) defines cancer health disparities as "adverse differences in cancer incidence, cancer prevalence, cancer mortality, cancer survivorship and burden of cancer or related health conditions that exist among specific population groups in the U.S."[10]

It is well documented that the incidence and outcome of various cancers are significantly impacted by race and ethnicity due to the inequalities in wealth, insurance status, risk factor exposures, and barriers precluding certain populations from accessing high-quality prevention, screening, and treatment modalities.[11]

For example, in one study, the five-year relative survival rate for all cancers combined diagnosed during 2009 through 2015 was 67 percent overall, 68 percent in whites, and 62 percent in Blacks, with Black patients having a lower stage-specific survival for most cancer types.[12] In another report, the relative risk of death after a cancer diagnosis was 33 percent higher in Black patients and 51 percent higher in American Indians/Alaska Natives than white patients.[12] Furthermore, cancer is the leading cause of death in many states for Hispanic Americans despite being the second cause of death nationally.[13]

### Addressing the Health Needs of Sexual and Gender Minority Patients

Additionally, glaring discrepancies affect sexual and gender minority (SGM) people. These are at least in part related to provider biases and deficits in education, insufficient collection of gender and sexual identification across cancer centers and tumor registries, and an overall lack of consensus guidelines on the approach and care for SGM populations.[14] This is despite accumulating data that SGM populations have an increased risk of certain cancers and are less likely to access cancer screening.[15] Despite this, the lack of standardized data collection on SGM people with cancer severely constrains the research on outcomes of this population after a cancer diagnosis, thereby limiting even more the generation of needs assessments and tailored interventional strategies to improve their well-being. This, ultimately, creates a discrepancy between clinical trial participants and real-world patients, and data is inappropriately extrapolated to treat all patients regardless of sexual/gender/racial/ethnic backgrounds.[16]

### Barriers to Access

Due to the unique structure of the healthcare system in the United States compared to other countries, there is a higher rate of uninsured people who lack access to healthcare, impeding access to high-quality and affordable cancer care. The system relies largely on employment-based private insurance with patients absorbing extra out-of-pocket costs through deductibles and co-payments. A for-profit system with limited access to Medicare and Medicaid results in a lack of universal coverage. The introduction of the Affordable Care Act (ACA) was one initiative geared toward expanding coverage, with favorable trends noted, but the changes in administration have weakened the effort and modified the original goal for the program. For example, Medicaid expansion states showed a decline in the number of uninsured patients with a new cancer diagnosis and a trend toward an early stage diagnosis of certain cancers.[17] Notably, there was a reduction in the disparities among sociodemographic subpopulations in the Medicaid expansion states.[18] Yet, even with the greater access to care afforded in states that have adopted the ACA, individuals living in rural areas face additional unique challenges related to healthcare access, including physical distance, limited healthcare facilities, and difficulty accessing subspecialists. Studies have demonstrated that individuals living in rural areas are more likely to be diagnosed with more advanced cancer stages than urban populations.[19] Additionally, the workforce is still not concentrated in rural areas, with only 11.6 percent of oncologists practicing in rural areas.[20] Furthermore, it is estimated that only 27 percent of U.S. patients with cancer have access to clinical trials, with geographical barriers playing a large role.[21] All of these barriers have become even more apparent during the COVID-19 pandemic.

### Government and Cancer Research Funding

Federal funding for cancer research has led to significant advances in cancer prevention, detection, diagnosis, treatment, and quality of life for patients, leading to a record number of people living with and beyond cancer in the United States today. In addition, federal funding has helped to address equity in cancer clinical trials. This was seen in one study by Unger and colleagues in which enrollment in clinical trials was evaluated by whether the studies were sponsored by the NCI or by industry.[22] Spanning fifteen different cancers, they reported that the rate of enrollment of Black volunteers was three-fold higher for trials sponsored by the NCI (9 percent versus 2.9 percent, $p < 0.001$).

Virtually every American has been touched by cancer, and voters in the United States overwhelmingly support greater investment in cancer research. The American Society of Clinical Oncology's National Cancer Opinion Survey found that 73 percent of Americans support the government spending more on finding treatments and cures for cancer—even if it means higher taxes or adding to the deficit.[23]

However, funding for cancer care and research is affected by past, current, and future administrations. Lengthy budget hearings and uncertainty are often seen when discussing funds for the NCI, in addition to the constant changes associated with each administration. Funding for the NCI has not kept pace with research opportunities. From 2013 to 2019, funding for the NCI increased by about 20 percent.[24] During the same timeframe, the number of grant applications increased by 50 percent, meaning promising science is going unfunded.[25] Low success rates for grant applications make it challenging to attract and retain talented cancer researchers, mainly because there is competition with fast-growing research departments in pharmaceutical companies, which are always willing to recruit new and promising researchers from academic oncology; the pharmaceutical companies can tout the fact that they do not have to compete for research funding.

Cancer research is the primary cause of improvement in cancer detection and survival rates. Making the NCI budget a priority and protecting it from the fluctuations associated with each government administration will assure discoveries and improvement in current practices continue.

## CANCER CARE IN THE TWENTY-FIRST CENTURY: THE EMERGING INFLUENCE OF PEOPLE WITH CANCER

The past decade has seen an emerging influence of people with cancer as major voices in research and policy making. People with cancer provide a perspective that only a handful of physicians can (as cancer survivors themselves). Issues like access to clinical trials, clinical trials design, and financial toxicity have now been brought to the forefront by the people that are affected the most by decisions that before were made behind closed doors. Indeed, patient advocates are now important members of the National Clinical Trials Network, with representation in the cooperative groups and disease site research committees.

Cancer patient advocates have a broad view of cancer research.[26] They are involved in many diverse cancer research committees, where they can help tackle old problems from new perspectives that often differ from policy, academic, medical, and scientific approaches.[27] In this role, patient advocates have transformed how we conduct cancer research by becoming active members of research teams, conducting and funding studies on their own and providing their perspective when new clinical trials results are presented.[28]

Patient advocacy organizations' role in the oncology healthcare delivery ecosystem is ever evolving and has moved well beyond its original role of solely advocating for services, research, care, and understanding.[29] The current field of patient advocacy has its roots in the patient rights movement of the 1970s, with groups like the National Welfare Rights Organization being instrumental in getting a patient bill of rights accepted by the Joint Commission on Accreditation of Healthcare Organizations in 1972.[30]

The transformation was further accelerated in 1991 with the U.S. Food Drug Administration Patient Representative Program's formation and has continued to expand over time, with patient advocates now being involved in the entire care continuum.[31]

Patient advocacy requires a multilevel approach to meet each patient's needs, and it can be difficult and labor-intensive, particularly for people receiving treatment for their cancer or recovering from recent radiation or surgery. For that reason, we advise that all healthcare providers become advocates to guide patients during treatments and be actively involved with state and national societies to generate policy changes and create a more inclusive environment for all people with cancer.

As of 2021, each cancer type has at least one community group, meeting on social media and independent of geographic location. Within these communities, people with cancer are helping each other navigate healthcare, pointing out disparities and, often, solutions borne only out of personal experience as it relates to disparities in care, the timeliness of treatment, and navigating clinical trials. In so doing they have moved well beyond their original patient supportive role and have become critical players in the oncology healthcare delivery and clinical research ecosystems.[32]

Social media platforms have changed how physicians and other healthcare providers interact with people with cancer and their caregivers.[33] Platforms like Twitter provide a direct channel of communication between scientists, patients, and caregivers.[34] Consequently, it provides a forum for patients to learn about their own cancers far beyond conversations with the medical professionals who treat them; patients develop expertise within their own right.

As the healthcare system continues to evolve and become more complex, so will the role of patient advocacy organizations. To address these challenges, there will be an even greater need for collaboration, innovation, increased infrastructure, support by national and international societies, the avoidance of overlap and duplication, and a laser focus on providing meaningful improvement in the availability, transparency, and affordability of healthcare.[35] The era in which people with cancer were excluded when large policy changes were made is part of the past; our patient advocates are here to stay. We all have the same goal: improving the care and outcomes of people with cancer.

# THE FUTURE OF CANCER CARE:
# IMAGINING THE POSSIBILITIES

"We make progress in society only if we stop cursing and complaining about its shortcomings and have the courage to do something about them."

—Elisabeth Kübler-Ross

There has been a growing recognition of the difference between healthcare equality and equity in cancer care in recent years. While equality entails providing everyone with the same resources, equity acknowledges that specific populations require additional support and resources to obtain the same opportunities for cancer detection and treatment.

In an updated statement on August 12, 2020, the American Society of Clinical Oncology[36] affirmed its commitment to achieving cancer health equity via the following four recommendations that aim to guide future activities and strategies:

1. Ensure equitable access to high-quality care
2. Ensure equitable access to research
3. Address structural barriers
4. Increase awareness and action[37]

## Shared Decision Making, Destigmatization of Cancer, and Survivorship Programs

Shared decision making, a core component of patient-centered communication, involves an open discussion between the clinician and the patient regarding the risks, benefits, and costs of caretaking regarding the patient's preferences and values. The Institute of Medicine recognizes this is an integral element of high-quality cancer care, ensuring individualized, informed, and evidence-based care that aligns with the patient's principles.[38] Shared decision making improves trust between clinician and patient, and promotes a better understanding of an individual's unique social determinants of health that impacts their care throughout the continuum of cancer care. This could be particularly challenging when language barriers exist, exacerbating disparities and increasing the risk of medical errors. Appropriate utilization of professional interpretation services, rather than reliance on family members or non-proficient staff, is vital.

When discussing stigma related to cancer, none is as apparent as that related to lung cancer. There are known genetic and environmental-related risk factors related to lung cancer, with smoking being an established cause. Unfortunately, the stigma associated with developing a smoking-related malignancy often leads to a "shame and blame" culture. Patients with lung cancer can often internalize these negative connotations, leading to increased depression rates, reduced screening, and delayed diagnosis.[39]

Workplace discrimination is the main challenge for cancer survivors looking to reenter the workforce.[40] This may include assumptions of lower productivity, demotions or lack of promotions, and inflexibility regarding requested time off for medical appointments. Increased awareness of discriminatory behaviors and anti-stigma legislations are imperative and require regulatory oversight. Providing education to employers about survivors' right to work and performance abilities following cancer therapies is vital. Supporting and promoting patient advocacy groups can help raise awareness, destigmatization, and education regarding appropriate resources and support networks.

## Legislation in Drug Pricing and Equitable Enrollment in Clinical Trials

Legislative and regulatory reforms are imperative in combating the exponential rise of cancer drug costs in the United States. There is a need for scrutiny to prevent profiteering, wastage, and cronyism. In the United Kingdom, for example, there are several cost control structures implemented by the National Health System. This includes the Voluntary Pricing and Access Scheme for branded drugs, which confines total (U.K.) health service pharmaceutical cost increases to 2 percent a year. Additionally, the National Institute for Health and Care Excellence can negotiate price reductions of certain medications. The Cancer Drug Fund also ensures a supply of new drugs at negotiated prices pending further data gathering regarding effectiveness.[41]

Other cost-lowering measures can include increasing use of generic drugs or biosimilars and reducing/preventing direct advertisements to the public by pharmaceutical companies. A more centralized healthcare system can allow for collective bargaining and joining of a global patent pool.[42] Government-driven price negotiations can help target drugs with low clinical benefit. Oncologists should adhere to evidence-based guidelines and minimize off-label use of cancer drugs except after careful deliberation. Healthcare policies such as the ACA expand coverage for necessary drugs and treatments and could further healthcare equity via the provision of increased insurance coverage to vulnerable populations including patients with preexisting conditions at the time of health insurance enrollment.[43]

The National Institutes of Health Revitalization Act of 1993 requires that medical research paid for by the National Institutes of Health (approximately

6 percent of U.S. clinical trials) includes women and minorities.[44] However, it does not provide adequate instruction on minority enrollment. The remainder of U.S. clinical trials (94 percent) are mostly unregulated in this manner. There has been an increased awareness regarding this complicated matter. The Eliminating Disparities in Clinical Trials report by the Intercultural Cancer Council stated that researchers must focus on the "three Rs": recruitment, retention, and return.[45] There are ongoing efforts by professional societies, pharmaceutical companies, and healthcare organizations to promote diverse recruitment and to collaborate with community practices to improve access to clinical trials.

## Diversification of the Oncology Workforce

Despite the diverse makeup of the U.S. population, the physician workforce lacks adequate racial and ethnic representation. According to the most recent census, 13 percent of the U.S. population is Black or African American, and 18 percent is Hispanic. In contrast, only 2.3 percent of practicing oncologists self-identified as Black or African American, and 5.8 percent of practicing oncologists self-identified as Hispanic. Additionally, only one-third of oncologists are women.[46] Specific challenges to underrepresented groups in medicine include few role models, paucity of mentorship, biases, and citizenship tax, leading to a prominent leaky pipeline phenomenon.

A greater effort is needed to bring equity to healthcare in the United States. One solution relies on greater diversity of the healthcare workforce, a stance supported by the 2009 Position Statement of the American Society of Clinical Oncology.[47] Diversification in the workforce can bring about equity in several ways. One, diversity in medical school matriculants is associated with a more culturally competent workforce. In a 2008 study of medical school students (n = 31,370), white students comprised of classes with higher proportion of underrepresented groups in medicine or nonwhite students were significantly more likely to self-rate as culturally competent and of having stronger attitudes regarding equitable access to care than those attending more homogenous classes.[48] The importance of having a clinician of your own racial background (race concordance) continues to be explored but is important. For example, in one study that assessed information processing, 105 volunteers met with a virtual doctor who performed a risk assessment for the development of lung cancer. Compared to information provided by a race-concordant doctor, volunteers were less accurate in their perceived risk of lung cancer when it came from a racially discordant doctor ($p = 0.048$).[49]

## CONCLUSIONS

In the United States, cancer care remains one of the settings where large health disparities are seen, from access to cancer screening to referral to end-of-life services. Despite many advances in diagnosis and treatment of cancer many disparities persist, further widening during the COVID-19 pandemic. Inclusion of minority populations in clinical trials, cost control of cancer drugs, and protected funds for cancer research are some of the initiatives that make a difference in cancer care equity. In order to achieve those goals, the involvement of all parties in cancer care is essential and is past due.

# 7

# "Sick and Tired of Being Sick and Tired"

## The History, Present, and Future of Healthcare Policy and Provision in U.S. Black Communities

*Arrianna Marie Planey and Max Jordan Nguemeni Tiako*

> "Medicine is a social science, and politics nothing but medicine at a larger scale."
>
> —Rudolf Virchow

## NO RIGHT TO HEALTHCARE

The title of this chapter alludes to Fannie Lou Hamer's famed 1964 speech, delivered in Harlem at an event organized to issue the Mississippi Freedom Democratic Party's challenge to the Democratic National Convention following their refusal to admit to the convention in Atlantic City the delegates of the Mississippi Freedom Democratic Party. In that speech she enumerated the struggles to secure rights for Black communities in the face of incrementalist politics that effectively maintained the status quo of profound racial and class inequity: "And you can always hear this long sob story: 'You know it takes time.' For three hundred years, we've given them time. And I've been tired so long, now I am sick and tired of being sick and tired, and we want a change."[1]

We open this chapter with this quote because so much remains to be done, and the urgency is still with us as Black communities bear the brunt of social and health inequities, which culminate in morbidity and premature mortality. In the United States, there is no effective, positive right to healthcare, and access to care is contoured by the intersections of racism, classism, ableism, and other forms of oppression. Overall, the patterning of healthcare provision can be characterized by Tudor Hart's (1971) Inverse Care Law: "the availability of good medical care tends to vary inversely with the need for it in the population served . . . [especially] where medical care is most exposed to market forces."[2]

Put another way, under "market conditions," healthcare resources—facilities and providers—are distributed according to demand (ability to pay), not need (underlying health status of population in service area). This is evidenced in the rationing of care by geographic location (health system preference for population dense and wealthy service areas), price (co-pays and deductibles on private plans), employment status (employer-sponsored insurance), age (Children's Health Insurance Plan, Medicare), disability and diagnostic status (Medicaid, Medicare in the case of end-stage renal disease), veteran status (U.S. Department of Veterans Affairs, Tricare), and income (Medicaid).[3] In the context of a system where employer-sponsored insurance predominates, racist employment discrimination, Black adults (and children in their care) continue to have higher rates of uninsurance.[4]

Moreover, the post-recession landscape is marked by inequity in health coverage eligibility, as many states—especially those in the Black belt and Mississippi Delta regions—have refused to expand Medicaid, which would extend eligibility to include adults making 138 percent of the federal poverty level. The downstream effects of these policy choices include disproportionate and accelerating rates of rural hospital closures between 2010 and 2019,[5] which exacerbates the ongoing crises of adverse maternal and infant outcomes,[6] and heavier burdens of chronic illness.[7]

Importantly, "market forces" in healthcare provision are not racially "neutral." The political economy of healthcare—evidenced in the path dependence of healthcare policies that condition access to healthcare on "work-readiness" and "willingness to pay," excepting those with documented disabilities or chronic illness—is contoured by the racist animus that historically undergirded the moral logic of "desert." Core to rationing in social and health policy is the concept of "desert"; that is, one must "deserve" the social investments in their health and well-being by being a "responsible" citizen, and that is determined by means-testing, medical gatekeeping, and other forms of rationing. "Desert" posits that individuals must bear the costs associated with outcomes of their health behaviors, rather than rely on a pool of social goods.[8] Indeed, the predominance of behavioral explanations for racial disparities in health status and outcomes are premised on the belief that the racialized Other has failed to live up to an obligation to live healthily and is thus less deserving than those who enjoy better health. Specifically, anti-Black racism posits Black people as undeserving by default.

This reasoning—that healthcare is not a *right*—was made explicit between 1862 and 1867, amid the debates over the creation and funding of the Freedmen's Bureau and its Medical Division, which provided hospital services to Freedmen.[9] Freedom was conditioned on "work-readiness" for the free labor economy, and this was reflected in the Freedmen's Bureau's four divisions: (1) the Land Division, which confiscated and allocated abandoned lands to freedmen; (2) the Educational Division, which established schools to educate freedmen and shape them into laborers; (3) the Legal Division, tasked with mediating disputes between former slaveowners and freedmen; and (4) the Medical Division, which attended to the health needs of freedmen, to return them to the state of health necessary for their participation in the free labor economy. In the fall of 1865, federal funds went toward twelve Bureau hospitals, staffed by eighty doctors, who served approximately four million formerly enslaved patients.[10] Unfortunately, most of these hospitals ceased operations because there was insufficient staffing, in part due to provider attitudes toward their patients. Further, the Civil War veterans' pension program, administered by the Freedmen's Bureau, carved out another "deserving" subset of the Black population—disabled men who served in the Union army, their widows, and children.[11] As Linda Faye Williams wrote, "[H]istorically, there has always been a strong belief in the United States that the government is under a moral obligation to provide for the aid and relief of those who have been disabled in its military service and for the support of widows and dependent relatives of the slain."[12]

## ILLNESS AS RACIAL PATHOLOGY

While earlier eighteenth-century theories of "innate black immunity" to Yellow Fever (a disease transmitted by the *Aedes aegypti* mosquito, whose expanded geographic range was enabled by the Transatlantic Slave Trade) posited that enslaved Black people were biologically distinct,[13] post–Civil War medical theories of "racial degeneracy" made the case for racial "difference" that would ostensibly lead to the eventual dying out of the "black race" due to the unsuitability of freedom.[14] This theory was rooted in the belief that forcible labor exerted a "civilizing" influence and suppressed the "innate" atavistic characteristics of Africans.

In the wake of Emancipation, white physicians' theories of racial pathology ("racial degeneracy") seemed to be confirmed by the ill health of freedmen who left the plantation for war-ravaged landscapes that were ripe for infectious disease transmission, with little more than the clothes on their backs. Malnutrition was common before Emancipation, and freedmen's mobility amid the

Civil War exacerbated their food insecurity, as they became more reliant on the provisions of Union Army officials and sympathetic abolitionists or foraging in unfamiliar and despoiled landscapes. The resulting effects of malnutrition on their immune system functioning likely exacerbated their susceptibility to infectious diseases, in conjunction with the unsanitary environments in which they found themselves (contaminated water supply from the corpses that riddled the landscape; tight quarters in the infirmaries and housing quarters; minimal shelter from the elements).

Moreover, theories of racial "difference" proved salient in the debates over the 1866 Freedmen's Bill, in which Radical Republicans insisted that able-bodied freedmen should be ineligible for federally funded medical assistance, asserting, "no person shall be deemed 'destitute,' 'suffering,' or 'dependent' upon the Government for support' within the meaning of this Act [the Freedmen's Bill of 1866], who, being able to find employment, could by proper industry and exertion avoid such destitution, suffering, or dependence."[15] The crux of this reasoning was that illness in Black communities was rooted in (1) their supposed innate "unwillingness" to participate in labor markets and that (2) work was curative and protective against poverty. This belief would underlie social policy for centuries, justifying work requirements for access to food (e.g., welfare reforms in the Personal Responsibility and Work Opportunity Reconciliation Act of 1996) and healthcare coverage (e.g., Medicaid work requirements attached to Medicaid expansion after the passage and implementation of the Affordable Care Act).

Moreover, the persistence of the racial essentialism in medicine, or biological explanations for conditions that were seemingly prevalent in Black communities, made it necessary for Black healthcare practitioners to defend their communities against the prevailing dogma in medicine.[16] For example, through the National Medical Association, a key organization for the professionalization of Black physicians in light of their exclusion from American Medical Association (AMA) and the American Psychiatric Association, Black psychiatrists emphasized what we now know as the "social determinants of health" as underlying causes of conditions like pellagra-induced dementia, neurasthenia, and other somatic conditions. In articles published between 1895 and 1940 in the *Journal of the National Medical Association*, Black physicians challenged prevailing "racial degeneracy" theories and made the case that these reflected profound inequities in food security, housing, sanitation, and disinvestment in infrastructure in Black communities, which were all patterned by racial and economic discrimination under Jim Crow.[17] The echoes of these debates persisted into the twentieth century, with racialized etiologies underlying the overdiagnosis of conditions like schizophrenia in Black patients.[18]

## HEALTHCARE WORKFORCE ISSUES AMID SEGREGATION

Under "market conditions," the site placement of healthcare facilities reflects firms' or health systems' tendency toward profit maximization. This includes clustering locations in high-income, high-density service areas. However, given the historical segregation of U.S. cities, health systems and practices were also incentivized to locate in whiter service areas, where incomes and rates of private insurance coverage tended to be higher—in other words, service areas with a "good" payor mix. This was exacerbated by the segregation of hospitals, and the underlying social patterning of environmental exposures due to residential segregation, which produced downstream inequities in health outcomes (increased incidence and prevalence of chronic conditions, such as asthma and cancers) in Black communities.[19] As a result, Black residents of segregated metros have longer travel distances to care, which is associated with lower utilization and later diagnosis. These inequities in access to care persisted after nearly 95 percent (396 out of 420) of historically Black-serving hospitals were either closed or converted in the twenty years following the implementation of Medicare and desegregation of U.S. hospitals, despite the prior use of Hill-Burton funds to build modern facilities.[20] The disproportionate effect of hospital closures on Black communities continues today, as the rate of rural hospital closures accelerated post-2010, particularly in states that did not expand Medicaid.[21] These closures interact with an already constrained clinical training landscape to reinforce shortages of healthcare workers—both nurses and physicians—who face limited placements (Figure 7.1).[22]

Moreover, the added context of the historical exclusion of Black healthcare providers from their respective professions partly explains divides between Black communities and healthcare provision. From the Civil War to the twentieth century, Black doctors, nurses, and midwives faced barriers to entry in their respective professions, including but not limited to admissions and licensure requirements erected by white-dominated professional associations, such as the AMA and Association of American Medical Colleges.[23] After the Civil War, Black physicians had to make the case that they were legitimate doctors and defend (or disavow) medicinal and therapeutic treatments provided within Black communities.[24]

Perhaps the most instructive example of these structural exclusions is Abraham Flexner's (1910) Carnegie Foundation–commissioned report, which, based on his audit of medical schools, recommended the closure of all but two of the medical schools that trained Black physicians: Howard and Meharry.[25] Historian Thomas J. Ward notes,

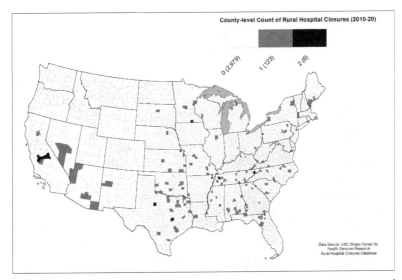

**Figure 7.1.    Map of rural hospital closures in the U.S. between 2010-2020, summed to the county level.** *Source*: **UNC Sheps Center for Health Services Research, Rural Hospital Closure Database. https://www.shepscenter.unc.edu/programs -projects/rural-health/rural-hospital-closures/**

The Flexner Report itself did not close down any medical schools; it had no power to do so. What made the report so devastating, was that the report was embraced by the American Medical Association & the nation's major philanthropies, who, in turn, did have the power to run the schools that did not meet Flexner's standards out of business.[26]

This was accomplished through the AMA's push for standardization in medical education, and the philanthropies' (Carnegie Foundation, Rockefeller, Julius Rosenwald Fund) withdrawal of support from medical schools that trained Black physicians.[27] As a result, all but two of the medical schools that trained Black physicians—Howard University in Washington, DC, and Meharry Medical College in Nashville, Tennessee—were closed. Still, in the Flexner Report and elsewhere, the continued existence of medical schools that trained Black physicians was justified on the grounds that the work of Black physicians and nurses was necessary boundary work (a metaphorical "cordon sanitaire") to keep pathologies in Black communities out of white communities.[28] In effect, the health inequities borne by Black communities were treated as a threat to a putatively white nation, and the role of the physician was to maintain the separation between Black and white communities by managing their health.

## THE WORK OF HEALTH JUSTICE: MOVING FORWARD

In addition to inequities in health outcomes, inequitable *healthcare* outcomes are well documented.[29] Many factors contribute to preventable disparate outcomes, including structural racism and healthcare providers' clinical decision making based in racist bias.[30] For example, studies have shown that Black patients are less likely to receive adequate treatment for acute, chronic, and postoperative pain.[31] A 2016 study of medical students and residents showed that false beliefs in a biological basis for race (e.g., "Blacks have thicker skin than whites") *were* associated with the tendency to rate Black patients' pain as lower than white patients' and, accordingly, make less accurate treatment recommendations.[32] These discredited biological notions of racial difference can be traced to chattel slavery.[33]

Healthcare organizations can contribute to addressing these issues by actively making changes and incorporating lessons from Black activist organizations that have existed within and adjacent to the healthcare system, such as the Black Panthers Party and Midwives' Collaborative Activism. These changes need to take place in health professionals' education, workforce development, socially conscious use of lobbying power, equitable distribution of resources in terms of patient care and community benefits, and constant evaluation of outcomes resulting from practices.

## TOWARD ANTI-RACIST PRAXIS IN HEALTH PROFESSIONS' EDUCATION

While some health professions' education has started to address racism through the implementation of implicit bias training, curricula and licensing exams still do not challenge the predominate belief in race-as-biology, which elide the detrimental effects of racism on the life prospects and health outcomes of negatively racialized people and communities.[34] For instance, medical students often rely on heuristics in the form of racial stereotypes and statistical discrimination (e.g., "young African American woman with dry cough" is often first associated with sarcoidosis) on licensing exams to identify pathology accurately.

As recently as 2017, a popular nursing textbook presented racial and ethnic stereotypes as guides for communication with and diagnosis of patients. The publishing company has since promised to remove these materials.[35] Given the portrayal of race in health professionals' education, scholars have suggested that critical race theory and structural competency be embedded in curricula.[36]

Currently, most attempts at addressing racism in medical curricula are secondary or tertiary in quality and quantity, relative to the rigor expected of students in biomedical topic areas, despite the fact that racism in medical care has life and death consequences.[37] While biochemistry and physiology may be taught by expert biochemists and physiologists, topics related to social inequity are rarely taught by expert social scientists. Instead, medical educators use a "conscripted curriculum," relying on students from underrepresented minority (URM) backgrounds to share personal accounts of racism and co-teach their overrepresented classmates. This practice obscures or displaces understandings of racism as a fundamental cause that shapes the social determinants of health, and thus, implications for healthcare delivery.[38]

If medical schools embraced their professed social missions, medical education would look very different. Medical schools would, for example, have more diverse ranks, train more graduates who go into primary care, and choose to practice in underserved communities.[39] Experts in social sciences, medical humanities, and communication would teach medical students on the subject matter, and equip trainees with the tools needed for continued self-education. In addition, medical librarians may also be an indispensable support for embedding resources on race, racism, and social determinants of health into medical school curricula. Moreover, to increase racial and socioeconomic diversity in medical school matriculants, scholars and advocates have pushed for schools to drop the Medical College Admission Test,[40] given that it, like most standardized tests, more readily measures socioeconomic status than it does students' ability to perform well in medical school.[41]

In terms of evaluations and career advancement opportunities in medical school, a few schools have begun to question the place of Alpha Omega Alpha, the elite medical honor society, after a study showed that with all other things equal, Black and Asian medical students were six times less likely to be inducted into Alpha Omega Alpha.[42] Researchers have also revealed disparities in grading of medical students, from distribution of "honors" grades, to the type of superlative adjectives used in evaluations, which all have an impact on evaluations for residency.[43] It is paramount for medical schools to create processes to evaluate and counter these biases, with sufficient resources in order to hold themselves accountable.

Beyond training institutions, governing bodies that set standards for health professionals' education must strengthen their commitment to health equity and diversifying the workforce. When they have, changes have ensued. For example, after the Liaison Committee on Medical Education introduced two diversity standards for accreditations, medical schools saw an increase in the percentages of women, Black, and Hispanic matriculants.[44] Black, Hispanic, Native, and Pacific Islander students are still underrepresented, suggesting that medical schools should be held to even higher standards by the Liaison Committee on Medical Education.[45]

## WORKFORCE DEVELOPMENT/RETENTION IN HEALTH PROFESSIONS

As with other racialized organizations, academic medicine facilitates the ascension of white scientists, while URM scientists face significant barriers.[46] Data shows stagnation in the representation of URMs among medical students over the years and decreasing representation of URMs among faculty with increasing levels on the academic medicine hierarchy.[47] Studies show disparities in promotion rates of URM physicians compared to their white counterparts: Black physicians in academic medicine are promoted from assistant to associate professor, and from associate to full professor at half the rate of white physicians.[48] Additionally, racial fatigue and discrimination experienced by physicians contributes to attrition and turnover rates.[49] Healthcare institutions—and especially academic medical centers—need to make robust investments to support minoritized health professionals, in addition to supports for increasing the workforce as we face looming shortages of healthcare providers.

Additionally, widespread adoption and implementation of interprofessional education and interprofessional models of care would address workplace dynamics including power struggles that are ultimately detrimental to patient care. Furthermore, healthcare professionals from different disciplines learning from one another during training and practice, and sharing responsibilities contribute to better outcomes. For instance, studies have shown the impact of midwifery on pregnancy and birth outcomes, including lower cesarean delivery rates among healthy birthing people.[50] Interprofessional education could facilitate an exchange of ideas and values. For instance, nurse-midwives have long advocated for policy and practice changes that would improve patients' birth experiences, including de-medicalized deliveries in birthing centers,[51] as well as addressing social conditions that drive disparities in infant mortality.[52] As Black and Indigenous women bear the brunt of the U.S. maternal morbidity and mortality crisis,[53] it is important that healthcare institutions innovate in models of care that favor interprofessional approaches to obstetrical care.

## LOBBYING POWER

We cannot understate the power and influence of healthcare sector lobbies in healthcare policy making. The AMA is among the ten largest lobbies in terms of spending, alongside the American Hospital Association (AHA).[54] In the past, however, the AMA harnessed its power to oppose progressive legislation that would contribute to addressing inequality, such as the passage of Medicaid and Medicare in the 1960s.[55] In 2019, both the AHA and the AMA opposed Medicare for All and other similarly expansive reforms to health insurance. On the other hand, the American Association of Pediatrics, which has a track record of advocacy regarding childhood poverty, recently issued its first policy statement on the impact of racism on child and adolescent health.[56] More recently, the American College of Physicians, internal medicine's professional body, endorsed Medicare for All.[57]

These professional healthcare organizations that have recently renewed their commitment to health equity on the heels of the national reckoning about racism should leverage their resources in order to improve health professionals' education and at the national level. A 2018 study showed that the Black Lives Matter movement (and its proponents' advocacy for anti-racist policy making) had a positive impact on white Americans' implicit and explicit attitudes toward Black people.[58] Thus, embracing anti-racism, and structural competency in the practice of medicine, as well as in undergraduate, graduate, and continuing medical education, could also work in favor of indirectly addressing racial bias and its impact on patient-provider encounters. This should similarly be adopted by professional bodies in healthcare that wield lobbying power, such as the American Nurses' Association. Beyond lobbying for healthcare-focused changes such as insurance, organizations like the AMA, the AHA, and the American Nurses' Association could further address health inequities by diversifying their lobbying portfolios in favor of policy areas that have significant upstream effects on health such as housing, climate, and education. These areas are already targeted by activist organizations, including the aforementioned Black Lives Matter, and collaborating with such organizations could contribute to holding the lobby arms of the professional bodies accountable to communities first.

## COMMUNITY RELATIONS: WHAT CAN BE DONE?

Over the last decade, healthcare organizations have increasingly invested in initiatives aimed at addressing social determinants of health to improve patient outcomes. These initiatives have been focused on addressing greatest areas of need at the individual level: housing, employment, food security, education, social and community context, and transportation. A 2019 study showed that at least $2.5 billion of health system funds were spent across these domains.[59] A study evaluating hospital expenditures on community benefits showed that spending on community health improvement initiatives was unrelated to community health needs, highlighting the need for healthcare organizations to improve in their community health initiatives.[60]

Furthermore, critics of hospital-based initiatives point out that addressing individual patients' social needs, while important, falls short of addressing the social determinants of health.[61] They also argue that nonprofit hospitals should invest more in community benefits, given that seven out of ten most profitable hospitals are "not-for-profit."[62] This tension between profitable academic medical centers and their surrounding communities is not new. In 1966, the Hough riots in Cleveland stopped the Cleveland Clinic's expansion plans and had a significant impact on the clinic's redistributive practices, most substantially in the form of loaning clinic personnel to the city's primary care system to relieve the pressure on public primary care centers.[63] Such community health centers are part of the Black Panther Party's legacy on U.S. healthcare, and larger academic medical centers located in urban areas should further embrace their model when it comes to designing outpatient care. For instance, a key feature of the Black Panther Party's free health clinics was the presence of community health workers that helped patients navigate social services.

Today, although some medical centers have included community health workers as part of their workforce to serve their most disadvantaged patients, more community health workers are needed.[64] This expansion, akin to the Panthers' clinics, could further provide employment opportunities for community members, an often-overlooked form of community benefits.[65] The U.S. healthcare sector accounts for nearly one-fifth of the nation's gross domestic product and accounts for the fastest growth in employment.

Still, in the healthcare sector, a significant proportion of individuals employed by healthcare institutions are paid low wages (less than $15 per hour), and job growth is concentrated among the lowest-paid, lowest-status positions. Specifically, one-fifth of hospital employees and over half of workers in home healthcare, nursing home, and residential care facilities are low-wage workers. Healthcare institutions, especially hospitals, which employ the largest number of low-wage workers, should commit to ensuring that all employees receive living wages. Half of Black and Latinx women healthcare workers earn less than $15 per hour, and more than a quarter do not receive employer-based insurance.[66] Inequality within the healthcare workforce is such that the lowest-income healthcare workers have nearly six-fold higher risk of deaths relative to the highest income healthcare workers, an income-mortality gradient steeper than that of non-healthcare workers.[67] This suggests that beyond expansion and job creation, healthcare institutions must ensure that they provide all employees with decent living wages and work benefits, especially to address racial disparities mortality and other health outcomes associated with poverty.

In keeping with the language used in their advertising, healthcare institutions have ample opportunities to follow through on their claims to being neighbors or community institutions. For example, healthcare institutions can expand existing "medical home" models to address both the medical and social needs of the patients that they serve, as well as strengthening community assets. This would require defining the "population" beyond the pool of insured patients within their service area in a given fiscal year and including the community itself.[68] This expansion and integration of medical home models with community asset building may include additional services such as childcare or after school programs. Such programming, however, should be designed in collaboration and partnership with various community stakeholders: individuals and faith-based and community-based organizations. Their input is crucial, as a recent study showed that medical homes may contribute to worsening racial disparities in healthcare delivery if not designed with the intentionality required to address varying patient needs.[69]

## CONCLUSION

In this chapter, we offer an abbreviated history of U.S. healthcare in relation to Black communities and end with a set of actionable steps that healthcare systems and academic medical institutions can implement to take strides toward racial equity and health equity in the communities they serve. Put simply, healthcare in the United States is rooted in a fraught history, and a future with healthcare equity requires change within healthcare systems, including but not limited to the leveraging of capital resources to bolster community assets, and the building up of the healthcare workforce as our aging population faces a growing shortage of healthcare workers.

In taking action to move toward healthcare equity, it is important to be attentive to the history of medicine and healthcare institutions—particularly in relation to Black communities. The institutions that historically provided charity care in exchange for the right to use their patients' bodies or biological materials as fodder for teaching and research are also the institutions that contribute to gentrification in historically Black neighborhoods. Similarly, the historically symbiotic relationship between biomedical research and practice and exploitation of community members in cumulatively disadvantaged and dispossessed communities shapes the orientation of medical education and practice to this day.

# 8

# Sexual and Gender Minority Health

## Meeting the Needs of Lesbian, Gay, Bisexual, Transgender, and Queer Patients

*Riordan Ledgerwood, Carl G. Streed Jr., and Jennifer Siegel*

The health professions have a long and sordid history of pathologizing and regulating the bodies of lesbian, gay, bisexual, transgender, and queer (LGBTQ) persons, more recently broadened to sexual and gender minority (SGM) persons.[1] Although the science of sexuality and gender has since at least the mid-nineteenth century acknowledged the existence of same-sex attraction, most clinicians of the time saw this an abnormality to be cured or resolved. Similarly, while the historical record acknowledges the existence of a diversity of gender identities and gender modalities throughout human existence, Western notions of binary, immutable categories for gender and sex have dictated what is "normal" and "allowable" at many points throughout history.[2] While the health professions have largely moved from pathologizing to acceptance and support of the full diversity of sexual and gender identities,[3] ensuring SGM persons are able to lead healthy lives that allow them to thrive requires health professionals to be both informed of the issues that affect SGM persons and to advocate with them in the public domain.

This chapter lays out historical context for the current landscape of SGM health and policy affecting the lives of SGM persons and communities. To begin, we will discuss the expansive language used to describe the sexual and gender identities that we all have.

## STAYING UP TO DATE ON LANGUAGE

"If a transvestite doesn't say I'm gay and I'm proud and I'm a transvestite, then nobody else is going to hop up there and say I'm gay and I'm proud and I'm a transvestite for them."

—Marsha P. Johnson

In this quotation by the prolific transgender activist Marsha P. Johnson, made famous through her role in the Stonewall riots of 1969, is the word "transvestite." In general, this word would no longer be deemed acceptable in most social circles as an appropriate word for a transgender or trans person. In Johnson's time, though, this was a word of power for those who embraced it.

Indeed, language changes with the times and what may be acceptable today will change by tomorrow. While it may sometimes feel difficult to keep current on best practices around terminology, there are many excellent resources from which to learn.[4] A guiding principle is to engage directly with members of SGM communities, to listen to the language used, and to mirror its use. For example, if a woman refers to her significant other as her wife, then it is acceptable and often encouraged to use that word. However, there will be exceptions to this rule, particularly in clinical professional spaces. The word "queer" provides a good example.

Historically, the word "queer" simply meant something that was odd, or not quite part of what was deemed normal at the time. Its use as a word to describe members of the SGM community began in 1914.[5] Its connotations as a derogatory slur were noted, and the word continues to be a slur used against community members.

Like many slurs within the SGM community, "queer" has been reclaimed and destigmatized by the community. Queer became a word that was "derogatory from the outside, not from within."[6] Use of the word remains acceptable only to community members: due to its history as a slur, use by a non-SGM-identified person brings the assumption of potential antagonistic intentions.

Further complicating language is the societal desire to label and categorize, even when existing categories may not accommodate the breadth of options needed for self-identification. Society is not yet comfortable without a label or word for an identity. For instance, a person with a "feminine" appearance who engages in sexual behaviors with women may not identify as a woman or a lesbian (indeed, this person may self-label their gender as nonbinary or agender; they may label their sexual identity as pansexual, etc.) but often society is quick to label that person with "she/her" pronouns and assume them to be a lesbian. It is important to understand that an individual is the only person that can designate or label their sexual and gender identities.

How does a well-meaning health professional figure out how to function in this ever-shifting landscape? A critical practice is to avoid assumptions, to practice utilizing gender-neutral language in the clinical space, and to develop comfort with normalizing questions about pronouns. Some examples of gender-neutral greetings include the following:[7] *"Welcome, thanks for coming. My name is Dr. Smith, and my pronouns are they/them. What name and pronouns should I use today?"* or *"Hello. My name is Dr. Smith. How would you like that I address you during the visit today?"*

Additional efforts can be made to limit assumptions about honorifics, family members/structures, sexual behaviors, names for body parts, and more. Asking patients for their preferred language will go a long way in creating a welcoming and affirming clinical space. Furthermore, it is important for all members of the health professional team/clinical office to receive training in inclusive language use.

Beyond optimizing language use, additional best practices for health professionals include developing paper and electronic forms that avoid assumptions about names/pronouns/relationships, working with electronic health records to optimize collection of sexual orientation/gender identity data, and developing processes for patients to provide their own information about key identifiers via patient portals.

By normalizing gender-neutral questions and avoiding assumptions in language, one can help eliminate stigma from the SGM community and deconstruct a long history of pathologizing by the medical establishment. It is worth noting here that while clinicians may have some discomfort in asking a patient their pronouns, sexual orientation, and/or gender identity,[8] patients across a variety of clinical and public health settings are more than willing to provide this information,[9] recognizing its value in various clinical scenarios. Table 8.1 provides additional details of key concepts regarding sexual and gender identity that are applicable to all persons without requiring memorization of the meaning of each term.[10]

## HOMOSEXUALITY AS A MENTAL DISORDER

Although the science of sexuality has since the mid-nineteenth century recognized the existence of homosexual or same-sex attraction, most doctors perceived such attraction as abnormal and believed that it could be resolved with surgery. At the turn of the twentieth century, medical doctors, psychiatrists,

**Table 8.1. Key Concepts Regarding Sexual and Gender Identity**

| Concept | Definition | Example |
|---------|-----------|---------|
| Sexual Orientation | Sexual orientation is the type of sexual, romantic, and/or physical attraction one feels for others, often labeled based on the gender relationship between the person and the people they are attracted to. Sexual and romantic attraction can be based on a variety of factors including, but not limited to, gender identity, gender expression/presentation, and sex assigned at birth. | Asexual Gay Lesbian Bisexual Pansexual Queer |
| Gender Identity | One's internal sense of being male, female, neither, both, or another gender. Everyone has a gender identity. For transgender and gender nonconforming people, their sex assigned at birth, or natal sex, and their internal sense of gender identity are not the same. | Man Woman Nonbinary Genderqueer |
| Gender Expression | Outward manifestations of one's gender identity that are socially and culturally derived. | Hair style Accessories Clothing |
| Gender Modality[1] | Refers to the correspondence of one's assigned sex at birth and one's gender identity. | Agender Cisgender Transgender |
| Sex Assigned at Birth | Designation assigned to someone at birth most frequently based on external genitalia. | Female Male Intersex |

1. Ashley, Florence. "'Trans' is my gender modality: A modest terminological proposal." In Laura Erickson-Schroth (Ed.). *Trans bodies, trans selves.* Oxford: Oxford University Press, 2021.

psychotherapists, and sexologists continued to develop theories regarding causes of and potential cures for sexual and gender variations. However, in the pre–World War II era, no single orthodox explanation emerged. It wasn't until 1952, with the publication of the first edition of the *Diagnostic and Statistical Manual of Mental Disorders*, that the American Psychiatric Association codified homosexuality as a mental illness. By the late 1960s, behavioral modification therapy tried to reinforce heterosexual behavior in manipulative ways. These methods included the use of commercial sex workers, orgasmic reconditioning, and emphasis on marriage to an opposite-sex partner. Psychological professionals also used various forms of aversion therapy, including electroshock, chemical, and deprivation therapy, to cause a "heterosexual adjustment." These medical interventions continue to be touted to SGM people as an opportunity to assimilate and live like cisgender, heterosexual Americans.[11]

Although medical opinions are often contingent on prevailing social and cultural attitudes, over the course of the second half of the twentieth century, some researchers and psychologists challenged the model of homosexuality as illness. Alfred Kinsey disputed prevailing psychiatric opinion that homosexuality was pathological. In 1948, Kinsey's *Sexual Behavior in the Human Male* revealed that over a third (37 percent) of American men had participated in same-sex sexual activity to the point of orgasm. Other health professionals in various fields soon followed. In 1951, ethologist Frank A. Beach and anthropologist Clellan Ford reported the acceptance of homosexuality in cultures they studied; psychologist Evelyn Hooker began publishing research in the 1950s reporting no discernable mental difference between homosexual and heterosexual men; and in 1961, psychiatrist Thomas Szasz published *The Myth of Mental Illness* in which he refuted the premises of mental illness as a model for explaining homosexuality.[12] Through a confluence of research of internal as well as external advocacy, the American Psychological Association (APA) finally, in 1973, removed homosexuality from the *Diagnostic and Statistical Manual of Mental Disorders*. It is worth noting that some of the most ardent advocacy from within the APA was from members who were not able to be out professional, including Dr. Anonymous, now known to be Dr. John Fryer, who spoke from behind a mask at the 1972 APA annual conference.

Concurrent with the pathologizing and depathologizing of nonheterosexual sexuality, the medical establishment's relationship to gender identity has experienced similar twists and turns over time. While historians have acknowledged a long record of persons with diverse sexual and gender identities,[13] the earliest record of research and clinical care regarding gender identity comes from *Institut für Sexualwissenschaft* (Institute of Sexual Research), opened in 1919 by Magnus Hirschfeld. Dr. Hirschfeld is credited with coining the term "transsexualism," defining a clinical category that Dr. Harry Benjamin would later expand upon in the United States. Unfortunately, Dr. Hirschfeld was targeted by Nazis for being Jewish and gay, and in 1933 the Institute of Sexual Research was destroyed along with much of the gender-affirming research of Dr. Hirschfeld and colleagues.

In the United States, the availability of gender-affirming medical and surgical care was beginning to come out thanks to the public advocacy of persons like Christine Jorgensen, who had undergone gender-affirming medical and surgical interventions both in New York and Copenhagen in the 1950s. More medical and surgical practices began to address gender-affirming care more openly in the 1960s to 1970s.[14] However, much progress in gender-affirming care would be rolled back with the closing of the Gender Identity Clinic at Johns Hopkins.[15] Despite this setback, gender-affirming care continued abroad as well as in fits and starts in the United States, particularly through the auspices of the Harry Benjamin International Gender Dysphoria Association, now known as the World Professional Association for Transgender Health. As the World Professional Association for Transgender Health has been leading and providing guidance on the care of transgender persons, the terminology and ways in which the medical establishment depends on these terms have evolved over time. For example, the International Classification of Disease has moved from "trans-sexualism," a term seen as pejorative and inaccurate, to "Gender Identity Disorder" in *International Classification of Disease* 9. Both terms pathologize gender identities that are not cisgender and reflect a focus of the medical establishment on "fixing" or "curing" conditions rather than providing support for individual traits, such as gender identity. Yet, regardless of the terms used or codes utilized for billing purposes, evidence-based and community-informed advocacy has ensured that gender-affirming care is recognized by nearly every major medical professional association as essential to the well-being of transgender persons.

The history of how "homosexuality" and "trans-sexualism" as clinical diagnoses and disorders created distrust between SGM communities and the medical system is critical to understand the current context of SGM health and well-being because the stigma of nonheterosexual and non-cisgender behaviors and identities persists to this day. Further distrust of the medical community increased in the 1980s with the advent of the AIDS crisis.

## "GAY-RELATED" DISEASES AND ADVOCACY FROM WITHIN

On the cover of the *Science Times* of the *New York Times* on May 11, 1982, below the fold, the title of a small article read, *NEW HOMOSEXUAL DISORDER WORRIES HEALTH OFFICIALS.*

The article discusses a new and emerging serious disorder of the immune system, one that was primarily affecting "male homosexuals" though noting heterosexual women and bisexual men were also affected by the disease. Despite this, the term used for the new disease was gay-related immune deficiency, the precursor name for what is now known as AIDS.

At that time, the disease was thought to be a result of "an accumulation of risk factors" and not a single infectious cause. Others postulated that the disease spread through sexual contact, though other methods of spread and drug reaction were not yet ruled out.

Within this article the words of Dr. Lawrence D. Mass, a physician in New York City, standout:[16] "Gay people whose lifestyle consists of anonymous sexual encounters are going to have to do some serious rethinking." Dr. Mass's words reinforced some common perceptions of the SGM community in the early 1980s, particularly the gay male community. In 1981, physicians simultaneously began observing strange, yet similar symptoms in some of their gay male patients. At first, due to the population affected it was referred to as "gay cancer" or the "gay plague," and frequently broadened to include other marginalized persons at risk of infection such as "the four Hs: Homosexuals, Heroin Users, Haitians, and Hemophiliacs."[17]

The inaction of the government led to a delay in the proper identification of the virus and test to diagnose the disease. By the time a test was developed to diagnose the disease, thousands had died.[18] It was not until 1984 and the discovery of the HIV virus by Robert Gallo that the disease started to be fully understood as something other than a gay-related illness.

While the general population was falsely reassured that this new disease would not affect them, gay and bisexual men were dying. Without help from the outside, SGM communities advocated for themselves and organized to fight the disease and provide education for others.

On a local and national level, members of the SGM community took a major hand in their own advocacy for better and more informed healthcare. This started with organizations like Gay Men's Health Crisis and ACT UP (AIDS Coalition to Unleash Power) in New York. Organizations aligned with medical communities with the goal of providing quality care to SGM communities.

GLMA: Health Professionals Advancing LGBTQ Equality was founded in 1981 as the American Association of Physicians for Human Rights (AAPHR). Originally this organization was created to combat discrimination faced by physicians over their sexual orientation. Over time the AAPHR broadened its focus to include discrimination encountered by patients as well. In 1994, with gradually increasing societal acceptance of the gay and lesbian community, the AAPHR changed its name to GLMA.[19] GLMA continues to advocate for LGBTQ equality within and outside the health professions.

Despite increased societal acceptance and a shift in the global pandemic toward heterosexual transmission, gay men still carry the blame for starting the AIDS epidemic in the United States. Further, sexual behavior associated with higher risk of HIV infection (e.g., unprotected anal intercourse), particularly among marginalized populations and members of communities of color, remains an ongoing driver of the HIV epidemic and itself reflects the impact of stigma around these intersecting identities.[20] This ongoing stigma and societal stress continue to negatively impact the healthcare of the SGM community.

As the AIDS crisis brought gay men and gay rights into the spotlight, discussions typically held behind closed doors were beginning to happen publicly. Human rights groups emboldened by the challenges of the 1980s and 1990s as well as increasing societal acceptance continued the fight for improved conditions for the SGM community.

## MARRIAGE EQUALITY

Advocacy in the late 1990s and early 2000s turned its attention from HIV to gaining additional legal standing typically denied to most SGM persons. In the United States, marriage as regulated by the state confers numerous rights and privileges, not least of which is recognition. After years of state-by-state advocacy, federal recognition for same-sex marriage was granted via the 2015 Supreme Court decision in *Obergefell v Hodges*, which ruled that same-sex couples have a fundamental right to be married.[21] Prior to the ruling, same-sex marriage had been established in thirty-six states, demonstrating the gradual but increasing acceptance of same-sex couples and families. While the focus on marriage at the expense of other issues (e.g., housing, economic opportunities, etc.) has been criticized within LGBTQ advocacy groups, marriage equality has offered a roadmap for advocacy efforts and demonstrates how great change may occur over a relatively short period of time.

## TRANS TIPPING POINT

"I stand before you this evening, a proud, African-American transgender woman."

—Laverne Cox

While gay, lesbian, and bisexual communities benefited from the additional public support conferred through marriage equality advocacy, transgender communities were often overlooked.[22] While some issues faced by transgender persons did overlap with the marriage equality movement, many issues specific to transgender persons and communities were treated as secondary priority among LGBTQ advocacy groups. Fortunately, this has improved somewhat over the past decade, much in part due to increased visibility of transgender people in the media.

Advocacy within the transgender community had once again, as it had with Marsha P. Johnson in the 1970s, found a powerful Black trans woman as a spokesperson. Laverne Cox spoke these words in 2014, having become a public figure through her role as an actress.[23] Through Cox's visibility as well as other prominent figures increasing their public presence, transgender activists and advocates started to gain traction on new policies supporting elimination of gender identity–based discrimination. In the last half of the 2020s, activists saw the overturn of multiple "Bathroom Bills," the removal of transgender-related exclusions from certain health insurance, and the reinstatement and the removal (in 2021) of the ban on serving openly in the military. However, even with these victories, increased visibility and public support, members of the SGM communities continue to struggle with barriers inside and outside of healthcare.

## THE COMMUNITY SPEAKS OUT ABOUT DISPARITIES IN CARE

As acceptance of SGM populations improved, organizations were better able to survey the SGM community to understand and address needs of the community. In 2009, Lambda Legal was the first to examine barriers to healthcare among SGM communities as well as among persons living with HIV on a national scale.

The report from Lambda Legal highlighted the stark realities faced by SGM patients when attempting to access healthcare. Almost 56 percent of lesbian, gay, or bisexual respondents had at least one instance of discrimination in care. Examples of discrimination included being refused care, having health professionals refuse to touch them, experiencing professionals using harsh or abusive language, and, at times, being physically assaulted. When transgender populations were queried, 70 percent of respondents had experienced discrimination in care. Furthermore, 90 percent of transgender respondents worried that there were not enough trained healthcare providers to care for them. And even these high numbers likely underestimate the level of barriers faced by SGM communities as it is well documented that those able to complete surveys are often among the more privileged within a given community.[24]

This pattern of discrimination was again noted in the 2015 U.S. Transgender Survey, the largest survey to date of transgender populations with over twenty-seven thousand respondents.[25] Overall, transgender respondents reported high levels of mistreatment, harassment, and violence in every aspect of life. Compared to the general U.S. population, respondents suffered from greater levels of economic hardship, job instability, homelessness, and physical and sexual assault. Along with these difficulties, those surveyed indicated greater levels of physical and mental health concerns.

A total of 39 percent of respondents experienced serious psychological distress in the month prior to completing the survey, compared to only 5 percent of the general U.S. population; rates of suicidality among transgender respondents were also nearly ten-fold that of the general population.[25] A third of the respondents had at least one negative experience related to being transgender in a healthcare setting. These unacceptable metrics are certainly driven by discrimination faced in healthcare settings as well as by transphobic local and national polices, which have been demonstrated to adversely impact the mental health of gender minority populations.

A more recent survey conducted in 2017 unfortunately demonstrates that these issues persist.[26] It again noted gaps in healthcare with 22 percent of transgender respondents lacking insurance and nearly 20 percent avoiding care for fear of discrimination and poor treatment. It also explored the impact of intersecting identities, finding that that SGM people of color were at least twice as likely as white SGM people to say they have been personally discriminated against when applying for jobs or interacting with police. Further, a recent research collection looking at the impact of the COVID-19 pandemic on SGM communities again draws similar conclusions noting that SGM communities experienced severe health impacts with disproportionate adverse health and economic outcomes among SGM persons of color.[27]

Access to care remains an important issue. Beyond the insurance barriers noted in these reports, most health centers and programs dedicated to SGM care are clustered in a limited number of urban areas.[28] This presents a challenge to more rural populations; patients have shared stories of being turned away after being told that the practice is not equipped to take care of transgender patients or simply are left with a disconnected call.

Further, as of this writing, gender-affirming care as well as participation in community activities, particularly for transgender youth, are being threatened. As of April 2021, Arkansas has banned access to gender-affirming care for transgender youth. At last count, five states (Arkansas, Idaho, Mississippi, South Dakota, and Tennessee) ban transgender youth participation in sports that match their gender identity. These initiatives are part of a larger effort by conservative political forces to scapegoat transgender persons. As experts in the health and well-being of youth of all gender identities, the role for health professionals to counter these efforts to harm transgender youth is clear.[29]

## RECOMMENDATIONS AND NEXT STEPS

While a great deal of progress has been made to ensure that SGM populations receive high-quality healthcare and, more importantly, enjoy rates of health and well-being like any other group, significant inequities remain. To close these gaps, change is needed at multiple levels both within and outside the walls of healthcare institutions.

At a local level, healthcare organizations should develop clear policies that prohibit bias and discrimination based on sexual orientation, gender identity, and gender expression. These policies should allow for reporting and a way to proactively address issues as they arise. Implementing procedures for routine collection of patient-reported sexual orientation/gender identity data is imperative such that institutions can capture the care needs of SGM populations. Finally, institutions can codify their efforts through seeking recognition or certification from efforts such as the Healthcare Equality Index.[30]

Education for all health professionals at every level of training continues to be a critical strategy for improving care of SGM populations. It has been well documented that medical education devotes insufficient time to inclusion of SGM topics in the curriculum; medical schools and residency programs can now draw from numerous publicly available tools to design educational materials to address these gaps.[31] Recognizing that most providers in practice will not have undergone adequate training in SGM healthcare, required continuing medical education in this area represents an opportunity to provide further education. And finally, education and significant cultural humility training should be required for all healthcare employees to include administrative and ancillary staff.

Research focused on questions important to SGM health is another critical tool for addressing health inequities. The National Institutes of Health and Agency for Healthcare Research and Quality have designated SGM communities as "a health disparity population for research" providing some needed financial resources for investigators.[32] However, current research and funding opportunities skew toward HIV-related studies.[33] Future efforts must address the full range of health needs of these populations. Further, more opportunities are needed for community-based participatory research to ensure that research questions and procedures are inclusive and responsive to the needs of SGM communities.[34]

Finally, health providers should not limit their advocacy to healthcare systems alone. Efforts are needed at the national level to ensure that overly broad religious exemptions for providers do not eliminate access to care, to ensure that access to gender-affirming care remains legal, and that nondiscrimination protections for SGM persons are enacted at the federal level. Legislation is needed to diminish additional barriers to well-being, such as financial, housing, parental/spousal rights, and job protection. Transgender youth face enormous societal stigma; action is needed to address the waves of current legislative proposals threatening access to affirming treatment, ability to play on sports teams, and more. Health professionals' voices are traditionally heard loudly in the advocacy sphere, and they should be raised to address these many challenges to health and well-being among SGM populations.

## CONCLUSION

Despite the struggles faced by SGM people in healthcare as well as in society, SGM community members have remained steadfast in caring and advocating for their own. Greater numbers of people than ever identify as SGM, particularly youth but increasingly persons of all ages. This increase, greater visibility in the media, and the reality that SGM individuals are more and more likely to be open in their families and communities has helped to limit prejudice and stigma. Within healthcare, SGM patients find themselves supported by allies and affirming policies much more regularly than in the past.

In recent years, the health professional community has worked to diminish healthcare inequities experienced by SGM populations. Though clearly more work is to be done to help improve the lives of SGM community members, the progress is encouraging and demonstrates that through collective action and effort, SGM people can experience the health and well-being they deserve.

# 9

## Immigrant Health

*Rheanna Platt and Altaf Saadi*

### BACKGROUND

International migration has increased considerably. Today, over 270 million people live in a country outside of their country of birth, compared to approximately 170 million in 2000.[1] While some people migrate out of choice for better economic opportunities, many others do so out of necessity, fleeing persecution from war, armed conflict, or human rights violations like torture, or in response to the adverse effects of climate change and natural disasters. In the context of international migration (hereafter, migration), the nomenclature is varied and terms like "migrants," "refugees," "asylum-seekers," and "undocumented" or "illegal" immigrants are used to describe people who are on the move, who have left their home countries, and have crossed borders.

In the United States, almost 14 percent of the United States population is foreign-born, 23 percent of whom are undocumented.[2] Latinx and Asian immigrants represent the fastest growing immigrant population in the United States.[3] The United States has the world's largest immigrant population, and, until policy changes under the Trump administration, led the world in resettling refugees.[4] At a time when the global refugee population is at its highest ever, asylum applications in the United States have also increased at record numbers.[5] Different legal statuses proffer different rights and access to federal and state services, thereby conferring unique health implications.

When most immigrants enter the United States, their health is generally better than that of U.S.-born people.[6] For many immigrants, the longer they stay in the United States, the worse their health becomes.[7] Refugees and asylum-seekers have unique health problems over and beyond the general immigrant population, owing to significant traumatic experiences endured during the migration journey, prolonged stays in refugee camps, and/or a lack of medical resources along this continuum of experience. There are many other types of immigrant status beyond refugee or asylum seeker status: noncitizens can be lawful permanent residents (i.e., green card holders), hold temporary legal status (e.g., as tourists or students), or may be considered undocumented or unauthorized (e.g., immigrants who overstay a visa or enter the country without permission). Understanding this nomenclature is an important first step to understanding the factors contributing to the health of this population.

## UNDERSTANDING THE MIGRATION NOMENCLATURE

The UN Migration Agency defines a *migrant* as any person who is moving or has moved across an international border or within a state away from their habitual place of residence regardless of the person's legal status. This umbrella term applies whether the movement is voluntary or not, the underlying causes of the movement, or what the length of the stay is after the move.[8] Like any other group of people, migrants differ in terms of their experiences, resources, vulnerabilities, and rights recognized by international and national laws. We include a table describing specific groups of migrants (Table 9.1).

In the United States, someone's "immigration status" spans dozens of visa types and other legal designations—and there are nuances within each that determine whether someone can become a U.S. citizen or legal permanent resident. For example, refugee status—determined outside of the United States, often involving the UN High Commissioner for Refugees—requires refugees to apply for permanent residency within a year of being admitted to the United States. Asylees, similarly, can apply for lawful permanent resident status, whereas individuals with Deferred Action for Childhood Arrivals status currently do not have a pathway to permanent residency or citizenship. It is important to note that immigration status exists outside a black-and-white reality. Immigration status is fluid and can be adjusted, even (if not often) subject to political whims. For example, nearly half of undocumented immigrants previously held proper documentation prior to becoming undocumented[9] and have the potential of gaining proper documents in the future like seeking and being granted asylum.

As we discuss the health effects of migration across the continuum of experience and of categories described, there are additional concepts important to

**Table 9.1.  Common Terms and Definitions Related to Migration**

| Category | Definition/Description |
|---|---|
| Refugee | • People who have been forced to leave or flee native country because of war, persecution, or violence<br>• Defined by the 1951 UN Refugee Convention and its accompanying 1967 Protocol as fleeing a specific kind of persecution based on "race, religion, nationality, membership of a particular social group or political opinion" |
| Asylum-Seeker | • A person seeking refuge due to persecution faced in their native country, but their claim has not yet been determined by the country in which they are seeking asylum<br>• In the United States, asylum-seekers are physically present in the United States or at a U.S. border and seeking permission to remain in the United States, compared to refugees whose status has been determined outside the country |
| Asylee | • Person who has been granted relief of asylum |
| Lawful Permanent Resident | • In the United States, also known as "green card" holder<br>• Noncitizens who are lawfully authorized to live permanently within the United States |
| Undocumented or Unauthorized Immigrant | • Foreign-born person who doesn't have a legal right to be or remain in the country they have crossed into<br>• Other terms used in the media is "illegal" immigrant, although the use of this term is contested on both legal and moral grounds. For example, it connotes criminality despite presence in the United States without documentation being considered a civil and not criminal offense |
| Deferred Action for Childhood Arrivals | • Available to certain people who came to the United States as children and meet several guidelines<br>• Neither in lawful status nor fully undocumented, having been given protection from deportation for a period of two years, subject to renewal<br>• Eligible for work authorization |

1. UN High Commissioner for Refugees. "What is a refugee." 2021. https://www.unhcr.org/en-us/what-is-a-refugee.html
2. U.S. Citizenship and Immigration Services. "Consideration of deferred action for childhood arrivals (DACA)." 2021. https://www.uscis.gov/humanitarian/humanitarian-parole/consideration-of-deferred-action-for-childhood-arrivals-daca

underscore. First, regardless of whether someone is granted asylum or refugee status, and regardless of a person's reasons for migration (e.g., fleeing persecution versus economic reasons), all individuals are entitled to have their human rights protected and respected. Second, while there are different legal categories of migrants, we would like to emphasize that these labels do not reflect whole identities, and no one can be known solely through their legal status.

## HEALTH EFFECTS ACROSS THE MIGRATION EXPERIENCE CONTINUUM

Migration comprises three stages: pre-migration, migration, and post-migration, during which there can exist many risks or protective factors for health.[10] A more recent model used to examine the course of migration, the Immigration Intercept Model,[11] identifies points or intercepts at which social or structural determinants play a role in health: (1) migration, (2) in the community, (3) detention, and (4) deportation and removal. In the following, we will briefly review considerations relevant to each stage or intercept.

### Pre-Migration

Traumatic events that may precipitate migration include war, economic desperation, political or other persecution, torture, natural disasters, climate change, and ongoing gang, community, and/or family violence in the context of unresponsive policing/law enforcement or governments. These events can lead to both short- and long-term physical and mental health outcomes.[12] For example, refugees and asylum seekers experience increased risk of depression or post-traumatic stress disorder.[13] Someone who has faced torture can experience complications depending on the torture technique, like nerve injury from being in a stressed position for hours or brain injury from being hit in the head or strangulated.[14]

Immigrants who move out of choice or to seek out better economic opportunities also have health consequences as a result of their pre-migration context, including the social circumstances they come from. For example, their educational background, whether they spoke English in their native country, and other social factors can inform how easily and quickly they adapt to life in the United States. Just as there are social determinants of health that influence their lived experience in the United States (see "In the Community" section), there are social determinants of health that are carried over from their time prior to living in the United States.

## Migration

Migration can be physically dangerous, involving desert or ocean crossings, physical or sexual victimization by smugglers or other travelers, which can all be compounded by dehydration or malnutrition. The process can also be lengthy: the average time refugees stay in camps is ten to twenty-six years.[15] Refugee camps can also be sites of victimization, malnutrition, and spread of disease.[16] Migration can also involve prolonged separation from family or other social supports critical to well-being—or, in the case of children, critical to normal development and schooling that in turn promotes long-term health and well-being.[17] Sometimes, migration occurs under uncertainty about whether one will relocate and even find refuge in a host country or return to their homeland. This uncertainty about the future carries health consequences by amplifying someone's stress response, compounding other health issues they may have.

## In the Community

The experience and health of immigrants in the community is shaped by factors including, but not limited to, their immigration status; state, local, and federal policies; community demographics and characteristics; and local and national public sentiment (e.g., toward immigrants or toward people or communities of color). These are all factors that have been shown to impact immigrants' health outcomes and how they seek out healthcare.

It can be helpful to conceptualize immigration status as a social determinant of health, meaning a social factor that affects access to resources that can promote and determine well-being. For example, undocumented immigrants are disproportionately affected by poverty, food and housing insecurity,[18] and challenges with healthcare access.[19] Even when a person and/or their child is eligible for resources like public assistance benefits, fear of being labeled a public charge (i.e., an individual who immigration officials determine is likely to become reliant on public assistance and therefore ineligible to become a legal permanent resident) can lead to a "chilling effect" on use of those resources;[20] people are left in a difficult calculus between their health and their immigration status. These effects have been magnified in the setting of changes to public charge rules made by the Trump administration and, in fact, were magnified before the changes were formally implemented in February 2020 because of surrounding rumors and fears.[21] In this way, we know that rumor alone, or perceptions of anti-immigrant policies, are sufficient to dissuade people from seeking healthcare.

Immigration status has impacts on the entire family, including citizen family members. As of 2016, there are more than five million citizen children in the United States with at least one undocumented parent.[22] Despite being eligible for benefits (e.g., insurance and food benefits), citizen children of undocumented parents are less likely to have insurance than citizen children of citizen parents; they are also less likely to access food benefits and more likely to be food insecure.[23] Researchers have described myriad ways in which a parent's undocumented status can impact a (citizen) child's development, including through use of public benefits and programs (including preschool), housing quality (due to lack of eligibility for federal housing), poverty and poor work conditions (leading to decreased ability to invest time and resources in children), and family processes (including periods of family separation, or parent stress that leads to changes in parenting behaviors).[24] In addition, parents may be less able to engage with their children's schools due to language barriers or fears that schools will identify or record parental immigration status (and therefore subject families to detention or deportation).[25] Fear about risks of family separation and/or parent deportation can impact children's mental and physical health.[26] It's important to know that it's not just undocumented immigrants who are subject to deportation: even legal permanent residents can be (and have been) deported, so many of these fears extend across immigration status type. Immigration status can change dramatically with federal policy (with downstream effects on other family members) so these risks wax and wane with shifting immigration policies at local, state, or federal levels.

Apart from policies directly impacting immigration status, public policy contexts have been described as either inclusive or potentially protective, or exclusive and potentially restrictive toward immigrants.[27] Inclusive public policies may view immigrants as having the potential to become U.S. citizens and productive community members.[28] Examples include in-state residency tuition benefits or healthcare benefits for undocumented individuals, in-state residency tuition policies have been associated with a decrease in rates of dropping out of high school,[29] and insurance eligibility expansion has been associated with outcomes such as increases in receipt of prenatal care and decrease in adverse birth outcomes.[30] Exclusive or restrictive policies curtail immigrant access to public services like education, healthcare, employment, and protections; they may also contribute to stress and discrimination in both immigrants and non-immigrants who are perceived to be immigrants because of their skin color, accent, or physical appearance.[31]

Exclusionary or inclusionary public policies may be reflective of local public sentiment toward immigrants. Public policies can be subtly discriminatory or overtly xenophobic (e.g., formation of anti-immigrant militia groups to patrol borders with Mexico).[32] Xenophobia can be both a deterrent to seeking healthcare and associated with negative outcomes like psychological distress, depression, bullying, being a victim of physical violence, and household financial strain. Xenophobia can also intersect with racism, itself a determinant of health.[33] Economic crisis and financial instability can lead governments to respond with stricter immigration laws[34] and can cause xenophobic sentiment to swell.[35]

The geography of settlement may also impact the health and well-being of its immigrant residents. Some immigrants and refugees settle in "traditional destinations" or established "enclaves," with an initial base of community support as well as familiar language and culture. Other "newer" destinations have fewer same-culture residents, potentially leading to a sense of isolation from both the culture of origin and the receiving culture.[36] In these newer destinations, there may be inadequate culturally and linguistically appropriate healthcare resources.[37]

The process of relating, interacting with, and adapting to a new culture (acculturation) can be stressful, particularly when people experience discrimination or experience barriers like limited proficiency in the language of the host culture.[38] Immigrants with low English proficiency face challenges navigating healthcare[39] and education systems in the United States,[40] and are more likely to work in hazardous conditions.[41] Other challenges relate to the loss of social and family networks from the country of origin—networks that can buffer the stress of acculturation.[42] Conflicts can arise when there are different rates or levels of acculturation—linguistic or otherwise—between family members. This is a phenomenon called acculturative family distancing (or an acculturative gap).[43] Acculturative family distancing has been associated with distress and negative mental health outcomes for both parents and children.[44]

Despite the many challenges faced by immigrant families, there is also substantial literature testifying to family resilience.[45] Many studies support a healthy immigrant effect or an "immigrant paradox" by which physical and mental health outcomes for immigrants are better than would be expected based on socioeconomic factors.[46] These findings extend to children, with some studies showing more positive developmental outcomes and academic attitudes in newly arrived immigrant children.[47] This may be reflective of family-level resilience, family attitudes, and cultural processes.[48] However, the paradox tends to diminish over time, with factors such as discrimination and family conflict being thought to contribute.[49] Exclusive or restrictive immigration public policies and enforcement may also contribute to deterioration of the immigrant paradox over time.[50]

## Detention, Deportation, and Remova

In the United States, there has been a nearly five-fold increase in immigrant detentions in the past twenty years.[51] Immigrants can be detained for unauthorized arrival or visa violations, when claims for asylum are received, and in the process of deportation. As mentioned previously, and contrary to popular belief, immigrants with legal permanent residency can also be detained and deported.[52] While many detention activities occur at the border, detentions have increased significantly in the U.S. interior through cooperation between local and state law enforcement and federal Immigrations and Customs Enforcement (ICE).

The degree of state and local cooperation with ICE has been associated with adverse impacts in immigrant communities (e.g., food insecurity).[53] The intersection of law enforcement and ICE also disproportionately impacts Black immigrants, who are comparatively more likely than non-Black immigrants to be deported due to a criminal conviction.[54]

In recent years, the federal government has increased immigration enforcement raids in workplaces, homes, and other community settings, leading to the detention (and, for some, deportation) of thousands of immigrants.[55] Immigration raids not only have economic, health, and psychological impacts on the detained individuals who are detained and their families, but impact immigrant communities as a whole, leading to fears about enrolling in health insurance and accessing healthcare,[56] poorer self-rated health,[57] and stress-related health outcomes such as low birth weight.[58] Deportation risk and fears have also been associated with reduced participation in public programs such as Medicaid[59] and Special Supplemental Nutrition Program for Women, Infants, and Children[60] for eligible citizen children. Perhaps related to public awareness of immigration enforcement raids and cooperation between ICE and local law enforcement, deportation fears and associated reticence to use health services have increased even among Latinx U.S. citizen adults in recent decades.[61]

The conditions of detention have raised alarms. Mistreatment includes sexual and physical abuse of both detained adults and detained children; overcrowding and outbreaks of infectious diseases[62] (compounded in the era of COVID-19);[63] inadequate access to food, water, and hygiene supplies;[64] twenty-four-hour lighting resulting in sleep deprivation; and harassment or mistreatment by detention officers.[65] Moreover, immigrants in detention, legal and human rights organizations, and medical and public health professionals have reported severe deficiencies in access to and quality of medical care,[66] exacerbated by inadequate access to interpretation.[67] In September 2020, there were reports of hysterectomies done without consent of women detained by ICE, prompting a congressional investigation and civil rights litigation.[68]

While immigration detention is classified civil rather than criminal,[69] conditions of detention centers have been compared to jails and many detention facilities are run by for-profit prison firms.[70] However, detainees lack constitutional protections available under criminal law (however limited they may be, such as the right to legal representation).[71] Lack of legal representation, and other conditions of detention, like the possibility of being detained indefinitely, contribute to uncertainty about the duration of detention not only on the part of the detainee, but also on the part of those left behind like spouses and children.

The conditions of detention are compounded by the psychological and financial implications of detention in terms of detainees' separation from family and social networks.[72] At times, detainee separation has been an explicit policy, as when the U.S. Department of Homeland Security formally adopted a policy in 2018 requiring federal prosecution of immigrants crossing the U.S. border without authorization. This policy led to forced separation of parents from their children while parents awaited prosecution and review of asylum cases. Children, some as young as infants and toddlers, and upward of 4,500 of them, were turned over to separate facilities operated by the Office of Refugee Resettlement.[73] Similar to reports of conditions inside adult detention centers, there were reports of grossly inadequate food, water, and sanitation for child detainees within the Office of Refugee Resettlement facilities.[74]

Unsurprisingly, studies of adults and children being held in immigration detention have found high rates of mental health conditions including depression and anxiety.[75] For refugees and asylum-seekers, who suffer disproportionately from trauma-related conditions such as post-traumatic stress disorder,[76] both the physical conditions of detention and symbolic meaning of detention (being treated like a criminal, being detained for indeterminate periods) can exacerbate underlying mental health conditions.[77]

After detention, immigrants may be released due to receiving an immigration benefit (e.g., being granted asylum status), posting bond, or being deported. Deportation has severe or even fatal consequences when individuals are forced to return to the dangerous circumstances they were trying to escape.[78] The consequences of deportation to families left behind are profound and include severe financial deprivation,[79] negative mental health outcomes,[80] and impacts on school attendance, engagement, and educational aspirations.[81] Formerly detained immigrants who are released to the community can experience a period of readjustment like community reentry following incarceration.[82] They also disproportionately return to impoverished communities and communities of color in the United States (Figure 9.1).

## RECOMMENDATIONS FOR PROMOTING EQUITABLE HEALTH AMONG IMMIGRANTS AND THEIR FAMILIES

The Social-Ecological Model[83] is one framework that describes multiple levels of influence on health and potential avenues for solutions. These levels include the individual, interpersonal, organizational, and public policy levels, as described in Table 9.2. Levels interact with and are codependent with one another. Individual-level knowledge (e.g., about the realities of the immigrant experience) is often a necessary first step to working toward the types of higher-level interventions that may have broader impact. Underlying all interventions, we emphasize the need for continual reassessment on multiple levels. On the individual and interpersonal levels, we should be aware of our own of racial and cultural biases and how these may inform our understanding of immigrant issues and, therefore, attitudes about, or interactions with, im-

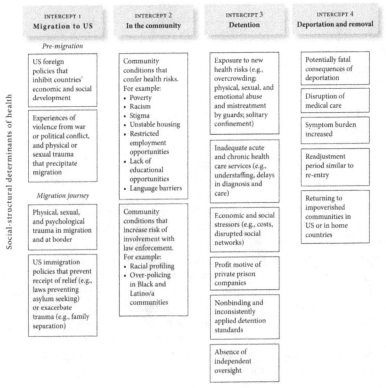

Figure 9.1.   Immigration intercept model. Copyright © Saadi et al. 2020

migrants. On the organizational and policy levels, it is important to recognize that immigration status is a *modifiable* social determinant of health.[84]

In Table 9.2, we further define levels and give examples of steps or interventions that a person (clinician or nonclinician) could take at that level.[85]

For someone not already steeped in the immigrant health space, a critical first step would be to begin by identifying what local organizations exist to offer direct services or policy advocacy around immigrant rights.[86] Local organizations can be an incredible first step to connecting to local and state efforts and leveraging to larger level policy advocacy if there is interest. National organizations involved in policy-level advocacy for immigrants include the National Immigration Law Center, the American Civil Liberties Union, and Kids in Need of Defense. Above all, the rallying cry "nothing about us without us!" is one that should be heeded equally in immigrant health advocacy just as it should be when seeking to reach equity for other populations.[87]

**Table 9.2. Recommendations for Actions to Promote Equitable Health**

| Level | Definition | Examples of Steps or Interventions That Could Be Taken |
|---|---|---|
| Individual | Knowledge, attitudes, biases, or skills | • Increasing knowledge about immigration, local immigrant communities<br>• Increasing knowledge about legal aspects of providing healthcare services to undocumented immigrants<br>• Increasing knowledge about collection and/or documentation of immigration information about patients |
| Interpersonal | Relationships with other people | • Attending trainings or reading about whether and how to talk to patients about immigration status without inciting fear or perpetuating stigma<br>• Emphasize confidentiality in interactions |
| Organizational | Organizations or social institutions (including healthcare organizations) serving or affecting immigrants | • Learning about or advocating for institutional policies and programs that promote psychological and physical safety for immigrants within organizations (both patients and workforce members), so that immigrants can make decisions not influenced by fear of immigration enforcement or fear of discrimination and stigma |

*(continued)*

**Table 9.2.** *(continued)*

| | Organizations or social institutions (including healthcare organizations) serving or affecting immigrants | • Ensuring that organizations are protected from onsite immigration enforcement to the fullest extent permitted by law<br>• Establishing a local medical-legal partnership or facilitating referrals to outside legal resources to address immigrants' legal needs |
|---|---|---|
| Public Policy | National, state, and local laws | • Increasing awareness of national, state, and local immigration laws<br>• Advocating for timely processing of asylum applications, against entry policies that discriminate based on religion and/or national origin<br>• Advocating for decrease in use of and oversight of immigration detention centers and prioritizing alternatives to detention<br>• Advocating for promotion of family unity<br>• Advocating for expanded access to public services for immigrants (including healthcare services)<br>• Advocating against cooperation of state and local law enforcement with federal immigration authorities<br>• Promoting standards across sectors (e.g., labor/employment, education) that protect immigrants regardless of immigration status[1] |

1. Berlinger, Nancy, and Rachel L. Zacharias. "Resources for teaching and learning about immigrant health care in health professions education." *AMA Journal of Ethics* 21, no. 1 (2019): 50–57; National Immigration Law Center. "Health care." 2021. https://www.nilc.org/issues/health-care/.
2. Berlinger, Nancy, and Rachel L. Zacharias. "Resources for teaching and learning about immigrant health care in health professions education." *AMA Journal of Ethics* 21, no. 1 (2019): 50–57; Doctors for Immigrants. "Our work." 2021. http://doctorsforimmigrants.com/ourwork/.
3. Costa, Daniel. California leads the way: A look at California laws that help protect labor standards for unauthorized immigrant workers. *Washington, DC: Economic Policy Institute*, 2018.

# 10

## Improving Healthcare for Disabled Patients

*Laura Calloway*

### INTRODUCTION

Like the polio and HIV epidemics have previously established, the COVID-19 pandemic is yet another reminder that health is not guaranteed, and that it is not a question of if you'll become disabled, but when. Both polio[1] and HIV[2] have demonstrated this, as they were mass disabling events, newly disabling previously able-bodied people, and adding additional health concerns for disabled people. COVID-19 is no different. It's estimated that 10 percent of COVID cases result in disability (a.k.a. Long Haulers),[3] which would equal millions of newly disabled Americans.[4] Due to the likelihood of continuing national health crises and new ones that have the potential to newly disable as well as cause additional issues for existing disabled people, it is imperative to create a healthcare system to serve them with dignity.

### DEFINING DISABILITY

Following are three models of disability. Although not all chronically ill people identify as disabled, because chronic illness is often disabling, any mention of disability for the remainder of the chapter can also be assumed to include chronic illness.

## Medical Model

Under the medical model of disability, impairment is treated as the individual's problem. Impairment is a wrong that must be fixed through medical treatments such as surgery, protheses, or other interventions, so that the individual in question may return to "good health."[5] Thus, under this model, disabled healthcare is an individual rather than collective issue.

## Social Model

In contrast to the medical model of disability, in the social model, disability is a function of both social and political dynamics wherein certain bodies are exemplified as deviant and abnormal. So disability is the socially constructed outcome of interplay between social and relational phenomenon, rather than simply a catastrophic event in or of the body.[6] As a result, the focus of the social model is collectivist, and more specifically on breaking down both the ideological and architectural obstacles that exclude disabled people from full societal participation.[7]

While the social model separates disability from impairment due to the assumption that disability is socially constructed, it is important to remember that "impairment itself is both a lived experience and an effect of discourse," meaning that impairment cannot be examined or understood without historical and political context, namely an understanding of inequities as a result of our current hierarchy of human value based on skin color.[8]

## Black Feminist Model

Because the hierarchy of human value is an influential part of the social construction of disability, it is important to consider the intersectional nature of oppression in disability frameworks.[9] The Black feminist model of disability is invaluable for this purpose as its foundation rests on a variety of vectors, such as race, gender, and power. Essentially, this framework decenters whiteness and the white male body (often the focus of disability studies) and places its focus on "how bodies are raced and how this intersects with disability, disease, and bodily sovereignty."[10] This framework addresses critiques of the medical model's limitations (especially of impairment as an individual problem to be medically corrected) by leaving room for individuals to exercise bodily autonomy through "treatment, cure, or resistance to medical intervention all together."[11]

# IMPROVING HEALTHCARE FOR DISABLED PEOPLE

Improving healthcare for disabled people requires a variety of approaches, but for the sake of this short chapter, four are included here:

1. Expanding accessibility to care locations, treatment options, and cost of care
2. Treating disabled people as experts about their lived experiences and goals
3. Reimagining health by accounting for both its structural and social determinants
4. Reevaluating digital infrastructure

## ACCESSIBILITY

### Meet Patients Where They Are

Access to healthcare is a critical public health concern. Patients should be able to receive care in their own communities and from their own communities in a way that is financially and emotionally supportive of their life goals. Primary care services can be provided effectively by physicians, nurse practitioners, physician assistants, pharmacists, and other advanced practice providers in a collaborative effort,[12] as long as clinics are accessible to community members. Having a variety of primary care practitioners available in a community increases the likelihood of patient visits.[13]

However, there are a variety of barriers to patient-centered local care, especially for disabled patients. First, being disabled is incredibly expensive and often means patients ration or forgo care.[14] In addition to disabled patients rationing care due to medical expenses, medical providers also ration care for disabled patients due to ableism and capitalism, creating a lower valuation for disabled lives (this logic is often visible in survival estimations and triage policies).[15] Charging for health insurance and subsequently discouraging "frivolous" use of care, restricting "expensive" care when a cheaper (but not necessarily adequate) alternative exists, enforcing step therapy and/or prior authorizations, designating certain care providers (and even specific healthcare professionals within individual care facilities) as out of network, maintaining formularies and preferred drug lists, requiring specialist referrals from a primary care providers, and cost sharing are also forms of healthcare rationing.[16]

Second, due to ableism in medical education, research, and practice, becoming a disabled health provider is difficult. Technical standards for medical school enrollees, such as requirements to be able to lift a patient, are one example.[17] Ableism in staffing, where practioners expect expect to work with disabled patients but not alongside them as colleagues, is another.[18] Additionally, due to stigma[19] around mental illness, healthcare providers experiencing mental health issues may leave them underreported and/or unaddressed, leading to burnout.[20] A lack of disabled healthcare providers is a detriment to disabled patients and healthcare as a whole because "medical school does not teach you to be a patient."[21]

Third, medical care locations are often inaccessible for an assortment of reasons including distance from public transit,[22] lack of accessible medical diagnostic equipment and examination rooms,[23] lack of accessible entrances, long distances from parking areas to the facility, lack of web accessibility for digital health services,[24] and hospital closure (most notable for rural and/or southern hospitals).[25]

Fourth, a key part of community-based care is patients being able to age in place in their communities. However, only 1 percent of current housing stock is fully accessible[26] (meaning a wheelchair user could live there independently).[27] In addition, what is available is often more expensive and disabled people have less wealth to pay to move into accessible housing or to modify their current housing.[28]

## Being Disabled is Expensive

As mentioned previously, there are a variety of additional costs that accompany being disabled. Sometimes, these are referred to as "hidden costs"; however, the costs are largely hidden only to able-bodied people. For disabled people, these costs are an additional price for admission.[29] A variety of tools, products, services, and medications are often required for a disabled person to accomplish their activities of daily living[30] such as, but not limited to, mobility aids (e.g., wheelchair, cane, orthopedic footwear), over-the-counter and prescription drugs, car modifications, adaptive clothing, fragrance-free skin care, allergen-free food items, prepared food, physical therapy, service animals, and home healthcare. These elements are largely direct financial costs of disability, but there are also indirect costs such as significant parking fees[31] due to frequent doctors' visits, loss of productivity due to medical appointments, and poorer health due to delay to diagnosis.[32]

In addition to being disabled costing more than being able bodied, disabled people are more likely to be in poverty, with 21 percent of disabled people living in poverty versus 13 percent of able-bodied people in 2016.[33] Further, disabled people of color (especially Black people[34] and Indigenous peoples[35]), queer disabled people, and anyone at those intersections[36] are more likely to live in poverty.

Not all disability costs are simply financial; many are related to time and energy,[37] such as managing medications and refills, meal planning, doing symptoms research, and scheduling appointments. The amount of physical, mental, and logistical work necessary to deal with disability can often feel like a full-time job, but since this work does not produce capital; it is not prioritized or valued by our capitalist society. Another cost is marriage equality. For some disabled people, marriage (or fitting the Supplemental Security Income definition of a couple) can mean a loss of crucial benefits, such as Supplemental Security Income, Medicare, or Medicaid.[38] This type of loss is devastating and potentially life threatening.[39]

## DISABLED PEOPLE'S LIVED EXPERIENCES ARE MEDICAL EXPERTISE

Patients are acutely aware of their bodies, and while it may be difficult to demonstrate the depth and breadth of their knowledge in a single doctor's appointment, patients' knowledge of the self should not be underestimated or undervalued. Health providers know disease, but given that providers may not be disabled people themselves, they may not know the specifics of living with a disease. Here then, patients are the experts[40] and should be centered as such.

Further, patient knowledge of potential prognoses, their drug interactions, symptom and disease progression, and any logistical issues with insurance coverage should be respected. Moreover, patients in pain (especially Black, fat, women, and those at the intersections)[41] must be believed. Lastly, treatment and care should focus on supporting patients so they (and their communities) can meet the goals they have set for their everyday lives.

## REIMAGINING HEALTH

Health should not be considered a moral entity that can be measured in binary terms of "good" or "bad"[42] where the individual, and more specifically individual behaviors, are the locus of change.[43] This is because it is unreasonable to expect individuals to be able to have direct control over

> many of the upstream determinants of health: governance, policy, and cultural
> or societal norms and values that shape who has access to health-promoting

resources and opportunities and who does not. . . . In other words, no matter how empowered, knowledgeable, or willing someone is to change their behavior, they may not be able to do so because of structural determinants of health inequities.[44]

Those least likely to have the power to access health-promoting resources experience health inequities due to racism, classism, colonialism, misogyny, homophobia, fatphobia, disability, and any intersection thereof.

These power dynamics are largely shaped by what is societally considered the ideal body, which can generally be defined as white, straight, abled, thin,[45] and cis. This creates a system of health comparison wherein the ideal body is the health goal (one that is unattainable for othered bodies). If the current status quo remains, then "health" is a status you are allowed to reach and/or maintain if you possess enough power.[46] Thus, relying on a system of health comparison frames health as an exclusionary construct, where minoritized bodies cannot be healthy.[47]

Further, when medical care is framed around the premise of the ideal body and provided in service to it, healthcare and health behaviors become a series of disciplinary practices patients perform on the way to this ideal. Here, the goal is to be perceived as healthy and, more importantly, good.[48] This goodness is impossible for those framed as having "unideal" bodies.

## REEVALUATING DIGITAL INFRASTRUCTURE

### Telemedicine and Telehealth Appointments

Having telehealth appointments available legitimizes the patient's home as a site of care rather than leaving onsite care as the only option. Using the home as a site of care has many patient benefits. First, because patients don't have to travel to appointments, they can avoid a variety of physical access barriers, such as the cost,[49] logistics,[50] and inaccessibility of public transportation;[51] parking fees; and inaccessible care facilities (e.g., building entrances, exam rooms, and equipment). Second, patients may feel more comfortable at home than they might in a traditional clinical setting, especially if they have experienced previous medical trauma (which is common for disabled people).[52] Third, patients have immediate access to their medications and can have them in front of them during their visit. Fourth, visits can be more of a communal process as caregivers and family members can be easily included in appointments. Fifth, patients can reduce their risk of exposure to respiratory illnesses.[53] In addition to using telemedicine for appointments, this technique can support additional purposes such as telemonitoring, symptoms screening, and chatbots (for frequently asked questions and recommending patients at risk see a medical professional).[60] With these benefits related to accessibility, telemedicine should be integral to care offerings during COVID-19 and beyond, especially for disabled adults who are more likely to experience one (or a combination of) the aforementioned accessibility issues (as able-bodiedness is both temporal and temporary).[54]

## The Limitations of Digital Medicine

Despite its merits, digital technologies are not an immediate equalizer. For example, the previously discussed improvements in accessibility facilitated by telemedicine can only be realized by patients with reliable access to an adequate internet connection and to a compatible internet connected device (smartphone, tablet, desktop, or laptop computer). Disabled people are three times as likely as able-bodied people to say they never go online. Further, disabled people who are online are less likely to have multiple internet-connected devices at home.[55]

One solution to the dearth of internet access experienced by disabled people (and other minoritized groups) is expanding the Federal Communications Commission's Lifeline Program[56] to ensure that households with incomes at or below 135 percent of the Federal Poverty Guidelines can receive low-cost phone or internet service. Because the Lifeline Program provides low-cost internet service, but not devices to access the service, funding to improve device availability would also be necessary.

Medical access issues experienced by poor people are mediated by the geographic area they live in. Because medical access issues of people in rural poverty differ[57] from those experiencing urban poverty, and health information technology usage differs between urban and rural residents,[58] any telemedicine and digital device funding program would need to address issues unique to both rural and urban areas.

Besides technology access and internet connectivity, successful telemedicine programs need to include support for deaf, hard of hearing, blind, low vision, and other disabled patients (through design approaches centering disabled user[59] such as user-sensitive inclusive design[60]). This must be addressed before the implementation of any telemedicine program[61] as such support ensures more equitable access than shoe horning in accessibility workarounds after a program is already running simply to meet legal requirements.[62] Along the same lines, creating "accessibility" using automated web solutions is wildly inadequate.[63] Lastly, support for languages other than English should be approached in a similarly preventative, rather than reactive, manner[64] with emphasis on onsite health interpreters to "advocate for patients if the patient's health, well-being, or dignity is at risk"[65] and bilingual patient navigators to assist patients in addressing barriers to care and navigating complex medical systems.[66]

In addition to ensuring that the multiplicity of patient access needs for effectively utilizing digital medicine are met, in order for digital medicine be a successful part of patient-centered care, a deeper understanding of and accountability for how technology shapes society (and how society shapes technology) is necessary. "Technology is a process, not a product,"[67] meaning that individual technologies, platforms, and services will likely come and go, but the social, privacy, and civil rights aftermaths of their implementation and use will not. A key issue underpinning all technological processes, especially those involving medical information, is surveillance potential. Health surveillance often increases during times of public health crisis,[68] but it is not exclusive to those occurrences. Rather, it is a key component of public health strategy.[69] Even when surveillance is conducted in service of the public good, individual and/or collective harm is possible.

A large component of this is the fact that collecting, storing, transmitting, and utilizing medical information, largely electronically, in a privacy-preserving manner is challenging.[70] Thus, only the minimum amount of health data required to complete a desired task should be collected. This strategy should also be applied to health-adjacent data, essentially anything that includes personally identifiable information, or information that can be used to trace individuals' identities.[71] Examples of personally identifiable information include name, address (street or email), social security number, fingerprints, and biometric data. Additionally, the same precautions are necessary for potential personally identifiable information, which includes partial identities leading to a full identity when combined (e.g., IP address, employment information,[72] and social media data[73]).

It is also critical to collect the minimum amount of data necessary in a way that minimizes harm for those whose data is centered under surveillance. To do so, those responsible for surveillance should "identify, evaluate, minimize, and disclose risks for harm"[74] prior to implementing surveillance mechanisms. In addition, monitoring for harm should be a continuous process, and harm mitigation should begin immediately after any harm is identified.[75] Cases of harm to disabled people due to oversurveillance include but are not limited to location tracking of mental health hotline users leading to police and other forms of carceral violence,[76] life insurance companies collecting health data from a customer's wearables in exchange for discounts,[77] and hospitals using algorithmic modeling to predict disease survival.[78]

Besides minimizing the overall amount of data collected, it is essential to follow security best practices for protecting any data necessary for patient care. These best practices include performing medical security audits and risk assessments of new devices and services before they are introduced to the market, limiting unauthorized access, employing multiple layers of security to minimize risk,[79] using data[80] and image encryption,[81] and instituting authentication protocols.[82] Following the aforementioned strategies is essential for protecting the privacy, bodily autonomy, and agency of the most marginalized patients, especially disabled people. Protecting the privacy of disabled patients ensures more privacy-preserving care for all.

## CONCLUSION

Improving healthcare for disabled patients is a multifaceted endeavor. To ensure success, accessibility must be expanded, disabled people need to be treated as experts, the concept of health should be re-imagined, and our digital infrastructure reexamined. Most importantly, the agency, bodily autonomy, goals, lived experiences, and privacy of disabled patients must be centered in the process, while also acknowledging both the social and structural factors that shape societal expectations for health and one's access to health-promoting resources.

# 11

## Pediatrics

*Ben Wormser and David M. Keller*

The U.S. healthcare system is built to deliver acute care to patients who request it and have the means to pay for it. Over the years, the system has evolved to provide preventive health services and chronic disease management through a patchwork of services, with little connection to the community, making it difficult to address the relationships, culture, and environment that affect children as they grow and develop. Healthy, thriving children are raised by families that are, in turn, supported by their community. A new healthcare system must be integrated with that community and financially incentivized to address the factors that affect child health outside of the clinic.

In 2004, the Institute of Medicine convened a workgroup to define "child health."[1] After deliberation, they determined that a healthy child is one who is able to "a) develop and realize their potential; b) satisfy their needs; and c) develop the capacities that allow them to interact successfully with their biological, physical, and social environments." A healthy child is prepared and able to live a fulfilling life, no matter how they define it. The support and resources required to develop such an ability rest in our most fundamental needs as humans: a safe, clean, and secure home to live in; access to healthy nutrition; regular exposure to rich spoken language; and a sense of security and trust with others, particularly adults. These environmental contributions to health intertwine with and differentially activate the genes each individual is born with to produce the physical, emotional, and behavioral patterns that shape an individual's health throughout their lifecourse.[2] A healthy community formalizes the physical supports, such as safe housing and access to nutrition, and the social supports, such as language and healthy interpersonal interactions, that promote health. It accomplishes this through robust educational opportunities for learning and social development, green spaces for physical activity, partnerships that promote agriculture and housing development, and customs that build social networks and provide rules for social etiquette.[3]

While healthy communities promote health, they can also mitigate the negative influences that are known to drive poor health.[4] Adverse childhood experiences represent stressors that children are exposed to early in life, such as abuse, neglect, or family dysfunction, that have been linked to worse adult health outcomes.[5] Subsequent research has identified factors that grow a child's resiliency in the face of adverse childhood experiences, allowing them to thrive despite the exposure. These include access to a family-centered medical home, a safe and supportive neighborhood environment, and healthy mothers.[6]

When communities do not have the resources or the structure to provide positive supports and to mitigate negative influences, we see child health worsen. This paucity of support often correlates with two overarching community experiences that are not distributed equally between communities. The first is poverty, which impedes access to nutrition and safe housing, infuses the body with toxic stress, and limits critical supports including transportation, communication technology, and adult supervision.[7] A total of 38.1 percent—nearly two in every five—children in the United States are poor or "near poor" (defined as families living within 150 percent of the poverty line).[8] The second is structural racism, which limits the distribution of resources to communities of color, increases their exposure to environmental toxins, and casts a false shadow of inferior self-worth over those who are subject to it. In this way, both poverty and systemic racism deprive children of the health-promoting aspects of community.

Given the considerable influence of community on child health, pediatric healthcare systems must be designed to work with communities to maximize the health and well-being of children effectively and equitably.[9] This means integrating with the surrounding community to coordinate existing services and to create new resources that meet the population's stated needs. Success would be a healthy community, integrated with and supported by the pediatric healthcare system, for every child.

Communities currently benefit from a wide variety of social service programs that affect child health. Many of these programs are funded through the federal and state governments, beginning with the robust promise of public education for every child (including Head Start, Early Head Start, and preschool in certain communities). Nutrition benefits are administered through the Supplemental Nutrition Assistance Program and the Special Supplemental

Nutrition Program for Women, Infants, and Children. Housing benefits are administered through the Housing Choice Voucher Program, and household financial support is available through the Earned Income Tax Credit. Publicly subsidized transportation enables access to all of these services and more. Pediatric healthcare providers have long recognized the importance of connecting patients to these programs and have established mechanisms to do so from within the healthcare system.[10] Sometimes, this is a formal program to provide warm handoffs between clinics and community resources. Other times, it is simply a list of resources that can be readily shared by clinic staff. Unfortunately, these services within the healthcare system have never been sustainably financed—an adverse effect of the healthcare system's current focus on paying for acute care management over preventive services—and further integration with community supports has subsequently been limited. A truly innovative practice might incorporate home- and community-based programs, such as nurse home visiting, school-based healthcare (both through a traditional school nurse and the more robust school-based health center), early childhood intervention services, and mental health counselors integrated into the community and clinic settings. The advantage of these programs is that they deliver support directly to where the child spends their time and become part of the child's surrounding community. These qualities also allow the programs to target multiple generations in the home or community, which makes them particularly effective.

Pediatricians have long been at the forefront of a movement for more preventive care. Their support of the Sheppard-Towner Maternal and Infant Welfare Act of 1921, which established federal funds for states to create educational preventive programs for families and their children, led them to leave the American Medical Association and to form their own organization, the American Academy of Pediatrics.[11] These programs were focused on education, nutrition, and prevention of chronic disease, which was a new concept at the time. These principles evolved into the modern-day well child visit, which focuses on health screening, development, vaccination, and age-appropriate anticipatory guidance.

Further attempts to develop a community-wide focus for pediatric care have taken different forms, including Federally Qualified Community Health Centers (FQHCs), Accountable Care Organizations (ACOs), and the Integrated Care for Kids (InCK) Model promoted by the Centers for Medicare and Medicaid Innovation.

FQHCs were created in 1965 by the Office of Economic Opportunity as demonstration projects intended to use comprehensive primary healthcare and community-based interventions to drive improved community health.[12]

They were placed in locations with the greatest need for healthcare—urban and rural areas with high poverty levels and low healthcare access. Today, they deliver financially accessible and culturally relevant care to 29.8 million patients per year, 30 percent of whom are children under the age of eighteen.[13] A total of 84 percent of FQHCs are recognized as patient-centered medical homes and deliver medical, behavioral, and dental care that is designed with the surrounding community in mind. Studies have demonstrated that this approach yields improved child health, meeting or even exceeding national rates for child health measures such as childhood immunizations, prenatal care, and low birth weight.[14] Roughly 10 percent of funding is also allocated toward "enabling" resources like transportation and translation services, which help to integrate services into the community.[15] The FQHC locations in impoverished communities also has the added benefit of stimulating the local economy.[16]

For all of their impact on community health, FQHCs have relied heavily on Medicaid financing and federal grants to remain operational. Medicaid provided 44 percent of the funding for FQHCs in 2017, with an additional 18 percent coming from federal grants.[17] One key to the success and survival of FQHCs is the Prospective Payment System within Medicaid. The Prospective Payment System ensures that Medicaid payments remain close to the cost of delivering care, which keeps FQHCs functioning while also ensuring that grant funding goes toward uninsured patients and unreimbursed services. Unfortunately, the Medicare and private insurers pay far less than the Prospective Payment System rate for similar services, limiting the extent to which FQHCs can extend their services beyond the Medicaid and uninsured populations.

ACOs were created by the Patient Protection and Affordable Care Act of 2010 and represent collections of healthcare providers who join together to provide integrated health services and care coordination for a defined population of patients.[18] These providers also assume financial risk for the health of their panel of patients, losing money when they become sick and require expensive care and sharing in the savings when they remain well and stay out of the hospital.

The first ACOs were focused on the adult population, as their care is more expensive and a reduction in costly care could more readily be achieved. Pediatric-focused ACOs eventually followed, often using a per-member, per-month pay scheme that allowed providers more flexibility to invest in how the community supported their patient's health. Pediatric ACOs could use the extra funding, for example, to hire community health workers who are able to connect patients to both clinical and social service resources within the community.

Nationwide Children's Hospital created an ACO called Partners For Kids in 2008 which has grown to cover over three hundred thousand low-income children in Columbus, Ohio.[19] This arrangement aligned financial incentives with ongoing community-based work in which the hospital had founded a nonprofit housing organization with an area faith-based organization. This nonprofit subsequently impacted over 389 residential properties and generated over $40 million of investment in the surrounding neighborhoods. Early analysis demonstrated improved health as a result of this effort, which could lead to financial gains for Partners For Kids and further investment in the community.[20]

While this example is encouraging, it should also be noted that it is often challenging to demonstrate a significant improvement in the cost of care for children. Their care is relatively inexpensive compared to older, sicker adults, and the return on investment of pediatric healthcare is typically recognized many years later during adulthood. Pediatric ACOs are also limited by focusing only on their panel of patients, which does not incentivize broad community-level investment that could benefit all children in the community, even those who are not included in the panel of patients. This presents a challenge to finding common ground with the public health system (which conducts many of the community programs) and to justifying community-wide investment. To improve collaboration, these organizations require shared financial interests and a shared definition of population health.

In 2018, the Centers for Medicare and Medicaid Innovation announced a new proposal for pediatric healthcare improvement called the InCK Model.[21] The InCK model is intended to test whether integration of clinical care and community supports under the umbrella of a new payment model will improve health outcomes and reduce healthcare expenditures. In 2019, InCK distributed $128 million to eight programs that will design child-centered and family-centered care coordination services. Each program includes their state's Medicaid agency, which will design the new payment model to promote sustainability. The InCK model will judge success based on the quality of care delivered, reductions in avoidable inpatient hospitalizations, and reductions in out-of-home placements for Medicaid and Children's Health Insurance Program beneficiaries ages twenty-one years and younger. Of note, the funding is only designated for clinical services, but can be used to coordinate service delivery. In this way, the healthcare system is investing in its connection to the strong community programs that already exist and improving cross-sector integration.

Early experiences with the InCK Model have demonstrated three important components of a successful system:[22] first, there must be a bridging organization designated to coordinate and communicate between partners. This is typically a healthcare organization or a public health department. Second, meaningful data must be shared between medical and social services institutions. This allows for collaboration on quality improvement across sectors and could lay the foundation of shared savings or revenue in the future. This is a particular issue when it comes to sharing data between healthcare organizations and schools, as the data is subject to competing privacy clauses—the Health Insurance Portability and Accountability Act in healthcare and the Family Educational Rights and Privacy Act in education.[23] Third, there must be alignment of payments to enable sustained cross-sector collaboration. This collective ownership and accountability feeds the survival of this program.[24]

The InCK model is a first step toward integration of healthcare and social services, but further change will be needed. Despite their altruistic missions and willingness to experiment with grant support, both healthcare institutions and social service programs depend on stable funding streams for sustainability. Full integration of social services and healthcare will not be attainable without shared funding streams that align the organizations and ensure their mutual financial health. As former president of the American Academy of Pediatrics, Dr. James Perrin, observes, "current US policies, which sharply divide case management and resources across the education, child welfare, and healthcare sectors, serve families poorly."[25]

A new pediatric healthcare system is needed: one that owns the health of all children and is fully integrated with the communities that support child health. This system will require three crucial components: universal health insurance coverage for children, shared funding streams between healthcare and social service programs based on mutually recognized measures, and a commitment to maternal health as the earliest determinant of child health.

Approximately 5.5 percent of children in the United States were uninsured in 2018.[26] This was a historically low proportion of children, primarily thanks to coverage provided by the combination of Medicaid, the Children's Health Insurance Program, employer-based insurance, and plans available through the marketplaces created by the Affordable Care Act. This legislation also ensured that all Medicaid recipients would receive the Early and Periodic Screening, Diagnostic, and Treatment benefits, which were originally created to ensure the fitness of America's young adults for military service.[27] But this still leaves one in twenty children without access to affordable healthcare. It also hides two additional complicating factors:[28] first, the coverage that is offered by each type of insurance varies drastically and can often be quite sparse, even for routine preventive care. Second, the eligibility for each insurance is dependent on the family's financial or employment status—two factors that change regularly and can force children to frequently switch between plans. This process of unenrolling and re-enrolling in health insurance is complicated and time intensive and often falls on families with the fewest reserves to devote to this effort. Social workers, advocates, healthcare providers, volunteers, and parents ultimately contribute significant time and energy to maintaining coverage that should be readily accessible and stable.

An additional benefit to universal healthcare coverage for children is that it promotes a focus on the health of an entire community. Health systems and insurers currently face the unusual challenge of designing programs and interventions that change the structural supports of a community, but only delivering them to the specific children who seek care at their institution. This creates disparities and dilutes the potential impact of such programs. Universal insurance coverage would incentivize the creation of supports that could be used by all children in the community.

Universal health insurance for children could be accomplished by expanding Medicaid coverage to all children.[29] This would involve fully federalizing Medicaid so that states would no longer be responsible for funding part of the program (a source of variability in access to the program across the United States) and raising Medicaid reimbursement rates to be equal to those of the Medicare program. Without needing to fund Medicaid, state governments could redirect money toward education and social programs that improve child health. Increased Medicaid funding would enable all pediatric providers to deliver the effective, community-based healthcare currently provided by FQHCs.

In order to achieve shared funding streams for healthcare and social services, there are two proposed funding mechanisms. The first is blended funding, in which funding from multiple sources is combined into one lump sum and then shared with all organizations that are delivering the services. Capitated payments, such as those used in an ACOs, work this way. The second is braided funding, in which individual organizations maintain their defined funding streams but direct them toward a shared initiative.[30] This particular mechanism is promising because it is very similar to the current funding design of many local, state, and federal programs. Pediatric patient-centered medical homes have already begun to use these funding mechanisms to create fully integrated mental health supports.[31] "Full integration" in this context means that mental health specialists are collocated with the physical health team, have access to the same electronic health records, have shared billing for services, and have regular contact with the patient and their family. A key prerequisite for shared funding is to identify common measures of community health off of which to define shared goals.

Currently, the most commonly used measures of health are narrow and disease specific: control of hypertension, receipt of all recommended immunizations, number of hospitalizations for an asthma exacerbation, and so on. These measures can often identify patients' struggles with a specific disease, but they do not describe a child's overall well-being and tend to suggest focused solutions for each disease-specific problem. These measures do not describe the role played by the patient's surrounding community, and they are only financially relevant to the healthcare industry. This creates two problems: first, these measures do not align with the upstream objectives of social service programs and second, they do not capture the return on investment that might occur outside of the healthcare sector.[32]

There has subsequently been an effort to create other measures that more broadly describe the health of a child as it is defined by the Institute of Medicine. These include such measures as kindergarten readiness, which measures a five-year-old child's developmental stage and physical well-being, and school absenteeism, which reflects both the child's physical health and community supports and can be directly linked to potential for future earnings and health.[33] The Early Developmental Instrument is a tool for measuring children's functioning at kindergarten entry; it is currently in widespread use in Canada and Australia.[34] It is based on a teacher's observations in the classroom, which make it easy to obtain and very accurate. The tool evaluates each child's development across five domains: physical health and well-being, social competence, emotional maturity, language and cognitive development, and general knowledge and communication skills. Individual student results are aggregated to provide a community-level description of child health at kindergarten entry. By using tools such as the Early Developmental Instrument and identifying other measures that describe health across generations, organizations from different sectors will be able to more readily collaborate on interventions because the return on investment of their funding is more apparent and the effects of their interventions are amplified by cross-sector partnerships.

Finally, any effort intended to improve child health must recognize the role that maternal health plays in the health of the child. This begins with preconception care and reproductive health counseling that uses a reproductive justice lens to ensure women can plan their pregnancies and optimize their health prior to becoming pregnant. This population has been challenging to address with a unified strategy because their care spans pediatric, adolescent, and adult healthcare organizations. The expansion of Medicaid coverage for all women to begin at the start of prenatal care and persist through the first year postpartum would allow for the same community-wide focus and integration with social services as universal pediatric coverage would have. It would also minimize the disruption of care experienced by the one in three U.S. women who change health insurance coverage between preconception and postpartum care.[35] This continuous coverage would enable mothers to receive all necessary care to promote optimal maternal and child health.[36] This should include contraceptive care in the postpartum period, screening and treatment for postpartum depression, and a robust suite of social services supports including home visiting and drug counseling, if needed.

A reorganization of the healthcare system toward working with communities to provide the foundational supports for child health will yield better health in the future, but also better economic outcomes. As Dr. Neal Halfon urges, "In this way, they should be considered an investment, rather than a cost."[37] The economic benefit of child health can be appreciated in several different ways.[38] Healthier children allow parents and families to focus on their well-being, leading to healthier, happier adults in the community. Healthier children also tend to become healthier, more productive adults in the future. In addition to productivity, better child health also reduces future costs through decreased use of the justice system, social services, and healthcare. Finally, there is a decreased loss of productive life years through incarceration, early death or disability, and severe mental health disease or drug addiction.[39]

In conclusion, a child's health and well-being are heavily influenced by the community in which they are raised. The healthcare system can be better designed with a focus on helping to create and support that community, as opposed to a focus on individual patient needs for only those who present to care. Universal healthcare coverage is nearly achievable for children and will have the benefit of establishing consistent coverage and benefits while also helping organizations to take a population health perspective in their delivery of health. In order to truly bring the community's resources together in the care of pediatric patients, braided and blended funding streams will increasingly be needed. Broad, community-based measures of child health will promote the development of this system and a focus on maternal health will pay dividends for child health. A new pediatric healthcare system is needed. It will make the United States healthier, stronger, and more financially secure by aligning the healthcare system with community supports for health.

# 12

## Latinx

*Briana Christophers, Edwin Nieblas-Bedolla, Maru Lozano, and María C. Mora Pinzón*

### WHO IS THE LATINX COMMUNITY?

The Latinx community comprises over sixty million people of Latin American heritage and represents approximately 18.5 percent of the U.S. population.[1] Over the last two decades, the number of individuals who identify as Latinx has continued to grow rapidly; by the year 2050, this community will include more than 120 million people or about 28.6 percent of the nation.[2] In 2014, one-quarter of individuals under the age of eighteen identified as Latinx or a similar characterization in the United States; this statistic is projected to be one-third of children and adolescents being of Latinx heritage by 2060.[2] These children will be mainly U.S.-born and likely to be proficient in English, rather than immigrants coming directly from Latin American countries.[3]

The Latinx community is an incredibly diverse group. The terms with which people identify have changed over time, including Hispanic, Latino, Latin@, and combining country of origin with American (e.g., Mexican American). The word "Latinx," which is in part influenced by the Nahuatl language of the indigenous people of Mexico, was designed to be an overarching classification to identify individuals with ancestral connections to Latin America while including gender nonbinary people.[4] In this chapter, when citing a study, we will use the word used in the article or publication to avoid misidentifications of populations. The Latinx community is affected by substantial and disproportionate health burdens, which we discuss in the following—but there exists the potential for significant improvement.

In considering the health disparities affecting the Latinx community, one must address the so-called Latino Paradox, the epidemiological observation that Latinx individuals appear to have equal or better health outcomes in some measures despite lower levels of income or education compared to other groups.[5] However, given the strong correlations between income, education, and health, these findings should be interpreted with caution. For example, there is evidence that Hispanic deaths may be historically underestimated in studies evaluating mortality in the U.S. population.[6] It is possible that the so-called paradox can be explained through such underreporting.

Culturally appropriate care respects diversity in the patient population, such as language, communication styles, beliefs, attitudes, and behaviors.[7] Culturally adapted care can include diversification of medical providers by race or ethnicity; adaptation of materials to reflect patients' culture, language, or literacy skills;[8] incorporation of norms about faith, food, family, or self-image into patient care; and implementation of patient involvement strategies.[9]

In the following, we discuss special considerations in the care of Latinx individuals, including care for Latinx children, interpreter and language services, and current health inequities from a preventive medicine and surgical care perspective.

## INVOLVING AN INTERPRETER

Clinician-patient encounters may be a single word away from potentially devastating consequences such as death or unnecessary permanent harm. In other non-life-threatening scenarios, discrepancy in understanding between patients and their providers may cause delay in diagnosis and treatment. These interactions are often influenced not only by language but also by sociocultural norms.[10] While caring for patients with limited English proficiency, it is therefore critical to acknowledge and provide the linguistic competency required for optimal care while simultaneously embracing *cultural humility*.[11]

Such humility is the "lifelong process of self-reflection and self-critique whereby the individual not only learns about another's culture, but one starts with an examination of her or his own beliefs and cultural identities."[12] This differs from cultural *competence* in the sense that the latter loosely refers to the ability to understand and communicate with patients across cultures.[13] Thus, the concept of cultural humility arises as a means to connect with a patient, and sometimes their family as well, in order to provide the best care possible.

Many interpreters may face resistance to their full involvement. For example, a Mexican woman demonstrated physical and emotional pain as she relayed her manager's abusive harassment to her physician through an interpreter. When the doctor asked her to give a number to her current level of pain, she hesitated. He then proceeded to yell at her saying, "What's the matter with you? Are you stupid? Don't you know what pain is?" At that point, the interpreter chose to play patient advocate by saying, "Doctor, if you can find a respectful way to ask the patient for the information, I'll be happy to continue." This example speaks to the existence of power imbalances in the patient-physician-interpreter dynamic, reinforcing the need healthcare providers to engage in cultural humility.

In a well-known case further illustrating this point, an eighteen-year-old Hispanic man became unconscious. His Spanish-speaking family used the word "*intoxicado*," which was then interpreted by the medical team as "intoxicated." The family was attempting to inform the providers that his symptoms might have been due to a hamburger he had eaten. This misinterpretation led to evaluations of substance use while the patient's symptoms were actually due to a ruptured brain aneurysm that was unfortunately found too late and left the patient quadriplegic. The patient and his family were awarded $71 million as damages for malpractice.[14] The event shows how one word, and its interpretation, can have enormous consequences. A book published years later argued that aside from cultural differences, stereotypes, power dynamics, and prejudice also played major roles in the outcome.[15]

In another illuminating and tragic case, a two-year-old girl fractured her clavicle after falling off her tricycle. The words in this case, "*se pegó*," were misinterpreted to have meant "she was hit" rather than "she hit herself." Subsequently, the mother, who had low English proficiency, was asked to sign a form in English which led to her daughter being placed in social services custody.[16]

In the end, providing interpreting services is more than just language. It means being a patient advocate, a potential bridge between cultures, to ensure all patients regardless of background are able to obtain just and equitable treatment.

## ACCESS AND USE OF PREVENTIVE SERVICES

Latinx people face barriers to accessing preventive services (e.g., inadequate insurance coverage, costs, logistics, health literacy) that result in underutilization and subsequent increased burden of preventable conditions.[17] Although lack of insurance is the most frequently described barrier, country of origin, acculturation, immigration status, education, and fear of discrimination also affect how Latinx individuals interact with the healthcare system.[18] Latinx people have higher levels of physician distrust than white individuals; however, these were significantly affected by location, education, and insurance status.[19] Similarly, individual physician characteristics (e.g., physician-patient ethnic concordance) might mediate levels of mistrust, but there is mixed evidence on how medical mistrust and discrimination affect use of healthcare services.[20]

In communications to promote preventive health, trusted sources such as friends and family are very effective. Radio and television are also effective in sharing information with individuals that have difficulty reading written materials. Messages should be tailored to the audience, and consideration of the use of cultural values to increase the relevance of the messages is necessary.[21]

One underused strategy is the use of health workers (*"promotores de salud"*) to raise awareness of chronic conditions and promote preventive measures. These are community members, commonly without a professional certificate or degree, who receive limited training to promote health through coaching and social support, connect individuals to care services, and assist in the self-management of chronic conditions.[22] Their success is derived from shared lived experiences with those they serve, allowing the sharing of health information while building trusting relationships and addressing the social needs of patients.

One study indicates that dollar invested in *promotores de salud* would return $2.47 to an average Medicaid payer within the fiscal year; these savings were a result of decreased hospital admissions and shorter hospital stays.[23] Other studies have confirmed the cost-effectiveness of this intervention and potential return on investment. Certainly, community health workers can be funded from a variety of sources, but sustainability and widespread use would require adjustments in reimbursement practices and value-based payment practices.

### Primary Prevention

*Mental Health*

Several environmental factors play important roles in the psychological development of Latinx children. First-generation immigrants are less likely to present mental health disorders than second or third generations, a phenomenon attributed to the immigrant paradox. U.S.-born adolescent children with at least one immigrant parent who had significant stress due to existing U.S. immigration policy were found to have higher anxiety, more sleep problems, and higher blood pressure.[24] As liaisons between their families and social services, Latinx children from mixed status may feel the weight of discrimination more heavily because their roles may require them to navigate complicated systems others often do not, especially in the aftermath of the 2016 election.[25] There is also a role for those in ambulatory care settings to reassure parents about their safety when they seek care for their children in the case of mixed-status families.[26] Latinx children and adolescents are also more likely to be exposed to community violence, which can trigger post-traumatic stress disorder.[27]

Considering that mental illness is stigmatized in the Latinx culture, it is important to identify culturally appropriate ways to address mental health and mental illness. The use of integrated behavioral health within primary care, and other programs such as pre-/postnatal visits that include psychological support and parenting skills might help.[28]

## Obesity

Obesity affects 43 percent of Latinx men and 51 percent of women, compared to 28 percent among non-Hispanic whites.[29] In 2013 to 2016 the prevalence of obesity within the Latinx youth population (eight to sixteen years) reached 23.6 percent, over seven percentage points higher than the prevalence in non-Latinx white youth.[30] In fact, Latinx male youths are at an increased risk of obesity and prediabetes between the ages of eight and sixteen years.[31]

Obesity is associated with lower physical activity levels, misconceptions about healthy eating, consumption of high sugary beverages and foods, and lack of access to supermarkets,[32] among other factors.[33] Work from the Texas Childhood Obesity Research Demonstration Study has found that maternal obesity as a pre- and perinatal factor is linked to a Latinx child's development of obesity.[34]

Using an ecological approach in a child's environment was associated with reducing and preventing obesity in Latinx children, in addition to promoting balanced nutrition behavior.[35] Similarly, effective strategies for adults include weight management programs with bicultural/bilingual professionals, family-centered approaches, clearing misconceptions, increasing health literacy, facilitating access to healthy foods, and increasing physical activity opportunities.[36]

## Diabetes

One epidemiological study found that 3.1 percent of Hispanic children had been diagnosed with type 2 diabetes mellitus by 2014, which is three times the proportion of non-Hispanic white children who received the same diagnosis.[37] Surgical interventions and culturally tailored programs have shown some efficacy in achieving glucose control and reducing the risk of developing type 2 diabetes in Latinx children, although more rigorous studies are needed with longer follow-up.[38]

## Vaccinations

Hispanic children aged nineteen to thirty-five months have rates of immunization for hepatitis, influenza, measles/mumps/rubella, varicella, and polio that are comparable to those seen in non-Hispanic white children.[39] In 2015, Hispanic women were 20 percent less likely to receive a human papillomavirus vaccine, as compared to non-Hispanic white women; however, some new evidence suggests that Latinx women are more likely to initiate vaccination but less likely to complete the vaccination series.[40]

Immunization rates for adults (e.g., influenza, pneumococcal pneumonia) are lower than those seen in non-Hispanic white adults, which has been mostly attributed to lack of insurance, lack of place to obtain routine medical care, and lack of information in the language of preference.[41]

Similar to what is seen in the use of preventive services, variations in vaccine hesitancy have been described according to country of origin, immigration status, education, health literacy, and insurance status. To increase vaccination uptake, it is important to identify trusted messengers and tailor messages to specific audiences (e.g., for Mexican men, messages that emphasize the financial impact of the disease that can be prevented by the vaccine can increase uptake).[42]

## Asthma

Latinx children are about two times more likely to have to visit an emergency room due to asthma than non-Latinx children.[43] There is evidence that the prevalence of asthma for Latinx youth may have plateaued and even decreased between 2001 and 2016, although the rates remain higher than those in non-Latinx white children.[44] However, within the identity group, there are differences in asthma prevalence: for example, Puerto Rican children appear to be affected at higher rates than Mexican American children.[45]

The disparities between Latinx and non-Latinx white children has been attributed, in part, to environmental racism. For example, Latinx children are more likely to be exposed to traffic-related pollution with an associated higher risk of developing asthma.[46] Therefore, addressing disparities in asthma rates will require an understanding of the specific risk factors that vary between groups in the Latinx community[47] and a comprehensive approach to reduce environmental exposures such as molds, fungi, cockroaches, and second-hand smoke. More work directed at educating children and families about asthma is needed to prevent exacerbations, hospitalizations, and missed days of school.[48]

## Secondary Prevention

*Cancer*

Overall, Latinx adults have lower incidence and mortality of cancers, but they have higher incidence of infection-related cancers (e.g., liver or cervical cancer). Additionally, Latinx individuals are less likely to receive cancer screenings than non-Latinx white people, which may contribute to higher rates of advanced-stage disease at presentation seen among some cancers, such as breast and prostate.[49] Strategies to improve cancer screening include increased access to health insurance and/or free low-cost screening services, outreach programs, use of community health workers or patient navigators, and modification of materials to be culturally appropriate.[50]

*Mental Health*

According to the Substance Abuse and Mental Health Services Administration, in 2019 approximately 18 percent of Latinx individuals reported having a mental illness, but only 34 percent of them received mental health services, which has been attributed to lack of insurance, lack of cultural competence of healthcare providers, and stigma.[51]

There is a hypothesized underdiagnosis and undertreatment of attention deficit/hyperactivity disorder for Latinx and African American children.[52] Fewer Latinx children are diagnosed with autism spectrum disorder, and they are diagnosed at an older age.[53] Some have undertaken efforts to develop a better understanding of which diagnostic indicators might be most helpful in diagnosing Latinx children. Based on the Childhood Autism Rating Scale items for children in Puerto Rico, the following items seem to be the most predictive of diagnosis: item 2, imitation; item 1, relating to people; item 5, object use; and item 4, body use. Some attribute this disparity to English not being spoken at home, or less community awareness of these diagnoses.[54]

## SURGICAL CARE

The Latino Paradox is relevant in surgical care as well. A large database that included approximately 3.5 million patients concluded that, overall, Hispanics that had undergone surgery had lower odds of thirty-day postoperative mortality or major morbidity, providing further supporting evidence for the Hispanic Paradox.[55] However, a recent study evaluating patients undergoing low-risk surgery noted worse outcomes in the Hispanic population compared to non-Hispanics—questioning this so-called paradox.[56]

Access to timely and adequate surgical care is another area of research among the Latinx population. One study evaluating Hispanic children requiring neuro-oncological surgery has shown that this group is 32 percent less likely than white children to be admitted to high-volume hospitals.[57] Adult Hispanic patients admitted for neurosurgical treatment of brain tumors were less likely to be seen at high-volume hospitals compared with non-Hispanic adults.[58] Access to surgical care among Latinx is an area of significant concern for both children and adults.

### Language-Concordant Care

Language-concordant care among Hispanic families that do not speak English fluently improves patient satisfaction and understanding among pediatric surgery patients.[59] Preoperative anxiety has been found to be higher among Spanish-speaking Latino parents of children undergoing surgery.[60] Further, Latino children receive around 30 percent less opioids for perioperative analgesia than white children, which could be due to language barriers between non-English speaking Latinx families and members of the surgical team in charge of the operation.[61]

### Diversity

Increasing diversity among the surgical workforce could improve outcomes for the Latinx population in surgery. However, Latinx people face major challenges in becoming surgeons.[62] Moreover, Latinx surgeons are less likely to remain in academia or hold positions of influence.[63] The improvement of surgical care for the Latinx community will likely require interventions aimed at a number of different levels, from community to institutional.

## CONCLUSION

The Latinx community is diverse in country of origin, language spoken, cultural practices, and race. However, given the groups status as minoritized within the context of the United States, there are important disparities and aspects of care to consider for their health and well-being. The importance of culturally competent care provided in the patient's native or most comfortable language cannot be overstated as ways of mitigating disparities.

# 13

# Seeking New Voices and Perspectives for Healthcare in America

## Recognizing and Overcoming Barriers of Language

*Nicholas Stienstra and Jennifer L. Barton*

### THE LANGUAGE DIVIDE

Isaias, a forty-five-year-old farmworker, arrives in clinic for a follow-up appointment for rheumatoid arthritis. One of many patients I will see this morning, he stands out partly for a memorable comment during a prior visit. "What would a doctor know about farm work?" he teased with a smile (via the interpreter), after I asked him to explain what kinds of physical tasks he was engaged in, hoping to better understand the limitations caused by his arthritis. Although my grandfather worked as a dairy farmer, I admitted to Isaias that I could not claim the same first-hand knowledge.

This was not the only obstacle to our mutual understanding that we faced. On the agenda was a discussion about choosing an additional medication for rheumatoid arthritis, to prevent joint damage that could lead to early disability (and loss of his livelihood). Because multiple medication options exist, it was important that we chose an option together that fit his situation.[1] An already complex discussion of potential harms and benefits, pills versus injections, was made more challenging by a language barrier. Isaias is grateful for the opportunity to raise his daughter, Jaqueline, with the prospect of going to college, a chance he never had. Although Jaqueline speaks both English and Spanish with ease, Isaias's grasp of English is limited to brief conversations at the post office or grocery store, and my Spanish is too rudimentary to ensure a nuanced discussion about immunosuppressive therapies.

A language barrier between clinicians and patients is not unusual. The U.S. Census Bureau estimates that more than sixty-seven million Americans speak a language other than English at home, with about twenty-five million (almost 8 percent of the 2019 population) having limited English proficiency (LEP): the "limited ability to read, speak, write or understand" the English language in a person whose first language is not English.[2] The most commonly spoken language in the United States after English is Spanish, followed by Chinese languages and languages from the Indian subcontinent, but there are close to four hundred spoken languages in the United States.[3] In terms of absolute numbers, the number of people with LEP is only likely to increase, as will interactions between people with LEP and the healthcare system.

Unfortunately, there is substantial evidence that LEP is a risk factor for worse healthcare quality and outcomes. While LEP is likely closely intertwined with other determinants of health like socioeconomic status, level of education, and other cultural considerations, language barriers have been implicated in worse access to healthcare resources, worse quality and outcomes when receiving healthcare, and reduced satisfaction and trust in the healthcare system.[4] Language barriers make it more difficult to elicit symptoms, lead to misunderstandings or inadequate understanding of diagnoses, expose patients to more invasive and expensive testing and treatment, and increase risk for adverse events and otherwise preventable injury.

The COVID-19 pandemic illustrated in stark terms that the inability to communicate accurately with clinicians due to language barriers can result in unnecessary or avoidable deaths.[5] Although not related to COVID, Mrs. Vu's story is unfortunately a representative example. Now a sixty-year-old woman originally from Vietnam, like my patient Isaias, she moved to the United States to give her family opportunities she never had. Otherwise a relatively healthy woman, she now lives with diabetes because of a surgery she had soon after coming to the United States that removed part of her pancreas, the result of an aggressive intervention to remove a pancreatic cyst. Although some pancreatic cysts develop into cancers, most do not, and so management usually relies on regular monitoring. Although she speaks English relatively fluently now, at the time she only understood that she needed surgery, and so went forward with the operation that in hindsight may have been unnecessary, and has left her with a chronic medical condition.

Language barriers also contribute to suboptimal control of chronic diseases. Patients with LEP who receive care from a clinician who doesn't speak the same language (language discordant) have been shown to be twice as likely to have poorly controlled diabetes compared with patients with a clinician who speaks the same language (language concordant).[6] This is not just true for diabetes. Studies of blood pressure and cholesterol management (other important risk factors for cardiovascular disease, the number one cause of death in the United States) as well as diseases like rheumatoid arthritis, similarly show better outcomes among patients who are language concordant with their clinicians.[7]

In addition to being at risk for lower-quality care, patients with LEP face reduced access to and use of primary care,[8] and increased use of emergency care for conditions that could be managed in ambulatory care settings. Treatment of a simple urinary tract infection in the emergency department (ED) may cost $2,000 compared with $200 for essentially the same treatment in an office setting.[9] In the ED, patients with LEP are also often exposed to unnecessary laboratory and imaging testing, which can further increase risk for adverse events and cost.[10] It is unsurprising that language barriers negatively impact satisfaction with care.[11]

In summary, patients like Isaias and Mrs. Vu face a healthcare system that does not serve them equally. A progressive healthcare system must examine how to mitigate this effect to improve quality and maximize available resources. We will next review solutions that have shown benefit for persons with LEP and the communities in which they live, and reflect on opportunities for further improvement.

## BRIDGING THE DIVIDE: EFFECTIVE INTERVENTIONS FOR LIMITED ENGLISH PROFICIENCY

The simplest solution to overcoming the barriers of LEP is access to a trained, third-person interpreter who is both proficient in the languages of the patient and clinician, and familiar with medical terminology and concepts. In reality, busy clinicians often turn to whomever is available, including bilingual medical staff or even family members. This risks impaired communication and presents ethical issues. Professional medical interpreters reduce the likelihood of errors in interpretation compared with nonprofessional (ad hoc) interpreters and eliminate many of the disparities previously discussed, leading to better understanding of diagnoses, equal rates of adherence to follow-up after ED visits, equal frequency of testing, equal rates of ED visits and hospital admissions, improved measurements of diabetes control and cardiovascular disease, and higher rates of patient satisfaction.[12]

Even when a professional interpreter is present during a clinical encounter, a patient with LEP may still face barriers at other points of contact with the healthcare system, at the lab or in radiology, or when scheduling a follow-up appointment. One potential solution to overcoming these barriers is the role of the patient navigator. Navigators often speak the same languages as the patients they interact with, but they also fulfill functions that go beyond traditional interpretation: helping set up appointments, providing reminder calls for medical appointments, and education about aspects of healthcare. Patient navigators have been shown to significantly increase rates of cancer screening among persons with LEP, and it is logical to conjecture that their benefits likely surpass those gained from interpretation on its own. A review of the bilingual patient navigator program at Seattle Children's Hospital reports patient navigators were better able to "build trust with a patient's family over time, to point out missed inferences . . . to alert providers to barriers to implementation of treatment plans, and to teach families basic skills such as preparing for a medical appointment and how to talk with doctors."[13] The role of patient navigators leads to more time spent with patients and their families and increased responsibility in their patient's care, which has traditionally limited their availability, though finding ways to increase access to navigators for patients with LEP would likely be beneficial.

Making healthcare decisions can be incredibly complex, even in one's primary language, so patients with LEP face a distinct disadvantage when trying to be informed and communicate decisions involving their care. An additional strategy to facilitate communication is to use a carefully designed, language-appropriate decision aid. A decision aid refers to any tool that is used to help people "make informed choices . . . that take into account their personal values and preferences."[14] Decision aids can take many forms. Published examples include informational videos informing Spanish-speaking patients about colorectal and prostate cancer screening options;[15] interactive learning modules with telenovela scenes to educate women with a new diagnosis of breast cancer and low health literacy on treatment options;[16] and a set of cards with key themes to facilitate discussion of medications for rheumatoid arthritis among English-, Spanish-, and Chinese-speaking patients and their rheumatologists.[17] When designed properly, decision aids can help persons with LEP better understand their options and communicate healthcare preferences.

While it is beyond the scope of this chapter, it is important to acknowledge that our healthcare system needs to actively shape itself to be more representative of the population it serves. Latinx physicians are significantly underrepresented in the United States, and this underrepresentation has worsened with time.[18] Similar considerations apply for African American physicians. While race/ethnicity is not a surrogate for LEP, it does illustrate the need for more clinicians from underrepresented minority groups. When both clinician and patient speak the same language competently (language concordance), there are multiple positive impacts on patient care, including improved patient knowledge of their diagnosis, improved utilization of healthcare resources, better care, and improved satisfaction.[19] Increasing the diversity and linguistic capacities of the clinician workforce to better reflect the population it serves is therefore an essential part of reducing disparities.

So far, we have identified effective interventions in reducing disparities in access and outcomes for patients with LEP. Why don't we use them more? Next, we will address existing limitations to implementation and identify potential strategies to successfully navigate those barriers.

## THE CHALLENGE OF CHANGE

"Today, our very survival depends on our ability to stay awake, to adjust to new ideas, to remain vigilant and to face the challenge of change."

—Rev. Martin Luther King, Jr.

Awareness of needed changes in our healthcare system is not enough. Collectively facing the "challenge of change" requires breaking down multiple barriers. Here we divide these obstacles into five common areas: barriers of focus, resources, workforce capabilities, research, and sustainability.

### Barriers of Focus

Focus in this context refers to competing priorities. While we can all agree that a progressive healthcare system should be equipped to provide equitable care for all persons, including those with LEP, access for patients with LEP is one metric among many to determine a system's overall success. Executive Order 13166, signed into law in 2000, made it mandatory for healthcare providers and facilities that receive federal funding to provide appropriate access to patients with LEP, setting standards to provide language assistance services at no cost to patients during all hours of operation.[20] This directive remains relevant today given ongoing health disparities and a growing LEP population, but efforts to improve access to language services in healthcare must remain an active priority. Table 13.1 lists examples of advocacy efforts that need to be prioritized to ensure improved healthcare access and quality for LEP populations.

**Table 13.1.  Examples of Advocacy Efforts**

| Stakeholder | Advocacy Required |
|---|---|
| Federal Government | –Ensure accountability through enforcing new and existing laws that promote equal access for patients with LEP (payment incentives/penalties)<br>–Fund research in areas that relate to health access and quality for persons with LEP<br>–Promote recognized standardized credentials for interpreters and patient navigators<br>–Engage with national professional organizations to encourage diversity in healthcare recruitment at all levels |
| National/State Healthcare Organizations | –Lobby for education/recruitment of a diverse provider and administrative workforce<br>–Encourage quality initiatives that promote access<br>–Expand language offerings for credentialing interpreters and navigators |
| Local Government | –Same as federal government advocacy<br>–Engage at-risk communities to promote better dialogue regarding health and education needs |
| Healthcare Executives | –Invest resources to ensure adequate availability for interpreter/patient navigator services<br>–Examine and publish data on differences in health outcome measures in patients with LEP at the system and practice level<br>–Promote quality improvement initiatives that address LEP disparities |
| Clinicians | –Offer interpreters at any interaction with patients where English proficiency is uncertain<br>–Make interpreter availability a requirement when joining a new practice<br>–Let professional organizations know how language discordance affects their practices |
| Patients/Caregivers | –Demonstrate and promote awareness that interpreter assistance is a right when receiving healthcare<br>–Try to discourage using family members for interpreting encounters with healthcare |
| Communities (through organizations) | –Promote awareness/education that interpreter access is a right when accessing healthcare<br>–Lobby for accountability from healthcare organizations and government funding |

Note: LEP = limited English proficiency.

## Resource Barriers

Economic cost is often viewed as the major obstacle to healthcare system change. Interpretation and patient navigation both require a specialized skill set that may be limited by availability and drive up costs. Given the wide array of languages spoken in the United States, one can imagine that finding an interpreter for a patient at the right time could be a difficult proposition, which only well-funded medical centers in major cities could provide. Rural facilities with fewer patients with LEP might not be able to ensure the same availability in a cost-effective way. Additionally, different types of healthcare services are disproportionally affected by language barriers. For example, a mental health visit that relies extensively on patient/clinician communication has different language requirements than a preoperative visit for a surgical procedure under general anesthesia. Hospitals and outpatient clinics currently provide interpretation service in two main ways: in-person interpreters, who are physically in the exam room, or remote interpreters (phone or video). Phone interpretation is usually facilitated by centralized call centers that offer interpreters with multiple languages as a service that can be purchased by a healthcare center. The benefits of this service are that a healthcare practice can theoretically access an interpreter in most commonly spoken languages within a matter of minutes, even in a physically remote area.

Before we assume that having professional interpreter and patient navigator services at every healthcare access point is a pipe dream, let's take a closer look at the costs and benefits. We've already highlighted that care for patients with LEP is associated with poorer outcomes, overtesting, increased risk for errors, and entry to healthcare systems at more expensive routes (ED versus primary care), all of which add societal costs to our current system. It is well known that the United States spends almost twice the amount per capita on healthcare compared with other wealthy countries (despite similar rates of utilization), but ranks among the worst in metrics like life expectancy and infant mortality.[21] There are many reasons for this, but waste is a key component, which raises the possibility that addressing disparities may be more cost-effective than is initially apparent. A study by Jacobs et al. reviewed the cost of care provided to patients in a Massachusetts health maintenance organization that included four healthcare centers serving over 120,000 patients before and after interpreter services were added. The average cost per enrollee only increased by $2.40 a year and was associated with a significant increase in preventive and primary care, which was deemed cost-effective.[22] Another study in a Chicago public hospital similarly found that interpreter services did not significantly impact hospital costs as the increased cost for interpreter services was offset by decreased ED visits.[23] A more recent literature review (including studies from Germany, South Africa, and Switzerland) had disparate results, with most reporting reduced costs due to fewer ED visits, reduced superfluous testing, and lower hospital admission rates, though increased treatment costs and increased office visits were reported by a minority of studies.[24] In studies that did report increased costs from treatment, it is important to consider whether this represents successful diagnosis and treatment that may have been missed without interpreters, potentially sparing yet higher cost (and morbidity) from delayed diagnoses.

While there are even fewer cost-effectiveness studies for patient navigator programs with patients with LEP, the patient navigator program at Seattle Children's Hospital showed significant returns on investment. Patient navigators helped Spanish- and Somali-speaking families provide care at home and prepare for appointments. Investigators estimated that for every dollar spent on the program, $6 were saved through avoidance of ED visits and admissions, and from fewer missed outpatient appointments.[25]

Overall, data support that the relative costs of interpreter services can be offset by reduced costs from more effective and efficient care. Despite these findings, more research is needed to better understand whether these results can be reproduced in other settings, and to quantify short- and longer-term cost-effectiveness.

Monetary cost is not the only limited resource. Limited clinician time with patients is another key concern. Interpreter use is frequently perceived to increase the amount of time during clinical encounters, though the data point to a more complicated story. A study by Kravitz et al. at the University of California Davis Medical Center found increased visit times for non-English speakers, though attributed the longer times to visits with physicians in training.[26] Fagan et al. found that clinicians requiring interpreters had longer clinic visit times, but that this effect was due to encounters where phone or ad hoc interpreters were used, not for visits with in-person interpreters.[27]

The impact of decision aids on time and cost-effectiveness can be difficult to study due to the variety of forms and settings these are used in, but their purpose (to elicit more effective communication and empower patients to guide their own treatment) is aligned. Unfortunately, decision aids are often not designed to meet the needs of vulnerable populations including LEP patients.[28] In a study by Dugas et al., only about 16 percent of projects designing decision aids specifically involved members of vulnerable populations.[29] Although it was often not the developer's intent *not* to include patients from vulnerable populations, it often takes more work and time to include these patients, and recognition that existing procedures to recruit patients into research (such as lengthy written consent forms) may not be conducive to inclusion.

Other barriers include building trust with the communities' investigators are trying to reach, and finding ways to limit time and transportation costs. One of the most significant challenges for developing and validating decision aids is finding ways to include the groups that are most likely to benefit from them, but also may be the most difficult to reach.

Even if professional interpreter services and decision aids do not significantly increase the time of visits, the perception that they do can be enough to discourage their use. One survey found that interpreters were used in less than 1 percent of interactions at outpatient visits with patients with LEP in Australia, even though Australia has a national fee-free interpreter service for medical professionals and pharmacists.[30] This problem is not unique to Australia. In the United States, even in a hospitalized setting (with more acutely ill patients) and twenty-four-hour access to phone interpreter services, only 43 percent of patients with LEP were asked if they wanted an interpreter, though low rates have been reported in outpatient and ED settings as well.[31] When asked, primary reasons for underuse of professional interpreters included trying to "get by," particularly with shorter visits and the use of ad hoc interpreters. Thus, even if universal on-demand professional interpretation is made available in a timely manner, it is unlikely to be sufficient without a corresponding shift in healthcare culture that prioritizes the use of professional interpretation as a requirement for interaction with patients with LEP. Systems must also engage patients and the communities they live in to educate and empower them about their rights to access healthcare interpretation as part of the care they receive.

### Workforce Capabilities

Ways to expand the healthcare workforce to better reflect the populations they serve, with increased linguistic capabilities that match the languages spoken in their communities, must be identified and promoted. For healthcare providers who are bilingual, the Clinical Cultural and Linguistic Assessment is currently considered the gold standard for validating proficiency in another language. It is a testing tool for about thirty languages that can be completed over the phone and is available twenty-four hours a day. In the field of medical interpretation, there are two national certifications (the Certification Commission for Healthcare Interpreters and the National Board for Certified Medical Interpreters), though the complete certifications at this time remain limited to only a few more widely spoken languages including Spanish and Chinese. Differences in training have been identified as a reason why some studies show less benefit from medical interpreters,[32] so it remains critical to find ways to standardize requirements of proficiency for medical interpreters and patient navigators, particularly in less widely spoken languages. Healthcare systems also need to implement more standard requirements to mandate when an interpreter is used, as both patients and clinicians may overestimate their abilities and similarly underestimate the importance of the topic they are trying to discuss.

### Barriers to Research

How do we improve access for and care of patients with LEP? A common difficulty in comparing studies that examine the effects of interpreters is the lack of consensus about the qualifications of a professional interpreter. Are interpreters who complete a forty-hour training program just as able to eliminate medical errors as those who have undergone more (or less) training? Which types of interpretation are more effective (e.g., interpreting word for word as a clinician or patient is speaking [simultaneous] versus the interpreter waiting for a party to finish speaking before interpreting [consecutive])? As we see more care delivered virtually, are the benefits of a remote interpreter equal to an in-person interpreter? The more specific we can be about what exactly is necessary to overcome barriers for persons with LEP, the more generalizable and valuable the research becomes. Medical care delivery in the United States lacks uniformity, with dozens of independent, unconnected systems that include (or exclude) patients across different geographic, economic, social, and cultural divides. Solutions to equalizing healthcare access and quality for patients with LEP will need to be tailored to the involved communities, though should be held to a shared standard. Healthcare systems will need to be convinced with models of successful implementation of interventions that have proven both effective and cost-effective. A recent editorial in the *British Medical Journal* called for "interventional studies that test the most effective behaviors of individual clinicians."[33] We must expand this to include interpreters, patient navigators, *and patients* to identify the strategies and contexts that work best. Acknowledging the limitations (and quantifiable benefits) of the tools we have to address disparities in healthcare experienced by persons with LEP is essential to find the best solutions for the range of diverse settings in which they will be needed.

### Barriers to Sustainability

As important as it is to find solutions that can be implemented now, efforts to improve LEP access to equitable and effective healthcare must also be sustainable and able to expand to meet the growing need. Interventions must be cost-effective and reduce medical waste and unnecessary care. It will also require a shift in current attitudes and recognition that access to interpreter services is a fixable source of disparity. Healthcare providers as a group must become more aware of the power they have to ensure patients with LEP are able to communicate on equal footing, and of the potential disparities introduced from even benign assumptions about English proficiency or efforts to conserve time for other patient care aspects. They should also demand the time and resources necessary to achieve this from employers and hospital systems. At the end of the day, addressing these disparities is in the system's interest too if it prevents wasteful or harmful care, and improves patient satisfaction and outcomes. At the same time, we must identify ways to educate people with LEP about their rights and empower them to expect and request language assistance in any healthcare setting.

## ENVISIONING THE FUTURE

At a time of much-needed collective reexamination of the ways in which our society perpetuates disparity (and the roles we play within it)—through systemic racism and diverging extremes of wealth and opportunity—it behooves us to apply the same introspection to our healthcare systems. People with LEP are just one demographic underserved by our current model, and they suffer worse healthcare outcomes as a result. While other chapters in this book may address many of the challenges we face in moving toward a more effective and equitable system, including patients with LEP does not require a novel therapy or surgical technique that has yet to be invented. Clinic and hospital visits with trained professional interpreters and patient navigators happen every day in this country, using shared decision making often supported by decision aids. But they don't happen enough or consistently enough at the right time, at the right place, or with the necessary people. We have effective tools, but we need to practice and refine the ways to incorporate them in current practice so that clinicians and patients can bridge language differences and achieve safe, timely, effective, and cost-effective care, while restructuring our current system to better reflect the ethnic and linguistic diversity that is already present in our society.

Achieving the change we want to see will require proponents from all sides of healthcare. This includes leaders at any part of the delivery system, but likely the most important voices are those of patients and their communities, as these are the voices that have traditionally been overlooked. Healthcare centers that receive federal funding have a legal requirement to provide access to patients with LEP, but we need to do better to normalize this to avoid stigma and make it more a standard part of care. Finding ways for healthcare organizations to reach out to communities with concentrations of patients with LEP to improve education and awareness about the right for interpreter services is at least a first step. A potentially useful example of communities taking proactive steps to inform themselves can be seen from social media groups like Việt Solidarity and Action Network and news aggregator sites like the Interpreter, which provide online spaces for the Vietnamese community to "share translated educational resources, combat disinformation, and discuss ways to engage with family and community members about systemic racism."[34] Similar groups are finding ways to engage with their own ethnic communities.

An increase in activism hints at the potential of involving greater numbers and diversity of people in manifesting systemic change to address chronic disparities in this country. Ensuring that patients with LEP are able to access a healthcare system that treats them equally and offers the outcomes it does to anyone else is an important part in making sure millions of people in this country have the chance to find their voice. It is up to us to listen for it.

# 14

## Progressive Healthcare for Seniors

### Redesigning How We Deliver Care for Older Adults

*Pooja Chandrashekar and Sachin Jain*

Mrs. J is a seventy-five-year-old woman who immigrated from Mexico and now lives in San Diego, California. She is divorced, having suffered decades of physical and emotional abuse from her ex-husband, and now lives with her son and his family. She grapples with a long list of medical conditions, including a history of falls, major depression, anxiety, lumbar degeneration, polyneuropathy, insomnia, irritable bowel syndrome, active hernia, and chronic pain.

Over the past five years, Mrs. J has spent much of her time making doctors' appointments. Shuffled from specialist to specialist, she has seen a total of eleven clinicians. None of them speak Spanish, which is Mrs. J's first and preferred language. They practice in separate clinical settings and have prescribed eighteen different medications. The side effects of these medications "made every day terrible" for Mrs. J, so she eventually stopped taking them, relying on home remedies to manage her health. When asked about her clinicians, Mrs. J becomes frustrated, saying "None of them understand me. They just keep giving me more medicine and telling me to see someone else. But none of it makes me feel better."

Mrs. J's experience is all too common. As the U.S. population ages, it is becoming clear that our healthcare system is fundamentally not designed for older adults, resulting in care that is unnecessary, ineffective, or harmful.

It is high time that we reengineer our approach to caring for this population. For the large part, we already know what patients like Mrs. J want—to remain active, independent, and at home for as long as possible. How then can we design a model of care that produces better health outcomes, costs less, and—most importantly—addresses what matters the most to older people?

## INTRODUCTION

Owing to medical advances and healthier lifestyles, the United States has a growing number of aging adults (age sixty-five or older) who are living longer than previous generations. According to the U.S. Census Bureau, older adults will make up more than 20 percent of the total population starting in 2030, outnumbering children for the first time in history. The number of people aged eighty-five and older will grow the fastest over the coming decades, reaching 4 percent of the population by 2050.

This demographic shift is one of the greatest challenges faced by the U.S. healthcare system. For one, an aging population will have different health needs, including more severe and complex health conditions. Older adults experience more chronic diseases, physical disabilities, and mental illnesses than younger populations, and managing these patients' multiple comorbid health conditions requires a coordinated approach to treatment. However, our fragmented healthcare system is not designed to help or incentivize clinicians to communicate with each other, placing older adults like Mrs. J at risk for overtreatment, adverse drug reactions, and preventable hospitalizations. Second, older adults have a unique set of social needs that influence their access to care and, ultimately, their outcomes. These include financial hardship, inability to access or afford nutritious food, unstable or unsafe housing, lack of reliable transportation, and social isolation. Although these social, economic, and environmental factors are critical to the health of older adults and their ability to live independently and age in place, few models of care meaningfully address them.

Our current approach to caring for older adults has produced dismal results. An analysis by the U.S. Department of Health and Human Service found that fewer than half of patients age sixty-five or older are up to date with preventive services despite regular checkups.[1] Older adults also receive less care for geriatric conditions such as dementia, urinary incontinence, and falls compared to care for general medical conditions like diabetes or hypertension that affect adults of all ages. Older adults are also at a higher risk of receiving inappropriate treatments. As patients move through the healthcare system and are shuffled from clinician to clinician, they tend to accumulate layers of drug therapy. More than 35 percent of older adults take five or more medications on a regular basis—a condition called medication polypharmacy.[2] Polypharmacy significantly increases the risk of adverse drug events.[3] Approximately 9 percent of all hospital admissions in older adults are associated with adverse drug reactions.[4] Along with producing poor outcomes, our fragmented, reactive approach to caring for older adults is also costly. Those over age sixty-five accounted for 34 percent of all healthcare expenditures in 2014.[5] By 2028, annual Medicare spending is projected to reach $1.6 trillion.[6] At this pace, the costs of caring for the aging population will soon overwhelm taxpayer-funded programs like Medicare and Medicaid, leading to higher costs for healthcare coverage and a corresponding decline in access to care for this vulnerable population.

Most importantly, the care we provide to older adults often fails to consider and integrate patients' perspectives, priorities, and experiences. For example, consider the problem of multiple medications in older adults. Older adults see medication-related problems as inseparable from their broader life context, describing the impact of medications on interpersonal relationships, emotional well-being, and activities that add meaning to life. In contrast, clinicians almost exclusively focus on issues such as nonadherence or adverse drug effects, often making no reference to the fear, communication, and the socioemotional impacts of medication use and showing little interest in learning about patients' perspectives. Clinicians fail to ask patients the simple question "What matters?"

A rapidly aging population will stress test our healthcare system like few other phenomena. The problems with our current approach to caring for older adults—poor quality, rising costs, and low patient satisfaction—will only be exacerbated in coming years. As we brace for this demographic shift, it is time that we envision a new model of care delivery for this vulnerable population. In this chapter, we begin by exploring the unique medical, psychological, and social needs of older adults and then describe why our current healthcare system is ill-equipped to meet these needs. Finally, we paint a vision for a new model of care; one tailored to the needs of older adults and dedicated to keeping patients healthy and independent.

## HEALTHCARE CHALLENGES FACING OLDER ADULTS IN THE UNITED STATES

Older adults have different healthcare needs than the rest of the population. Broadly speaking, these needs can be broken down into three categories: medical, psychological, and social. In this section, we discuss each of these categories, focusing on those needs that are most important to helping older adults age in place and live a meaningful, active, and independent life.

## Medical Needs of Older Adults

First, older adults have a high burden of chronic diseases such as diabetes, heart disease, cancer, arthritis, and dementia. About 80 percent of adults aged sixty-five and older in the United States suffer from multiple chronic conditions.[7] Chronic diseases take a significant toll on older adults and reduce quality of life, making it difficult to perform daily tasks and causing physical, emotional, and financial strain. They are also a leading cause of death in this population; four chronic diseases—heart disease, cancer, stroke, and diabetes—are responsible for almost two-thirds of all deaths among older people each year.

Chronic disease also places older adults at a higher risk for disability. According to the Centers for Disease Control and Prevention, about 40 percent of adults age sixty-five and older have one of the following types of disabilities: hearing (difficulty hearing), vision (difficulty seeing), cognition (difficulty concentrating, remembering, or making decisions), mobility (difficulty walking or climbing stairs), self-care (difficulty dressing or bathing), and independent living (difficulty performing errands alone).[8] The impacts of disabilities are far-reaching and limit the ability of older adults to live independently and in the community. As a result, older adults frequently need assistance performing activities of daily living, the basic self-care activities needed to live an independent life. By 2050, it is expected that two-thirds of elderly in the United States will need assistance for this reason.[9]

Another important medical problem among older adults is falls. Falls are exceedingly common—about one in four older adults fall each year[10]—and are the leading cause of injury and death in this age group. Around 20 percent of falls result in a serious injury, including broken bones and head injuries.[11] People may begin to limit their activities after a fall, leading to a more sedentary lifestyle and muscle atrophy that increases their risk of falling again. They also have enormous financial consequences—in the United States, the annual cost of direct care associated with falls among the elderly is $57.5 billion.[12] Common causes of falls include the normal changes of aging that impair balance and strength, functional disability, poor lighting or rugs in the home, and side effects of medications (especially in patients taking multiple medications). Because of their prevalence and devastating consequences, falls are considered a public health concern in the aging population.

## Psychological Needs of Older Adults

It is important to treat the mental health needs of older adults with the same urgency as physical health. It is estimated that around 20 percent of people aged fifty-five or older experience some type of mental health concern.[13] The most common conditions include mood disorders (e.g., depression, bipolar disorder), anxiety, and severe cognitive impairment. Substance use is also an emerging concern among older adults: nearly one million older adults in the United States live with a substance use disorder,[14] and rates of alcohol, prescription drug, and illicit substance misuse continue to climb in this population. Despite their prevalence, mental health and substance use disorders are often untreated or undertreated. This is due to several reasons. First, few clinicians have the adequate training to address depression, anxiety, and substance use disorders in older adults. As a result, many attribute the symptoms of mental health conditions (e.g., difficulty sleeping, poor appetite, weight changes) to the normal changes of aging or another medical condition. Second, there is significant stigma associated with seeking help for mental health conditions, especially in older generations where being labeled as a "psychiatric patient" is still loaded with shame.

Untreated mental health and substance use problems among older adults are associated with increased mortality, increased levels of disability and impairment, higher risk of suicide, compromised quality of life, and increased caregiver stress.

### Social Needs of Older Adults

It is widely recognized that environmental, social, and economic conditions—collectively called the "social determinants of health"—influence the ability of older adults to live a healthy and meaningful life. Compared to the rest of the population, older adults have significant unmet social needs. A recent survey of 1,590 adults aged fifty and older revealed that 51 percent have at least one unmet social need, including strained financial resources, loneliness, food insecurity, inadequate transportation, mobility challenges, and living alone.[15]

Loneliness and social isolation, in particular, are important to the care of older adults. Loneliness is the feeling of being alone regardless of social contact, while social isolation refers to the lack of social connections. A report from the National Academies of Sciences, Engineering, and Medicine shows that over 33 percent of adults age forty-five and older feel lonely, and nearly 25 percent of adults age sixty-five and older experience social isolation. Older adults are at a higher risk for loneliness and social isolation due to living alone, chronic illness, hearing and vision loss, and the loss of family and friends.[16] Though difficult to measure, there is growing evidence that loneliness and social isolation put older adults at a higher risk for dementia and other serious medical conditions.

## A NEW VISION FOR THE FUTURE:
## IMPROVING CARE DELIVERY FOR OLDER ADULTS

The structure and function of our healthcare system can be traced back to the beginning of the twentieth century. At the time, infectious diseases were rampant; breakthroughs in laboratory science provided clinicians with a new and powerful set of tools for treating these diseases. A model focused on acute care makes sense in this context given the prominence of acute infectious disease. But it makes little sense a century later, in the context of an aging population with a high burden of chronic disease, mental illness, and social needs. Meeting the health needs of an aging America requires a fundamentally different approach to care delivery.

### Put Geriatricians at the Helm

In a 2015 essay, Dr. Louise Aronson, a geriatrician at the University of California, San Francisco, described her chance meeting with Eva, an elderly woman waiting for a ride.[17] When Eva's taxi did not arrive, Dr. Aronson offered to drop her home. Eva lived alone in an apartment on one of San Francisco's famous hills. As Dr. Aronson helped her up the forty-nine dimly lit steps to her apartment, she learned that Eva had been hospitalized twice in the past year. Eva had a host of chronic diseases, but these recent hospitalizations had really derailed her life as a small business owner.

Eva received her medical care at the University of California, San Francisco, so Dr. Aronson logged into the electronic health record to look at her chart the next morning (with her permission). She saw that Eva had made thirty visits to the medical center in the past year and was taking a total of seventeen medications. Her doctors provided excellent, evidence-based care, but they did not address Eva's most important needs. None of them evaluated her joints and gait, did a functional assessment, treated her pain, or referred her to a social worker. None of them commented on the number of doctors or medications Eva had—and most importantly, no one asked Eva what matters to her.

Most doctors would have taken the same approach—they simply did not have the specific knowledge or skills needed to care for older adults. Eva's story highlights the importance of putting geriatricians, primary care doctors who specialize in the care and treatment of older people, at the helm of caring for this population.

What makes geriatric care so different from traditional primary care? First, geriatricians are trained to evaluate issues that are critical to the health of older adults but which often go unaddressed, including frailty, cognition, polypharmacy, functionality, and nutrition. They understand how illness in an elderly person is different from illness in a younger person and can determine the best treatments for an aging adult. Second, by nature of their training, geriatricians "treat the whole person" rather than focusing on discrete disease processes. To do this, they integrate everything about the patient as a person—their broader life context, priorities, and goals—into their approach to treatment. Third, geriatricians work in tandem with other clinicians to address patients' medical, psychological, and social needs—all with the aim of helping patients remain active, independent, and at home for as long as possible. This is important because older patients often receive fragmented care from multiple clinicians across different care settings.

Integrating geriatricians into models of care has a real impact. In one study of older adults hospitalized at the Oregon Health and Science University Hospital, an inpatient geriatric consultation program resulted in significant reductions in intensive care unit days, daily charges, inappropriate medication use, and use of physical restraints, along with increased end-of-life planning.[18] The model was so successful that it has since been expanded and adopted by other academic medical institutions.

However, geriatric care should begin in primary care offices, not after patients have already suffered one or more catastrophic health events. Instead of waiting for older adults to suffer a fall that lands them in the hospital and *then* matching them with a geriatrician, what if we prevented the patient from falling in the first place?

Geriatricians should be at the helm of a care delivery model for older adults. They have the right expertise to treat older patients, specialized training in coordinating care across settings, and experience working with different health professionals. A good example of how to do this in practice is the Geriatrics Primary Care program at the Department of Veterans Affairs Boston Healthcare System, where an onsite geriatrician and geriatric nurse case manager work with primary care physicians (PCPs) to manage and coordinate the care of older patients as they age.[19] Preliminary data shows patients enrolled in the program had significantly fewer visits to specialists, suggesting this approach can reduce care fragmentation.

Eva's story has a happy ending. Dr. Aronson helped her get on a geriatrics practice waitlist and, eleven months later, Eva was paired with a geriatrician who elicited her health and life goals, treated her joint pain, simplified her medication regimen, and arranged for a caregiver. Several years later, Eva has not had any more hospitalizations and is still living at home in her beloved apartment. She is a testament to the power of geriatric medicine.

**Meet Patients Where They Are**

Where care is delivered is as important as who is delivering the care. Right now, when older adults have an acute health concern, they come to the clinic or, in severe enough cases, the hospital emergency room. For young healthy patients, this model makes sense. But for frail and vulnerable older adults, many of whom have impaired mobility and lack access to reliable transportation, getting to a clinic or hospital can be difficult or even dangerous. Moreover, hospitalizations place older adults at increased risk for a host of conditions, including delirium, malnutrition, pressure ulcers, falls, infection, functional decline, and depression.

Because many older adults do not have the support or resources to manage their medical conditions at home, they end up making up more visits to the emergency room. After each hospitalization, they may leave more frail and disabled than before, racking up enormous costs in the process. It is no surprise that older adults make up an outsized portion of emergency department (ED) visits in this country. In fact, a recent study showed that frequent geriatric utilizers of the ED represented just 5.7 percent of patients in the ED, but accounted for 21.2 percent of all ED visits.[20]

What if we flipped this model on its head and instead of expecting older adults to come to us, we took our services to them? Meeting patients where they are—at home, through telemedicine, or in the community—is a powerful way to improve the care of frail and vulnerable adults and forestall the need for more expensive care in hospitals and other institutional settings.

We know that the majority of older adults prefer to remain at home for as long as possible. Thus, home-based care is one of the most promising opportunities to improve care, lower costs, and allow patients to age in place and maintain their independence. For example, consider Independence at Home, a five-year Medicare demonstration that tested the effectiveness of home-based primary care.[21] Early results show that participating programs reduced ED visits, hospitalizations, and thirty-day readmissions for homebound patients, leading to savings of an average of $2,700 per beneficiary per year and increased patient and caregiver satisfaction.

Some of the best candidates for home-based care are homebound and chronically ill patients. In a survey of 2,009 adults conducted by CareMore Health, an integrated health plan and care delivery system for Medicare Advantage and Medicaid patients, 64 percent expressed interest in house calls.[22] House calls are defined as a team of health professionals visiting a homebound or chronically ill patient's home to deliver medical care, medication consultations, and social services.

Given this interest, CareMore pioneered the Home-Based Integrated Model for high-need, high-cost patients in Connecticut. In this model, members of the "Home Team" provide preventive, chronic disease management, urgent, and postdischarge care in the comfort of the patient's home. They assess a patient's physical and mental health, check to see if they are taking their medications, and address their social needs (which become far more apparent in a home visit).[23]

To understand the impact of shifting care to the home, look at Oscar. Oscar suffers from multiple chronic diseases and, prior to joining CareMore, was visiting the ED almost every week for complications related to chronic kidney disease. In their first visit, the CareMore team used his kitchen strainer to explain how his kidneys filter blood. In conversations that took place in Oscar's living room, the team spoke with his brother, a close friend from church, and personal care assistant to come up with a plan for managing his diabetes and blood pressure. Today, Oscar's kidney function is stable and his story is just one example: in one year, hospital admissions and ED visits for patients in the CareMore Home-Based Model went down 12.5 percent and 27.2 percent, respectively.

Another population that benefits from home-based care is patients receiving palliative care. It is well-known that palliative care—which focuses on providing relief from the symptoms, pain, and stress of serious illness—leads to improved quality of life, reduces symptoms and risks associated with treatment and hospitalization, and decreases costs of care. Struck by the challenges of end-of-life care for his dying grandmother, Brad Smith founded Aspire Health to bring the benefits of palliative care to patients' homes. Aspire Health sends clinicians to patients' homes to manage symptoms, help caregivers navigate difficult treatment options, and provide emotional and spiritual support. It is a model that demonstrates the promise of home-based care for older adults suffering from serious illness or nearing the end of life.[24]

Telemedicine is another avenue to meet older adults in the comfort of their own homes. There is a widespread misconception that older patients have no interest in telemedicine or cannot use these technologies. However, the success of telemedicine during the COVID-19 pandemic showed us that older adults can and will use these technologies to access care. But we should be thoughtful about which patients would benefit from virtual care. If conducted over video, these visits require patients to have the knowledge to get online, use audiovisual equipment, and communicate without the cues available in person. Though many older adults are willing and eager to learn to use telemedicine, it may be challenging or even impossible for some. These include patients with disabilities, technological inexperience, or social isolation. For these patients, geriatric models of care such as home visits are critical.

Despite the importance of meeting patients where they are, there are several reasons why older adults may prefer to visit a clinic in person. For some, receiving care at home can be a reminder of illness and invasion of privacy. Instead of telemedicine, some patients may enjoy the social aspect of seeking care outside the home and interacting with clinicians. Thus, patients should certainly have the option to visit a clinic in person. However, we should remember that many patients in this age group lack access to reliable transportation. Recognizing this problem, CareMore forged a partnership with Lyft to enable caregivers to schedule rides for patients ahead of appointments. They saw remarkable reductions in no-shows and savings of more than $1 million in one year. A care delivery model designed for older adults should offer free transportation for patients in need of these services to and from in-person clinic appointments.[25]

All in all, the imperative to meet patients where they are and reduce usage of high-cost settings such as the ED requires matching patients to the right setting (e.g., home-based care, telemedicine, clinic) based on each patient's unique constellation of needs, preferences, and barriers to accessing care.

## Integrate Behavioral Health into Medical Care

The behavioral health needs of older adults often go unaddressed by current models of care. Untreated mental illness can lead to poor physical and social functioning, along with worsening of other chronic diseases. Traditionally, the responsibility of addressing mental illness and substance use disorders in older adults has fallen on nonmental health specialists such as PCPs. However, PCPs are vastly underequipped to manage mental health conditions for this population. In one survey of PCPs, more than two-thirds reported being unable to access effective mental health services for their older patients.[26]

We need to rethink the way we deliver behavioral health for older adults. Rather than expecting PCPs to both treat patients' medical conditions and manage their mental health, a better solution is an integrated approach that brings together the unique and complementary expertise of mental health professionals and PCPs to address the full spectrum of patients' health needs. In this approach, a behavioral health specialist works with a patient's PCP to identify, treat, and manage mental health problems in the primary care setting. Integrated mental healthcare, sometimes called "collaborative care," has been shown to produce better outcomes for patients, increase access to treatment, reduce the stigma of seeking help for mental illness, and reduce costs.

However, just enabling better access to behavioral health specialists is not enough. Lifestyle management is critical to mental health, and we need to support older patients in making the choices that can help them achieve their happiest and healthiest selves. For example, managing an older patient's substance use disorder is about more than connecting them to a behavioral health specialist who identifies the problem. Older adults often have limited social support and need longitudinal, high-touch coaching and mentoring to reduce substance use.

One excellent example of integrating behavioral health, lifestyle coaching, and medical care is Iora Health, an innovative primary care provider network that has built a new model of relationship-focused primary care.[27] At Iora, patients are matched with a behavioral health specialist, a "Health Coach," and PCP. Together, they manage a patient's medical and behavioral health and empower them to take control of their own health. While behavioral health specialists provide expert mental health counseling, assessment, and referrals in the clinic, Health Coaches (usually community health workers) manage patients' health outside the clinic. Iora sees Health Coaches as the connection that ties it all together—they help seniors come up with a health plan, make lifestyle changes, and serve as a bridge between them and their doctors.

To ensure the mental health of older adults does not fall to the wayside, a care delivery model for the geriatric population should consist of a behavioral health specialist, a "coach" who manages patients' health outside the clinic, and a PCP familiar with the mental health issues affecting older patients.

### Address Both Medical and Nonmedical Needs

For the most part, our healthcare system is built on an episodic, acute care model. We have what some experts call a "sick care" system, meaning we wait for patients to get sick rather than preventing them from getting sick in the first place. And in our narrow focus on treating disease, we neglect to consider and address the multitude of social factors that predispose some patients to poor health.

Instead, a model of care for older adults should focus on chronic disease prevention and management. It is well established that small changes to unhealthy behaviors can prevent or delay the onset of chronic conditions. Therefore, we need to partner with patients from day one to screen for preventable illness and match patients with a trained professional (such as a Health Coach or community health worker) who can ensure patients have the knowledge and support to make these lifestyle changes.

But what about our highest-need, highest-cost patients, those with multiple chronic conditions and co-occurring behavioral and social complexity? For these patients, preventive screening and lifestyle modifications are hardly enough. In recent years, complex care management has emerged as a promising model to improve outcomes and reduce costs for this population.

Broadly speaking, complex care management is defined as assisting patients and caregivers in managing medical and behavioral health conditions, addressing the psychological and social drivers of health, and coordinating medical and social services. These programs can take many shapes and forms. For example, one oft-discussed example of complex care management is the Camden Coalition's "hotspotting" program that uses hospital admissions data to identify "superutilizers" and then coordinate these patients' outpatient care and social services in the months following discharge. However, a recent randomized controlled trial showed that it did not reduce readmissions rates.[28]

There are several lessons to be learned here. As with most efforts to address the social determinants of health, the Camden Coalition program used a "one-size-fits-all" approach instead of matching the right services to the right patients at the right time.

Now consider a complex care management program that CareMore pioneered for older adults in Memphis, Tennessee. They began by carefully identifying patients most likely to benefit from complex care management—this meant patients with the highest healthcare utilization, multiple chronic conditions, or those nominated by their care team. Each patient was then matched with a PCP, community health worker, and social worker. Together, this team developed a care plan tailored to a patient's specific set of medical, behavioral, and social needs. There was also frequent, structured follow-up. The community health worker called patients regularly to check in and troubleshoot barriers, and patients were also scheduled for monthly in-person visits.

For complex care management to work, coordinating care across multiple settings is also important. The CareMore model relies on extensivists. Extensivists are hospital-based physicians who care for patients during and after a hospitalization, making sure that no information is missed during the transition from hospital to outpatient care.[29]

Older adults enrolled in the CareMore complex care management program had lower total medical expenditures, fewer hospital admissions, and shorter hospital stays compared to patients who received usual care. Thus, complex care management can work—if designed for the right patients and tailored to meet each patient's medical and nonmedical needs.

Integrating community health workers and social workers into care teams is critical. However, if we want to really address the social determinants of health, we need to look further upstream and start in patients' communities. Oak Street Health, a Chicago-based network of primary care centers for low-income seniors, is a good example of this.[30] Oak Street calls themselves a "social determinants practice," but how did they build their model to address social determinants? For one, their centers are not designed like usual primary care offices. Rather, they are located in the neighborhoods where patients live, work, and play. Each has a community center, café, computer lab, and event space, signaling their commitment to holistic, community-based care. Second, they form meaningful partnerships with community-based organizations. These partnerships range from fresh produce sales at their centers to helping patients find stable housing.

At the core of addressing patients' social needs is trust. Any care delivery model for older adults is only as good at its people and the relationships they are able to build with patients. This is especially important for a population with significant unmet social needs and should be front and center in decisions about hiring people and building partnerships.

### Choose the Right Business Model

For all of these ideas to work, we need a business model that allows for true value-based care—that is, care designed to keep patients healthy and out of the hospital. Right now, care for older adults is based on a fee-for-service chassis that incentivizes more clinic visits, more hospitalizations, and more unnecessary treatments and procedures. It is the reason why our country's seniors are trapped in a cycle of increased utilization, poor outcomes, and increased costs. And given our rapidly aging population, it is inching our healthcare system closer to a financially unsustainable future.

One model that is becoming increasingly popular among care delivery organizations dedicated to reforming care for older adults is Medicare Advantage. A Medicare Advantage plan uses capitation, meaning providers receive a fixed amount of money (a "capitated" payment) to care for each patient rather than being paid based on the number of patients they see or the number of procedures they perform. As a result, they are incentivized to lower the cost of the care without compromising quality. This makes Medicare Advantage the perfect chassis to care for older adults with high healthcare utilization. Moreover, it rewards innovation; organizations and clinicians are incentivized to design and test new approaches to delivering care for a population that is desperately in need of innovation.

ChenMed, a network of primary care centers dedicated to providing concierge-level care for seniors, has long seen the benefits of Medicare Advantage trickle into patient care.[31] Medicare Advantage has enabled ChenMed to help seniors consistently enjoy more health days, fewer inpatient hospital admissions, and fewer emergency room visits than in county-specific averages reported by the Centers for Medicare and Medicaid Services. Other organizations, including CareMore and Iora, have seen similar advantages with Medicare Advantage compared to the usual fee-for-service model.

## CONCLUSION

We have a responsibility to transform care for frail and vulnerable older adults in this country. Though it might be impossible to cure Mrs. J's multiple chronic conditions, we can help her stay healthy, independent, and at home for as long as possible. We have all the ingredients at our disposal—excellent clinicians, an understanding of what older adults need, and the medical and social resources to meet those needs. It is high time that we use them to build the progressive model of healthcare delivery that patients like Mrs. J deserve.

# Notes

## CHAPTER 1

1. Lynch, Julia. "Why framing inequality as a health problem may make it harder to fight," November 1, 2016. https://items.ssrc.org/why-framing-inequality-as-a-health-problem-may-make-it-harder-to-fight/? Accessed June 18, 2021.
2. Beck, Ulrich, Scott Lash, and Brian Wynne. *Risk society: Towards a new modernity.* Volume 17. Sage, 1992.
3. Greenhalgh, Trisha, Mustafa F. Ozbilgin, Barbara Prainsack, and Sara Shaw. "Moral entrepreneurship, the power-knowledge nexus, and the Cochrane 'crisis.'" *Journal of evaluation in clinical practice* 25, no. 5 (2019): 717–25.
4. Carel, Havi, and Ian James Kidd. "Epistemic injustice in healthcare: A philosophial analysis." *Medicine, Health Care and Philosophy* 17, no. 4 (2014): 529–40.
5. Petrou, P., G. Samoutis, and C. Lionis. "Single-payer or a multipayer health system: a systematic literature review." *Public Health* 163 (2018): 141–52.

## CHAPTER 2

1. Wilson, Yolonda, Amina White, Akilah Jefferson, and Marion Danis. "Intersectionality in clinical medicine: The need for a conceptual framework." *The American Journal of Bioethics* 19, no. 2 (2019): 8–19.
2. Chisholm, Marie A., and Joseph T. DiPiro. "Pharmaceutical manufacturer assistance programs." *Archives of internal medicine* 162, no. 7 (2002): 780–84.

# CHAPTER 3

1. Booker, S. Q., T. A. Baker, D. K. Esiaka, J. A. Minahan, I. J. Engel, K. Banerjee, and M. Poitevien. (under review). "Advancing pain (disparities) research: Acknowledging the past while paving the way for the future."

2. Institute of Medicine. *Relieving pain in America: A blueprint for transforming prevention, care, education, and research.* Washington, DC: The National Academies Press, 2011.

3. Farrell, M. M., and S. J. Gibson. Psychosocial aspects of pain in older people. In R. H. Dworkin and W. S. Breitbart (Eds.). *Psychosocial aspects of pain: A handbook for healthcare providers, progress in pain research and management* (pp. 495–518). Seattle: IASP Press, 2004.

4. Treede, Rolf-Detlef, Winfried Rief, Antonia Barke, Qasim Aziz, Michael I. Bennett, Rafael Benoliel, Milton Cohen, et al. "A classification of chronic pain for ICD-11." *Pain* 156, no. 6 (2015): 1003.

5. Green, Carmen R., Karen O. Anderson, Tamara A. Baker, Lisa C. Campbell, Sheila Decker, Roger B. Fillingim, Donna A. Kaloukalani, et al. "The unequal burden of pain: Confronting racial and ethnic disparities in pain." *Pain Medicine* 4, no. 3 (2003): 277–94.

6. Reid, M. Carrington, Christopher Eccleston, and Karl Pillemer. "Management of chronic pain in older adults." *BMJ* 350 (2015).

7. Siddall, Philip J., and Michael J. Cousins. "Persistent pain as a disease entity: Implications for clinical management." *Anesthesia and Analgesia* 99, no. 2 (August 2004): 510–20; Aronowitz, Shoshana V., Catherine C. Mcdonald, Robin C. Stevens, and Therese S. Richmond. "Mixed studies review of factors influencing receipt of pain treatment by injured black patients." *Journal of Advanced Nursing* 76, no. 1 (2020): 34–46.

8. Hoffman, Kelly M., Sophie Trawalter, Jordan R. Axt, and M. Norman Oliver. "Racial bias in pain assessment and treatment recommendations, and false beliefs about biological differences between blacks and whites." *Proceedings of the National Academy of Sciences* 113, no. 16 (2016): 4296–301.

9. Shavers, Vickie L., Alexis Bakos, and Vanessa B. Sheppard. "Race, ethnicity, and pain among the US adult population." *Journal of Health Care for the Poor and Underserved* 21, no. 1 (2010): 177–220; Centers for Disease Control and Prevention. "Health disparities among racial/ethnic populations." Community Health and Program Services. 2008. http://www.cdc.gov/NCCDPHP/DACH/chaps/disparities/index.htm.

10. Commission on Social Determinants of Health. *Closing the gap in a generation: Health equity through action on the social determinants of health: Final report of the commission on social determinants of health.* Washington, DC: World Health Organization, 2008; Solar, O., and A. Irwin. "A conceptual framework for action on the social determinants of health." Social Determinants of Health Discussion Paper 2, World Health Organization, 2010. https://www.who.int/sdhconference/resources/Conceptualframe workforactiononSDH_eng.pdf; Marmot, Michael, and Richard Wilkinson, eds. *Social determinants of health.* Second edition. Oxford: Oxford University Press, 2005; Adler,

Nancy E., and Judith Stewart. "Preface to *The biology of disadvantage: Socioeconomic status and health.*" *Annals of the New York Academy of Sciences* 1186, no. 1 (February 1, 2010): 1–4.

11. Rubin, I. Leslie. "Social determinants of health." In I. Leslie Rubin, Joav Merrick, Donald E. Greydanus, and Dilip R. Patel (Eds.). *Healthcare for people with intellectual and developmental disabilities across the lifespan* (pp. 1919–32). Cham: Springer International Publishing, 2016; Rasanathan, K., and A. Sharkey. "Global health promotion and the social determinants of health." In R. S. Zimmerman, R. J. DiClemente, and J. K. Andrus (Eds.). *Introduction to global health promotion.* San Francisco, CA: Jossey-Bass Public Health, 2016; Interagency Pain Research Coordinating Committee. "National Pain Strategy: a comprehensive population health-level strategy for pain." Washington, DC: US Department of Health and Human Services, National Institutes of Health, 2016.

12. Hughes, M. Courtney, Tamara A. Baker, Hansol Kim, and Elise G. Valdes. "Health behaviors and related disparities of insured adults with a healthcare provider in the United States, 2015–2016." *Preventive Medicine* 120 (2019): 42–49.

13. Green, Carmen R., S. Khady Ndao-Brumblay, Brady West, and Tamika Washington. "Differences in prescription opioid analgesic availability: comparing minority and white pharmacies across Michigan." *The Journal of Pain* 6, no. 10 (2005): 689–99.

14. Jefferson, Kevin, Tammie Quest, and Katherine A. Yeager. "Factors associated with black cancer patients' ability to obtain their opioid prescriptions at the pharmacy." *Journal of Palliative Medicine* 22, no. 9 (2019): 1143–48. Gladyshev, Timothy V., and Vadim N. Gladyshev. "A disease or not a disease? Aging as a pathology." *Trends in Molecular Medicine* 22, no. 12 (2016): 995–96.

15. Baker, Tamara A., Olivio J. Clay, Vicki Johnson-Lawrence, Jacquelyn A. Minahan, Chivon A. Mingo, Roland J. Thorpe, Fernando Ovalle, and Michael Crowe. "Association of multiple chronic conditions and pain among older black and white adults with diabetes mellitus." *BMC Geriatrics* 17, no. 1 (2017): 1–9.

16. Cherry, Barbara J., Laura Zettel-Watson, Renee Shimizu, Ian Roberson, Dana N. Rutledge, and Caroline J. Jones. "Cognitive performance in women aged 50 years and older with and without fibromyalgia." *Journals of Gerontology Series B: Psychological Sciences and Social Sciences* 69, no. 2 (2014): 199–208; Covinsky, Kenneth E., Karla Lindquist, Dorothy D. Dunlop, and Edward Yelin. "Pain, functional limitations, and aging." *Journal of the American Geriatrics Society* 57, no. 9 (2009): 1556–61; Wilkie, Ross, Abdelouahid Tajar, and John McBeth. "The onset of widespread musculoskeletal pain is associated with a decrease in healthy ageing in older people: A population-based prospective study." *PLoS One* 8, no. 3 (2013): e59858; Andrews, James S., Irena Stijacic Cenzer, Edward Yelin, and Kenneth E. Covinsky. "Pain as a risk factor for disability or death." *Journal of the American Geriatrics Society* 61, no. 4 (2013): 583–89.

17. Stubbs, Brendon, Pat Schofield, Tarik Binnekade, Sandhi Patchay, Amir Sepehry, and Laura Eggermont. "Pain is associated with recurrent falls in community-dwelling older adults: Evidence from a systematic review and meta-analysis." *Pain Medicine* 15, no. 7 (2014): 1115–28; Zimmer, Zachary, and Anna Zajacova. "Persistent, consistent,

and extensive: The trend of increasing pain prevalence in older Americans." *The Journals of Gerontology: Series B* 75, no. 2 (2020): 436–47.

18. Grol-Prokopczyk, Hanna. "Sociodemographic disparities in chronic pain, based on 12-year longitudinal data." *Pain* 158, no. 2 (2017): 313.

19. Reyes-Gibby, Cielito C., Lu Ann Aday, Knox H. Todd, Charles S. Cleeland, and Karen O. Anderson. "Pain in aging community-dwelling adults in the United States: non-Hispanic whites, non-Hispanic blacks, and Hispanics." *The Journal of Pain* 8, no. 1 (2007): 75–84; Vaughn, Ivana A., Ellen L. Terry, Emily J. Bartley, Nancy Schaefer, and Roger B. Fillingim. "Racial-ethnic differences in osteoarthritis pain and disability: A meta-analysis." *The Journal of Pain* 20, no. 6 (2019): 629–44; Janevic, Mary R., Sara J. McLaughlin, Alicia A. Heapy, Casey Thacker, and John D. Piette. "Racial and socioeconomic disparities in disabling chronic pain: Findings from the health and retirement study." *The Journal of Pain* 18, no. 12 (2017): 1459–67.

20. Meghani, Salimah H., Rosemary C. Polomano, Raymond C. Tait, April H. Vallerand, Karen O. Anderson, and Rollin M. Gallagher. "Advancing a national agenda to eliminate disparities in pain care: Directions for health policy, education, practice, and research." *Pain Medicine* 13, no. 1 (2012): 5–28; Elder, Glen H., Monica Kirkpatrick Johnson, and Robert Crosnoe. "The emergence and development of life course theory." In *Handbook of the Life Course* (pp. 3–19). Boston, MA: Springer, 2003.

21. Stowe, James D., and Teresa M. Cooney. "Examining Rowe and Kahn's concept of successful aging: Importance of taking a life course perspective." *The Gerontologist* 55, no. 1 (2015): 43–50; Gee, Gilbert C., and Chandra L. Ford. "Structural racism and health inequities: Old issues, New Directions1." *Du Bois Review: Social Science Research on Race* 8, no. 1 (2011): 115.

22. Krieger, Nancy. "Measures of racism, sexism, heterosexism, and gender binarism for health equity research: From structural injustice to embodied harm-An ecosocial analysis." *Annual Review of Public Health* 41 (2019): 37–62.

23. Geronimus, Arline T., Margaret Hicken, Danya Keene, and John Bound. "'Weathering' and age patterns of allostatic load scores among blacks and whites in the United States." *American Journal of Public Health* 96, no. 5 (2006): 826–33.

24. Phelan, Jo C., and Bruce G. Link. "Is racism a fundamental cause of inequalities in health?" *Annual Review of Aociology* 41 (2015): 311–30; Gee, Gilbert C., Katrina M. Walsemann, and Elizabeth Brondolo. "A life course perspective on how racism may be related to health inequities." *American Journal of Public Health* 102, no. 5 (2012): 967–74.

25. Taylor, Janiece L. Walker, Claudia M. Campbell, Roland J. Thorpe Jr., Keith E. Whitfield, Manka Nkimbeng, and Sarah L. Szanton. "Pain, racial discrimination, and depressive symptoms among African American women." *Pain Management Nursing* 19, no. 1 (2018): 79–87.

26. Umberson, Debra. "Black deaths matter: Race, relationship loss, and effects on survivors." *Journal of Health and Social Behavior* 58, no. 4 (2017): 405–20.

27. Keefe, Francis J., Laura Porter, Tamara Somers, Rebecca Shelby, and Anava V. Wren. "Psychosocial interventions for managing pain in older adults: outcomes and clinical implications." *British Journal of Anaesthesia* 111, no. 1 (2013): 89–94.

28. Bowleg, Lisa. 2020. "Reframing mass incarceration as a social-structural driver of health inequity." *American Journal of Public Health* 110 (S1): S11–12.

29. Ruiz, D. S., A. Kopak. "The consequences of parental incarceration for African American mothers, children, and grandparent caregivers." *Journal of Pan African Studies* 7, no. 6 (2014): 9–25.

30. Booker, S. Q., T. A. Baker, D. K. Esiaka, J. A. Minahan, I. J. Engel, K. Banerjee, and M. Poitevien. (under review). "Advancing pain (disparities) research: Acknowledging the past while paving the way for the future."

31. Booker, S. Q., T. A. Baker, D. K. Esiaka, J. A. Minahan, I. J. Engel, K. Banerjee, and M. Poitevien. (under review). "Advancing pain (disparities) research: Acknowledging the past while paving the way for the future."

32. Institute of Medicine. *Relieving pain in America: A blueprint for transforming prevention, care, education, and research.* Washington, DC: The National Academies Press, 2011.

33. Institute of Medicine. *Relieving pain in America: A blueprint for transforming prevention, care, education, and research.* Washington, DC: The National Academies Press, 2011.

## CHAPTER 4

1. Peterson, Cora, Mengyao Li, Likang Xu, Christina A. Mikosz, and Feijun Luo. "Assessment of annual cost of substance use disorder in US hospitals." *JAMA Network Open* 4, no. 3 (2021): e210242–e210242.

2. Tervalon, Melanie, and Jann Murray-Garcia. "Cultural humility versus cultural competence: A critical distinction in defining physician training outcomes in multicultural education." *Journal of Healthcare for the Poor and Underserved* 9, no. 2 (1998): 117–25.

3. Saloner, Brendan, Emma E. McGinty, Leo Beletsky, Ricky Bluthenthal, Chris Beyrer, Michael Botticelli, and Susan G. Sherman. "A public health strategy for the opioid crisis." *Public Health Reports* 133, no. 1 suppl (2018): 24S–34S.

4. Bassuk, Ellen L., Justine Hanson, R. Neil Greene, Molly Richard, and Alexandre Laudet. "Peer-delivered recovery support services for addictions in the United States: A systematic review." *Journal of Substance Abuse Treatment* 63 (2016): 1–9.

5. Ashford, Robert D., Austin M. Brown, Georgeanne Dorney, Nancy McConnell, Justin Kunzelman, Jessica McDaniel, and Brenda Curtis. "Reducing harm and promoting recovery through community-based mutual aid: Characterizing those who engage in a hybrid peer recovery community organization." *Addictive Behaviors* 98 (2019): 106037.

6. Ashford, Robert D., Brenda Curtis, and Austin M. Brown. "Peer-delivered harm reduction and recovery support services: initial evaluation from a hybrid recovery community drop-in center and syringe exchange program." *Harm Reduction Journal* 15, no. 1 (2018): 1–9.

7. Greenfield, Brenna L., and Kamilla L. Venner. "Review of substance use disorder treatment research in Indian country: Future directions to strive toward health equity." *The American Journal of Drug and Alcohol Abuse* 38, no. 5 (2012): 483–92.

8. Duran, Eduardo, and Bonnie Duran. *Native American postcolonial psychology.* New York: SUNY Press, 1995.

9. Gone, Joseph P., and Patrick E. Calf Looking. "American Indian culture as substance abuse treatment: Pursuing evidence for a local intervention." *Journal of Psychoactive Drugs* 43, no. 4 (2011): 291–96; Gone, Joseph P., and Patrick E. Calf Looking. "The Blackfeet Indian culture camp: Auditioning an alternative indigenous treatment for substance use disorders." *Psychological Services* 12, no. 2 (2015): 83.

10. Dickerson, Daniel L., Kamilla L. Venner, Bonnie Duran, Jeffery J. Annon, Benjamin Hale, and George Funmaker. "Drum-assisted recovery therapy for Native Americans (DARTNA): Results from a pretest and focus groups." *American Indian and Alaska Native Mental Health Research (Online)* 21, no. 1 (2014): 35.

11. Tingey, Lauren, Francene Larzelere, Novalene Goklish, Summer Rosenstock, Larissa Jennings Mayo-Wilson, Elliott Pablo, Warren Goklish, et al. "Entrepreneurial, economic, and social well-being outcomes from an RCT of a youth entrepreneurship education intervention among Native American adolescents." *International Journal of Environmental Research and Public Health* 17, no. 7 (2020): 2383.

12. Barlow, Allison, Britta Mullany, Nicole Neault, Novalene Goklish, Trudy Billy, Ranelda Hastings, Sherilynn Lorenzo, et al. "Paraprofessional-delivered home-visiting intervention for American Indian teen mothers and children: 3-year outcomes from a randomized controlled trial." *American Journal of Psychiatry* 172, no. 2 (2015): 154–62.

13. National Harm Reduction Coalition. "Principles of harm reduction." https://harmreduction.org/about-us/principles-of-harm-reduction/.

14. National Harm Reduction Coalition. "Principles of harm reduction." https://harmreduction.org/about-us/principles-of-harm-reduction/.

15. Fernandes, Ricardo M., Maria Cary, Gonçalo Duarte, Gonçalo Jesus, Joana Alarcão, Carla Torre, Suzete Costa, João Costa, and António Vaz Carneiro. "Effectiveness of needle and syringe programmes in people who inject drugs–An overview of systematic reviews." *BMC Public Health* 17, no. 1 (2017): 1–15.

16. amfFAR. "Opioid and health indicators database." https://opioid.amfar.org/indicator/num; Dasgupta, Sharoda, Dita Broz, Mary Tanner, Monita Patel, Brandon Halleck, Philip J. Peters, Paul J. Weidle, et al. "Changes in reported injection behaviors following the public health response to an HIV outbreak among people who inject drugs: Indiana, 2016." *AIDS and Behavior* 23, no. 12 (2019): 3257–66.

17. Stop the Addiction Fatality Epidemic Project. "Naloxone Awareness Project state rules." 2020. https://www.safeproject.us/naloxone-awareness-project/state-rules/.

18. Kerr, Thomas, Sanjana Mitra, Mary Clare Kennedy, and Ryan McNeil. "Supervised injection facilities in Canada: past, present, and future." *Harm Reduction Journal* 14, no. 1 (2017): 1–9.

19. Bayoumi, Ahmed M., and Gregory S. Zaric. "The cost-effectiveness of Vancouver's supervised injection facility." *CMAJ* 179, no. 11 (2008): 1143–51.

20. Wood, Evan, Thomas Kerr, J. Stoltz, Z. Qui, R. Zhang, J. S. G. Montaner, and M. W. Tyndall. "Prevalence and correlates of hepatitis C infection among users of North America's first medically supervised safer injection facility." *Public Health* 119, no. 12 (2005): 1111–15.

21. Bayoumi, Ahmed M., and Gregory S. Zaric. "The cost-effectiveness of Vancouver's supervised injection facility." *CMAJ* 179, no. 11 (2008): 1143–51.

22. National Academies of Sciences, Engineering and Medicine. *Medications for opioid use disorder save lives.* Washington, DC: The National Academies Press, 2019.

23. Rao, H., H. Mahadevappa, P. Pillay, M. Sessay, A. Abraham, and J. Luty. "A study of stigmatized attitudes towards people with mental health problems among health professionals." *Journal of Psychiatric and Mental Health Nursing* 16, no. 3 (2009): 279–84.

24. Oxford University Press. "Stigma." https://www.oxfordreference.com/view /10.1093/oi/authority.20111007171501221.

25. Rao, H., H. Mahadevappa, P. Pillay, M. Sessay, A. Abraham, and J. Luty. "A study of stigmatized attitudes towards people with mental health problems among health professionals." *Journal of Psychiatric and Mental Health Nursing* 16, no. 3 (2009): 279–84.

26. Srivastava, A. Benjamin. "Impaired physicians: Obliterating the stigma." *American Journal of Psychiatry Residents Journal* 13, no. 3 (2018): 4–6.

27. Grappone, Gretchen. "Overcoming stigma." 2018. https://www.nami.org/Blogs /NAMI-Blog/October-2018/Overcoming-Stigma.

28. Livingston, James D., Teresa Milne, Mei Lan Fang, and Erica Amari. "The effectiveness of interventions for reducing stigma related to substance use disorders: A systematic review." *Addiction* 107, no. 1 (2012): 39–50.

29. Grappone, Gretchen. "Overcoming stigma." 2018. https://www.nami.org/Blogs /NAMI-Blog/October-2018/Overcoming-Stigma.

30. Grappone, Gretchen. "Overcoming stigma." 2018. https://www.nami.org/Blogs /NAMI-Blog/October-2018/Overcoming-Stigma.

31. Saitz, Richard, Shannon C. Miller, David A. Fiellin, and Richard N. Rosenthal. "Recommended use of terminology in addiction medicine." *Journal of Addiction Medicine* 15, no. 1 (2021): 3–7.

32. Health in Justice. "Home." https://www.healthinjustice.org/.

33. Sawyer, Wendy, and Peter Wagner. "Mass incarceration: The whole pie 2020." https://www.prisonpolicy.org/reports/pie2020.html.

34. National Research Council. *The growth of incarceration in the United States: Exploring causes and consequences.* Washington, DC: The National Academies Press, 2014.

35. Mackey, Katherine, Stephanie Veazie, Johanna Anderson, Donald Bourne, and Kim Peterson. "Barriers and facilitators to the use of medications for opioid use disorder: A rapid review." *Journal of General Internal Medicine* (2020): 1–10.

36. Friedmann, Peter D., Randall Hoskinson Jr., Michael Gordon, Robert Schwartz, Timothy Kinlock, Kevin Knight, Patrick M. Flynn, et al. "Medication-assisted treatment in criminal justice agencies affiliated with the criminal justice-drug abuse

treatment studies (CJ-DATS): Availability, barriers, and intentions." *Substance Abuse* 33, no. 1 (2012): 9–18.

37. Streisel, S. E. "Intent to refer: Exploring bias toward specific medication-assisted treatments by community corrections employees." *Substance Use & Misuse* 53, no. 14 (2018): 2421–30.

38. Mitchell, Shannon Gwin, Jennifer Willet, Laura B. Monico, Amy James, Danielle S. Rudes, Jill Viglioni, Robert P. Schwartz, Michael S. Gordon, and Peter D. Friedmann. "Community correctional agents' views of medication-assisted treatment: Examining their influence on treatment referrals and community supervision practices." *Substance Abuse* 37, no. 1 (2016): 127–33.

39. Khatri, Utsha G., Benjamin A. Howell, and Tyler N. A. Winkelman. "Medicaid expansion increased medications for opioid use disorder among adults referred by criminal justice agencies: Study examines receipt of medications for opioid use disorder among individuals people referred by criminal justice agencies and other sources before and after Medicaid expansion." *Health Affairs* 40, no. 4 (2021): 562–70.

## CHAPTER 5

1. Harris, Gardiner. "Talk doesn't pay, so psychiatry turns instead to drug therapy." *The New York Times*, March 5, 2011. https://www.nytimes.com/2011/03/06/health/policy/06doctors.html.

2. Bishop, Tara F., Matthew J. Press, Salomeh Keyhani, and Harold Alan Pincus. "Acceptance of insurance by psychiatrists and the implications for access to mental health care." *JAMA Psychiatry* 71, no. 2 (2014): 176–81.

3. Thomas, Christopher R., and Charles E. Holzer III. "The continuing shortage of child and adolescent psychiatrists." *Journal of the American Academy of Child & Adolescent Psychiatry* 45, no. 9 (2006): 1023–31.

4. Anderson, L. Elizabeth, Minghua L. Chen, James M. Perrin, and Jeanne Van Cleave. "Outpatient visits and medication prescribing for US children with mental health conditions." *Pediatrics* 136, no. 5 (2015): e1178–e1185.

5. Merikangas, Kathleen Ries, Jian-ping He, Marcy Burstein, Joel Swendsen, Shelli Avenevoli, Brady Case, Katholiki Georgiades, Leanne Heaton, Sonja Swanson, and Mark Olfson. "Service utilization for lifetime mental disorders in US adolescents: Results of the National Comorbidity Survey–Adolescent Supplement (NCS-A)." *Journal of the American Academy of Child & Adolescent Psychiatry* 50, no. 1 (2011): 32–45.

6. Miller, Lauren M., Michael A. Southam-Gerow, and Robert B. Allin. "Who stays in treatment? Child and family predictors of youth client retention in a public mental health agency." *Child & Youth Care Forum* 37, no. 4 (2008): 153–70.

7. Kronsberg, Hal, and Amie Bettencourt. "Patterns of student treatment attendance and dropout in an urban school-based mental health program." *School Mental Health* 12, no. 3 (2020): 610–25.

8. Metzl, Jonathan M., and Helena Hansen. "Structural competency: theorizing a new medical engagement with stigma and inequality." *Social Science & Medicine* 103 (2014): 126–33.

9. Kronsberg, Hal, Amie F. Bettencourt, Carol Vidal, and Rheanna E. Platt. "Education on the social determinants of mental health in child and adolescent psychiatry fellowships." *Academic Psychiatry* (2020): 1–5.

10. Weist, Mark D., Olga M. Acosta, and Eric A. Youngstrom. "Predictors of violence exposure among inner-city youth." *Journal of Clinical Child Psychology* 30, no. 2 (2001): 187–98.

11. McLaughlin, Katie A., Karestan C. Koenen, Eric D. Hill, Maria Petukhova, Nancy A. Sampson, Alan M. Zaslavsky, and Ronald C. Kessler. "Trauma exposure and posttraumatic stress disorder in a national sample of adolescents." *Journal of the American Academy of Child & Adolescent Psychiatry* 52, no. 8 (2013): 815–30.

12. D'Andrea, Wendy, Julian Ford, Bradley Stolbach, Joseph Spinazzola, and Bessel A. van der Kolk. "Understanding interpersonal trauma in children: Why we need a developmentally appropriate trauma diagnosis." *American Journal of Orthopsychiatry* 82, no. 2 (2012): 187.

13. Goenjian, Armen K., David Walling, Alan M. Steinberg, Ida Karayan, Louis M. Najarian, and Robert Pynoos. "A prospective study of posttraumatic stress and depressive reactions among treated and untreated adolescents 5 years after a catastrophic disaster." *American Journal of Psychiatry* 162, no. 12 (2005): 2302–08.

14. Teicher, Martin H., and Jacqueline A. Samson. "Childhood maltreatment and psychopathology: A case for ecophenotypic variants as clinically and neurobiologically distinct subtypes." *American Journal of Psychiatry* 170, no. 10 (2013): 1114–33.

15. Duckworth, Angela. "Grit: The power of passion and perseverance." Presented at the TED Talks Education, April 2013. https://www.ted.com/talks/angela_lee_duckworth_grit_the_power_of_passion_and_perseverance?language=en.

16. University of New Hampshire and United States of America. "National survey of children's exposure to violence (NATSCEV I), final report." 2014. https://ojjdp.ojp.gov/library/publications/national-survey-childrens-exposure-violence-natscev-i-final-report.

17. De Souza Briggs, Xavier, Susan J. Popkin, and John Goering. *Moving to opportunity: The story of an American experiment to fight ghetto poverty.* Oxford University Press, 2010.

18. Kessler, Ronald C., Greg J. Duncan, Lisa A. Gennetian, Lawrence F. Katz, Jeffrey R. Kling, Nancy A. Sampson, Lisa Sanbonmatsu, Alan M. Zaslavsky, and Jens Ludwig. "Associations of housing mobility interventions for children in high-poverty neighborhoods with subsequent mental disorders during adolescence." *JAMA* 311, no. 9 (2014): 937–47.

19. Clampet-Lundquist, Susan, Kathryn Edin, Jeffrey R. Kling, and Greg J. Duncan. "Moving teenagers out of high-risk neighborhoods: How girls fare better than boys." *American Journal of Sociology* 116, no. 4 (2011): 1154–89.

20. Baltimore City Health Department. "Community health assessment Baltimore City." September 20, 2017. https://health.baltimorecity.gov/sites/default/files/health /attachments/Baltimore%20City%20CHA%20-%20Final%209.20.17.pdf.

21. Erikson, Erik H. *Identity: Youth and crisis.* New York: W. W. Norton & Company, 1968.

22. Stearns, Elizabeth, and Elizabeth J. Glennie. "Opportunities to participate: Extracurricular activities' distribution across and academic correlates in high schools." *Social Science Research* 39, no. 2 (2010): 296–309.

23. Horrigan, John. "Baltimore's digital divide: Gaps in internet connectivity and the impact on low-income city residents." The Abell Foundation, May 2020. https://abell.org/sites/default/files/files/2020_Abell_digital%20divide_full%20report _FINAL_web%20(dr).pdf.

24. Cooper, Harris, Barbara Nye, Kelly Charlton, James Lindsay, and Scott Greathouse. "The effects of summer vacation on achievement test scores: A narrative and meta-analytic review." *Review of Educational Research* 66, no. 3 (1996): 227–68.

25. Cassidy, Jude. "Emotion regulation: Influences of attachment relationships." *Monographs of the Society for Research in Child Development* 59, no. 2–3 (1994): 228–49.

26. Alexander, Michelle. *The New Jim Crow: Mass incarceration in the age of colorblindness.* New York: New Press, 2010.

27. National Association for the Advancement of Colored People. "Criminal justice fact sheet." 2021. https://naacp.org/resources/criminal-justice-fact-sheet.

28. Wildeman, Christopher. "Parental imprisonment, the prison boom, and the concentration of childhood disadvantage." *Demography* 46, no. 2 (2009): 265–80.

29. Governor's Office of Children. "Reducing the impact of incarceration on Maryland's children, families, and communities." 2015. https://goc.maryland.gov /wp-content/uploads/sites/8/2015/10/Reducing-Impact-of-Incarceration-Final-LMB -Presentation.pdf.

30. Lee, Rosalyn D., Xiangming Fang, and Feijun Luo. "The impact of parental incarceration on the physical and mental health of young adults." *Pediatrics* 131, no. 4 (2013): e1188–e1195.

31. Merikangas, Kathleen Ries, Jian-ping He, Marcy Burstein, Sonja A. Swanson, Shelli Avenevoli, Lihong Cui, Corina Benjet, Katholiki Georgiades, and Joel Swendsen. "Lifetime prevalence of mental disorders in US adolescents: results from the National Comorbidity Survey Replication–Adolescent Supplement (NCS-A)." *Journal of the American Academy of Child & Adolescent Psychiatry* 49, no. 10 (2010): 980–89.

## CHAPTER 6

1. Hughes, Cathy, and Nichola Kane. *Multidisciplinary care.* London: RCOG Press, 2008.

2. Siegel, Rebecca L., Kimberly D. Miller, Ann Goding Sauer, Stacey A. Fedewa, Lynn F. Butterly, Joseph C. Anderson, Andrea Cercek, Robert A. Smith, and Ahmedin

Jemal. "Colorectal cancer statistics, 2020." *CA: A Cancer Journal for Clinicians* 70, no. 3 (2020): 145–64.

3. Smith, Sonali M., Kerri Wachter, Howard A. Burris III, Richard L. Schilsky, Daniel J. George, Douglas E. Peterson, Melissa L. Johnson, et al. "Clinical cancer advances 2021: ASCO's report on progress against cancer." *Journal of Clinical Oncology* 39, no. 10 (2021): 1165–84.

4. Laviana, Aaron A., Amy N. Luckenbaugh, and Matthew J. Resnick. "Trends in the cost of cancer care: Beyond drugs." *Journal of Clinical Oncology* 38, no. 4 (2020): 316.

5. Kantarjian, Hagop M., Tito Fojo, Michael Mathisen, and Leonard A. Zwelling. "Cancer drugs in the United States: Justum Pretium—the just price." *Journal of Clinical Oncology* 31, no. 28 (2013): 3600.

6. Vokinger, Kerstin N., Thomas J. Hwang, Thomas Grischott, Sophie Reichert, Ariadna Tibau, Thomas Rosemann, and Aaron S. Kesselheim. "Prices and clinical benefit of cancer drugs in the USA and Europe: A cost–benefit analysis." *The Lancer Oncology* 21, no. 5 (2020): 664–70.

7. Viale, Pamela Hallquist. "The American Society of Clinical Oncology reports on the state of cancer care in America: 2017." *Journal of the Advanced Practitioner in Oncology* 8, no. 5 (2017): 458.

8. Al-Shamsi, Humaid O., Marwan Al-Hajeili, and Sadir Alrawi. "Chasing the cure around the globe: Medical tourism for cancer care from developing countries." *Journal of Global Oncology* 4 (2018).

9. Foley, Brittany M., Jack M. Haglin, Joshua Ray Tanzer, and Adam EM Eltorai. "Patient care without borders: A systematic review of medical and surgical tourism." *Journal of Travel Medicine* 26, no. 6 (2019): taz049.

10. Polite, Blase N., Lucile L. Adams-Campbell, Otis W. Brawley, Nina Bickell, John M. Carethers, Christopher R. Flowers, Margaret Foti, et al. "Charting the future of cancer health disparities research: A position statement from the American Association for Cancer Research, the American Cancer Society, the American Society of Clinical Oncology, and the National Cancer Institute." *Cancer Research* 77, no. 17 (2017): 4548–55.

11. Bach, Peter B., Deborah Schrag, Otis W. Brawley, Aaron Galaznik, Sofia Yakren, and Colin B. Begg. "Survival of blacks and whites after a cancer diagnosis." *JAMA* 287, no. 16 (2002): 2106–13; Howlader, N., A. M. Noone, M. Krapcho, N. Neyman, R. Aminou, W. Waldron, S. F. Altekruse, C. L. Kosary, J. Ruhl, Z. Tatalovich, H. Cho, A. Mariotto, M. P. Eisner, D. R. Lewis, H. S. Chen, E. J. Feuer, K. A. Cronin, B. K. Edwards (Eds). "SEER cancer statistics review, 1975-2008, National Cancer Institute. Bethesda, MD." 2011. https://seer.cancer.gov/csr/1975_2008/.

12. Jemal, Ahmedin, Elizabeth M. Ward, Christopher J. Johnson, Kathleen A. Cronin, Jiemin Ma, A. Blythe Ryerson, Angela Mariotto, et al. "Annual report to the nation on the status of cancer, 1975–2014, featuring survival." *JNCI: Journal of the National Cancer Institute* 109, no. 9 (2017): djx030.

13. Siegel, Rebecca L., Stacey A. Fedewa, Kimberly D. Miller, Ann Goding-Sauer, Paulo S. Pinheiro, Dinorah Martinez-Tyson, and Ahmedin Jemal. "Cancer statistics for hispanics/latinos, 2015." *CA: A Cancer Journal for Clinicians* 65, no. 6 (2015): 457–80.

14. Kano, Miria, Nelson Sanchez, Irene Tamí-Maury, Benjamin Solder, Gordon Watt, and Shine Chang. "Addressing cancer disparities in SGM populations: Recommendations for a national action plan to increase SGM health equity through researcher and provider training and education." *Journal of Cancer Education* 35, no. 1 (2020): 44–53.

15. Quinn, Gwendolyn P., Julian A. Sanchez, Steven K. Sutton, Susan T. Vadaparampil, Giang T. Nguyen, B. Lee Green, Peter A. Kanetsky, and Matthew B. Schabath. "Cancer and lesbian, gay, bisexual, transgender/transsexual, and queer/questioning (LGBTQ) populations." *CA: A Cancer Journal for Clinicians* 65, no. 5 (2015): 384–400; Charkhchi, Paniz, Matthew B. Schabath, and Ruth C. Carlos. "Modifiers of cancer screening prevention among sexual and gender minorities in the Behavioral Risk Factor Surveillance System." *Journal of the American College of Radiology* 16, no. 4 (2019): 607–20.

16. Guerrero, Santiago, Andrés López-Cortés, Alberto Indacochea, Jennyfer M. García-Cárdenas, Ana Karina Zambrano, Alejandro Cabrera-Andrade, Patricia Guevara-Ramírez, Diana Abigail González, Paola E. Leone, and César Paz-y-Miño. "Analysis of racial/ethnic representation in select basic and applied cancer research studies." *Scientific Reports* 8, no. 1 (2018): 1–8; Duma, Narjust, Jesus Vera Aguilera, Jonas Paludo, Candace L. Haddox, Miguel Gonzalez Velez, Yucai Wang, Konstantinos Leventakos, et al. "Representation of minorities and women in oncology clinical trials: review of the past 14 years." *Journal of Oncology Practice* 14, no. 1 (2018): e1–e10; Kwiatkowski, Kat, Kathryn Coe, John C. Bailar, and G. Marie Swanson. "Inclusion of minorities and women in cancer clinical trials, a decade later: Have we improved?" *Cancer* 119, no. 16 (2013): 2956–63.

17. Han, Xuesong, K. Robin Yabroff, Elizabeth Ward, Otis W. Brawley, and Ahmedin Jemal. "Comparison of insurance status and diagnosis stage among patients with newly diagnosed cancer before vs after implementation of the Patient Protection and Affordable Care Act." *JAMA Oncology* 4, no. 12 (2018): 1713–20.

18. Jemal, Ahmedin, Chun Chieh Lin, Amy J. Davidoff, and Xuesong Han. "Changes in insurance coverage and stage at diagnosis among nonelderly patients with cancer after the Affordable Care Act." *Journal of Clinical Oncology* 35, no. 35 (2017): 3906–15.

19. Schootman, Mario, Edward Kinman, and Dione Farria. "Rural-urban differences in ductal carcinoma in situ as a proxy for mammography use over time." *The Journal of Rural Health* 19, no. 4 (2003): 470–76; Eberhardt, Mark S., and Elsie R. Pamuk. "The importance of place of residence: examining health in rural and nonrural areas." *American Journal of Public Health* 94, no. 10 (2004): 1682–86.

20. Polite, Blase N., Jerome E. Seid, Laura A. Levit, M. Kelsey Kirkwood, Caroline Schenkel, Suanna S. Bruinooge, Stephen S. Grubbs, Deborah Y. Kamin, and Richard L. Schilsky. "A new look at the state of cancer care in America." *Journal of Oncology Practice* 14, no. 7 (2018): 397–99.

21. Donia, Marco, Marie Louise Kimper-Karl, Katrine Lundby Høyer, Lars Bastholt, Henrik Schmidt, and Inge Marie Svane. "The majority of patients with metastatic melanoma are not represented in pivotal phase III immunotherapy trials." *European Journal of Cancer* 74 (2017): 89–95.

22. Unger, Joseph M., Dawn L. Hershman, Cathee Till, Lori M. Minasian, Raymond U. Osarogiagbon, Mark E. Fleury, and Riha Vaidya. "'When offered to participate': A systematic review and meta-analysis of patient agreement to participate in cancer clinical trials." *JNCI: Journal of the National Cancer Institute* 113, no. 3 (2021): 244–57.

23. Neumann, Peter J., Jennifer A. Palmer, Eric Nadler, ChiHui Fang, and Peter Ubel. "Cancer therapy costs influence treatment: A national survey of oncologists." *Health Affairs* 29, no. 1 (2010): 196–202; Altice, Cheryl K., Matthew P. Banegas, Reginald D. Tucker-Seeley, and K. Robin Yabroff. "Financial hardships experienced by cancer survivors: A systematic review." *JNCI: Journal of the National Cancer Institute* 109, no. 2 (2017).

24. Neta, Gila, Mindy Clyne, and David A. Chambers. "Dissemination and implementation research at the National Cancer Institute: A review of funded studies (2006–2019) and opportunities to advance the field." *Cancer Epidemiology and Prevention Biomarkers* 30, no. 2 (2021): 260–67.

25. Carter, Ashley J. R., and Cecine N. Nguyen. "A comparison of cancer burden and research spending reveals discrepancies in the distribution of research funding." *BMC Public Health* 12, no. 1 (2012): 1–12.

26. Collyar, Deborah. "How have patient advocates in the United States benefited cancer research?" *Nature Reviews Cancer* 5, no. 1 (2005): 73–78.

27. Collyar, Deborah. "How have patient advocates in the United States benefited cancer research?" *Nature Reviews Cancer* 5, no. 1 (2005): 73–78.

28. Varmus, Harold. "The new era in cancer research." *Science* 312, no. 5777 (2006): 1162–65; Collyar, Deborah. "How have patient advocates in the United States benefited cancer research?" *Nature Reviews Cancer* 5, no. 1 (2005): 73–78.

29. National Academies of Sciences, Engineering, and Medicine. "Integrating social care into the delivery of healthcare: Moving upstream to improve the nation's health." 2019; Epstein, Ronald M., Kevin Fiscella, Cara S. Lesser, and Kurt C. Stange. "Why the nation needs a policy push on patient-centered healthcare." *Health Affairs* 29, no. 8 (2010): 1489–95; Addario, Bonnie J., Ana Fadich, Jesme Fox, Linda Krebs, Deborah Maskens, Kathy Oliver, Erin Schwartz, Gilliosa Spurrier-Bernard, and Timothy Turnham. "Patient value: Perspectives from the advocacy community." *Health Expectations* 21, no. 1 (2018): 57–63; Addario, Bonnie, Jan Geissler, Marcia K. Horn, Linda U. Krebs, Deborah Maskens, Kathy Oliver, Ananda Plate, Erin Schwartz, and Nicole Willmarth. "Including the patient voice in the development and implementation of patient-reported outcomes in cancer clinical trials." *Health Expectations* 23, no. 1 (2020): 41–51.

30. Morrissey, Megan H. "The Downtown Welfare Advocate Center: A case study of a welfare rights organization." *Social Service Review* 64, no. 2 (1990): 189–207.

31. Perfetto, Eleanor M., Laurie Burke, Elisabeth M. Oehrlein, and Robert S. Epstein. "Patient-focused drug development: A new direction for collaboration." *Medical Care* 53, no. 1 (2015): 9–17; Anderson, Margaret, and K. Kimberly McCleary. "On the path to a science of patient input." *Science Translational Medicine* 8, no. 336 (2016): 336ps11–336ps11.

32. Addario, Bonnie. "SC31. 02 The role of patient advocacy groups." *Journal of Thoracic Oncology* 12, no. 1 (2017): S147–S148; Addario, Bonnie, Jan Geissler, Marcia K. Horn, Linda U. Krebs, Deborah Maskens, Kathy Oliver, Ananda Plate, Erin Schwartz, and Nicole Willmarth. "Including the patient voice in the development and implementation of patient-reported outcomes in cancer clinical trials." *Health Expectations* 23, no. 1 (2020): 41–51.

33. Smailhodzic, Edin, Wyanda Hooijsma, Albert Boonstra, and David J. Langley. "Social media use in healthcare: A systematic review of effects on patients and on their relationship with healthcare professionals." *BMC Health Services Research* 16, no. 1 (2016): 1–14.

34. Hawn, Carleen. "Take two aspirin and tweet me in the morning: How Twitter, Facebook, and other social media are reshaping healthcare." *Health Affairs* 28, no. 2 (2009): 361–68.

35. Addario, Bonnie, Jan Geissler, Marcia K. Horn, Linda U. Krebs, Deborah Maskens, Kathy Oliver, Ananda Plate, Erin Schwartz, and Nicole Willmarth. "Including the patient voice in the development and implementation of patient-reported outcomes in cancer clinical trials." *Health Expectations* 23, no. 1 (2020): 41–51; Addario, Bonnie. "SC31. 02 The role of patient advocacy groups." *Journal of Thoracic Oncology* 12, no. 1 (2017): S147–S148.

36. Patel, Manali I., Ana Maria Lopez, William Blackstock, Katherine Reeder-Hayes, E. Allyn Moushey, Jonathan Phillips, and William Tap. "Cancer disparities and health equity: A policy statement from the American Society of Clinical Oncology." *Journal of Clinical Oncology* 38, no. 29 (2020): 3439–48.

37. Patel, Manali I., Ana Maria Lopez, William Blackstock, Katherine Reeder-Hayes, E. Allyn Moushey, Jonathan Phillips, and William Tap. "Cancer disparities and health equity: A policy statement from the American Society of Clinical Oncology." *Journal of Clinical Oncology* 38, no. 29 (2020): 3439–48.

38. Levit, Laura A., Erin Balogh, Sharyl J. Nass, and Patricia Ganz, eds. *Delivering high-quality cancer care: Charting a new course for a system in crisis.* Washington, DC: National Academies Press, 2013.

39. Ostroff, Jamie S., Kristen E. Riley, Megan J. Shen, Thomas M. Atkinson, Timothy J. Williamson, and Heidi A. Hamann. "Lung cancer stigma and depression: Validation of the Lung Cancer Stigma Inventory." *Psycho-Oncology* 28, no. 5 (2019): 1011–17.

40. Stergiou-Kita, Mary, Cheryl Pritlove, and Bonnie Kirsh. "The 'Big C'—stigma, cancer, and workplace discrimination." *Journal of Cancer Survivorship* 10, no. 6 (2016): 1035–50.

41. Taylor, David G. "The political economics of cancer drug discovery and pricing." *Drug Discovery Today* (2020).

42. Sarpel, Umut, Bruce C. Vladeck, Celia M. Divino, and Paul E. Klotman. "Fact and fiction: Debunking myths in the US healthcare system." *Annals of Surgery* 247, no. 4 (2008): 563–69.

43. Brooks, Gabriel A., J. Russell Hoverman, and Carrie H. Colla. "The Affordable Care Act and cancer care delivery." *Cancer Journal* 23, no. 3 (2017): 163.

44. Duma, Narjust, Jesus Vera Aguilera, Jonas Paludo, Candace L. Haddox, Miguel Gonzalez Velez, Yucai Wang, Konstantinos Leventakos, et al. "Representation of minorities and women in oncology clinical trials: Review of the past 14 years." *Journal of Oncology Practice* 14, no. 1 (2018): e1–e10; Duma, Narjust, Tariq Azam, Irbaz Bin Riaz, Miguel Gonzalez-Velez, Sikander Ailawadhi, and Ronald Go. "Representation of minorities and elderly patients in multiple myeloma clinical trials." *The Oncologist* 23, no. 9 (2018): 1076.

45. Herrera, Angelica P., Shedra Amy Snipes, Denae W. King, Isabel Torres-Vigil, Daniel S. Goldberg, and Armin D. Weinberg. "Disparate inclusion of older adults in clinical trials: Priorities and opportunities for policy and practice change." *American Journal of Public Health* 100, no. S1 (2010): S105–S112.

46. American Society of Clinical Oncology. "Facts and figures: Diversity in oncology." 2018; Velazquez Manana, Ana I., Ryan Leibrandt, and Narjust Duma. "Trainee and workforce diversity in hematology and oncology: Ten years later what has changed?" *Journal of Clinical Oncology* 38 (2020): 11000.

47. Surbone, Antonella. "A review of cultural attitudes about cancer." In *Global oncology in global perspectives on cancer: Incidence, care and clinical experience*, volume one (pp. 19–40). Santa Barbara: Praeger Press, 2015; Goss, Elizabeth, Ana Maria Lopez, Carol L. Brown, Dana S. Wollins, Otis W. Brawley, and Derek Raghavan. "American society of clinical oncology policy statement: Disparities in cancer care." *Journal of Clinical Oncology* 27, no. 17 (2009): 2881–85.

48. Saha, Somnath, Gretchen Guiton, Paul F. Wimmers, and LuAnn Wilkerson. "Student body racial and ethnic composition and diversity-related outcomes in US medical schools." *JAMA* 300, no. 10 (2008): 1135–45.

49. Persky, Susan, Kimberly A. Kaphingst, Vincent C. Allen Jr., and Ibrahim Senay. "Effects of patient-provider race concordance and smoking status on lung cancer risk perception accuracy among African-Americans." *Annals of Behavioral Medicine* 45, no. 3 (2013): 308–17.

## CHAPTER 7

1. Hamer, Fannie Lou. "I'm Sick and Tired of Being Sick and Tired—Dec. 20, 1964." https://awpc.cattcenter.iastate.edu/2019/08/09/im-sick-and-tired-of-being-sick-and-tired-dec-20-1964/.

2. Hart, J. T. "The inverse care law." *The Lancet* 297, no. 7696 (1971): 405–12.

3. Hoffman, Kelly M., Sophie Trawalter, Jordan R. Axt, and M. Norman Oliver. "Racial bias in pain assessment and treatment recommendations, and false beliefs about

biological differences between Blacks and whites." *Proceedings of the National Academy of Sciences of the United States of America* 113, no. 16 (2016): 4296–301.

4. Quadagno, J. *One nation, uninsured: Why the U.S. has no national health insurance.* Oxford, UK: Oxford University Press, 2005.

5. Friedman, Ari B., D. Daphne Owen, and Victoria E. Perez. "Trends in hospital ED closures nationwide and across Medicaid expansion, 2006-2013." *The American Journal of Emergency Medicine* 34, no. 7 (2016): 1262–64; Lindrooth, Richard C., Marcelo C. Perraillon, Rose Y. Hardy, and Gregory J. Tung. "Understanding the relationship between Medicaid expansions and hospital closures." *Health Affairs* 37, no. 1 (2018): 111–20.

6. Kozhimannil, Katy B., Ifeoma Muoto, Blair G. Darney, Aaron B. Caughey, and Jonathan M. Snowden. "Early elective delivery disparities between non-Hispanic black and white women after statewide policy implementation." *Women's Health Issues* 28, no. 3 (2018): 224–31.

7. Kaufman, B. G., Whitaker, R., Pink, G., and Holmes, G. M. (2020). "Half of rural residents at high risk of serious illness due to COVID-19, creating stress on rural hospitals." *The Journal of Rural Health* 36, no. 4 (2020): 584–90.

8. Brown, R. C. H. "Moral responsibility for (un)healthy behavior." *Journal of Medical Ethics* 39 (2013): 695–98.

9. Downs, Jim. *Sick from freedom: African-American illness and suffering during the Civil War and Reconstruction.* Oxford: Oxford University Press, 2012; Williams, Linda Faye. *Constraint of race: Legacies of white skin privilege in America.* University Park, PA: Penn State Press, 2010.

10. Downs, Jim. *Sick from freedom: African-American illness and suffering during the Civil War and Reconstruction.* Oxford: Oxford University Press, 2012.

11. Williams, Linda Faye. *Constraint of race: Legacies of white skin privilege in America.* University Park, PA: Penn State Press, 2010.

12. Williams, Linda Faye. *Constraint of race: Legacies of white skin privilege in America.* University Park, PA: Penn State Press, 2010.

13. Hogarth, Rana A. *Medicalizing Blackness: Making racial difference in the Atlantic world, 1780–1840.* Chapel Hill, NC: UNC Press Books, 2017.

14. Summers, Martin. "Diagnosing the ailments of Black citizenship: African American physicians and the politics of mental illness, 1895–1940." In Laurie B. Green, John Mckiernan-González, and Martin Summers (Eds.). *Precarious prescriptions: Contested histories of race and health in North America.* Minneapolis, MN: University of Minnesota Press, 2014.

15. Downs, Jim. *Sick from freedom: African-American illness and suffering during the Civil War and Reconstruction.* Oxford: Oxford University Press, 2012.

16. Summers, Martin. "Diagnosing the ailments of Black citizenship: African American physicians and the politics of mental illness, 1895–1940." In Laurie B. Green, John Mckiernan-González, and Martin Summers (Eds.). *Precarious prescriptions: Contested histories of race and health in North America.* Minneapolis, MN: University of Minnesota Press, 2014.

17. Summers, Martin. "Diagnosing the ailments of Black citizenship: African American physicians and the politics of mental illness, 1895–1940." In Laurie B. Green, John Mckiernan-González, and Martin Summers (Eds.). *Precarious prescriptions: Contested histories of race and health in North America.* Minneapolis, MN: University of Minnesota Press, 2014.

18. Metzl, Jonathan M. *The protest psychosis: How schizophrenia became a black disease.* Boston: Beacon Press, 2010.

19. White, K., J. S. Haas, and D. R. Williams. "Elucidating the role of place in health care disparities: The example of racial/ethnic residential segregation." *Health Services Research* 47, No. 3 (2012): 1278–99.

20. Smith, D. B. *The power to heal: Civil rights, Medicare, and the struggle to transform America's health care system.* Nashville, TN: Vanderbilt University Press, 2016.

21. Thomas S. R., G. Pink, and K. Reiter. "Characteristics of communities served by rural hospitals predicted to be at high risk of financial distress in 2019." North Carolina Rural Health Research Program. Findings Brief. April 2019.

22. Harvey-Wingfield, A. *Flatlining: Race, work, and health care in the new economy.* Berkeley: University of California Press, 2019.

23. Long, G. (2014). "'I studied and practiced medicine without molestation': African American doctors in the first tears of freedom." In Laurie B. Green, John Mckiernan-González, and Martin Summers (Eds.). *Precarious prescriptions: Contested histories of race and health in North America.* Minneapolis, MN: University of Minnesota Press, 2014; Ward, T. J. *Black physicians in the Jim Crow south.* Fayetteville, AR: University of Arkansas Press, 2003; Hine, D. C. *Black women in white: Racial conflict and cooperation in the nursing profession, 1890–1950.* Bloomington, IN: Indiana University Press, 1989.

24. Long, G. (2014). "'I studied and practiced medicine without molestation': African American doctors in the first tears of freedom." In Laurie B. Green, John Mckiernan-González, and Martin Summers (Eds.). *Precarious prescriptions: Contested histories of race and health in North America.* Minneapolis, MN: University of Minnesota Press, 2014.

25. Ward, T. J. *Black physicians in the Jim Crow south.* Fayetteville, AR: University of Arkansas Press, 2003.

26. Ward, T. J. *Black physicians in the Jim Crow south.* Fayetteville, AR: University of Arkansas Press, 2003.

27. Hine, D. C. *Black women in white: Racial conflict and cooperation in the nursing profession, 1890-1950.* Bloomington, IN: Indiana University Press, 1989; Smith, S. L. *Sick and tired of being sick and tired: Black women's health activism in America, 1890-1950.* Philadelphia, PA: University of Pennsylvania Press, 1995; Savitt, T. "Abraham Flexner and the Black medical schools." *Journal of the National Medical Association* 98, no. 9 (2006): 1415–24.

28. Summers, Martin. "Diagnosing the ailments of Black citizenship: African American physicians and the politics of mental illness, 1895-1940." In eds Laurie B. Green, John Mckiernan-González, and Martin Summers (Eds.). *Precarious prescriptions:*

*Contested histories of race and health in North America*. Minneapolis, MN: University of Minnesota Press, 2014.

29. Smedley, Brian D., Adrienne Y. Stith, and Alan R. Nelson. *Unequal treatment: Confronting racial and ethnic disparities in health care*. Washington, DC: National Academies Press, 2003.

30. Khosla, Natalia N., Sylvia P. Perry, Corinne A. Moss-Racusin, Sara E. Burke, and John F. Dovidio. "A comparison of clinicians' racial biases in the United States and France." *Social Science and Medicine* 206 (2018): 31–37; Santoro, Taylor N., and Jonathan D. Santoro. "Racial bias in the US opioid epidemic: A review of the history of systemic bias and implications for care." *Cureus* 10, no. 12 (2018): e3733.

31. Goyal, M. K., N. Kuppermann, S. D. Cleary, S. J. Teach, and J. M. Chamberlain. "Racial disparities in pain management of children with appendicitis in emergency departments." *JAMA Pediatrics* 169 (2015): 996–1002; Johnson, J. D., I. V. Asiodu, C. P. McKenzie, C. Tucker, K. P. Tully, K. Bryant, S. Verbiest, and A. M. Stuebe. "Racial and ethnic inequities in postpartum pain evaluation and management." *Obstetrics & Gynecology* 134 (2019): 1155–62.

32. Hoffman, B. *Health care for some: Rights and rationing in the United States since 1930*. Chicago: University of Chicago Press, 2012.

33. Washington, H. "Profitable wonders: Antebellum medical experimentation with slaves and freedmen." In *Medical apartheid: The dark history of medical experimentation on Black Americans from colonial times to the present*. New York: Doubleday, 2006.

34. Ripp, Kelsey, and Lundy Braun. "Race/ethnicity in medical education: An analysis of a question bank for step 1 of the United States medical licensing examination." *Teaching and Learning in Medicine* 29, no. 2 (2017): 115–22; Tsai, Jennifer, Laura Ucik, Nell Baldwin, Christopher Hasslinger, and Paul George. "Race matters? Examining and rethinking race portrayal in preclinical medical education." *Academic Medicine* 19, No. 7 (2016): 916–20.

35. Jaschik, Scott. "Anger over stereotypes in textbook." Retrieved May 1, 2020. https://www.insidehighered.com/news/2017/10/23/nursing-textbook-pulled-over-stereotypes.

36. Metzl, Jonathan M., and Helena Hansen. "Structural competency: Theorizing a new medical engagement with stigma and inequality." *Social Science & Medicine* 103 (2014): 126–33; Tsai, Jennifer, and Ann Crawford-Roberts. "A call for critical race theory in medical education." *Academic Medicine* 92, no. 8 (2017): 1072–73.

37. Olsen, Lauren D. "The conscripted curriculum and the reproduction of racial inequalities in contemporary U.S. medical education." *Journal of Health and Social Behavior* 60, no. 1 (2019): 55–68.

38. Phelan J. C., and B. G. Link. "Is racism a fundamental cause of inequalities in health?" *Annual Review of Sociology* 41 (2015): 311–30; White, Kellee, Jennifer S. Haas, and David R. Williams. "Elucidating the role of place in healthcare disparities: the example of racial/ethnic residential segregation." *Health Services Research* 47, no. 3 (2012): 1278–99.

39. Mullan, Fitzhugh. "Social mission in health professions education: Beyond Flexner." *JAMA* 318, no. 2 (2017): 122–23; Mullan, Fitzhugh, Candice Chen, Stephen

Petterson, Gretchen Kolsky, and Michael Spagnol. "The social mission of medical education: Ranking the schools." *Annals of Internal Medicine* 152, no. 12 (2010): 804–11.

40. Genao, Inginia, and Jacob Gelman. "The MCAT's restrictive effect on the minority physician pipeline: A legal perspective." *Annals of Internal Medicine* 169, no. 6 (2018): 403–04.

41. Lucey, Catherine Reinis, and Aaron Saguil. "The consequences of structural racism on MCAT scores and medical school admissions." *Academic Medicine* 95, no. 3 (2020): 351–56; Rubright, Jonathan D., Michael Jodoin, and Michael A. Barone. "Examining demographics, prior academic performance, and United States medical licensing examination scores." *Academic Medicine* 94, no. 3 (2019): 364–70.

42. Boatright, Dowin H., Elizabeth A. Samuels, Laura Cramer, Jeremiah Cross, Mayur Desai, Darin Latimore, and Cary P. Gross. "Association between the liaison committee on medical education's diversity standards and changes in percentage of medical student sex, race, and ethnicity." *JAMA* 320, no. 21 (2018): 2267–69; Wijesekera, Thilan P., Margeum Kim, Edward Z. Moore, Olav Sorenson, and David A. Ross. "All other things being equal: Exploring racial and gender disparities in medical school honor society induction." *Academic Medicine* 94, no. 4 (2019): 562–69.

43. Bullock, Justin L., Cindy J. Lai, Tai Lockspeiser, Patricia S. O'Sullivan, Paul Aronowitz, Deborah Dellmore, Cha-Chi Fung, Christopher Knight, and Karen E. Hauer. "In pursuit of honors." *Academic Medicine* 94 (2019): S48–56; Low, Daniel, Samantha W. Pollack, Zachary C. Liao, Ramoncita Maestas, Larry E. Kirven, Anne M. Eacker, and Leo S. Morales. "Racial/ethnic disparities in clinical grading in medical school." *Teaching and Learning in Medicine* 31, no. 5 (2019): 487–96.

44. Boatright, Dowin, David Ross, Patrick O'Connor, Edward Moore, and Marcella Nunez-Smith. "Racial disparities in medical student membership in the Alpha Omega Alpha honor society." *JAMA Internal Medicine* 177, no. 5 (2017): 659–65.

45. Lett, Lanair Amaad, H. Moses Murdock, Whitney U. Orji, Jaya Aysola, and Ronnie Sebro. "Trends in racial/ethnic representation among US medical students." *JAMA Network Open* 2, no. 9 (2019): e1910490.

46. Ray, Victor. "A theory of racialized organizations." *American Sociological Review* 84, no. 1 (2019): 26–53; Wingfield, Adia Harvey. *Flatlining: Race, work, and healthcare in the new economy.* Berkeley: University of California Press, 2019.

47. Lett, Lanair Amaad, Whitney U. Orji, and Ronnie Sebro. "Declining racial and ethnic representation in clinical academic medicine: A longitudinal study of 16 US medical specialties." *PLOS One* 13, no. 11 (2018): e0207274.

48. Nunez-Smith, Marcella, Maria M. Ciarleglio, Teresa Sandoval-Schaefer, Johanna Elumn, Laura Castillo-Page, Peter Peduzzi, and Elizabeth H. Bradley. "Institutional variation in the promotion of racial/ethnic minority faculty at US medical schools." *American Journal of Public Health* 102, no. 5 (2012): 852–58.

49. Orom, Heather, Teresa Semalulu, and Willie Underwood. "The social and learning environments experienced by underrepresented minority medical students: A narrative review." *Academic Medicine* 88, no. 11 (2013): 1765–77.

50. Davis, Lorna G., Gayle L. Riedmann, Melissa Sapiro, John P. Minogue, and Ralph R. Kazer. "Cesarean section rates in low-risk private patients managed by

certified nurse-midwives and obstetricians." *Journal of Nurse-Midwifery* 39, no. 2 (1994): 91–97; Vedam, Saraswathi, Kathrin Stoll, Marian MacDorman, Eugene Declercq, Renee Cramer, Melissa Cheyney, Timothy Fisher, Emma Butt, Y. Tony Yang, and Holly Powell Kennedy. "Mapping integration of midwives across the United States: Impact on access, equity, and outcomes." *PLoS One* 13, no. 2 (2018).

51. Leslie, Mayri Sagady, and Amy Romano. "Appendix: Birth can safely take place at home and in birthing centers." *Journal of Perinatal Education* 16, no. 1 (2007): 81–88.

52. Maldonado, Linda Tina. 2013. "Midwives' collaborative activism in two U.S. cities, 1970-1990." Publicly Accessible Penn Dissertations 896.

53. Petersen, Emily E., Nicole L. Davis, David Goodman, Shanna Cox, Carla Syverson, Kristi Seed, Carrie Shapiro-Mendoza, William M. Callaghan, and Wanda Barfield. "Racial/ethnic disparities in pregnancy-related deaths—United States, 2007–2016." *Morbidity and Mortality Weekly Report* 68, no. 35 (2019): 762–65.

54. American Hospital Association. "Statement of the AHA for the Committee on Rules of the U.S. House of Representatives 'Medicare for All Act of 2019' | AHA." 2019. Retrieved February 2, 202. https://www.aha.org/lettercomment/2019-04-30-statement-aha-committee-rules-us-house-representatives-medicare-all-act.

55. Rogers, N. "'Caution: The AMA may be dangerous to your health': The student health organizations (SHO) and American medicine, 1965–1970." *Radical History Review* 80 (2001): 5–34.

56. Trent, Maria, Danielle G. Dooley, Jacqueline Dougé, Maria E. Trent, Robert M. Cavanaugh, Amy E. Lacroix, Jonathon Fanburg, Maria H. Rahmandar, Laurie L. Hornberger, Marcie B. Schneider, Sophia Yen, Lance Alix Chilton, Andrea E. Green, Kimberley Jo Dilley, Juan Raul Gutierrez, James H. Duffee, Virginia A. Keane, Scott Daniel Krugman, Carla Dawn McKelvey, Julie Michelle Linton, Jacqueline Lee Nelson, Gerri Mattson, Cora C. Breuner, Elizabeth M. Alderman, Laura K. Grubb, Janet Lee, Makia E. Powers, Maria H. Rahmandar, Krishna K. Upadhya, and Stephenie B. Wallace. "The impact of racism on child and adolescent health." *Pediatrics* 144, no. 2 (2019).

57. Doherty, Robert, Thomas G. Cooney, Ryan D. Mire, Lee S. Engel, and Jason M. Goldman. "Envisioning a better U.S. health care system for all: A call to action by the American College of Physicians." *Annals of Internal Medicine.* 172, no. 2 Supplement (2020): S3.

58. Sawyer, Jeremy, and Anup Gampa. "Implicit and explicit racial attitudes changed during Black Lives Matter." *Personality & Social Psychology Bulletin* 44, no. 7 (2018): 1039–59.

59. Horwitz, Leora I., Carol Chang, Harmony N. Arcilla, and James R. Knickman. "Quantifying health systems' investment in social determinants of health, by sector, 2017–19." *Health Affairs* 39, no. 2 (2020): 192–98.

60. Singh, Simone R., Gary J. Young, Shoou Yih, Daniel Lee, Paula H. Song, and Jeffrey A. Alexander. "Analysis of hospital community benefit expenditures' alignment with community health needs: Evidence from a national investigation of tax-exempt hospitals." *American Journal of Public Health* 105, no. 5 (2015): 914–21.

61. Castrucci, Brian, and John Auerbach. "Meeting individual social needs falls short of addressing social determinants of health." *Policy & Practice* 77, no. 2 (2019): 25–27; Murray, Genevra F., Hector P. Rodriguez, and Valerie A. Lewis. "Upstream with a small paddle: How ACOs are working against the current to meet patients' social needs." *Health Affairs* 39, no. 2 (2020):199–206.

62. Koh, Howard K., Amy Bantham, Alan C. Geller, Mark A. Rukavina, Karen M. Emmons, Pamela Yatsko, and Robert Restuccia. "Anchor institutions: Best practices to address social needs and social determinants of health." *American Journal of Public Health* 110, no. 3 (2020): e1–8.

63. Chowkwanyun, Merlin. "Cleveland versus the Clinic: The 1960s riots and community health reform." *American Journal of Public Health* 108, no. 11 (2018): 1494–502.

64. Morabia, Alfredo. "Unveiling the Black Panther Party legacy to public health." *American Journal of Public Health* 106, no. 10 (2016): 1732–33; Nelson, Alondra. *Body and soul: The Black Panther Party and the fight against medical racism.* Minneapolis: University of Minnesota Press, 2011.

65. Kangovi, Shreya, Nandita Mitra, David Grande, Judith A. Long, and David A. Asch. "Evidence-based community health worker program addresses unmet social needs and generates positive return on investment." *Health Affairs (Project Hope)* 39, no. 2 (2020): 207–13.

66. Himmelstein, K. E. W., and A. S. Venkataramani. "Economic vulnerability among US female healthcare workers: Potential impact of a $15-per-hour minimum wage." *American Journal of Public Health* 109 (2019): 198–205.

67. Matta, S., P. Chatterjee, and A. S. Venkataramani. "The income-based mortality gradient among US health care workers: Cohort study. *Journal of General Internal Medicine Gen.* (2020): 1–3.

68. Wiley, L. F., and G. W. Matthews. "Health care system transformation and integration: A call to action for public health." *The Journal of Law, Medicine & Ethics* 45, no. 1 supplement (2017): 94–97.

69. Swietek, Karen E., Bradley N. Gaynes, George L. Jackson, Morris Weinberger, and Marisa Elena Domino. "Effect of the patient-centered medical home on racial disparities in quality of care." *Journal of General Internal Medicine* (2020): 1–10.

## CHAPTER 8

1. McHarry, Kirwan. "Trans bodies, trans selves: A resource for the transgender community by L. Erickson-Schroth." *Journal of Homosexuality* 65, no. 13 (2018): 1934–36; Streed Jr., Carl G., J. Seth Anderson, Chris Babits, and Michael A. Ferguson. "Changing medical practice, not patients-Putting an end to conversion therapy." *The New England Journal of Medicine* 381, no. 6 (2019): 500–502.

2. Manion, Jen. *Female husbands: A trans history.* Cambridge: Cambridge University Press, 2020; Beemyn, Genny. "Transgender history in the United States." In Laura

Erickson-Schroth (ed.). *Trans bodies, trans selves: A resource for the transgender community.* Oxford: Oxford University Press, 2014: 501–36.

3. Slagstad, Ketil. "The political nature of sex-transgender in the history of medicine." *The New England Journal of Medicine* 384, no. 11 (2021): 1070–74.

4. Center of Excellence for Transgender Health. "Guidelines for the primary and gender-affirming care of transgender and gender nonbinary people," June 17, 2017. https://transcare.ucsf.edu/sites/transcare.ucsf.edu/files/Transgender-PGACG-6-17-16 .pdf; Makadon, Harvey J., Kenneth H. Mayer, Jennifer Potter, Hilary Goldhammer, eds. *Fenway guide to lesbian, gay, bisexual, and transgender health.* Second edition. Boston: The Fenway Institute, 2015.

5. Sayers, William. "The etymology of queer." *ANQ: A Quarterly Journal of Short Articles, Notes and Reviews* 18, no. 2 (2005): 17–19.

6. Partridge, E., T. Dalzell, and T. Victor. *The concise new partridge dictionary of slang and unconventional English.* New York: Routledge, 2015.

7. Cahill, Sean, Robbie Singal, Chris Grasso, Dana King, Kenneth Mayer, Kellan Baker, and Harvey Makadon. "Do ask, do tell: High levels of acceptability by patients of routine collection of sexual orientation and gender identity data in four diverse American community health centers." *PloS one* 9, no. 9 (2014): e107104.

8. Haider, Adil, Rachel R. Adler, Eric Schneider, Tarsicio Uribe Leitz, Anju Ranjit, Christina Ta, Adele Levine, et al. "Assessment of patient-centered approaches to collect sexual orientation and gender identity information in the emergency department: The EQUALITY study." *JAMA network open* 1, no. 8 (2018): e186506.

9. Streed, Carl G., Chris Grasso, Sari L. Reisner, and Kenneth H. Mayer. "Sexual orientation and gender identity data collection: Clinical and public health importance." *American Journal of Public Health* 110, no. 7 (2020): 991–93; Fredriksen-Goldsen, Karen I., and Hyun-Jun Kim. "Count me in: Response to sexual orientation measures among older adults." *Research on Aging* 37, no. 5 (2015): 464–80.

10. Ashley, Florence. "'Trans' is my gender modality: A modest terminological proposal." In Laura Erickson-Schroth (ed.). *Trans bodies, trans selves: A resource for the transgender community.* Oxford: Oxford University Press, 2021.

11. Terry, Jennifer. *An American obsession: Science, medicine, and homosexuality in modern society.* Chicago: University of Chicago Press, 1999.

12. Bayer, Ronald. *Homosexuality and American psychiatry: The politics of diagnosis.* Princeton: Princeton University Press, 1987.

13. Manion, Jen. *Female husbands: A trans history.* Cambridge: Cambridge University Press, 2020; Beemyn, Genny. "Transgender history in the United States." In Laura Erickson-Schroth (Ed.). *Trans bodies, trans selves: A resource for the transgender community.* Oxford: Oxford University Press, 2014: 501–36.

14. Siotos, Charalampos, Paula M. Neira, Brandyn D. Lau, Jill P. Stone, James Page, Gedge D. Rosson, and Devin Coon. "Origins of gender affirmation surgery: The history of the first gender identity clinic in the United States at Johns Hopkins." *Annals of Plastic Surgery* 83, no. 2 (2019): 132–36.

15. Nutt, A. E. "Long shadow cast by psychiatrist on transgender issues finally recedes at Johns Hopkins." *The Washington Post,* 2017. https://www.washington

post.com/national/health-science/long-shadow-cast-by-psychiatrist-on-transgender
-issues-finally-recedes-at-johns-hopkins/2017/04/05/e851e56e-0d85-11e7-ab07
-07d9f521f6b5_story.html.

16. Altman, Lawrence K. "New homosexual disorder worries health officials." *The New York Times*, May 11, 1982, C1–6.

17. Cantwell Jr., A. R. "Gay cancer, emerging viruses, and AIDS." *New Dawn (Melbourne)* (1998).

18. Miller, Neil. *Out of the past: Gay and lesbian history from 1869 to the present.* New York: Vintage Books, 1995.

19. McElroy, Jane A., Jenna J. Wintemberg, and Kenneth A. Haller. "Advancing healthcare for lesbian, gay, bisexual, and transgender patients in Missouri." *Missouri Medicine* 112, no. 4 (2015): 262.

20. Centers for Disease Control and Prevention. "Estimated HIV incidence and prevalence in the United States, 2014–2018." *HIV Surveillance Supplemental Report* 25, no. 1 (2020).

21. Solomon, Marc. *Winning marriage: The inside story of how same-sex couples took on the politicians and pundits-and won.* Lebanon, NH: University Press of New England, 2015.

22. Johnson, Chris. "10 years later, firestorm over gay-only ENDA vote still informs movement." *Washington Blade.* November 6, 2017. https://www.washingtonblade.com/2017/11/06/10-years-later-firestorm-over-gay-only-enda-vote-still-remembered/.

23. Steinmetz, Katy. "The transgender tipping point." *Time* 183, no. 22 (2014): 38–46.

24. Legal, Lambda. "When healthcare isn't caring: Lambda Legal's survey of discrimination against LGBT people and people with HIV." *New York: Lambda Legal* (2010): 1–26.

25. James, S. E., S. Herman, S. Rankin, M. Keisling, L. Mottet, and M. Anaf. "The report of the 2015 transgender survey." 2016. National Center for Transgender Equality, Washington, DC.

26. National Public Radio, the Robert Wood Johnson Foundation, and Harvard T.H. Chan School of Public Health. "Discrimination in America: Experiences and views of LGBTQ Americans." November 2017. https://legacy.npr.org/documents/2017/nov/npr-discrimination-lgbtq-final.pdf.

27. Drabble, Laurie A., and Michele J. Eliason. "Introduction to special issue: Impacts of the COVID-19 pandemic on LGBTQ+ health and well-being." *Journal of Homosexuality* (2021): 1–15.

28. Martos, Alexander J., Patrick A. Wilson, and Ilan H. Meyer. "Lesbian, gay, bisexual, and transgender (LGBT) health services in the United States: Origins, evolution, and contemporary landscape." *PloS One* 12, no. 7 (2017): e0180544.

29. Coles, Mandy. "Pediatrician sees life-changing benefits of gender care—and foresees great harm of Ark.'s anti-trans law." *Boston Globe.* April 8, 2021. https://www.bostonglobe.com/2021/04/08/opinion/pediatrician-sees-life-changing-benefits-gender-care-foresees-great-harm-arks-anti-trans-law/.

30. Human Rights Campaign Foundation. "Healthcare equality index: Promoting equitable and inclusive care for lesbian, gay, bisexual, transgender and queer patients and their families. 2020. https://hrc-prod-requests.s3-us-west-2.amazonaws.com/resources /HEI-2020-FinalReport.pdf?mtime=20200830220806&focal=none.

31. Obedin-Maliver, Juno, Elizabeth S. Goldsmith, Leslie Stewart, William White, Eric Tran, Stephanie Brenman, Maggie Wells, David M. Fetterman, Gabriel Garcia, and Mitchell R. Lunn. "Lesbian, gay, bisexual, and transgender–related content in undergraduate medical education." *JAMA* 306, no. 9 (2011): 971–77; Streed Jr., Carl G., Mitchell R. Lunn, Jennifer Siegel, and Juno Obedin-Maliver. "Meeting the patient care, education, and research missions: Academic medical centers must comprehensively address sexual and gender minority health." *Academic Medicine: Journal of the Association of American Medical Colleges* 96, no. 6 (2020): 822–27; Hollenbach, Andrew D., Kristen L. Eckstrand, and Alice Domurat Dreger, eds. *Implementing curricular and institutional climate changes to improve healthcare for individuals who are LGBT, gender nonconforming, or born with DSD: a resource for medical educators.* Washington, DC: Association of American Medical Colleges, 2014.

32. Pérez-Stable, Eliseo J. "Director's message: Sexual and gender minorities formally designated as a health disparity population for research purposes." National Institutes of Health, October 6, 2016. http://www.nimhd.nih.gov/about/directors -corner/message.html?utm_medium=email&utm_source=govdelivery.

33. Sexual and Gender Minority Research Office. "Sexual and gender minority populations in NIH-supported research." August 28, 2019. https://grants.nih.gov/grants /guide/notice-files/NOT-OD-19-139.html.

34. Noonan, Emily J., Susan Sawning, Ryan Combs, Laura A. Weingartner, Leslee J. Martin, V. Faye Jones, and Amy Holthouser. "Engaging the transgender community to improve medical education and prioritize healthcare initiatives." *Teaching and Learning in Medicine* 30, no. 2 (2018): 119–32.

## CHAPTER 9

1. United Nations. "World migration report 2020." (2020). https://www.un.org/sites /un2.un.org/files/wmr_2020.pdf.

2. Budiman, Abby. "Key findings about US immigrants." Pew Research Centre (2020).

3. Batalova, Jeanne, Brittany Blizzard., and J. Bolter. "Frequently requested statistics on immigrants and immigration in the United States 2020." 2020. https://www .migrationpolicy.org/article/frequently-requested-statistics-immigrants-and-immi gration-united-states.

4. Blizzard, Brittany, and Jeanne Batalova. "Refugees and asylees in the United States." June 13, 2019. https://www.migrationpolicy.org/article/refugees-and-asylees -united-states-2018.

5. TRAC. "Record number of asylum cases in FY 2019." January 8, 2020. https://trac.syr.edu/immigration/reports/588/.

6. National Research Council Panel on Race, Ethnicity, and Health in Later Life; Anderson NB, Bulatao RA, and Cohen B (Eds.). *Critical perspectives on racial and ethnic differences in health in late life*. Washington, DC: National Academies Press, 2004.

7. Commodore-Mensah, Yvonne, Nwakaego Ukonu, Olawunmi Obisesan, Jonathan Kumi Aboagye, Charles Agyemang, Carolyn M. Reilly, Sandra B. Dunbar, and Ike S. Okosun. "Length of residence in the United States is associated with a higher prevalence of cardiometabolic risk factors in immigrants: a contemporary analysis of the National Health Interview Survey." *Journal of the American Heart Association* 5, no. 11 (2016): e004059.

8. International Organization for Migration. "Who is a migrant?" 2019. https://www.iom.int/who-is-a-migrant.

9. Pew Research Center. "Modes of entry for the unauthorized migrant population." 2006. https://www.pewresearch.org/hispanic/2006/05/22/modes-of-entry-for-the-unauthorized-migrant-population/.

10. Drachman, Diane. "A stage-of-migration framework for service to immigrant populations." *Social Work* 37, no. 1 (1992): 68–72.

11. Saadi, Altaf, Maria-Elena De Trinidad Young, Caitlin Patler, Jeremias Leonel Estrada, and Homer Venters. "Understanding US immigration detention: Reaffirming rights and addressing social-structural determinants of health." *Health and Human Rights* 22, no. 1 (2020): 187.

12. Castañeda, Heide, Seth M. Holmes, Daniel S. Madrigal, Maria-Elena DeTrinidad Young, Naomi Beyeler, and James Quesada. "Immigration as a social determinant of health." *Annual Review of Public Health* 36 (2015): 375–92; Schütte, Stefanie, François Gemenne, Muhammad Zaman, Antoine Flahault, and Anneliese Depoux. "Connecting planetary health, climate change, and migration." *The Lancet Planetary Health* 2, no. 2 (2018): e58–e59.

13. Henkelmann, Jens-R., Sanne de Best, Carla Deckers, Katarina Jensen, Mona Shahab, Bernet Elzinga, and Marc Molendijk. "Anxiety, depression and post-traumatic stress disorder in refugees resettling in high-income countries: systematic review and meta-analysis." *BJPsych Open* 6, no. 4 (2020); Steel, Zachary, Tien Chey, Derrick Silove, Claire Marnane, Richard A. Bryant, and Mark Van Ommeren. "Association of torture and other potentially traumatic events with mental health outcomes among populations exposed to mass conflict and displacement: A systematic review and meta-analysis." *JAMA* 302, no. 5 (2009): 537–49.

14. Moreno, A., and M. A. Grodin. "Torture and its neurological sequelae." *Spinal cord* 40, no. 5 (2002): 213–23; McMurry, Hannah S., Darren C. Tsang, Nicole Lin, Stephen N. Symes, Chuanhui Dong, and Teshamae S. Monteith. "Head injury and neuropsychiatric sequelae in asylum seekers." *Neurology* 95, no. 19 (2020): e2605–e2609.

15. Ferris, Elizabeth. "When refugee displacement drags on, is self-reliance the answer?" *Brookings Institute* (2018): 1–3.

16. Pumariega, Andres J, and Eugenio Rothe. "Leaving no children or families outside: The challenges of immigration." *The American journal of Orthopsychiatry* 80, no. 4 (2010): 505–15; Willen, Sarah S., Michael Knipper, César E. Abadía-Barrero, and Nadav Davidovitch. "Syndemic vulnerability and the right to health." *The Lancet* 389, no. 10072 (2017): 964–77.

17. Pumariega, Andres J, and Eugenio Rothe. "Leaving no children or families outside: the challenges of immigration." *The American Journal of Orthopsychiatry* 80, no. 4 (2010): 505–15.

18. Yoshikawa, Hirokazu, and Ariel Kalil. "The effects of parental undocumented status on the developmental contexts of young children in immigrant families." *Child Development Perspectives* 5, no. 4 (2011): 291–97; Walsemann, Katrina M., Annie Ro, and Gilbert C. Gee. "Trends in food insecurity among California residents from 2001 to 2011: Inequities at the intersection of immigration status and ethnicity." *Preventive Medicine* 105 (2017): 142–48.

19. Bustamante, Arturo Vargas, Hai Fang, Jeremiah Garza, Olivia Carter-Pokras, Steven P. Wallace, John A. Rizzo, and Alexander N. Ortega. "Variations in healthcare access and utilization among Mexican immigrants: The role of documentation status." *Journal of Immigrant and Minority Health* 14, no. 1 (2012): 146–55.

20. Perreira, Krista M., and Juan M. Pedroza. "Policies of exclusion: Implications for the health of immigrants and their children." *Annual Review of Public Health* 40 (2019): 147–66.

21. Haley, Jennifer M., Genevieve M. Kenney, Hamutal Bernstein, and Dulce Gonzalez. "One in five adults in immigrant families with children reported chilling effects on public benefit receipt in 2019." Urban Institute, *Washington, DC*, 2020.

22. Perreira, Krista M., and Juan M. Pedroza. "Policies of exclusion: Implications for the health of immigrants and their children." *Annual Review of Public Health* 40 (2019): 147–66.

23. Perreira, Krista M., and Juan M. Pedroza. "Policies of exclusion: Implications for the health of immigrants and their children." *Annual Review of Public Health* 40 (2019): 147–66.

24. Yoshikawa, Hirokazu, and Ariel Kalil. "The effects of parental undocumented status on the developmental contexts of young children in immigrant families." *Child Development Perspectives* 5, no. 4 (2011): 291–97.

25. Suárez-Orozco, Carola, Hirokazu Yoshikawa, Robert Teranishi, and Marcelo Suárez-Orozco. "Growing up in the shadows: The developmental implications of unauthorized status." *Harvard Educational Review* 81, no. 3 (2011): 438–73.

26. Eskenazi, Brenda, Carolyn A. Fahey, Katherine Kogut, Robert Gunier, Jacqueline Torres, Nancy A. Gonzales, Nina Holland, and Julianna Deardorff. "Association of perceived immigration policy vulnerability with mental and physical health among US-born Latino adolescents in California." *JAMA Pediatrics* 173, no. 8 (2019): 744–53.

27. Philbin, Morgan M., Morgan Flake, Mark L. Hatzenbuehler, and Jennifer S. Hirsch. "State-level immigration and immigrant-focused policies as drivers of Latino health disparities in the United States." *Social Science & Medicine* 199 (2018): 29–38.

28. Perreira, Krista M., and Juan M. Pedroza. "Policies of exclusion: Implications for the health of immigrants and their children." *Annual Review of Public Health* 40 (2019): 147–66.

29. Potochnick, Stephanie. "How states can reduce the dropout rate for undocumented immigrant youth: The effects of in-state resident tuition policies." *Social Science Research* 45 (2014): 18–32.

30. Swartz, Jonas J., Jens Hainmueller, Duncan Lawrence, and Maria I. Rodriguez. "Expanding prenatal care to unauthorized immigrant women and the effects on infant health." *Obstetrics and Gynecology* 130, no. 5 (2017): 938.

31. Philbin, Morgan M., Morgan Flake, Mark L. Hatzenbuehler, and Jennifer S. Hirsch. "State-level immigration and immigrant-focused policies as drivers of Latino health disparities in the United States." *Social Science & Medicine* 199 (2018): 29–38.

32. Pumariega, Andres J., and Eugenio Rothe. "Leaving no children or families outside: The challenges of immigration." *The American Journal of Orthopsychiatry* 80, no. 4 (2010): 505–15.

33. Suleman, Shazeen, Kent D. Garber, and Lainie Rutkow. "Xenophobia as a determinant of health: An integrative review." *Journal of Public Health Policy* 39, no. 4 (2018): 407–23.

34. Martinez, Omar, Elwin Wu, Theo Sandfort, Brian Dodge, Alex Carballo-Dieguez, Rogeiro Pinto, Scott Rhodes, Eva Moya, and Silvia Chavez-Baray. "Evaluating the impact of immigration policies on health status among undocumented immigrants: A systematic review." *Journal of Immigrant and Minority Health* 17, no. 3 (2015): 947–70.

35. White, Alexandre I. R. "Historical linkages: Epidemic threat, economic risk, and xenophobia." *The Lancet* 395, no. 10232 (2020): 1250–51.

36. Pumariega, Andres J., and Eugenio Rothe. "Leaving no children or families outside: The challenges of immigration." *The American Journal of Orthopsychiatry* 80, no. 4 (2010): 505–15.

37. Negi, Nalini J., Patrice Forrester, Marilyn Calderon, Katherine Esser, and Danielle Parrish. "'We are at full capacity': Social care workers persisting through work-related stress in a new immigrant settlement context in the United States." *Health & Social Care in the Community* 27, no. 5 (2019): e793–e801.

38. Sam, David L., and John W. Berry. "Acculturation: When individuals and groups of different cultural backgrounds meet." *Perspectives on Psychological Science* 5, no. 4 (2010): 472–81.

39. Yeheskel, Ariel, and Shail Rawal. "Exploring the 'patient experience' of individuals with limited English proficiency: A scoping review." *Journal of Immigrant and Minority Health* 21, no. 4 (2019): 853–78.

40. Kim, Won. "Long-term English language learners' educational experiences in the context of high-stakes accountability." *Teachers College Record* 119, no. 9 (2017): 1–32.

41. Orrenius, Pia M., and Madeline Zavodny. "Do immigrants work in riskier jobs?" *Demography* 46, no. 3 (2009): 535–51.

42. Pumariega, Andres J., and Eugenio Rothe. "Leaving no children or families outside: The challenges of immigration." *The American Journal of Orthopsychiatry* 80, no. 4 (2010): 505–15.

43. Pumariega, Andres J., and Eugenio Rothe. "Leaving no children or families outside: The challenges of immigration." *The American Journal of Orthopsychiatry* 80, no. 4 (2010): 505–15.

44. Hwang, Wei-Chin. "Acculturative family distancing: Theory, research, and clinical practice." *Psychotherapy: Theory, Research, Practice, Training* 43, no. 4 (2006): 397.

45. Linton, Julie M., Ricky Choi, and Fernando Mendoza. "Caring for children in immigrant families: Vulnerabilities, resilience, and opportunities." *Pediatric Clinics* 63, no. 1 (2016): 115–30.

46. Shor, Eran, David Roelfs, and Zoua M. Vang. "The 'Hispanic mortality paradox' revisited: Meta-analysis and meta-regression of life-course differentials in Latin American and Caribbean immigrants' mortality." *Social Science & Medicine* 186 (2017): 20–33; Alarcón, Renato D., Amrita Parekh, Milton L. Wainberg, Cristiane S. Duarte, Ricardo Araya, and María A. Oquendo. "Hispanic immigrants in the USA: Social and mental health perspectives." *The Lancet Psychiatry* 3, no. 9 (2016): 860–70.

47. Marks, Amy K., Kida Ejesi, and Cynthia García Coll. "Understanding the US immigrant paradox in childhood and adolescence." *Child Development Perspectives* 8, no. 2 (2014): 59–64.

48. Perreira, Krista M., and Juan M. Pedroza. "Policies of exclusion: Implications for the health of immigrants and their children." *Annual Review of Public Health* 40 (2019): 147–66; Marks, Amy K., Kida Ejesi, and Cynthia García Coll. "Understanding the US immigrant paradox in childhood and adolescence." *Child Development Perspectives* 8, no. 2 (2014): 59–64.

49. Cook, Benjamin, Margarita Alegría, Julia Y. Lin, and Jing Guo. "Pathways and correlates connecting Latinos' mental health with exposure to the United States." *American Journal of Public Health* 99, no. 12 (2009): 2247–54.

50. Perreira, Krista M., and Juan M. Pedroza. "Policies of exclusion: Implications for the health of immigrants and their children." *Annual Review of Public Health* 40 (2019): 147–66.

51. Moinester, Margot. "Beyond the border and into the heartland: Spatial patterning of US immigration detention." *Demography* 55, no. 3 (2018): 1147–93.

52. Saadi, Altaf, Maria-Elena De Trinidad Young, Caitlin Patler, Jeremias Leonel Estrada, and Homer Venters. "Understanding US immigration detention: Reaffirming rights and addressing social-structural determinants of health." *Health and Human Rights* 22, no. 1 (2020): 187.

53. Potochnick, Stephanie, Jen-Hao Chen, and Krista Perreira. "Local-level immigration enforcement and food insecurity risk among Hispanic immigrant families with children: National-level evidence." *Journal of Immigrant and Minority Health* 19, no. 5 (2017): 1042–49.

54. Saadi, Altaf, Maria-Elena De Trinidad Young, Caitlin Patler, Jeremias Leonel Estrada, and Homer Venters. "Understanding US immigration detention: Reaffirming

rights and addressing social-structural determinants of health." *Health and Human Rights* 22, no. 1 (2020): 187.

55. Perreira, Krista M., and Juan M. Pedroza. "Policies of exclusion: Implications for the health of immigrants and their children." *Annual Review of Public Health* 40 (2019): 147–66.

56. Hacker, Karen, Jocelyn Chu, Carolyn Leung, Robert Marra, Alex Pirie, Mohamed Brahimi, Margaret English, Joshua Beckmann, Dolores Acevedo-Garcia, and Robert P. Marlin. "The impact of immigration and customs enforcement on immigrant health: Perceptions of immigrants in Everett, Massachusetts, USA." *Social Science & Medicine* 73, no. 4 (2011): 586–94.

57. Lopez, William D., Daniel J. Kruger, Jorge Delva, Mikel Llanes, Charo Ledón, Adreanne Waller, Melanie Harner, et al. "Health implications of an immigration raid: Findings from a Latino community in the Midwestern United States." *Journal of Immigrant and Minority Health* 19, no. 3 (2017): 702–08.

58. Novak, Nicole L., Arline T. Geronimus, and Aresha M. Martinez-Cardoso. "Change in birth outcomes among infants born to Latina mothers after a major immigration raid." *International Journal of Epidemiology* 46, no. 3 (2017): 839–49.

59. Vargas, Edward D. "Immigration enforcement and mixed-status families: The effects of risk of deportation on Medicaid use." *Children and Youth Services Review* 57 (2015): 83–89.

60. Vargas, Edward D., and Maureen A. Pirog. "Mixed-status families and WIC uptake: The effects of risk of deportation on program use." *Social Science Quarterly* 97, no. 3 (2016): 555–72.

61. Pedraza, Franciso I., Vanessa Cruz Nichols, and Alana MW LeBrón. "Cautious citizenship: The deterring effect of immigration issue salience on healthcare use and bureaucratic interactions among Latino US citizens." *Journal of Health Politics, Policy and Law* 42, no. 5 (2017): 925–60; Asad, Asad L. "Latinos' deportation fears by citizenship and legal status, 2007 to 2018." *Proceedings of the National Academy of Sciences* 117, no. 16 (2020): 8836–44.

62. Alvarez, P. "5,200 people in ICE custody quarantined for exposure to mumps or chicken pox." CNN, 2019.

63. Meyer, Jaimie P., Carlos Franco-Paredes, Parveen Parmar, Faiza Yasin, and Matthew Gartland. "COVID-19 and the coming epidemic in US immigration detention centres." *The Lancet Infectious Diseases* 20, no. 6 (2020): 646–48.

64. Bochenek, Michael. *In the freezer: Abusive conditions for women and children in US immigration holding cells.* New York: Human Rights Watch, 2018.

65. Wong, Tom, Sebastian Bonilla, and Anna Coleman. "Seeking asylum: Part 1." U.S. Immigration Policy Center, August 28, 2019. https://usipc.ucsd.edu/publications/usipc-seeking-asylum-part-1-final.pdf.

66. Venters, Homer D., and Allen S. Keller. "The immigration detention health plan: An acute care model for a chronic care population." *Journal of Healthcare for the Poor and Underserved* 20, no. 4 (2009): 951–57; Venters, Homer D., Mary Foote, and Allen S. Keller. "Medical advocacy on behalf of detained immigrants." *Journal of Immigrant and Minority Health* 13, no. 3 (2011): 625–28.

67. Venters, Homer D., Mary Foote, and Allen S. Keller. "Medical advocacy on behalf of detained immigrants." *Journal of Immigrant and Minority Health* 13, no. 3 (2011): 625–28.

68. Dickerson, Caitlin. "Inquiry ordered into claims immigrants had unwanted gynecology procedures." *The New York Times*, 2020.

69. Torrey, Philip L. "Rethinking immigration's mandatory detention regime: Politics, profit, and the meaning of custody." *U. Mich. JL Reform* 48 (2014): 879.

70. Saadi, Altaf, and Lello Tesema. "Privatisation of immigration detention facilities." *The Lancet* 393, no. 10188 (2019): 2299.

71. Saadi, Altaf, Maria-Elena De Trinidad Young, Caitlin Patler, Jeremias Leonel Estrada, and Homer Venters. "Understanding US immigration detention: Reaffirming rights and addressing social-structural determinants of health." *Health and Human Rights* 22, no. 1 (2020): 187.

72. Saadi, Altaf, Maria-Elena De Trinidad Young, Caitlin Patler, Jeremias Leonel Estrada, and Homer Venters. "Understanding US immigration detention: Reaffirming rights and addressing social-structural determinants of health." *Health and Human Rights* 22, no. 1 (2020): 187.

73. Office of Inspector General. "DHS lacked technology needed to successfully account for separated migrant families." Homeland Security, November 25, 2019. https://www.oig.dhs.gov/sites/default/files/assets/2019-11/OIG-20-06-Nov19.pdf.

74. Attansasio, Cedar, Garance Burke, and Martha Mendoza. "Lawyers: 250 children held in bad conditions at Texas border." Associated Press, 2019. https://apnews.com/article/texas-immigration-us-news-ap-top-news-border-patrols-a074f375e643408cb9b8d1a5fc5acf6a.

75. MacLean, Sarah A., Priscilla O. Agyeman, Joshua Walther, Elizabeth K. Singer, Kim A. Baranowski, and Craig L. Katz. "Mental health of children held at a United States immigration detention center." *Social Science & Medicine* 230 (2019): 303–8; von Werthern, Martha, Katy Robjant, Zoe Chui, Rachel Schon, Livia Ottisova, Claire Mason, and Cornelius Katona. "The impact of immigration detention on mental health: a systematic review." *BMC Psychiatry* 18, no. 1 (2018): 1–19; Keller, Allen S., Barry Rosenfeld, Chau Trinh-Shevrin, Chris Meserve, Emily Sachs, Jonathan A. Leviss, Elizabeth Singer, et al. "Mental health of detained asylum seekers." *The Lancet* 362, no. 9397 (2003): 1721–23.

76. Rousseau, Cécile, and Rochelle L. Frounfelker. "Mental health needs and services for migrants: An overview for primary care providers." *Journal of Travel Medicine* 26, no. 2 (2019): tay150.

77. Cleveland, Janet, Rachel Kronick, Hanna Gros, and Cécile Rousseau. "Symbolic violence and disempowerment as factors in the adverse impact of immigration detention on adult asylum seekers' mental health." *International Journal of Public Health* 63, no. 8 (2018): 1001–08.

78. Human Rights Watch. "Deported to danger: United States deportation policies expose Salvadorans to death and abuse." February 5, 2020. https://www.hrw.org/sites/default/files/report_pdf/elsalvador0220_web_0.pdf.

79. Artiga, Samantha, and Barbara Lyons. "Family consequences of detention/deportation: Effects on finances, health, and well being." Henry J. Kaiser Family Foundation, San Francisco, CA, 2018.

80. Morris, Juliana E., and Daniel Palazuelos. "The health implications of deportation policy." *Journal of Healthcare for the Poor and Underserved* 26, no. 2 (2015): 406–9.

81. Macías, Luis Fernando, and Bruce Anthony Collet. "Separated by removal: The impact of parental deportation on Latina/o children's postsecondary educational goals." *Diaspora, Indigenous, and Minority Education* 10, no. 3 (2016): 169–81.

82. Patler C. "Blurring the borders of stigma: Socioeconomic reintegration among noncitizens following imprisonment." Presentation at UC Davis Hemispheric Institute on the Americas, University of California, Davis, 2018.

83. National Center for Injury Prevention and Control, Division of Violence Prevention. "The Social-Ecological Model: A framework for prevention." U.S. Department of Health and Human Services, January 28, 2021. https://www.cdc.gov/violenceprevention/about/social-ecologicalmodel.html.

84. Berlinger, Nancy, and Rachel L. Zacharias. "Resources for teaching and learning about immigrant healthcare in health professions education." *AMA Journal of Ethics* 21, no. 1 (2019): 50–57.

85. National Immigration Law Center. "Health care." 2021. https://www.nilc.org/issues/health-care/.

86. Doctors for Immigrants. "Our work." 2021. http://doctorsforimmigrants.com/ourwork/.

87. Costa, Daniel. "California leads the way: A look at California laws that help protect labor standards for unauthorized immigrant workers." Economic Policy Institute, 2018. https://www.epi.org/publication/california-immigrant-labor-laws.

## CHAPTER 10

1. Nair, Aparna. "Public health campaigns and the 'threat' of disability." Wellcome Collection, September 8, 2020. https://wellcomecollection.org/articles/X1YhrRAAAEt_izkW.

2. Aubrecht, Katie, Christine Kelly, and Carla Rice, eds. *The aging–disability nexus.* Vancouver: UBC Press, 2020; Huang, Ya-Lin A., Emma L. Frazier, Stephanie L. Sansom, Paul G. Farnham, Ram K. Shrestha, Angela B. Hutchinson, Jennifer L. Fagan, Abigail H. Viall, and Jacek Skarbinski. "Nearly half of US adults living with HIV received federal disability benefits in 2009." *Health Affairs* 34, no. 10 (2015): 1657–65.

3. Greenhalgh, Trisha, Matthew Knight, Maria Buxton, and Laiba Husain. "Management of post-acute covid-19 in primary care." *BMJ* 370 (2020).

4. UCLA Office of Information Technology. "Is COVID-19 a mass disabling event?" https://dcp.ucla.edu/covid-19-mass-disabling-event.

5. Bailey, Moya, and Izetta Autumn Mobley. "Work in the intersections: A black feminist disability framework." *Gender & Society* 33, no. 1 (2019): 19–40.

6. Mintz, Susannah B. *Unruly bodies: Life writing by women with disabilities.* Raleigh: University of North Carolina Press, 2007.

7. Mintz, Susannah B. *Unruly bodies: Life writing by women with disabilities.* Raleigh: University of North Carolina Press, 2007.

8. Crear-Perry, Joia. "You can't have quality without equity." March 18, 2020. http://www.ihi.org/communities/blogs/you-can-t-have-quality-without-equity.

9. Bailey, Moya. "Work in the intersections: A Black feminist disability framework." *Moya Bailey.* October 16, 2018. https://www.moyabailey.com/2018/10/16/work-in-the intersections-a-black-feminist-disability-framework/.

10. Bailey, Moya, and Izetta Autumn Mobley. "Work in the intersections: A black feminist disability framework." *Gender & Society* 33, no. 1 (2019): 19–40.

11. Bailey, Moya, and Izetta Autumn Mobley. "Work in the intersections: A black feminist disability framework." *Gender & Society* 33, no. 1 (2019): 19–40.

12. Fodeman, Jason, and Phil Factor. "Solutions to the primary care physician shortage." *The American Journal of Medicine* 128, no. 8 (2015): 800–801.

13. Berenbrok, Lucas A., Nico Gabriel, Kim C. Coley, and Inmaculada Hernandez. "Evaluation of frequency of encounters with primary care physicians vs visits to community pharmacies among Medicare beneficiaries." *JAMA Network Open* 3, no. 7 (2020): e209132–e209132.

14. Herkert, Darby, Pavithra Vijayakumar, Jing Luo, Jeremy I. Schwartz, Tracy L. Rabin, Eunice DeFilippo, and Kasia J. Lipska. "Cost-related insulin underuse among patients with diabetes." *JAMA Internal Medicine* 179, no. 1 (2019): 112–14.

15. Bustillo, Yolanda, and Rachel Perler. "Balancing health care rationing and disability rights in a pandemic." January 15, 2021. https://blog.petrieflom.law.harvard.edu/2021/01/15/health-care-rationing-disability-rights-covid/.

16. Davis, Elizabeth. "How healthcare rationing in the United States affects even you." Verywell Health, April 17, 2021. https://www.verywellhealth.com/how-health-care-rationing-in-the-us-affects-even-you-1738482.

17. Joy, Kevin. "'A seat at the table': Why U-M's medical school wants more students with disabilities." University of Michigan Office of Diversity, Equity and Inclusion, October 12, 2017. https://labblog.uofmhealth.org/med-u/a-seat-at-table-why-u-ms-medical-school-wants-more-students-disabilities.

18. Shpigelman, Carmit-Noa, Cheryl Zlotnick, and Rachel Brand. "Attitudes toward nursing students with disabilities: Promoting social inclusion." *Journal of Nursing Education* 55, no. 8 (2016): 441–49; Calloway, Kristy, and Darcy Copeland. "Acute care nurses' attitudes toward nursing students with disabilities: A focused ethnography." *Nurse Education in Practice* 51 (2021): 102960.

19. Mehta, Swapnil S., and Matthew L. Edwards. "Suffering in silence: Mental health stigma and physicians' licensing fears." *American Journal of Psychiatry Residents* (2018).

20. Bakhamis, Lama, David P. Paul III, Harlan Smith, and Alberto Coustasse. "Still an epidemic: The burnout syndrome in hospital registered nurses." *The Healthcare Manager* 38, no. 1 (2019): 3–10; Chesnut, Renae J., Iqbal I. Atcha, Duc P. Do, Kristopher Harrell, Amy Holland, Monica L. Miller, Kelly M. Shields, et al. "Report of

the 2016–2017 student affairs standing committee." *American Journal of Pharmaceutical Education* 81, no. 8 (2017).

21. Wong, Alice, ed. *Disability visibility: First-person stories from the twenty-first century*. New York: Vintage, 2020.

22. Mattson, Jeremy. "Transportation, distance, and healthcare utilization for older adults in rural and small urban areas." *Transportation research record* 2265, no. 1 (2011): 192–99; Gaskin, Darrell J., Gniesha Y. Dinwiddie, Kitty S. Chan, and Rachael R. McCleary. "Residential segregation and the availability of primary care physicians." *Health Services Research* 47, no. 6 (2012): 2353–76.

23. U.S. Department of Justice. "Access to medical care for individuals with mobility disabilities." July 2010. https://www.ada.gov/medcare_mobility_ta/medcare_ta.htm.

24. Bureau of Internet Accessibility. "Why web accessibility is important to hospitals." May 17, 2018. https://www.boia.org/blog/why-web-accessibility-is-important-to-hospitals.

25. McCarthy, Sean, Dylana Moore, W. Andrew Smedley, Brandon M. Crowley, Shannon W. Stephens, Russell L. Griffin, Lauren C. Tanner, and Jan O. Jansen. "Impact of rural hospital closures on health-care access." *Journal of Surgical Research* 258 (2021): 170–78.

26. Lu, Wendy. "Emily Barker wants accessibility to become the norm." *The Huffington Post*. https://www.huffpost.com/entry/emily-barker-accessibility-art-fashion-world_n_6021ff7bc5b6f38d06e68557.

27. HUD User. "Assessing the accessibility of America's housing stock for physically disabled persons." https://www.huduser.gov/portal/pdredge/pdr_edge_research_101315.html.

28. Franklin, April. "Accessible housing still tough to find 30 years after Americans with Disabilities Act." WXXI News, January 28, 2021. https://www.wxxinews.org/post/accessible-housing-still-tough-find-30-years-after-americans-disabilities-act.

29. Mitra, Sophie, Michael Palmer, Hoolda Kim, Daniel Mont, and Nora Groce. "Extra costs of living with a disability: A review and agenda for research." *Disability and Health Journal* 10, no. 4 (2017): 475–84.

30. Evans, Dominick. "Life with a disability is seriously expensive," June 30, 2015. https://www.dominickevans.com/2015/06/life-with-a-disability-is-seriously-expensive/.

31. Lee, Anna, Kanan Shah, and Fumiko Chino. "Assessment of parking fees at National Cancer Institute–designated cancer treatment centers." *JAMA Oncology* 6, no. 8 (2020): 1295–97.

32. Flynn, Caitlin. "For years, doctors told me anxiety was making me sick, then I was diagnosed with lupus." Popsugar.com, May 4, 2020. https://www.popsugar.com/fitness/Why-Took-Years-Me-Diagnosed-Lupus-46093200.

33. Bureau of Internet Accessibility. "Disability statistics in the United States." November 29, 2018. https://www.boia.org/blog/disability-statistics-in-the-united-states.

34. Shanell Thompson. "Looking at race, poverty and disability." National Disability Institute, November 29, 2018. https://www.nationaldisabilityinstitute.org/blog/looking-at-race-poverty-and-disability/.

35. Cornell, Stephen. *Indigenous peoples, poverty and self-determination in Australia, New Zealand, Canada and the United States*. Tuscon, AZ: Native Nations Institute for Leadership, Management, and Policy, 2006.

36. Patterson, Emmett, Margaret Hughes, Andrew Cray, and Hannah Hussey. "Disability justice is LGBT justice: A conversation with movement leaders." Center for American Progress. July 30, 2015. https://www.americanprogress.org/issues/lgbtq rights/news/2015/07/30/118531/disability-justice-is-lgbt-justice-a-conversation-with -movement leaders/.

37. Miserandino, Christine. "The spoon theory." *But you dont look sick? Support for those with invisible illness or chronic illness* (blog). April 25, 2013. https://butyoudont looksick.com/articles/written-by-christine/the-spoon-theory/; Peterson, Ashley L. "Applying spoon theory to mental illness." Mental health @ home. January 28, 2019. https://mentalhealthathome.org/2019/01/28/spoon-theory-mental-illness/.

38. Pulrang, Andrew. "A simple fix for one of disabled people's most persistent, pointless injustices." *Forbes*. August 31, 2020. https://www.forbes.com/sites /andrewpulrang/2020/08/31/a-simple-fix-for-one-of-disabled-peoples-most-persis tent-pointless-injustices/?sh=2a817d9b6b71.

39. Stasio, B. J. "'People with disabilities and the federal marriage penalties.' Impact feature issue on sexuality and people with intellectual, developmental and other disabilities, Spring/Summer 2010." https://publications.ici.umn.edu/impact/23-2 /people-with-disabilities-and-the-federal-marriage-penalties.

40. Wong, Warren. "How to honor patients' lived experience: Learning from community based organizations." July 18, 2017. http://www.ihi.org/communities/blogs/how -to-honor-patients-lived-experience-learning-from-community-based-organizations.

41. Fassler, Joe. "How doctors take women's pain less seriously." *The Atlantic* 15 (2015); Trawalter, Sophie. "Black Americans are systematically under-treated for pain. Why?" Frank Batten School of Leadership and Public Policy. June 30, 2020. https:// batten.virginia.edu/about/news/black-americans-are-systematically-under-treated -pain-why; Zhang, Sarah. "The long history of discrimination in pain medicine." *The Atlantic* (2017).

42. Marquisele, Mercedes. "Twitter/ @marquisele: The priority is to sever the link between healthfulness and inherent worth, between healthfulness and moral alignment, between the relentless pursuit of health and the right to be treated with respect. (4/x)." May 11, 2021, 9:36 AM.

43. Goldberg, Daniel S. "Social justice, health inequalities and methodological individualism in US health promotion." *Public Health Ethics* 5, no. 2 (2012): 104–15; Woolf, Steven H., and Paula Braveman. "Where health disparities begin: The role of social and economic determinants—and why current policies may make matters worse." *Health Affairs* 30, no. 10 (2011): 1852–59.

44. Crear-Perry, Joia, Rosaly Correa-de-Araujo, Tamara Lewis Johnson, Monica R. McLemore, Elizabeth Neilson, and Maeve Wallace. "Social and structural determinants of health inequities in maternal health." *Journal of Women's Health* 30, no. 2 (2021): 230–35.

45. Cottom, Tressie McMillan, Roxane Gay, Sabrina Strings, and Sonya Renee Taylor. "The fat tax." Hear to slay. 56:03-56:34. February 9, 2021. https://luminary podcasts.com/listen/roxane-gay-and-dr-tressie%20mcmillan-cottom/hear-to-slay/the -fat-tax/a5495e99-fc26-47ee-89bc-e1faf4b921da?country=US.

46. D'Ignazio, Catherine, and Lauren Klein. "The power chapter." *Data feminism*, March 20, 2020. https://data-feminism.mitpress.mit.edu/pub/vi8obxh7/release/3.

47. Marquisele, Mercedes. "Twitter/ @marquisele: * = health is a loaded af ideal and I agree with @DashaunLH's view that Black/fat/disabled/queer/trans bodies cannot be healthy because "health" exists in inherent opposition to these embodiments; it is an exclusionary construct. (5/x) May 11, 2021, 9:39 AM.

48. Nair, Aparna. "Public health campaigns and the 'threat' of disability." Wellcome Collection. September 8, 2020. https://wellcomecollection.org/articles/X1Yhr RAAAEt_izkW; Strings, Sabrina. *Fearing the black body: The racial origins of fat phobia.* New York: NYU Press, 2019.

49. Powers, George M., Lex Frieden, and Vinh Nguyen. "Telemedicine: Access to healthcare for people with disabilities." *Houston Journal of Health Law & Policy* 17 (2017): 7.

50. Young, Daniel, and Elizabeth Edwards. "Telehealth and disability: Challenges and opportunities for care." National Health Law Program. May 6, 2020. https:// healthlaw.org/telehealth-and-disability-challenges-and-opportunities-for-care/.

51. Thomas, Stephanie. "Adapt rides again in Phoenix." *Incitement, incitement,* Spring 1987. https://adapt.org/wp-content/uploads/2017/04/incit03-2.pdf.

52. Hall, Michelle Flaum, and Scott E. Hall. "When treatment becomes trauma: Defining, preventing, and transforming medical trauma." *America Counseling Association* 73 (2013).

53. Vidal-Alaball, Josep, Ruthy Acosta-Roja, Nuria Pastor Hernández, Unai Sanchez Luque, Danielle Morrison, Silvia Narejos Pérez, Jesús Perez-Llano, Angels Salvador Vèrges, and Francesc López Seguí. "Telemedicine in the face of the COVID-19 pandemic." *Atencion primaria* 52, no. 6 (2020): 418–22.

54. Aubrecht, Katie, Christine Kelly, and Carla Rice, eds. *The aging–disability nexus.* Vancouver: UBC Press, 2020.

55. Anderson, Monica, and Andrew Perrin. 2017. "Disabled Americans less likely to use technology." Pew Research Center. https://www.pewresearch.org/fact-tank /2017/04/07/disabled-americans-are-less-likely-to-use-technology/.

56. Roberts, Eric T., and Ateev Mehrotra. "Assessment of disparities in digital access among Medicare beneficiaries and implications for telemedicine." *JAMA Internal Medicine* 180, no. 10 (2020): 1386–89.

57. Weeks, Elizabeth. "Medicalization of rural poverty: Challenges for access." *The Journal of Law, Medicine & Ethics* 46, no. 3 (2018): 651–57.

58. Greenberg, Alexandra J., Danielle Haney, Kelly D. Blake, Richard P. Moser, and Bradford W. Hesse. "Differences in access to and use of electronic personal health information between rural and urban residents in the United States." *The Journal of Rural Health* 34 (2018): s30–s38.

59. Shinohara, Kristen, Cynthia L. Bennett, and Jacob O. Wobbrock. "How designing for people with and without disabilities shapes student design thinking." *Proceedings of the 18th International ACM SIGACCESS Conference on Computers and Accessibility* (2016): 229–37.

60. Newell, Alan F., Peter Gregor, Maggie Morgan, Graham Pullin, and Catriona Macaulay. "User-sensitive inclusive design." *Universal Access in the Information Society* 10, no. 3 (2011): 235–43.

61. Annaswamy, Thiru M., Monica Verduzco-Gutierrez, and Lex Frieden. "Tele-medicine barriers and challenges for persons with disabilities: COVID-19 and beyond." *Disability and Health Journal* 13, no. 4 (2020): 100973.

62. Weeks, Elizabeth. "Medicalization of rural poverty: Challenges for access." *The Journal of Law, Medicine & Ethics* 46, no. 3 (2018): 651–57.

63. Girma, Haben. 2021. "Avoid AccessiBe and other companies claiming quick and easy AI accessibility." May 5, 2021. https://www.youtube.com/watch?v=R12Z1Sp-u4U; Glaser, April. "Blind people, advocates slam company claiming to make websites ADA compliant." May 9, 2021. https://www.nbcnews.com/tech/innovation/blind-people-advocates-slam-company-claiming-make-websites-ada-compliant-n1266720.

64. Hsieh, Elaine. "Not just 'getting by': Factors influencing providers' choice of interpreters." *Journal of General Internal Medicine* 30, no. 1 (2015): 75–82.

65. Crezee, Ineke H. M., and Cynthia E. Roat. "Bilingual patient navigator or healthcare interpreter: What's the difference and why does it matter?" *Cogent Medicine* 6, no. 1 (2019): 181087776.

66. Freeman, Harold P., and Rian L. Rodriguez. "History and principles of patient navigation." *Cancer* 117, no. S15 (2011): 3537–40.

67. Donovan, Joan. "Twitter/ @BostonJoan: What I mean is that technology is a process, not a product. Facebook will come and go and so will Google and Twitter. Researchers have to see the horizon and then anticipate (as @alondra teaches) what comes next. History is the guide, social science our compass." April 21, 2021, 9:03 AM. https://twitter.com/BostonJoan/status/1384855329096282112.

68. Langmuir, Alexander D. "The surveillance of communicable diseases of national importance." *New England Journal of Medicine* 268, no. 4 (1963): 182–92.

69. Nsubuga, P., M. E. White, S. B. Thacker, et al. "Public health surveillance: A tool for targeting and monitoring interventions." In D. T. Jamison, J. G. Breman, A. R. Measham, et al., (Eds.). *Disease control priorities in developing countries.* Second edition. Washington, DC: The International Bank for Reconstruction and Development /The World Bank, 2006.

70. Kanwal, Tehsin, Adeel Anjum, and Abid Khan. "Privacy preservation in e-health cloud: Taxonomy, privacy requirements, feasibility analysis, and opportunities." *Cluster Computing* 24, no. 1 (2021): 293–317.

71. McCallister, Erika, Tim Grance, and Karen Scarfone. *Guide to protecting the confidentiality of personally identifiable information.* Gaithersburg, MD: National Institute of Standards and Technology, 2010.

72. Onik, Md Mehedi Hassan, Nasr Al-Zaben, Jinhong Yang, Nam-Yong Lee, and Chul-Soo Kim. "Risk identification of personally identifiable information from col-

lective mobile app data." *2018 International Conference on Computing, Electronics & Communications Engineering (iCCECE)* (2018): 71–76.

73. Abad, Zahra Shakeri Hossein, Adrienne Kline, Madeena Sultana, Mohammad Noaeen, Elvira Nurmambetova, Filipe Lucini, Majed Al-Jefri, and Joon Lee. "Digital public health surveillance: A systematic scoping review." *NPJ Digital Medicine* 4, no. 1 (2021): 1–13.

74. World Health Organization. "WHO guidelines on ethical issues in public health surveillance." New York, 2017.

75. World Health Organization. "WHO guidelines on ethical issues in public health surveillance." New York, 2017.

76. Harris, L. "The new national mental health crisis line wants to track your location." Disability Visibility Project. April 19, 2021. https://disabilityvisibilityproject.com/2021/04/19/the-new-national-mental-health-crisis-line-wants-to-track-your-location/.

77. Chen, Angela. "What happens when life insurance companies track fitness data?" *The Verge*, September 26, 2018. https://www.theverge.com/2018/9/26/17905390/john-hancock-life-insurance-fitness-tracker-wearables-science-health.

78. Ross, Casey. "Hospitals are using AI to predict the decline of Covid-19 patients—before knowing it works." *STAT*, April 24, 2020. https://www.statnews.com/2020/04/24/coronavirus-hospitals-use-ai-to-predict-patient-decline-before-knowing-it-works/#:~:text=Dozens%20of%20hospitals%20across,those%20with%20the%20new%20disease.

79. Chacko, Anil, and Thaier Hayajneh. "Security and privacy issues with IoT in healthcare." *EAI Endorsed Transactions on Pervasive Health and Technology* 4, no. 14 (2018).

80. Hall, Joseph L., and Deven McGraw. "For telehealth to succeed, privacy and security risks must be identified and addressed." *Health Affairs* 33, no. 2 (2014): 216–21.

81. Pavithra, V., and Jeyamala Chandrasekaran. "Developing security solutions for telemedicine applications: Medical image encryption and watermarking." In *Research anthology on telemedicine efficacy, adoption, and impact on healthcare delivery*, pp. 612–31. Hershey, PA: IGI Global, 2021.

82. Razali, Rina Azlin, and Norziana Jamil. "A quick review of security issues in telemedicine." *2020 8th International Conference on Information Technology and Multimedia (ICIMU)* (2020): 162–65.

## CHAPTER 11

1. National Research Council and Institute of Medicine. *Children's health, the nation's wealth: Assessing and improving child health*. Washington, DC, 2004.

2. Halfon, Neal, Kandyce Larson, Michael Lu, Ericka Tullis, and Shirley Russ. "Lifecourse health development: Past, present and future." *Maternal and Child Health Journal* 18, no. 2 (2014): 344–65; Shonkoff, Jack P., Andrew S. Garner, Benjamin S.

Siegel, Mary I. Dobbins, Marian F. Earls, Laura McGuinn, John Pascoe, David L. Wood, Committee on Psychosocial Aspects of Child and Family Health, and Committee on Early Childhood, Adoption, and Dependent Care. "The lifelong effects of early childhood adversity and toxic stress." *Pediatrics* 129, no. 1 (2012): e232–e246.

   3. Masten, Ann S., and J. Douglas Coatsworth. "The development of competence in favorable and unfavorable environments: Lessons from research on successful children." *American Psychologist* 53, no. 2 (1998): 205; Touloumakos, Anna K., and Alexia Barrable. "Adverse childhood experiences: The protective and therapeutic potential of nature." *Frontiers in Psychology* 11 (2020).

   4. Yule, Kristen, Jessica Houston, and John Grych. "Resilience in children exposed to violence: A meta-analysis of protective factors across ecological contexts." *Clinical Child and Family Psychology Review* 22, no. 3 (2019): 406–31.

   5. Dube, Shanta R., Vincent J. Felitti, Maxia Dong, Wayne H. Giles, and Robert F. Anda. "The impact of adverse childhood experiences on health problems: Evidence from four birth cohorts dating back to 1900." *Preventive Medicine* 37, no. 3 (2003): 268–77; Felitti, Vincent J., Robert F. Anda, Dale Nordenberg, David F. Williamson, Alison M. Spitz, Valerie Edwards, and James S. Marks. "Relationship of childhood abuse and household dysfunction to many of the leading causes of death in adults: The Adverse Childhood Experiences (ACE) study." *American Journal of Preventive Medicine* 14, no. 4 (1998): 245–58.

   6. Ross, Nancy, Robert Gilbert, Sara Torres, Kevin Dugas, Philip Jefferies, Sheila McDonald, Susan Savage, and Michael Ungar. "Adverse childhood experiences: Assessing the impact on physical and psychosocial health in adulthood and the mitigating role of resilience." *Child Abuse & Neglect* 103 (2020): 104440.

   7. Beck, Andrew F., Megan M. Tschudy, Tumaini R. Coker, Kamila B. Mistry, Joanne E. Cox, Benjamin A. Gitterman, Lisa J. Chamberlain, et al. "Determinants of health and pediatric primary care practices." *Pediatrics* 137, no. 3 (2016).

   8. National Academies of Sciences, Engineering, and Medicine. *A roadmap to reducing child poverty*. Washington, DC: National Academies Press, 2019.

   9. Stille, Christopher, Renee M. Turchi, Richard Antonelli, Michael D. Cabana, Tina L. Cheng, Danielle Laraque, and James Perrin. "The family-centered medical home: specific considerations for child health research and policy." *Academic Pediatrics* 10, no. 4 (2010): 211–17.

   10. Beck, Andrew F., Megan M. Tschudy, Tumaini R. Coker, Kamila B. Mistry, Joanne E. Cox, Benjamin A. Gitterman, Lisa J. Chamberlain. et al. "Determinants of health and pediatric primary care practices." *Pediatrics* 137, no. 3 (2016).

   11. Baker, Jeffrey P. "Women and the invention of well child care." *Pediatrics* 94, no. 4 (1994): 527–31.

   12. Shin, Peter, Jessica Sharac, and Sara Rosenbaum. "Community health centers and Medicaid at 50: An enduring relationship essential for health system transformation." *Health Affairs* 34, no. 7 (2015): 1096–104.

   13. Health Resources and Services Administration. "Health center program: Impact and growth." 2020. https://bphc.hrsa.gov/about/healthcenterprogram/index.html; Health Resources and Services Administration. *National Health Center Data*. 2019.

14. Lebrun-Harris, Lydie A., Judith A. Mendel Van Alstyne, and Alek Sripipatana. "Influenza vaccination among US pediatric patients receiving care from federally funded health centers." *Vaccine* 38, no. 39 (2020): 6120–26; Shi, Leiyu, Lydie A. Lebrun, Jinsheng Zhu, Arthur S. Hayashi, Ravi Sharma, Charles A. Daly, Alek Sripipatana, and Quyen Ngo-Metzger. "Clinical quality performance in US health centers." *Health Services Research* 47, no. 6 (2012): 2225–49.

15. Shin, Peter, Jessica Sharac, and Sara Rosenbaum. "Community health centers and Medicaid at 50: An enduring relationship essential for health system transformation." *Health Affairs* 34, no. 7 (2015): 1096–104.

16. Lewis, Corinne, Yaphet Getachew, Melinda Abrams, and Michelle Doty. "Changes at community health centers, and how patients are benefiting." The Commonwealth Fund, August 20, 2019. https://www.commonwealthfund.org/publica tions/issue-briefs/2019/aug/changes-at-community-health-centers-how-patients-are -benefiting.

17. Rosenbaum, Sara, Jessica Sharac, Peter Shin, and Jennifer Tolbert. "Community health center financing: The role of Medicaid and Section 330 grant funding explained." Kaiser Family Foundation, March 26, 2019. https://www.kff.org/medicaid /issue-brief/community-health-center-financing-the-role-of-medicaid-and-section -330-grant-funding-explained/.

18. Kaiser Commission on Medicaid and the Uninsured. *Emerging Medicaid accountable care organizations: The role of managed care.* https://www.kff.org/wp-content /uploads/2013/01/8319.pdf.

19. Kelleher, Kelly J., Jennifer Cooper, Katherine Deans, Pam Carr, Richard J. Brilli, Steven Allen, and William Gardner. "Cost saving and quality of care in a pediatric accountable care organization." *Pediatrics* 135, no. 3 (2015): e582–e589.

20. Chisolm, Deena J., Claire Jones, Elisabeth D. Root, Millie Dolce, and Kelly J. Kelleher. "A community development program and reduction in high-cost health care use." *Pediatrics* 146, no. 2 (2020).

21. Alley, Dawn E., Nina C. Ashford, and Ashley M. Gavin. "Payment innovations to drive improvements in pediatric care—the Integrated Care for Kids Model." *JAMA Pediatrics* 173, no. 8 (2019): 717–18.

22. Wang, Gary X., Heather R. Frank, Taruni S. Santanam, Erica Zeng, Madhulika Vulimiri, Mark McClellan, and Charlene A. Wong. "Pediatric accountable health communities: Insights on needed capabilities and potential solutions." *Healthcare* 8, no. 4 (2020): 100481..

23. Kiel, Joan M., and Laura M. Knoblauch. "HIPAA and FERPA: Competing or collaborating?" *Journal of Allied Health* 39, no. 4 (2010): 161E–165E.

24. Sherry, Melissa, Jennifer L. Wolff, Jeromie Ballreich, Eva DuGoff, Karen Davis, and Gerard Anderson. "Bridging the silos of service delivery for high-need, high-cost individuals." *Population Health Management* 19, no. 6 (2016): 421–28.

25. Perrin, James M., Greg Duncan, Angela Diaz, and Kelly Kelleher. "Principles and policies to strengthen child and adolescent health and well-being: Study describes National Academies of Sciences, Engineering, and Medicine reports on poverty,

188

mental, emotional, and behavioral health, adolescence, and young family health and education." *Health Affairs* 39, no. 10 (2020): 1677–83.

26. Alker, Joan C., Genevieve M. Kenney, and Sara Rosenbaum. "Children's health insurance coverage: Progress, problems, and priorities for 2021 and beyond: Study examines children's health insurance coverage." *Health Affairs* 39, no. 10 (2020): 1743–51.

27. Keller, David, and Lisa J. Chamberlain. "Children and the Patient Protection and Affordable Care Act: Opportunities and challenges in an evolving system." *Academic Pediatrics* 14, no. 3 (2014): 225–33.

28. Alker, Joan C., Genevieve M. Kenney, and Sara Rosenbaum. "Children's health insurance coverage: Progress, problems, and priorities for 2021 and beyond: Study examines children's health insurance coverage." *Health Affairs* 39, no. 10 (2020): 1743–51.

29. Perrin, James M., Genevieve M. Kenney, and Sara Rosenbaum. "Medicaid and child health equity." *The New England Journal of Medicine* 383, no. 27 (2020): 2595–98.

30. Association of Government Accountants. "Blended and braided funding: A guide for policy makers and practitioners." December 2014. https://www.agacgfm.org/Intergov/More-Tools/Blended-and-Braided-Funding-A-Guide-for-Policy-Ma.aspx.

31. Ader, Jeremy, Christopher J. Stille, David Keller, Benjamin F. Miller, Michael S. Barr, and James M. Perrin. "The medical home and integrated behavioral health: Advancing the policy agenda." *Pediatrics* 135, no. 5 (2015): 909–17.

32. Wang, Gary X., Heather R. Frank, Taruni S. Santanam, Erica Zeng, Madhulika Vulimiri, Mark McClellan, and Charlene A. Wong. "Pediatric accountable health communities: Insights on needed capabilities and potential solutions." *Healthcare* 8, no. 4 (2020): 100481.

33. Allison, Mandy A., and Elliott Attisha. "The link between school attendance and good health." *Pediatrics* 143, no. 2 (2019).

34. Halfon, Neal, Efren Aguilar, Lisa Stanley, Emily Hotez, Eryn Block, and Magdalena Janus. "Measuring equity from the start: Disparities in the health development of US kindergartners: Study examines disparities in the health development of US kindergartners." *Health Affairs* 39, no. 10 (2020): 1702–09.

35. Daw, J. R., K. B. Kozhimannil, and L. K. Admon. "High rates of perinatal insurance churn persist after the ACA." *Health Affairs Blog.* 2019.

36. McKinney, Jessica, Laura Keyser, Susan Clinton, and Carrie Pagliano. "ACOG Committee Opinion No. 736: Optimizing postpartum care." *Obstetrics & Gynecology* 132, no. 3 (2018): 784–85.

37. Halfon, Neal, Kandyce Larson, Michael Lu, Ericka Tullis, and Shirley Russ. "Lifecourse health development: Past, present and future." *Maternal and Child Health Journal* 18, no. 2 (2014): 344–65.

38. Conti, G., and J. J. Heckman. "Economics of child well-being." In A. Ben-Arieh, F. Casas, I. Frønes, and J. E. Korbin (Eds.). *Handbook of child well-being: Theories, methods and policies in global perspective*, pp. 363–401. Dordrecht: Springer

Netherlands, 2014; Flanagan, Patricia, Patrick M. Tigue, and James Perrin. "The value proposition for pediatric care." *JAMA Pediatrics* 173, no. 12 (2019): 1125–26.

39. Currie, Janet. "What we say and what we do: Why US investments in children's health are falling short: Study examines US investments in children's health." *Health Affairs* 39, no. 10 (2020): 1684–92.

## CHAPTER 12

1. U.S. Census Bureau. "QuickFacts: United States." 2019. https://www.census .gov/quickfacts/fact/table/US/RHI725219#qf-headnote-b.

2. Colby, Sandra L., and Jennifer M. Ortman. "Projections of the size and composition of the US population: 2014 to 2060. Population estimates and projections. Current population reports. P25-1143." U.S. Census Bureau, Washington, DC, 2015.

3. Flores, Antonio. "2015, Hispanic population in the United States statistical portrait." Pew Research Center, September 18, 2017. https://www.pewresearch.org /hispanic/2017/09/18/2015-statistical-information-on-hispanics-in-united-states/.

4. Salinas Jr., Cristobal. "The complexity of the 'x' in Latinx: How Latinx/a/o students relate to, identify with, and understand the term Latinx." *Journal of Hispanic Higher Education* 19, no. 2 (2020): 149–68.

5. Smith, David P., and Benjamin S. Bradshaw. "Rethinking the Hispanic paradox: Death rates and life expectancy for US non-Hispanic White and Hispanic populations." *American Journal of Public Health* 96, no. 9 (2006): 1686–92.

6. Smith, David P., and Benjamin S. Bradshaw. "Rethinking the Hispanic paradox: Death rates and life expectancy for US non-Hispanic White and Hispanic populations." *American Journal of Public Health* 96, no. 9 (2006): 1686–92.

7. Agency for Healthcare Research and Quality. "Improving cultural competence to reduce health disparities for priority populations." U.S. Department of Health and Human Services, July 8, 2014. https://effectivehealthcare.ahrq.gov/products/cultural-competence/research-protocol.

8. Pottie, K., A. Hadi, J. Chen, V. Welch, and K. Hawthorne. "Realist review to understand the efficacy of culturally appropriate diabetes education programmes." *Diabetic Medicine* 30, no. 9 (2013): 1017–25.

9. Chowdhary, N., A. T. Jotheeswaran, A. Nadkarni, S. D. Hollon, M. King, M. J. D. Jordans, A. Rahman, H. Verdeli, R. Araya, and V. Patel. "The methods and outcomes of cultural adaptations of psychological treatments for depressive disorders: A systematic review." *Psychological Medicine* 44, no. 6 (2014): 1131–46; County Health Rankings. "Culturally adapted health care." UW Population Health Institute, January 31, 2020. https://www.countyhealthrankings.org/take-action-to-improve-health/what -works-for-health/strategies/culturally-adapted-health-care; Kong, Angela, Lisa M. Tussing-Humphreys, Angela M. Odoms-Young, Melinda R. Stolley, and Marian L. Fitzgibbon. "Systematic review of behavioural interventions with culturally adapted

strategies to improve diet and weight outcomes in African American women." *Obesity Reviews* 15 (2014): 62–92.

10. Wear, Delese, and Lois LaCivita Nixon. "The spirit catches you and you fall down: A Hmong child, her American doctors, and the collision of two cultures: [commentary]." *Academic Medicine* 76, no. 6 (2001): 620.

11. Stubbe, Dorothy E. "Practicing cultural competence and cultural humility in the care of diverse patients." *Focus* 18, no. 1 (2020): 49–51.

12. Tervalon, Melanie, and Jann Murray-Garcia. "Cultural humility versus cultural competence: A critical distinction in defining physician training outcomes in multicultural education." *Journal of Healthcare for the Poor and Underserved* 9, no. 2 (1998): 117–25.

13. Cushman, Linda F., Marlyn Delva, Cheryl L. Franks, Ana Jimenez-Bautista, Joyce Moon-Howard, Jim Glover, and Melissa D. Begg. "Cultural competency training for public health students: Integrating self, social, and global awareness into a master of public health curriculum." *American Journal of Public Health* 105, no. S1 (2015): S132–S140.

14. Ku, Leighton, and Glenn Flores. "Pay now or pay later: Providing interpreter services in healthcare." *Health Affairs* 24, no. 2 (2005): 435–44.

15. Price-Wise, Gail. *An intoxicating error: Mistranslation, medical malpractice, and prejudice.* Cork: BookBaby, 2015.

16. Flores, Glenn, Milagros Abreu, Ilan Schwartz, and Maria Hill. "The importance of language and culture in pediatric care: Case studies from the Latino community." *The Journal of Pediatrics* 137, no. 6 (2000): 842–48; Flores, Glenn, and Emmanuel Ngui. "Racial/ethnic disparities and patient safety." *Pediatric Clinics* 53, no. 6 (2006): 1197–215.

17. CDC Vital Signs. "Hispanic health." Centers for Disease Control and Prevention, Office of Minority Health and Health Equity, May 5, 2015. https://www.cdc.gov/vitalsigns/hispanic-health/index.html; Alcalá, Héctor E., Stephanie L. Albert, Dylan H. Roby, Jacob Beckerman, Philippe Champagne, Ron Brookmeyer, Michael L. Prelip, et al. "Access to care and cardiovascular disease prevention: A cross-sectional study in 2 Latino communities." *Medicine* 94, no. 34 (2015); De Jesus, Maria, and Chenyang Xiao. "Predicting healthcare utilization among Latinos: Health locus of control beliefs or access factors?" *Health Education & Behavior* 41, no. 4 (2014): 423–30.

18. Chen, Jie, Arturo Vargas-Bustamante, Karoline Mortensen, and Alexander N. Ortega. "Racial and ethnic disparities in healthcare access and utilization under the Affordable Care Act." *Medical Care* 54, no. 2 (2016): 140; Savas, Lara S., Sally W. Vernon, John S. Atkinson, and Maria E. Fernández. "Effect of acculturation and access to care on colorectal cancer screening in low-income Latinos." *Journal of Immigrant and Minority Health* 17, no. 3 (2015): 696–703; Miller, Kimberly D., Ann Goding Sauer, Ana P. Ortiz, Stacey A. Fedewa, Paulo S. Pinheiro, Guillermo Tortolero-Luna, Dinorah Martinez-Tyson, Ahmedin Jemal, and Rebecca L. Siegel. "Cancer statistics for hispanics/latinos, 2018." *CA: A Cancer Journal for Clinicians* 68, no. 6 (2018): 425–45.

19. Armstrong, Katrina, Karima L. Ravenell, Suzanne McMurphy, and Mary Putt. "Racial/ethnic differences in physician distrust in the United States." *American Journal of Public Health* 97, no. 7 (2007): 1283–89.

20. Abraído-Lanza, Ana F., Amarilis Céspedes, Shaira Daya, Karen R. Flórez, and Kellee White. "Satisfaction with healthcare among Latinas." *Journal of Healthcare for the Poor and Underserved* 22, no. 2 (2011): 491; Sohler, Nancy Lynn, Lisa K. Fitzpatrick, Rebecca G. Lindsay, Kathryn Anastos, and Chinazo O. Cunningham. "Does patient–provider racial/ethnic concordance influence ratings of trust in people with HIV infection?" *AIDS and Behavior* 11, no. 6 (2007): 884–96; Casagrande, Sarah Stark, Tiffany L. Gary, Thomas A. LaVeist, Darrell J. Gaskin, and Lisa A. Cooper. "Perceived discrimination and adherence to medical care in a racially integrated community." *Journal of General Internal Medicine* 22, no. 3 (2007): 389–95; Benjamins, Maureen R. "Race/ethnic discrimination and preventive service utilization in a sample of whites, blacks, Mexicans, and Puerto Ricans." *Medical Care* (2012): 870–76.

21. Elder, John P., Guadalupe X. Ayala, Deborah Parra-Medina, and Gregory A. Talavera. "Health communication in the Latino community: Issues and approaches." *Annual Review of Public Health* 30 (2009): 227–51.

22. Kok, Maryse C., Marjolein Dieleman, Miriam Taegtmeyer, Jacqueline E. W. Broerse, Sumit S. Kane, Hermen Ormel, Mandy M. Tijm, and Korrie A. M. De Koning. "Which intervention design factors influence performance of community health workers in low-and middle-income countries? A systematic review." *Health Policy and Planning* 30, no. 9 (2015): 1207–27; Hartzler, Andrea L., Leah Tuzzio, Clarissa Hsu, and Edward H. Wagner. "Roles and functions of community health workers in primary care." *The Annals of Family Medicine* 16, no. 3 (2018): 240–45.

23. Kangovi, Shreya, Nandita Mitra, David Grande, Judith A. Long, and David A. Asch. "Evidence-based community health worker program addresses unmet social needs and generates positive return on investment: A return on investment analysis of a randomized controlled trial of a standardized community health worker program that addresses unmet social needs for disadvantaged individuals." *Health Affairs* 39, no. 2 (2020): 207–13.

24. Stolbach, Bradley C., and Seeba Anam. "Racial and ethnic health disparities and trauma-informed care for children exposed to community violence." *Pediatric Annals* 46, no. 10 (2017): e377–e381; Eskenazi, Brenda, Carolyn A. Fahey, Katherine Kogut, Robert Gunier, Jacqueline Torres, Nancy A. Gonzales, Nina Holland, and Julianna Deardorff. "Association of perceived immigration policy vulnerability with mental and physical health among US-born Latino adolescents in California." *JAMA Pediatrics* 173, no. 8 (2019): 744–53.

25. Singer, Margaret A., Manuela Gutierrez Velez, Scott D. Rhodes, and Julie M. Linton. "Discrimination against mixed-status families and its health impact on Latino children." *The Journal of Applied Research on Children: Informing Policy for Children at Risk* 10, no. 1 (2018).

26. Trent, M., D. G. Dooley, and J. Douge. "The impact of racism on child and adolescent health." *Pediatrics* 144, no. 2 (2019): e20191765.

27. Lee, July, Janine Bruce, and Nancy Ewen Wang. "Opportunities for supporting Latino immigrants in emergency and ambulatory care settings." *Journal of Community Health* 46, no. 3 (2021): 494–501.

28. Bridges, Ana J., Arthur R. Andrews III, Bianca T. Villalobos, Freddie A. Pastrana, Timothy A. Cavell, and Debbie Gomez. "Does integrated behavioral healthcare reduce mental health disparities for Latinos? Initial findings." *Journal of Latina/o Psychology* 2, no. 1 (2014): 37; Flynn, Amy, Erika Gaitan, Rebecca Stocker, Elizabeth Showalter, and Karen Sautter Errichetti. "Enhanced integrated behavioral health model improves depressive symptoms in a low-income, uninsured, primarily Hispanic population served by a free and charitable clinic." *International Journal of Integrated Care* 20, no. 4 (2020).

29. National Center for Health Statistics. "National health and nutrition examination durvey." U.S. Department of Health and Human Services, February 25, 2019. https://www.cdc.gov/nchs/data/factsheets/factsheet_nhanes.pdf.

30. Ogden, Cynthia L., Margaret D. Carroll, Hannah G. Lawman, Cheryl D. Fryar, Deanna Kruszon-Moran, Brian K. Kit, and Katherine M. Flegal. "Trends in obesity prevalence among children and adolescents in the United States, 1988–1994 through 2013–2014." *JAMA* 315, no. 21 (2016): 2292–99.

31. Isasi, Carmen R., Christina M. Parrinello, Guadalupe X. Ayala, Alan M. Delamater, Krista M. Perreira, Martha L. Daviglus, John P. Elder, et al. "Sex differences in cardiometabolic risk factors among Hispanic/Latino youth." *The Journal of Pediatrics* 176 (2016): 121–27.

32. Hsieh, Stephanie, Ann C. Klassen, Frank C. Curriero, Laura E. Caulfield, Lawrence J. Cheskin, Jaimie N. Davis, Michael I. Goran, Marc J. Weigensberg, and Donna Spruijt-Metz. "Built environment associations with adiposity parameters among overweight and obese Hispanic youth." *Preventive Medicine Reports* 2 (2015): 406–12.

33. Perez, Lilian G., Elva M. Arredondo, John P. Elder, Simón Barquera, Brian Nagle, and Christina K. Holub. "Evidence-based obesity treatment interventions for Latino adults in the US: A systematic review." *American Journal of Preventive Medicine* 44, no. 5 (2013): 550–60; Albert, Stephanie L., Brent A. Langellier, Mienah Z. Sharif, Alec M. Chan-Golston, Michael L. Prelip, Rosa Elena Garcia, Deborah C. Glik, Thomas R. Belin, Ron Brookmeyer, and Alexander N. Ortega. "A corner store intervention to improve access to fruits and vegetables in two Latino communities." *Public Health Nutrition* 20, no. 12 (2017): 2249–59; MacNell, Lillian, Sinikka Elliott, Annie Hardison-Moody, and Sarah Bowen. "Black and Latino urban food desert residents' perceptions of their food environment and factors that influence food shopping decisions." *Journal of Hunger & Environmental Nutrition* 12, no. 3 (2017): 375–93.

34. Salahuddin, Meliha, Adriana Pérez, Nalini Ranjit, Steven H. Kelder, Sarah E. Barlow, Stephen J. Pont, Nancy F. Butte, and Deanna M. Hoelscher. "Predictors of severe obesity in low-income, predominantly Hispanic/Latino children: The Texas childhood obesity research demonstration study." *Preventing Chronic Disease* 14 (2017): E141.

35. Kiraly, Carmen, Melanie T. Turk, Melissa A. Kalarchian, and Cheryl Shaffer. "Applying ecological frameworks in obesity intervention studies in Hispanic/Latino

youth: A systematic review." *Hispanic Health Care International* 15, no. 3 (2017): 130–42.

36. Beck, Amy L., Esti Iturralde, Julissa Haya-Fisher, Sarah Kim, Victoria Keeton, and Alicia Fernandez. "Barriers and facilitators to healthy eating among low-income Latino adolescents." *Appetite* 138 (2019): 215–22; Lindberg, Nangel M., Victor J. Stevens, Sonia Vega-López, Tia L. Kauffman, Mariana Rosales Calderón, and María Antonieta Cervantes. "A weight-loss intervention program designed for Mexican–American women: Cultural adaptations and results." *Journal of Immigrant and Minority Health* 14, no. 6 (2012): 1030–39.

37. Ogden, Cynthia L., Cheryl D. Fryar, Craig M. Hales, Margaret D. Carroll, Yutaka Aoki, and David S. Freedman. "Differences in obesity prevalence by demographics and urbanization in US children and adolescents, 2013–2016." *JAMA* 319, no. 23 (2018): 2410–18.

38. Cruz, Paulina, and Andrea Granados. "Type 2 diabetes in Latino youth: A clinical update and current challenges." *Current Problems in Pediatric and Adolescent Healthcare* 49, no. 1 (2019): 16–22. McCurley, Jessica L., Margaret A. Crawford, and Linda C. Gallo. "Prevention of type 2 diabetes in US hispanic youth: A systematic review of lifestyle interventions." *American Journal of Preventive Medicine* 53, no. 4 (2017): 519–32; Caballero, A. Enrique. "Cultural competence in diabetes mellitus care: An urgent need." *Insulin* 2, no. 2 (2007): 80–91.

39. Hill, Holly A., Laurie D. Elam-Evans, David Yankey, James A. Singleton, and Yoonjae Kang. "Vaccination coverage among children aged 19–35 months—United States, 2016." *Morbidity and Mortality Weekly Report* 66, no. 43 (2017): 1171.

40. Williams, Walter W., Peng-Jun Lu, Alissa O'Halloran, David K. Kim, Lisa A. Grohskopf, Tamara Pilishvili, Tami H. Skoff, et al. "Surveillance of vaccination coverage among adult populations—United States, 2014." *Morbidity and Mortality Weekly Report: Surveillance Summaries* 65, no. 1 (2016): 1–36; Spencer, Jennifer C., William A. Calo, and Noel T. Brewer. "Disparities and reverse disparities in HPV vaccination: A systematic review and meta-analysis." *Preventive Medicine* 123 (2019): 197–203.

41. FluVaxView. "Flu vaccination coverage, United States, 2019–20 influenza season." U.S. Department of Health and Human Services, October 1, 2020. https://www.cdc.gov/flu/fluvaxview/coverage-1920estimates.htm#additional.

42. Snyder, V. Nelly Salgado de, Deliana Garcia, Roxana Pineda, Jessica Calderon, Dania Diaz, Alondra Morales, and Brenda Perez. "Exploring why adult Mexican males do not get vaccinated: Implications for COVID-19 preventive actions." *Hispanic Journal of Behavioral Sciences* 42, no. 4 (2020): 515–27; National Academies of Sciences, Engineering and Medicine. *Strategies for building xonfidence in the COVID-19 vaccines.* Washington, DC: The National Academies Press, 2021.

43. Urquhart, Audrey, and Philippa Clarke. "US racial/ethnic disparities in childhood asthma emergent healthcare use: National Health Interview Survey, 2013–2015." *Journal of Asthma* 57, no. 5 (2020): 510–20.

44. Akinbami, Lara J., Alan E. Simon, and Lauren M. Rossen. "Changing trends in asthma prevalence among children." *Pediatrics* 137, no. 1 (2016).

45. Lara, Marielena, Lara Akinbami, Glenn Flores, and Hal Morgenstern. "Heterogeneity of childhood asthma among Hispanic children: Puerto Rican children bear a disproportionate burden." *Pediatrics* 117, no. 1 (2006): 43–53.

46. Weaver, Garrett M., and W. James Gauderman. "Traffic-related pollutants: Exposure and health effects among Hispanic children." *American Journal of Epidemiology* 187, no. 1 (2018): 45–52.

47. Arcoleo, Kimberly, Flavio Marsiglia, Denise Serebrisky, Juliana Rodriguez, Colleen Mcgovern, and Jonathan Feldman. "Explanatory model for asthma disparities in Latino children: Results from the Latino Childhood Asthma Project." *Annals of Behavioral Medicine* 54, no. 4 (2020): 223–36.

48. Carrillo, Genny, Maria J. Perez-Patron, Rose L. Lucio, Lucia Cabrera, Alyssa Trevino, Xiaohui Xu, and Nelda Mier. "The benefits and challenges of managing asthma in Hispanic families in South Texas: A mixed-methods study." *Frontiers in Public Health* 5 (2017): 150.

49. American Cancer Society. "Cancer facts and figures for Hispanics/Latinos 2018-2020." 2020. https://www.cancer.org/content/dam/cancer-org/research/cancer-facts-and-statistics/cancer-facts-and-figures-for-hispanics-and-latinos/cancer-facts-and-figures-for-hispanics-and-latinos-2018-2020.pdf.

50. Mojica, Cynthia M., Deborah Parra-Medina, and Sally Vernon. "Peer reviewed: Interventions promoting colorectal cancer screening among Latino men: A systematic review." *Preventing Chronic Disease* 15 (2018); Gorin, Sherri Sheinfeld, and Julia E. Heck. "Cancer screening among Latino subgroups in the United States." *Preventive Medicine* 40, no. 5 (2005): 515–26; Larkey, Linda K., Julie A. Gonzalez, Lily E. Mar, and Namino Glantz. "Latina recruitment for cancer prevention education via community based participatory research strategies." *Contemporary Clinical Trials* 30, no. 1 (2009): 47–54; Navarro, Ana M., Rema Raman, Lori J. McNicholas, and Oralia Loza. "Diffusion of cancer education information through a Latino community health advisor program." *Preventive Medicine* 45, no. 2-3 (2007): 135–38.

51. Substance Abuse and Mental Health Services Administration. "2019 NSDUH detailed tables." U.S. Department of Health and Human Services, September 11, 2020. https://www.samhsa.gov/data/report/2019-nsduh-detailed-tables; American Psychiatric Association. "Mental health disparities: Diverse populations." 2021. https://www.psychiatry.org/psychiatrists/cultural-competency/education/mental-health-facts.

52. Morgan, Paul L., Marianne M. Hillemeier, George Farkas, and Steve Maczuga. "Racial/ethnic disparities in ADHD diagnosis by kindergarten entry." *Journal of Child Psychology and Psychiatry* 55, no. 8 (2014): 905–13.

53. Coker, Tumaini R., Marc N. Elliott, Sara L. Toomey, David C. Schwebel, Paula Cuccaro, Susan Tortolero Emery, Susan L. Davies, Susanna N. Visser, and Mark A. Schuster. "Racial and ethnic disparities in ADHD diagnosis and treatment." *Pediatrics* 138, no. 3 (2016).

54. Linares-Orama, Nicolas, Katherine Miranda, and Annette Romero. "Identifying robust autism indicators for Latino children." *Puerto Rico Health Sciences Journal* 38, no. 2 (2019); Rothe, Eugenio M. "Considering cultural diversity in the management

of ADHD in Hispanic patients." *Journal of the National Medical Association* 97, no. 10 Suppl (2005): 17S.

55. Betancourt-Garcia, Monica M., Kristina Vatcheva, Prateek K. Gupta, Ricardo D. Martinez, Joseph B. McCormick, Susan P. Fisher-Hoch, and R. Armour Forse. "The effect of Hispanic ethnicity on surgical outcomes: An analysis of the NSQIP database." *The American Journal of Surgery* 217, no. 4 (2019): 618–33.

56. Eguia, Emanuel, Adrienne N. Cobb, Eric J. Kirshenbaum, Majid Afshar, and Paul C. Kuo. "Racial and ethnic postoperative outcomes after surgery: The Hispanic paradox." *Journal of Surgical Research* 232 (2018): 88–93.

57. Mukherjee, Debraj, Thomas Kosztowski, Hasan A. Zaidi, George Jallo, Benjamin S. Carson, David C. Chang, and Alfredo Quiñones-Hinojosa. "Disparities in access to pediatric neurooncological surgery in the United States." *Pediatrics* 124, no. 4 (2009): e688–e696.

58. Curry Jr., William T., Bob S. Carter, and Fred G. Barker. "Racial, ethnic, and socioeconomic disparities in patient outcomes after craniotomy for tumor in adult patients in the United States, 1988–2004." *Neurosurgery* 66, no. 3 (2010): 427–38.

59. Dunlap, Jonathan L., Joshua D. Jaramillo, Raji Koppolu, Robert Wright, Fernando Mendoza, and Matias Bruzoni. "The effects of language concordant care on patient satisfaction and clinical understanding for Hispanic pediatric surgery patients." *Journal of Pediatric Surgery* 50, no. 9 (2015): 1586–89.

60. Mamtora, Pragati H., Zeev N. Kain, Robert S. Stevenson, Brenda Golianu, Jeannie Zuk, Jeffrey I. Gold, and Michelle A. Fortier. "An evaluation of preoperative anxiety in Spanish-speaking and Latino children in the United States." *Pediatric Anesthesia* 28, no. 8 (2018): 719–25.

61. Jimenez, Nathalia, Ms Kristy Seidel, Lynn D. Martin, Frederick P. Rivara, and Anne M. Lynn. "Perioperative analgesic treatment in Latino and non-Latino pediatric patients." *Journal of Healthcare for the Poor and Underserved* 21, no. 1 (2010): 229.

62. Ulloa, Jesus G., Omar Viramontes, Gery Ryan, Kenneth Wells, Melinda Maggard-Gibbons, and Gerardo Moreno. "Perceptual and structural facilitators and barriers to becoming a surgeon: A qualitative study of African-American and Latino surgeons." *Academic Medicine: Journal of the Association of American Medical Colleges* 93, no. 9 (2018): 1326.

63. Abelson, Jonathan S., Natalie Z. Wong, Matthew Symer, Gregory Eckenrode, Anthony Watkins, and Heather L. Yeo. "Racial and ethnic disparities in promotion and retention of academic surgeons." *The American Journal of Surgery* 216, no. 4 (2018): 678–82.

## CHAPTER 13

1. Hargraves, Ian G., Victor M. Montori, Juan P. Brito, Marleen Kunneman, Kevin Shaw, Christina LaVecchia, Michael Wilson, Laura Walker, and Bjorg Thorsteinsdottir. "Purposeful SDM: A problem-based approach to caring for patients with shared decision making." *Patient Education and Counseling* 102, no. 10 (2019): 1786–92.

2. U.S. Census Bureau. "Detailed languages spoken at home and ability to speak English for the population 5 years and over: 2009-2013." October 2015. https://www.census.gov/data/tables/2013/demo/2009-2013-lang-tables.html; LEP.gov. "Limited English proficiency." U.S. Department of Justice, 2021. https://www.lep.gov/.

3. Rumbaut, Rubén G., and Douglas S. Massey. "Immigration and language diversity in the United States." *Daedalus* 142, no. 3 (2013): 141–54.

4. Divi, Chandrika, Richard G. Koss, Stephen P. Schmaltz, and Jerod M. Loeb. "Language proficiency and adverse events in US hospitals: A pilot study." *International Journal for Quality in Healthcare* 19, no. 2 (2007): 60–67; John-Baptiste, Ava, Gary Naglie, George Tomlinson, Shabbir MH Alibhai, Edward Etchells, Angela Cheung, Moira Kapral, et al. "The effect of English language proficiency on length of stay and in-hospital mortality." *Journal of General Internal Medicine* 19, no. 3 (2004): 221–28; Hines, Anika L., Roxanne M. Andrews, Ernest Moy, Marguerite L. Barrett, and Rosanna M. Coffey. "Disparities in rates of inpatient mortality and adverse events: Race/ethnicity and language as independent contributors." *International Journal of Environmental Research and Public Health* 11, no. 12 (2014): 13017–34.

5. Kaplan, Joshua. "Hospitals have left many COVID-19 patients who don't speak English alone, confused and without proper care." *ProPublica* (2020).

6. Fernandez, Alicia, Dean Schillinger, E. Margaret Warton, Nancy Adler, Howard H. Moffet, Yael Schenker, M. Victoria Salgado, Ameena Ahmed, and Andrew J. Karter. "Language barriers, physician-patient language concordance, and glycemic control among insured Latinos with diabetes: The Diabetes Study of Northern California (DISTANCE)." *Journal of General Internal Medicine* 26, no. 2 (2011): 170–76.

7. Diamond, Lisa, Karen Izquierdo, Dana Canfield, Konstantina Matsoukas, and Francesca Gany. "A systematic review of the impact of patient–physician non-English language concordance on quality of care and outcomes." *Journal of General Internal Medicine* 34, no. 8 (2019): 1591–606; Barton, J. L., L. Trupin, D. Schillinger, S. A. Gansky, C. Tonner, M. Margaretten, V. Chernitskiy, J. Graf, J. Imboden, and E. Yelin. "Racial and ethnic disparities in disease activity and function among persons with rheumatoid arthritis from university-affiliated clinics." *Arthritis Care & Research* 63, no. 9 (2011): 1238–46.

8. Anderson, Timothy S., Leah S. Karliner, and Grace A. Lin. "Association of primary language and hospitalization for ambulatory care sensitive conditions." *Medical Care* 58, no. 1 (2020): 45.

9. Infection Control Today. "ER visits for UTIs add almost $4 billion a year in unnecessary healthcare costs." May 6, 2013. https://www.infectioncontroltoday.com/view/er-visits-utis-add-almost-4-billion-year-unnecessary-healthcare-costs.

10. Waxman, Matthew A., and M. Andrew Levitt. "Are diagnostic testing and admission rates higher in non-English-speaking versus English-speaking patients in the emergency department?" *Annals of Emergency Medicine* 36, no. 5 (2000): 456–61; Stowell, Jeffrey R., Levi Filler, Marya S. Sabir, Albert T. Roh, and Murtaza Akhter. "Implications of language barrier on the diagnostic yield of computed tomography in pulmonary embolism." *The American Journal of Emergency Medicine* 36, no. 4 (2018): 677–79.

11. Diamond, Lisa, Karen Izquierdo, Dana Canfield, Konstantina Matsoukas, and Francesca Gany. "A systematic review of the impact of patient–physician non-English language concordance on quality of care and outcomes." *Journal of General Internal Medicine* 34, no. 8 (2019): 1591–606.

12. Karliner, Leah S., Elizabeth A. Jacobs, Alice Hm Chen, and Sunita Mutha. "Do professional interpreters improve clinical care for patients with limited English proficiency? A systematic review of the literature." *Health Services Research* 42, no. 2 (2007): 727–54.

13. Crezee, Ineke HM, and Cynthia E. Roat. "Bilingual patient navigator or healthcare interpreter: What's the difference and why does it matter?" *Cogent Medicine* 6, no. 1 (2019): 181087776.

14. Drug and Therapeutics Bulletin. "An introduction to patient decision aids." *BMJ* 23, no. 347 (2013):f4147.

15. Reuland, Daniel S., Linda K. Ko, Alicia Fernandez, Laura C. Braswell, and Michael Pignone. "Testing a Spanish-language colorectal cancer screening decision aid in Latinos with limited English proficiency: Results from a pre-post trial and four month follow-up survey." *BMC Medical Informatics and Decision Making* 12, no. 1 (2012): 1–8; Chan, Evelyn CY, Stephanie L. McFall, Theresa L. Byrd, Patricia Dolan Mullen, Robert J. Volk, John Ureda, Jessica Calderon-Mora, Pat Morales, Adriana Valdes, and L. Kay Bartholomew. "A community-based intervention to promote informed decision making for prostate cancer screening among Hispanic American men changed knowledge and role preferences: A cluster RCT." *Patient Education and Counseling* 84, no. 2 (2011): e44–e51.

16. Jibaja-Weiss, Maria L., Robert J. Volk, Thomas S. Granchi, Nancy E. Neff, Emily K. Robinson, Stephen J. Spann, Noriaki Aoki, Lois C. Friedman, and J. Robert Beck. "Entertainment education for breast cancer surgery decisions: A randomized trial among patients with low health literacy." *Patient Education and Counseling* 84, no. 1 (2011): 41–48.

17. Barton, Jennifer L., Christopher J. Koenig, Gina Evans-Young, Laura Trupin, Jennie Anderson, Dana Ragouzeos, Maggie Breslin, et al. "The design of a low literacy decision aid about rheumatoid arthritis medications developed in three languages for use during the clinical encounter." *BMC Medical Informatics and Decision Making* 14, no. 1 (2014): 1–14.

18. Sánchez, G., T. Nevarez, W. Schink, and D.E. Hayes-Bautista. "Latino physicians in the United States, 1980–2010: A thirty-year overview from the censuses." *Academic Medicine* 90, no. 7 (2015): 906–12.

19. Diamond, Lisa, Karen Izquierdo, Dana Canfield, Konstantina Matsoukas, and Francesca Gany. "A systematic review of the impact of patient–physician non-English language concordance on quality of care and outcomes." *Journal of General Internal Medicine* 34, no. 8 (2019): 1591–606.

20. Coren, Joshua S., Frank A. Filipetto, and Lucia Beck Weiss. "Eliminating barriers for patients with limited English proficiency." *The Journal of the American Osteopathic Association* 109, no. 12 (2009): 634–40.

21. Papanicolas, Irene, Liana R. Woskie, and Ashish K. Jha. "Health care spending in the United States and other high-income countries." *JAMA* 319, no. 10 (2018): 1024–39.

22. Jacobs, Elizabeth A., Donald S. Shepard, Jose A. Suaya, and Esta-Lee Stone. "Overcoming language barriers in healthcare: Costs and benefits of interpreter services." *American Journal of Public Health* 94, no. 5 (2004): 866–69.

23. Jacobs, Elizabeth A., Laura S. Sadowski, and Paul J. Rathouz. "The impact of an enhanced interpreter service intervention on hospital costs and patient satisfaction." *Journal of General Internal Medicine* 22, no. 2 (2007): 306–11.

24. Brandl, Eva J., Stefanie Schreiter, and Meryam Schouler-Ocak. "Are trained medical interpreters worth the cost? A review of the current literature on cost and cost-effectiveness." *Journal of Immigrant and Minority Health* 22, no. 1 (2020): 175–81.

25. Seattle Children's Hospital Foundation. "Seattle Children's Patient Navigator pilot and evaluation." March 13, 2013. https://www.phpda.org/projects/childrens-navigator-grant-and-clegg-evaluation-of-navigator-grant.

26. Kravitz, Richard L., L. Jay Helms, Rahman Azari, Deirdre Antonius, and Joy Melnikow. "Comparing the use of physician time and healthcare resources among patients speaking English, Spanish, and Russian." *Medical Care* (2000): 728–38.

27. Fagan, Mark J., Joseph A. Diaz, Steven E. Reinert, Christopher N. Sciamanna, and Dylan M. Fagan. "Impact of interpretation method on clinic visit length." *Journal of General Internal Medicine* 18, no. 8 (2003): 634–38.

28. Grabinski, Victoria F., Terence M. Myckatyn, Clara N. Lee, Sydney E. Philpott-Streiff, and Mary C. Politi. "Importance of shared decision-making for vulnerable populations: Examples from postmastectomy breast reconstruction." *Health Equity* 2, no. 1 (2018): 234–38.

29. Dugas, Michèle, Marie-Ève Trottier, Selma Chipenda Dansokho, Gratianne Vaisson, Thierry Provencher, Heather Colquhoun, Maman Joyce Dogba, et al. "Involving members of vulnerable populations in the development of patient decision aids: A mixed methods sequential explanatory study." *BMC Medical Informatics and Decision Making* 17, no. 1 (2017): 1–11.

30. Phillips, Christine B., and Joanne Travaglia. "Low levels of uptake of free interpreters by Australian doctors in private practice: Secondary analysis of national data." *Australian Health Review* 35, no. 4 (2011): 475–79.

31. Schenker, Yael, Eliseo J. Pérez-Stable, Dana Nickleach, and Leah S. Karliner. "Patterns of interpreter use for hospitalized patients with limited English proficiency." *Journal of General Internal Medicine* 26, no. 7 (2011): 712–17.

32. Karliner, Leah S., Elizabeth A. Jacobs, Alice Hm Chen, and Sunita Mutha. "Do professional interpreters improve clinical care for patients with limited English proficiency? A systematic review of the literature." *Health Services Research* 42, no. 2 (2007): 727–54.

33. Khoong, Elaine C., and Alicia Fernandez. "Language, culture and preventable readmissions: pragmatic, intervention studies needed." *BMJ* (2019): 859–61.

34. Nguyen, Terry. "How young people are combating anti-Black racism in their immigrant communities." Vox Media, June 22, 2020. https://www.vox.com/21295540 /second-generation-immigrants-black-lives-matter.

## CHAPTER 14

1. Centers for Disease Control and Prevention, Administration on Aging, Agency for Healthcare Research and Quality, and Centers for Medicare and Medicaid Services. "Enhancing use of clinical preventive services among older adults." https://www.cdc .gov/aging/pdf/Clinical_Preventive_Services_Closing_the_Gap_Report.pdf.
2. Young, E. H., S. Pan, A. G. Yap, K. R. Reveles, and K. Bhakta. "Polypharmacy prevalence in older adults seen in United States physician offices from 2009 to 2016." *Plos One* 16, no. 8 (2021): e0255642.
3. Shah, B. M., and E. R. Hajjar. "Polypharmacy, adverse drug reactions, and geriatric syndromes." *Clinics in Geriatric Medicine* 28, no. 2 (2012): 173–86.
4. Oscanoa, T. J., F. Lizaraso, and A. Carvajal. "Hospital admissions due to adverse drug reactions in the elderly. A meta-analysis." *European Journal of Clinical Pharmacology* 73, no. 6 (2017): 759–70.
5. Centers for Medicaid & Medicare Services. "NHE fact sheet." https://www.cms .gov/Research-Statistics-Data-and-Systems/Statistics-Trends-and-Reports/National HealthExpendData/NHE-Fact-Sheet.
6. Keehan, S. P., G. A. Cuckler, J. A. Poisal, A. M. Sisko, S. D. Smith, A. J. Madison, K. E. Rennie, J. A. Fiore, and J. C. Hardesty. "National health expenditure projections, 2019–28: Expected rebound in prices drives rising spending growth: National health expenditure projections for the period 2019–2028." *Health Affairs* 39, no. 4 (2020): 704–14.
7. Hajat, C., and E. Stein. "The global burden of multiple chronic conditions: A narrative review." *Preventive Medicine Reports* 12 (2018): 284–93.
8. Centers for Disease Control and Prevention. "Prevalence of disabilities and health care access by disability status and type among adults—United States, 2016." https://www.cdc.gov/ncbddd/disabilityandhealth/features/kf-adult-prevalence-disabil ities.html.
9. Congressional Budget Office. "Rising demand for long-term services and supports for elderly people." https://www.cbo.gov/publication/44363.
10. Burns, E., and R. Kakara. "Deaths from falls among persons aged ≥65 years—United States, 2007–2016." *MMWR* 67 (2018): 509–14.
11. United Health Foundation. "Falls—ages 65+." https://www.americashealthrank ings.org/explore/senior/measure/falls_sr/state/U.S.
12. Centers for Disease Control and Prevention. "Cost of older adult falls." https:// www.cdc.gov/falls/data/fall-cost.html#:~:text=Falls%20among%20adults%20age%20 65,spent%20related%20to%20fatal%20falls.

13. Centers for Disease Control and Prevention. "The state of mental health and aging in America." https://www.cdc.gov/aging/pdf/mental_health.pdf.

14. National Institute on Drug Abuse. "Substance use in older adults. Facts." https://www.drugabuse.gov/publications/substance-use-in-older-adults-drugfacts.

15. AARP Foundation and IMPAQ International. "Older adults and unmet social needs: Prevalence and health implications." https://impaqint.com/sites/default/files/files/SDOH%20among%20older%20adults%202017_IssueBrief_COR2.pdf.

16. National Academies of Sciences, Engineering, and Medicine. *Social isolation and loneliness in older adults: Opportunities for the health care system.* Washington, DC: National Academies Press, 2020.

17. Aronson, L. "Necessary steps: How health care fails older patients, and how it can be done better." *Health Affairs* 34, no. 3 (2015): 528–32.

18. Bernstein, J. M., P. Graven, K. Drago, K. Dobbertin, and E. Eckstrom. "Higher quality, lower cost with an innovative geriatrics consultation service." *Journal of the American Geriatrics Society* 66, no. 9 (2018): 1790–95.

19. Engel, P. A., J. Spencer, T. Paul, and J. B. Boardman. "The geriatrics in primary care demonstration: Integrating comprehensive geriatric care into the medical home: preliminary data." *Journal of the American Geriatrics Society* 64, no. 4 (2016): 875–79.

20. Castillo, E. M., J. J. Brennan, J. Howard, R. Y. Hsia, C. Chalmers, T. C. Chan, and K. J. Ko. "Factors associated with geriatric frequent users of emergency departments." *Annals of Emergency Medicine* 74, no. 2 (2019): 270–75.

21. Li, Evelyn, Laura Kimmey, and Valeria Cheh. "Evaluation of the independence at home demonstration: An examination of the first five years—appendices." https://www.hhs.gov/guidance/sites/default/files/hhs-guidance-documents/IndependenceAtHome-YearFiveEvaluationReportAppendices_3_2_20.pdf.

22. CareMore Health. "Could the house call make a comeback? CareMore Health survey findings say 'yes.'" https://www.caremore.com/Media/Details.aspx?id=%7Bbea38131-fc2e-43b2-a0d8-ac13c954c4da%7D.

23. Jain, S. H. "CareMore health tackles the unmet challenges of the aging population." *Generations* 42, no. 1 (2018): 14–18.

24. Patel, K., and D. Masi. "Palliative care in the era of health care reform." *Clinics in Geriatric Medicine* 31, no. 2 (2015): 265–70.

25. Powers, B. W., S. Rinefort, and S. H. Jain. "Nonemergency medical transportation: Delivering care in the era of Lyft and Uber." *JAMA* 316, no. 9 (2016): 921–22.

26. Cunningham, P. J. "Beyond parity: Primary care physicians' perspectives on access to mental health care: More PCPs have trouble obtaining mental health services for their patients than have problems getting other specialty services." *Health Affairs* 28, Suppl. 1 (2009): w490–501.

27. Howe, M. "Profile: Iora Health transactional vs. relationship-based care." *Nursing Management* 48, no. 5 (2017): 26–31.

28. Finkelstein, A., A. Zhou, S. Taubman, and J. Doyle. "Health care hotspotting—a randomized, controlled trial." *New England Journal of Medicine* 382, no. 2 (2020): 152–62.

29. Garg, V., S. W. Chang, E. Condon, T. Rhone, R. Pottharst, and S. H. Jain. "Adapting a senior-focused care strategy to Medicaid." *NEJM Catalyst* 2, no. 5 (2016).
30. Sommers, C., L. Ferrie, and G. Myers. "How can ninjas save primary care?" *NEJM Catalyst* 2, no. 5 (2016).
31. Tanio, C., and C. Chen. "Innovations at Miami practice show promise for treating high-risk Medicare patients." *Health Affairs* 32, no. 6 (2013): 1078–82.

# Bibliography

Abad, Zahra Shakeri Hossein, Adrienne Kline, Madeena Sultana, Mohammad Noaeen, Elvira Nurmambetova, Filipe Lucini, Majed Al-Jefri, and Joon Lee. "Digital public health surveillance: A systematic scoping review." *NPJ digital medicine* 4, no. 1 (2021): 1–13.

Abelson, Jonathan S., Natalie Z. Wong, Matthew Symer, Gregory Eckenrode, Anthony Watkins, and Heather L. Yeo. "Racial and ethnic disparities in promotion and retention of academic surgeons." *The American Journal of Surgery* 216, no. 4 (2018): 678–82.

Abraído-Lanza, Ana F., Amarilis Céspedes, Shaira Daya, Karen R. Flórez, and Kellee White. "Satisfaction with health care among Latinas." *Journal of Health Care for the Poor and Underserved* 22, no. 2 (2011): 491.

Addario, Bonnie J., Ana Fadich, Jesme Fox, Linda Krebs, Deborah Maskens, Kathy Oliver, Erin Schwartz, Gilliosa Spurrier-Bernard, and Timothy Turnham. "Patient value: Perspectives from the advocacy community." *Health Expectations* 21, no. 1 (2018): 57–63.

Addario, Bonnie, Jan Geissler, Marcia K. Horn, Linda U. Krebs, Deborah Maskens, Kathy Oliver, Ananda Plate, Erin Schwartz, and Nicole Willmarth. "Including the patient voice in the development and implementation of patient-reported outcomes in cancer clinical trials." *Health Expectations* 23, no. 1 (2020): 41–51.

Addario, Bonnie. "SC31. 02 The role of patient advocacy groups." *Journal of thoracic oncology* 12, no. 1 (2017): S147–S148.

Ader, Jeremy, Christopher J. Stille, David Keller, Benjamin F. Miller, Michael S. Barr, and James M. Perrin. "The medical home and integrated behavioral health: Advancing the policy agenda." *Pediatrics* 135, no. 5 (2015): 909–17.

Adler, Nancy E., and Judith Stewart. "Preface to *The biology of disadvantage: Socio-economic status and health.*" *Annals of the New York Academy of Sciences* 1186, no. 1 (February 1, 2010): 1–4.

Agency for Healthcare Research and Quality. "Improving cultural competence to reduce health disparities for priority populations." U.S. Department of Health and Human Services, July 8, 2014. https://effectivehealthcare.ahrq.gov/products/cultural -competence/research-protocol.

Akinbami, Lara J., Alan E. Simon, and Lauren M. Rossen. "Changing trends in asthma prevalence among children." *Pediatrics* 137, no. 1 (2016).

Alarcón, Renato D., Amrita Parekh, Milton L. Wainberg, Cristiane S. Duarte, Ricardo Araya, and María A. Oquendo. "Hispanic immigrants in the USA: Social and mental health perspectives." *The Lancet Psychiatry* 3, no. 9 (2016): 860–70.

Albert, Stephanie L., Brent A. Langellier, Mienah Z. Sharif, Alec M. Chan-Golston, Michael L. Prelip, Rosa Elena Garcia, Deborah C. Glik, Thomas R. Belin, Ron Brookmeyer, and Alexander N. Ortega. "A corner store intervention to improve access to fruits and vegetables in two Latino communities." *Public Health Nutrition* 20, no. 12 (2017): 2249–59.

Alcalá, Héctor E., Stephanie L. Albert, Dylan H. Roby, Jacob Beckerman, Philippe Champagne, Ron Brookmeyer, Michael L. Prelip, et al. "Access to care and cardiovascular disease prevention: A cross-sectional study in 2 Latino communities." *Medicine* 94, no. 34 (2015).

Alexander, Michelle. *The new Jim Crow: Mass incarceration in the age of colorblindness.* New York: New Press, 2010.

Alker, Joan C., Genevieve M. Kenney, and Sara Rosenbaum. "Children's health insurance coverage: Progress, problems, and priorities for 2021 and beyond: Study examines children's health insurance coverage." *Health Affairs* 39, no. 10 (2020): 1743–51.

Alley, Dawn E., Nina C. Ashford, and Ashley M. Gavin. "Payment innovations to drive improvements in pediatric care—the Integrated Care for Kids Model." *JAMA Pediatrics* 173, no. 8 (2019): 717–18.

Allison, Mandy A., and Elliott Attisha. "The link between school attendance and good health." *Pediatrics* 143, no. 2 (2019).

Al-Shamsi, Humaid O., Marwan Al-Hajeili, and Sadir Alrawi. "Chasing the cure around the globe: Medical tourism for cancer care from developing countries." *Journal of Global Oncology* 4 (2018).

Altice, Cheryl K., Matthew P. Banegas, Reginald D. Tucker-Seeley, and K. Robin Yabroff. "Financial hardships experienced by cancer survivors: A systematic review." *JNCI: Journal of the National Cancer Institute* 109, no. 2 (2017).

Altman, Lawrence K. "New homosexual disorder worries health officials." *The New York Times* 11 (1982): C1–6. https://www.nytimes.com/1982/05/11/science/new -homosexual-disorder-worries-health-officials.html.

Alvarez, P. "5,200 people in ICE custody quarantined for exposure to mumps or chicken pox." CNN, 2019.

American Cancer Society. "Cancer facts and figures for Hispanics/Latinos 2018-2020." 2020. https://www.cancer.org/content/dam/cancer-org/research/cancer-facts-and

-statistics/cancer-facts-and-figures-for-hispanics-and-latinos/cancer-facts-and-fig ures-for-hispanics-and-latinos-2018-2020.pdf.

American Hospital Association. (2019). "Statement of the AHA for the committee on rules of the U.S. House of Representatives 'Medicare for All Act of 2019' | AHA." https://www.aha.org/lettercomment/2019-04-30-statement-aha-committee-rules -us-house-representatives-medicare-all-act.

American Psychiatric Association. "Mental health disparities: Diverse populations." 2021. https://www.psychiatry.org/psychiatrists/cultural-competency/education /mental-health-facts.

American Society of Clinical Oncology. "Facts and figures: diversity in oncology." *American Society of Clinical Oncology.* 2018. https://www.asco.org/news-initiatives /current-initiatives/diversity-oncology-initiative/facts-figures.

amFAR. "Syringe exchange programs." https://opioid.amfar.org/indicator/num.

Anderson, L. Elizabeth, Minghua L. Chen, James M. Perrin, and Jeanne Van Cleave. "Outpatient visits and medication prescribing for US children with mental health conditions." *Pediatrics* 136, no. 5 (2015): e1178–e1185.

Anderson, Margaret, and K. Kimberly McCleary. "On the path to a science of patient input." *Science Translational Medicine* 8, no. 336 (2016): 336ps11.

Anderson, Monica, and Andrew Perrin. 2017. "Disabled Americans less likely to use technology." Pew Research Center. https://www.pewresearch.org/fact-tank /2017/04/07/disabled-americans-are-less-likely-to-use-technology/.

Anderson, Timothy S., Leah S. Karliner, and Grace A. Lin. "Association of primary language and hospitalization for ambulatory care sensitive conditions." *Medical Care* 58, no. 1 (2020): 45.

Andrews, James S., Irena Stijacic Cenzer, Edward Yelin, and Kenneth E. Covinsky. "Pain as a risk factor for disability or death." *Journal of the American Geriatrics Society* 61, no. 4 (2013): 583–89.

Annaswamy, Thiru M., Monica Verduzco-Gutierrez, and Lex Frieden. "Telemedicine barriers and challenges for persons with disabilities: COVID-19 and beyond." *Disability and Health Journal* 13, no. 4 (2020): 100973.

Arcoleo, Kimberly, Flavio Marsiglia, Denise Serebrisky, Juliana Rodriguez, Colleen Mc-govern, and Jonathan Feldman. "Explanatory model for asthma disparities in Latino children: Results from the Latino Childhood Asthma Project." *Annals of Behavioral Medicine* 54, no. 4 (2020): 223–36.

Armstrong, Katrina, Karima L. Ravenell, Suzanne McMurphy, and Mary Putt. "Racial/ ethnic differences in physician distrust in the United States." *American Journal of Public Health* 97, no. 7 (2007): 1283–89.

Aronowitz, Shoshana V., Catherine C. Mcdonald, Robin C. Stevens, and Therese S. Richmond. "Mixed studies review of factors influencing receipt of pain treatment by injured black patients." *Journal of Advanced Nursing* 76, no. 1 (2020): 34–46.

Artiga, Samantha, and Barbara Lyons. "Family consequences of detention/deportation: Effects on finances, health, and well being." Henry J. Kaiser Family Foundation, San Francisco, CA, 2018.

Asad, Asad L. "Latinos' deportation fears by citizenship and legal status, 2007 to 2018." *Proceedings of the National Academy of Sciences* 117, no. 16 (2020): 8836–44.

Ashford, Robert D., Austin M. Brown, Georgeanne Dorney, Nancy McConnell, Justin Kunzelman, Jessica McDaniel, and Brenda Curtis. "Reducing harm and promoting recovery through community-based mutual aid: Characterizing those who engage in a hybrid peer recovery community organization." *Addictive Behaviors* 98 (2019): 106037.

Ashford, Robert D., Brenda Curtis, and Austin M. Brown. "Peer-delivered harm reduction and recovery support services: Initial evaluation from a hybrid recovery community drop-in center and syringe exchange program." *Harm Reduction Journal* 15, no. 1 (2018): 1–9.

Ashley, Florence. "'Trans' is my gender modality: A modest terminological proposal." In Laura Erickson-Schroth (ed.). *Trans bodies, trans selves.* Second edition. Oxford: Oxford University Press, 2021.

Association of Government Accountants. "Blended and braided funding: A guide for policy makers and practitioners." December 2014. https://www.agacgfm.org/Intergov/More-Tools/Blended-and-Braided-Funding-A-Guide-for-Policy-Ma.aspx.

Attansasio, Cedar, Garance Burke, and Martha Mendoza. "Lawyers: 250 children held in bad conditions at Texas border." Associated Press, 2019. https://apnews.com/article/texas-immigration-us-news-ap-top-news-border-patrols-a074f375e643408cb9b8d1a5fc5acf6a.

Aubrecht, Katie, Christine Kelly, and Carla Rice, eds. *The aging–disability nexus.* Vancouver: UBC Press, 2020.

Bach, Peter B., Deborah Schrag, Otis W. Brawley, Aaron Galaznik, Sofia Yakren, and Colin B. Begg. "Survival of blacks and whites after a cancer diagnosis." *JAMA* 287, no. 16 (2002): 2106–13.

Bailey, Moya. "Work in the intersections: A Black feminist disability framework." *Moya Bailey* (blog). October 16, 2018. https://www.moyabailey.com/2018/10/16/work-in-the intersections-a-black-feminist-disability-framework/.

Bailey, Moya, and Izetta Autumn Mobley. "Work in the intersections: A black feminist disability framework." *Gender & Society* 33, no. 1 (2019): 19–40.

Baker, Jeffrey P. "Women and the invention of well child care." *Pediatrics* 94, no. 4 (1994): 527–31.

Baker, Tamara A., Olivio J. Clay, Vicki Johnson-Lawrence, Jacquelyn A. Minahan, Chivon A. Mingo, Roland J. Thorpe, Fernando Ovalle, and Michael Crowe. "Association of multiple chronic conditions and pain among older black and white adults with diabetes mellitus." *BMC Geriatrics* 17, no. 1 (2017): 1–9.

Bakhamis, Lama, David P. Paul III, Harlan Smith, and Alberto Coustasse. "Still an epidemic: The burnout syndrome in hospital registered nurses." *The Health Care Manager* 38, no. 1 (2019): 3–10.

Baltimore City Health Department. "Community health assessment Baltimore City." September 20, 2017. https://health.baltimorecity.gov/sites/default/files/health/attachments/Baltimore%20City%20CHA%20-%20Final%209.20.17.pdf.

Barlow, Allison, Britta Mullany, Nicole Neault, Novalene Goklish, Trudy Billy, Ranelda Hastings, Sherilynn Lorenzo, et al. "Paraprofessional-delivered home-visiting intervention for American Indian teen mothers and children: 3-year outcomes from a randomized controlled trial." *American Journal of Psychiatry* 172, no. 2 (2015): 154–62.

Barton, J. L., L. Trupin, D. Schillinger, S. A. Gansky, C. Tonner, M. Margaretten, V. Chernitskiy, J. Graf, J. Imboden, and E. Yelin. "Racial and ethnic disparities in disease activity and function among persons with rheumatoid arthritis from university-affiliated clinics." *Arthritis Care & Research* 63, no. 9 (2011): 1238–46.

Barton, Jennifer L., Christopher J. Koenig, Gina Evans-Young, Laura Trupin, Jennie Anderson, Dana Ragouzeos, Maggie Breslin, et al. "The design of a low literacy decision aid about rheumatoid arthritis medications developed in three languages for use during the clinical encounter." *BMC Medical Informatics and Decision Making* 14, no. 1 (2014): 1–14.

Bassuk, Ellen L., Justine Hanson, R. Neil Greene, Molly Richard, and Alexandre Laudet. "Peer-delivered recovery support services for addictions in the United States: A systematic review." *Journal of Substance Abuse Treatment* 63 (2016): 1–9.

Batalova, Jeanne, Brittany Blizzard., and J. Bolter. "Frequently requested statistics on immigrants and Iimmigration in the United States 2020." 2020. https://www.migrationpolicy.org/article/frequently-requested-statistics-immigrants-and-immigration-united-states.

Bayer, Ronald. *Homosexuality and American psychiatry: The politics of diagnosis.* Princeton: Princeton University Press, 1987.

Bayoumi, Ahmed M., and Gregory S. Zaric. "The cost-effectiveness of Vancouver's supervised injection facility." *CMAJ* 179, no. 11 (2008): 1143–51.

Beck, Amy L., Esti Iturralde, Julissa Haya-Fisher, Sarah Kim, Victoria Keeton, and Alicia Fernandez. "Barriers and facilitators to healthy eating among low-income Latino adolescents." *Appetite* 138 (2019): 215–22.

Beck, Andrew F., Megan M. Tschudy, Tumaini R. Coker, Kamila B. Mistry, Joanne E. Cox, Benjamin A. Gitterman, Lisa J. Chamberlain, et al. "Determinants of health and pediatric primary care practices." *Pediatrics* 137, no. 3 (2016).

Beck, Ulrich, Scott Lash, and Brian Wynne. *Risk society: Towards a new modernity.* Thousand Oaks, CA: Sage, 1992.

Beemyn, Genny. "Transgender history in the United States." In Laura Erickson-Schroth (Ed.). *Trans bodies, trans selves: A resource for the transgender community*, pp. 501–36. Oxford: Oxford University Press, 2014.

Benjamins, Maureen R. "Race/ethnic discrimination and preventive service utilization in a sample of whites, blacks, Mexicans, and Puerto Ricans." *Medical Care* (2012): 870–76.

Berenbrok, Lucas A., Nico Gabriel, Kim C. Coley, and Inmaculada Hernandez. "Evaluation of frequency of encounters with primary care physicians vs visits to community pharmacies among Medicare beneficiaries." *JAMA Network Open* 3, no. 7 (2020): e209132.

Berlinger, Nancy, and Rachel L. Zacharias. "Resources for teaching and learning about immigrant health care in health professions education." *AMA Journal of Ethics* 21, no. 1 (2019): 50–57.

Betancourt-Garcia, Monica M., Kristina Vatcheva, Prateek K. Gupta, Ricardo D. Martinez, Joseph B. McCormick, Susan P. Fisher-Hoch, and R. Armour Forse. "The effect of Hispanic ethnicity on surgical outcomes: An analysis of the NSQIP database." *The American Journal of Surgery* 217, no. 4 (2019): 618–33.

Bishop, Tara F., Matthew J. Press, Salomeh Keyhani, and Harold Alan Pincus. "Acceptance of insurance by psychiatrists and the implications for access to mental health care." *JAMA Psychiatry* 71, no. 2 (2014): 176–81.

Blizzard, Brittany, and Jeanne Batalova. "Refugees and asylees in the United States." June 13, 2019. https://www.migrationpolicy.org/article/refugees-and-asylees-united-states-2018.

Boatright, Dowin H., Elizabeth A. Samuels, Laura Cramer, Jeremiah Cross, Mayur Desai, Darin Latimore, and Cary P. Gross. "Association between the Liaison Committee on Medical Education's diversity standards and changes in percentage of medical student sex, race, and ethnicity." *JAMA* 320, no. 21 (2018): 2267–69.

Boatright, Dowin, David Ross, Patrick O'Connor, Edward Moore, and Marcella Nunez-Smith. "Racial disparities in medical student membership in the Alpha Omega Alpha honor society." *JAMA Internal Medicine* 177, no. 5 (2017): 659–65.

Bochenek, Michael. *In the freezer: Abusive conditions for women and children in US immigration holding cells*. New York: Human Rights Watch, 2018.

Booker, S. Q., T. A. Baker, D. K. Esiaka, J. A. Minahan, I. J. Engel, K. Banerjee, and M. Poitevien. (under review). "Advancing pain (disparities) research: Acknowledging the past while paving the way for the future."

Bowleg, Lisa. 2020. "Reframing mass incarceration as a social-structural driver of health inequity." *American Journal of Public Health* 110 (S1): S11–12.

Brandl, Eva J., Stefanie Schreiter, and Meryam Schouler-Ocak. "Are trained medical interpreters worth the cost? A review of the current literature on cost and cost-effectiveness." *Journal of Immigrant and Minority Health* 22, no. 1 (2020): 175–81.

Bridges, Ana J., Arthur R. Andrews III, Bianca T. Villalobos, Freddie A. Pastrana, Timothy A. Cavell, and Debbie Gomez. "Does integrated behavioral health care reduce mental health disparities for Latinos? Initial findings." *Journal of Latina/o Psychology* 2, no. 1 (2014): 37.

Brooks, Gabriel A., J. Russell Hoverman, and Carrie H. Colla. "The Affordable Care Act and cancer care delivery." *Cancer Journal* 23, no. 3 (2017): 163.

Brown, R. C. H. "Moral responsibility for (un)healthy behavior." *Journal of Medical Ethics* 39 (2013): 695–98.

Budiman, Abby. "Key findings about US immigrants." Pew Research Center (2020).

Bullock, Justin L., Cindy J. Lai, Tai Lockspeiser, Patricia S. O'Sullivan, Paul Aronowitz, Deborah Dellmore, Cha-Chi Fung, Christopher Knight, and Karen E. Hauer. "In pursuit of honors." *Academic Medicine* 94 (2019): S48–56.

Bureau of Internet Accessibility. "Disability statistics in the United States." November 29, 2018. https://www.boia.org/blog/disability-statistics-in-the-united-states.

Bureau of Internet Accessibility. "Why web accessibility is important to hospitals." May 17, 2018. https://www.boia.org/blog/why-web-accessibility-is-important-to-hospitals.

Bustamante, Arturo Vargas, Hai Fang, Jeremiah Garza, Olivia Carter-Pokras, Steven P. Wallace, John A. Rizzo, and Alexander N. Ortega. "Variations in healthcare access and utilization among Mexican immigrants: The role of documentation status." *Journal of Immigrant and Minority Health* 14, no. 1 (2012): 146–55.

Bustillo, Yolanda, and Rachel Perler. "Balancing health care rationing and disability rights in a pandemic." January 15, 2021. https://blog.petrieflom.law.harvard.edu/2021/01/15/health-care-rationing-disability-rights-covid/.

Caballero, A. Enrique. "Cultural competence in diabetes mellitus care: An urgent need." *Insulin* 2, no. 2 (2007): 80–91.

Cahill, Sean, Robbie Singal, Chris Grasso, Dana King, Kenneth Mayer, Kellan Baker, and Harvey Makadon. "Do ask, do tell: High levels of acceptability by patients of routine collection of sexual orientation and gender identity data in four diverse American community health centers." *PloS One* 9, no. 9 (2014): e107104.

Calloway, Kristy, and Darcy Copeland. "Acute care nurses' attitudes toward nursing students with disabilities: A focused ethnography." *Nurse Education in Practice* 51 (2021): 102960.

Cantwell Jr., A. R. "Gay cancer, emerging viruses, and AIDS." *New Dawn (Melbourne)* (1998).

Carel, Havi, and Ian James Kidd. "Epistemic injustice in healthcare: A philosophial analysis." *Medicine, Health Care and Philosophy* 17, no. 4 (2014): 529–40.

Carrillo, Genny, Maria J. Perez-Patron, Rose L. Lucio, Lucia Cabrera, Alyssa Trevino, Xiaohui Xu, and Nelda Mier. "The benefits and challenges of managing asthma in Hispanic families in South Texas: A mixed-methods study." *Frontiers in Public Health* 5 (2017): 150.

Carter, Ashley J. R., and Cecine N. Nguyen. "A comparison of cancer burden and research spending reveals discrepancies in the distribution of research funding." *BMC Public Health* 12, no. 1 (2012): 1–12.

Casagrande, Sarah Stark, Tiffany L. Gary, Thomas A. LaVeist, Darrell J. Gaskin, and Lisa A. Cooper. "Perceived discrimination and adherence to medical care in a racially integrated community." *Journal of General Internal Medicine* 22, no. 3 (2007): 389–95.

Cassidy, Jude. "Emotion regulation: Influences of attachment relationships." *Monographs of the Society for Research in Child Development* 59, no. 2-3 (1994): 228–49.

Castañeda, Heide, Seth M. Holmes, Daniel S. Madrigal, Maria-Elena DeTrinidad Young, Naomi Beyeler, and James Quesada. "Immigration as a social determinant of health." *Annual Review of Public Health* 36 (2015): 375–92.

Castrucci, Brian, and John Auerbach. "Meeting individual social needs falls short of addressing social determinants of health." *Policy & Practice* 77, no. 2 (2019): 25–27.

CDC Vital Signs. "Hispanic health." Centers for Disease Control and Prevention, Office of Minority Health and Health Equity, May 5, 2015. https://www.cdc.gov/vitalsigns/hispanic-health/index.html.

Center of Excellence for Transgender Health. "Guidelines for the primary and gender-affirming care of transgender and gender nonbinary people." June 17, 2017. https://transcare.ucsf.edu/sites/transcare.ucsf.edu/files/Transgender-PGACG-6-17-16.pdf.

Centers for Disease Control and Prevention. "Health disparities and strategies reports." Health Equity, 2018. https://www.cdc.gov/minorityhealth/chdir/index.html.

Centers for Disease Control and Prevention. "Estimated HIV incidence and prevalence in the United States, 2014–2018." *HIV surveillance supplemental report* 25, no. 1 (2020). http://www.cdc.gov/hiv/library/reports/hiv-surveillance.html.

Chacko, Anil, and Thaier Hayajneh. "Security and privacy issues with IoT in healthcare." *EAI Endorsed Transactions on Pervasive Health and Technology* 4, no. 14 (2018).

Chan, Evelyn C. Y., Stephanie L. McFall, Theresa L. Byrd, Patricia Dolan Mullen, Robert J. Volk, John Ureda, Jessica Calderon-Mora, Pat Morales, Adriana Valdes, and L. Kay Bartholomew. "A community-based intervention to promote informed decision making for prostate cancer screening among Hispanic American men changed knowledge and role preferences: A cluster RCT." *Patient Education and Counseling* 84, no. 2 (2011): e44–e51.

Charkhchi, Paniz, Matthew B. Schabath, and Ruth C. Carlos. "Modifiers of cancer screening prevention among sexual and gender minorities in the Behavioral Risk Factor Surveillance System." *Journal of the American College of Radiology* 16, no. 4 (2019): 607–20.

Chen, Angela. "What happens when life insurance companies track fitness data?" The Verge. September 26, 2018. https://www.theverge.com/2018/9/26/17905390/john-hancock-life-insurance-fitness-tracker-wearables-science-health.

Chen, Jie, Arturo Vargas-Bustamante, Karoline Mortensen, and Alexander N. Ortega. "Racial and ethnic disparities in health care access and utilization under the Affordable Care Act." *Medical Care* 54, no. 2 (2016): 140.

Cherry, Barbara J., Laura Zettel-Watson, Renee Shimizu, Ian Roberson, Dana N. Rutledge, and Caroline J. Jones. "Cognitive performance in women aged 50 years and older with and without fibromyalgia." *Journals of Gerontology Series B: Psychological Sciences and Social Sciences* 69, no. 2 (2014): 199–208.

Chesnut, Renae J., Iqbal I. Atcha, Duc P. Do, Kristopher Harrell, Amy Holland, Monica L. Miller, Kelly M. Shields, et al. "Report of the 2016-2017 student affairs standing committee." *American Journal of Pharmaceutical Education* 81, no. 8 (2017).

Chisholm, Marie A., and Joseph T. DiPiro. "Pharmaceutical manufacturer assistance programs." *Archives of Internal Medicine* 162, no. 7 (2002): 780–84.

Chisolm, Deena J., Claire Jones, Elisabeth D. Root, Millie Dolce, and Kelly J. Kelleher. "A community development program and reduction in high-cost health care use." *Pediatrics* 146, no. 2 (2020).

Chowdhary, N., A. T. Jotheeswaran, A. Nadkarni, S. D. Hollon, M. King, M. J. D. Jordans, A. Rahman, H. Verdeli, R. Araya, and V. Patel. "The methods and outcomes of cultural adaptations of psychological treatments for depressive disorders: A systematic review." *Psychological Medicine* 44, no. 6 (2014): 1131–46.

Chowkwanyun, Merlin. "Cleveland versus the clinic: The 1960s riots and community health reform." *American Journal of Public Health* 108, no. 11 (2018): 1494–502.

Clampet-Lundquist, Susan, Kathryn Edin, Jeffrey R. Kling, and Greg J. Duncan. "Moving teenagers out of high-risk neighborhoods: How girls fare better than boys." *American Journal of Sociology* 116, no. 4 (2011): 1154–89.

Cleveland, Janet, Rachel Kronick, Hanna Gros, and Cécile Rousseau. "Symbolic violence and disempowerment as factors in the adverse impact of immigration detention on adult asylum seekers' mental health." *International Journal of Public Health* 63, no. 8 (2018): 1001–08.

Coker, Tumaini R., Marc N. Elliott, Sara L. Toomey, David C. Schwebel, Paula Cuccaro, Susan Tortolero Emery, Susan L. Davies, Susanna N. Visser, and Mark A. Schuster. "Racial and ethnic disparities in ADHD diagnosis and treatment." *Pediatrics* 138, no. 3 (2016).

Colby, Sandra L., and Jennifer M. Ortman. "Projections of the size and composition of the US population: 2014 to 2060. Population estimates and projections. Current population reports. P25-1143." U.S. Census Bureau, Washington, DC, 2015.

Coles, Mandy. "Pediatrician sees life-changing benefits of gender care—and foresees great harm of Ark.'s anti-trans law." *Boston Globe*, April 8, 2021. https://www.bostonglobe.com/2021/04/08/opinion/pediatrician-sees-life-changing-benefits-gender-care-foresees-great-harm-arks-anti-trans-law/.

Collyar, Deborah. "How have patient advocates in the United States benefited cancer research?" *Nature Reviews Cancer* 5, no. 1 (2005): 73–78.

Commission on Social Determinants of Health. *Closing the gap in a generation: Health equity through action on the social determinants of health: Final report of the commission on social determinants of health*. Washington, DC: World Health Organization, 2008.

Commodore-Mensah, Yvonne, Nwakaego Ukonu, Olawunmi Obisesan, Jonathan Kumi Aboagye, Charles Agyemang, Carolyn M. Reilly, Sandra B. Dunbar, and Ike S. Okosun. "Length of residence in the United States is associated with a higher prevalence of cardiometabolic risk factors in immigrants: A contemporary analysis of the National Health Interview Survey." *Journal of the American Heart Association* 5, no. 11 (2016): e004059.

Conti, G., and J. J. Heckman. "Economics of child well-being." In A. Ben-Arieh, F. Casas, I. Frønes, and J. E. Korbin (eds.). *Handbook of child well-being: Theories, methods and policies in global perspective*, pp. 363–401. Dordrecht: Springer Netherlands, 2014.

Cook, Benjamin, Margarita Alegría, Julia Y. Lin, and Jing Guo. "Pathways and correlates connecting Latinos' mental health with exposure to the United States." *American Journal of Public Health* 99, no. 12 (2009): 2247–54.

Cooper, Harris, Barbara Nye, Kelly Charlton, James Lindsay, and Scott Greathouse. "The effects of summer vacation on achievement test scores: A narrative and meta-analytic review." *Review of Educational Research* 66, no. 3 (1996): 227–68.

Coren, Joshua S., Frank A. Filipetto, and Lucia Beck Weiss. "Eliminating barriers for patients with limited English proficiency." *The Journal of the American Osteopathic Association* 109, no. 12 (2009): 634–40.

Cornell, Stephen. *Indigenous peoples, poverty and self-determination in Australia, New Zealand, Canada and the United States.* Tuscon, AZ: Native Nations Institute for Leadership, Management, and Policy, 2006.

Costa, Daniel. "California leads the way: A look at California laws that help protect labor standards for unauthorized immigrant workers." Economic Policy Institute, 2018. https://www.epi.org/publication/california-immigrant-labor-laws.

Cottom, Tressie McMillan, Roxane Gay, Sabrina Strings, and Sonya Renee Taylor. "The fat tax." Hear to Slay. 56:03-56:34. February 9, 2021. https://luminarypod casts.com/listen/roxane-gay-and-dr-tressie%20mcmillan-cottom/hear-to-slay/the-fat-tax/a5495e99-fc26-47ee-89bc-e1faf4b921da?country=US.

County Health Rankings. "Culturally adapted health care." UW Population Health Institute, January 31, 2020. https://www.countyhealthrankings.org/take-action-to-improve-health/what-works-for-health/strategies/culturally-adapted-health-care.

Cousins, Michael J. "Persistent pain: A disease entity." *Journal of Pain and Symptom Management* 33, no. 2 (2007): S4–S10.

Covinsky, Kenneth E., Karla Lindquist, Dorothy D. Dunlop, and Edward Yelin. "Pain, functional limitations, and aging." *Journal of the American Geriatrics Society* 57, no. 9 (2009): 1556–61.

Crear-Perry, Joia. "You can't have quality without equity." March 18, 2020. http://www.ihi.org/communities/blogs/you-can-t-have-quality-without-equity.

Crear-Perry, Joia, Rosaly Correa-de-Araujo, Tamara Lewis Johnson, Monica R. McLemore, Elizabeth Neilson, and Maeve Wallace. "Social and structural determinants of health inequities in maternal health." *Journal of Women's Health* 30, no. 2 (2021): 230–35.

Crezee, Ineke H. M., and Cynthia E. Roat. "Bilingual patient navigator or healthcare interpreter: What's the difference and why does it matter?" *Cogent Medicine* 6, no. 1 (2019): 181087776.

Cruz, Paulina, and Andrea Granados. "Type 2 diabetes in Latino youth: A clinical update and current challenges." *Current Problems in Pediatric and Adolescent Health Care* 49, no. 1 (2019): 16–22.

Currie, Janet. "What we say and what we do: Why US investments in children's health are falling short: Study examines US investments in children's health." *Health Affairs* 39, no. 10 (2020): 1684–92.

Curry Jr., William T., Bob S. Carter, and Fred G. Barker. "Racial, ethnic, and socioeconomic disparities in patient outcomes after craniotomy for tumor in adult patients in the United States, 1988–2004." *Neurosurgery* 66, no. 3 (2010): 427–38.

Cushman, Linda F., Marlyn Delva, Cheryl L. Franks, Ana Jimenez-Bautista, Joyce Moon-Howard, Jim Glover, and Melissa D. Begg. "Cultural competency training for public health students: Integrating self, social, and global awareness into a master of public health curriculum." *American Journal of Public Health* 105, no. S1 (2015): S132–S140.

D'Ignazio, Catherine, and Lauren Klein. "The power chapter." Data Feminism, March 20, 2020. https://data-feminism.mitpress.mit.edu/pub/vi8obxh7/release/3.

D'Andrea, Wendy, Julian Ford, Bradley Stolbach, Joseph Spinazzola, and Bessel A. van der Kolk. "Understanding interpersonal trauma in children: Why we need a developmentally appropriate trauma diagnosis." *American Journal of Orthopsychiatry* 82, no. 2 (2012): 187.

Dasgupta, Sharoda, Dita Broz, Mary Tanner, Monita Patel, Brandon Halleck, Philip J. Peters, Paul J. Weidle, et al. "Changes in reported injection behaviors following the public health response to an HIV outbreak among people who inject drugs: Indiana, 2016." *AIDS and Behavior* 23, no. 12 (2019): 3257–66.

Davis, Elizabeth. "How healthcare rationing in the United States affects even you." Verywell Health, April 17, 2021. https://www.verywellhealth.com/how-health-care-rationing-in-the-us-affects-even-you-1738482.

Davis, Lorna G., Gayle L. Riedmann, Melissa Sapiro, John P. Minogue, and Ralph R. Kazer. "Cesarean section rates in low-risk private patients managed by certified nurse-midwives and obstetricians." *Journal of Nurse-Midwifery* 39, no. 2 (1994): 91–97.

Daw, J. R., K. B. Kozhimannil, and L. K. Admon. "High rates of perinatal insurance churn persist after the ACA." *Health Affairs Blog* (2019).

De Jesus, Maria, and Chenyang Xiao. "Predicting health care utilization among Latinos: Health locus of control beliefs or access factors?" *Health Education & Behavior* 41, no. 4 (2014): 423–30.

de Souza Briggs, Xavier, Susan J. Popkin, and John Goering. *Moving to opportunity: The story of an American experiment to fight ghetto poverty.* Oxford: Oxford University Press, 2010.

Diamond, Lisa, Karen Izquierdo, Dana Canfield, Konstantina Matsoukas, and Francesca Gany. "A systematic review of the impact of patient–physician non-English language concordance on quality of care and outcomes." *Journal of General Internal Medicine* 34, no. 8 (2019): 1591–606.

Dickerson, Caitlin. "Inquiry ordered into claims immigrants had unwanted gynecology procedures." *The New York Times*, 2020.

Dickerson, Daniel L., Kamilla L. Venner, Bonnie Duran, Jeffery J. Annon, Benjamin Hale, and George Funmaker. "Drum-assisted recovery therapy for Native Americans (DARTNA): Results from a pretest and focus groups." *American Indian and Alaska Native Mental Health Research (Online)* 21, no. 1 (2014): 35.

Divi, Chandrika, Richard G. Koss, Stephen P. Schmaltz, and Jerod M. Loeb. "Language proficiency and adverse events in US hospitals: A pilot study." *International Journal for Quality in Health Care* 19, no. 2 (2007): 60–67.

Doctors for Immigrants. "Our work." 2021. http://doctorsforimmigrants.com/our work/.

Doherty, Robert, Thomas G. Cooney, Ryan D. Mire, Lee S. Engel, and Jason M. Goldman. "Envisioning a better U.S. health care system for all: A call to action by the American College of Physicians." *Annals of internal medicine* 172, no. 2 Supplement (2020): S3.

Donia, Marco, Marie Louise Kimper-Karl, Katrine Lundby Høyer, Lars Bastholt, Henrik Schmidt, and Inge Marie Svane. "The majority of patients with metastatic melanoma are not represented in pivotal phase III immunotherapy trials." *European Journal of Cancer* 74 (2017): 89–95.

Donovan, Joan. "Twitter/ @BostonJoan: What I mean is that technology is a process, not a product. Facebook will come and go and so will Google and Twitter. Researchers have to see the horizon and then anticipate (as @alondra teaches) what comes next. History is the guide, social science our compass." April 21, 2021, 9:03 AM. https://twitter.com/BostonJoan/status/1384855329096282112.

Downs, Jim. *Sick from freedom: African-American illness and suffering during the Civil War and Reconstruction.* Oxford: Oxford University Press, 2012.

Drabble, Laurie A., and Michele J. Eliason. "Introduction to special Issue: Impacts of the COVID-19 pandemic on LGBTQ+ health and well-being." *Journal of Homosexuality* (2021): 1–15.

Drachman, Diane. "A stage-of-migration framework for service to immigrant populations." *Social Work* 37, no. 1 (1992): 68–72.

Drug and Therapeutics Bulletin. "An introduction to patient decision aids." *BMJ* 347 (2013): f4147.

Dube, Shanta R., Vincent J. Felitti, Maxia Dong, Wayne H. Giles, and Robert F. Anda. "The impact of adverse childhood experiences on health problems: Evidence from four birth cohorts dating back to 1900." *Preventive Medicine* 37, no. 3 (2003): 268–77.

Duckworth, Angela. "Grit: The power of passion and perseverance." Presented at the TED Talks Education, April 2013. https://www.ted.com/talks/angela_lee_duckworth_grit_the_power_of_passion_and_perseverance?language=en.

Dugas, Michèle, Marie-Ève Trottier, Selma Chipenda Dansokho, Gratianne Vaisson, Thierry Provencher, Heather Colquhoun, Maman Joyce Dogba, et al. "Involving members of vulnerable populations in the development of patient decision aids: A mixed methods sequential explanatory study." *BMC Medical Informatics and Decision Making* 17, no. 1 (2017): 1–11.

Duma, Narjust, Jesus Vera Aguilera, Jonas Paludo, Candace L. Haddox, Miguel Gonzalez Velez, Yucai Wang, Konstantinos Leventakos, et al. "Representation of minorities and women in oncology clinical trials: Review of the past 14 years." *Journal of Oncology Practice* 14, no. 1 (2018): e1–e10.

Duma, Narjust, Tariq Azam, Irbaz Bin Riaz, Miguel Gonzalez-Velez, Sikander Ailawadhi, and Ronald Go. "Representation of minorities and elderly patients in multiple myeloma clinical trials." *The Oncologist* 23, no. 9 (2018): 1076.

Dunlap, Jonathan L., Joshua D. Jaramillo, Raji Koppolu, Robert Wright, Fernando Mendoza, and Matias Bruzoni. "The effects of language concordant care on patient satisfaction and clinical understanding for Hispanic pediatric surgery patients." *Journal of Pediatric Surgery* 50, no. 9 (2015): 1586–89.

Duran, Eduardo, and Bonnie Duran. *Native American postcolonial psychology.* Albany, NY: SUNY Press, 1995.

Eberhardt, Mark S., and Elsie R. Pamuk. "The importance of place of residence: Examining health in rural and nonrural areas." *American Journal of Public Health* 94, no. 10 (2004): 1682–86.

Eguia, Emanuel, Adrienne N. Cobb, Eric J. Kirshenbaum, Majid Afshar, and Paul C. Kuo. "Racial and ethnic postoperative outcomes after surgery: The Hispanic paradox." *Journal of Surgical Research* 232 (2018): 88–93.

Elder, Glen H., Monica Kirkpatrick Johnson, and Robert Crosnoe. "The emergence and development of life course theory." In *Handbook of the life course*, pp. 3–19. Boston: Springer, 2003.

Elder, John P., Guadalupe X. Ayala, Deborah Parra-Medina, and Gregory A. Talavera. "Health communication in the Latino community: Issues and approaches." *Annual Review of Public Health* 30 (2009): 227–51.

Epstein, Ronald M., Kevin Fiscella, Cara S. Lesser, and Kurt C. Stange. "Why the nation needs a policy push on patient-centered health care." *Health Affairs* 29, no. 8 (2010): 1489–95.

Erikson, Erik H. *Identity: Youth and crisis.* New York: WW Norton & Company, 1968.

Eskenazi, Brenda, Carolyn A. Fahey, Katherine Kogut, Robert Gunier, Jacqueline Torres, Nancy A. Gonzales, Nina Holland, and Julianna Deardorff. "Association of perceived immigration policy vulnerability with mental and physical health among US-born Latino adolescents in California." *JAMA Pediatrics* 173, no. 8 (2019): 744–53.

Evans, Dominick. "Life with a disability is seriously expensive." June 30, 2015. https://www.dominickevans.com/2015/06/life-with-a-disability-is-seriously-expensive/.

Fagan, Mark J., Joseph A. Diaz, Steven E. Reinert, Christopher N. Sciamanna, and Dylan M. Fagan. "Impact of interpretation method on clinic visit length." *Journal of General Internal Medicine* 18, no. 8 (2003): 634–38.

Farrell, M. M., and S. J. Gibson. "Psychosocial aspects of pain in older people." In R. H. Dworkin and W. S. Breitbart (Eds.). *Psychosocial aspects of pain: A handbook for health care providers, progress in pain research and management*, pp. 495–518. Seattle: IASP Press, 2004.

Fassler, Joe. "How doctors take women's pain less seriously." *The Atlantic* 15 (2015).

Felitti, Vincent J., Robert F. Anda, Dale Nordenberg, David F. Williamson, Alison M. Spitz, Valerie Edwards, and James S. Marks. "Relationship of childhood abuse and household dysfunction to many of the leading causes of death in adults: The Adverse Childhood Experiences (ACE) Study." *American Journal of Preventive Medicine* 14, no. 4 (1998): 245–58.

Fernandes, Ricardo M., Maria Cary, Gonçalo Duarte, Gonçalo Jesus, Joana Alarcão, Carla Torre, Suzete Costa, João Costa, and António Vaz Carneiro. "Effectiveness of needle and syringe programmes in people who inject drugs–An overview of systematic reviews." *BMC Public Health* 17, no. 1 (2017): 1–15.

Fernandez, Alicia, Dean Schillinger, E. Margaret Warton, Nancy Adler, Howard H. Moffet, Yael Schenker, M. Victoria Salgado, Ameena Ahmed, and Andrew J. Karter. "Language barriers, physician-patient language concordance, and glycemic control among insured Latinos with diabetes: The Diabetes Study of Northern California (DISTANCE)." *Journal of General Internal Medicine* 26, no. 2 (2011): 170–76.

Ferris, Elizabeth. "When refugee displacement drags on, is self-reliance the answer?" *Brookings Institute* (2018): 1–3.

Flanagan, Patricia, Patrick M. Tigue, and James Perrin. "The value proposition for pediatric care." *JAMA Pediatrics* 173, no. 12 (2019): 1125–26.

Flores, Antonio. "2015, Hispanic population in the United States statistical portrait." Pew Research Center, September 18, 2017. https://www.pewresearch.org /hispanic/2017/09/18/2015-statistical-information-on-hispanics-in-united-states/.

Flores, Glenn, and Emmanuel Ngui. "Racial/ethnic disparities and patient safety." *Pediatric Clinics* 53, no. 6 (2006): 1197–215.

Flores, Glenn, Milagros Abreu, Ilan Schwartz, and Maria Hill. "The importance of language and culture in pediatric care: Case studies from the Latino community." *The Journal of Pediatrics* 137, no. 6 (2000): 842–48.

FluVaxView. "Flu vaccination coverage, United States, 2019–20 influenza season." U.S. Department of Health and Human Services, October 1, 2020. https://www.cdc .gov/flu/fluvaxview/coverage-1920estimates.htm#additional.

Flynn, Amy, Erika Gaitan, Rebecca Stocker, Elizabeth Showalter, and Karen Sautter Errichetti. "Enhanced integrated behavioral health model improves depressive symptoms in a low-income, uninsured, primarily Hispanic population served by a free and charitable clinic." *International Journal of Integrated Care* 20, no. 4 (2020).

Flynn, Caitlin. "For years, doctors told me anxiety was making me sick, then I was diagnosed with lupus." Popsugar.com, May 4, 2020. https://www.popsugar.com /fitness/Why-Took-Years-Me-Diagnosed-Lupus-46093200.

Fodeman, Jason, and Phil Factor. "Solutions to the primary care physician shortage." *The American Journal of Medicine* 128, no. 8 (2015): 800–801.

Foley, Brittany M., Jack M. Haglin, Joshua Ray Tanzer, and Adam EM Eltorai. "Patient care without borders: A systematic review of medical and surgical tourism." *Journal of Travel Medicine* 26, no. 6 (2019): taz049.

Franklin, April. "Accessible housing still tough to find 30 years after Americans with Disabilities Act." WXXI News, January 28, 2021. https://www.wxxinews.org/post /accessible-housing-still-tough-find-30-years-after-americans-with-disabilities-act.

Fredriksen-Goldsen, Karen I., and Hyun-Jun Kim. "Count me in: Response to sexual orientation measures among older adults." *Research on Aging* 37, no. 5 (2015): 464–80.

Freeman, Harold P., and Rian L. Rodriguez. "History and principles of patient navigation." *Cancer* 117, no. S15 (2011): 3537–40.

Friedman, Ari B., D. Daphne Owen, and Victoria E. Perez. "Trends in hospital ED closures nationwide and across Medicaid expansion, 2006-2013." *The American Journal of Emergency Medicine* 34, no. 7 (2016): 1262–64.

Friedmann, Peter D., Randall Hoskinson Jr., Michael Gordon, Robert Schwartz, Timothy Kinlock, Kevin Knight, Patrick M. Flynn, et al. "Medication-assisted treatment in criminal justice agencies affiliated with the criminal justice-drug abuse treatment studies (CJ-DATS): Availability, barriers, and intentions." *Substance Abuse* 33, no. 1 (2012): 9–18.

Gaskin, Darrell J., Gniesha Y. Dinwiddie, Kitty S. Chan, and Rachael R. McCleary. "Residential segregation and the availability of primary care physicians." *Health Services Research* 47, no. 6 (2012): 2353–76.

Gee, Gilbert C., and Chandra L. Ford. "Structural racism and health inequities: Old issues, new directions." *Du Bois Review: Social Science Research on Race* 8, no. 1 (2011): 115.

Gee, Gilbert C., Katrina M. Walsemann, and Elizabeth Brondolo. "A life course perspective on how racism may be related to health inequities." *American Journal of Public Health* 102, no. 5 (2012): 967–74.

Genao, Inginia, and Jacob Gelman. "The MCAT's restrictive effect on the minority physician pipeline: A legal perspective." *Annals of Internal Medicine* 169, no. (2018): 403–4.

Geronimus, Arline T., Margaret Hicken, Danya Keene, and John Bound. "'Weathering' and age patterns of allostatic load scores among blacks and whites in the United States." *American Journal of Public Health* 96, no. 5 (2006): 826–33.

Girma, Haben. "Avoid AccessiBe and other companies claiming quick and easy AI accessibility." May 5, 2021. https://www.youtube.com/watch?v=R12Z1Sp-u4U.

Gladyshev, Timothy V., and Vadim N. Gladyshev. "A disease or not a disease? Aging as a pathology." *Trends in Molecular Medicine* 22, no. 12 (2016): 995–96.

Glaser, April. "Blind people, advocates slam company claiming to make websites ADA compliant." May 9, 2021. https://www.nbcnews.com/tech/innovation/blind -people-advocates-slam-company-claiming-make-websites-ada-compliant -n1266720.

Goenjian, Armen K., David Walling, Alan M. Steinberg, Ida Karayan, Louis M. Najarian, and Robert Pynoos. "A prospective study of posttraumatic stress and depressive reactions among treated and untreated adolescents 5 years after a catastrophic disaster." *American Journal of Psychiatry* 162, no. 12 (2005): 2302–08.

Goldberg, Daniel S. "Social justice, health inequalities and methodological individualism in US health promotion." *Public Health Ethics* 5, no. 2 (2012): 104–15.

Gone, Joseph P., and Patrick E. Calf Looking. "American Indian culture as substance abuse treatment: Pursuing evidence for a local intervention." *Journal of Psychoactive Drugs* 43, no. 4 (2011): 291–96.

Gone, Joseph P., and Patrick E. Calf Looking. "The Blackfeet Indian culture camp: Auditioning an alternative indigenous treatment for substance use disorders." *Psychological Services* 12, no. 2 (2015): 83.

Gorin, Sherri Sheinfeld, and Julia E. Heck. "Cancer screening among Latino subgroups in the United States." *Preventive Medicine* 40, no. 5 (2005): 515–26.

Goss, Elizabeth, Ana Maria Lopez, Carol L. Brown, Dana S. Wollins, Otis W. Brawley, and Derek Raghavan. "American society of clinical oncology policy statement: Disparities in cancer care." *Journal of Clinical Oncology* 27, no. 17 (2009): 2881–85.

Governor's Office of Children. "Reducing the impact of incarceration on Maryland's children, families, and communities." 2015. https://goc.maryland.gov/wp-content /uploads/sites/8/2015/10/Reducing-Impact-of-Incarceration-Final-LMB-Presenta tion.pdf.

Goyal, M. K., N. Kuppermann, S. D. Cleary, S. J. Teach, and J. M. Chamberlain. "Racial disparities in pain management of children with appendicitis in emergency departments." *JAMA Pediatrics* 169 (2015): 996–1002.

Grabinski, Victoria F., Terence M. Myckatyn, Clara N. Lee, Sydney E. Philpott-Streiff, and Mary C. Politi. "Importance of shared decision-making for vulnerable populations: Examples from postmastectomy breast reconstruction." *Health Equity* 2, no. 1 (2018): 234–38.

Grappone, Gretchen. "Overcoming stigma." 2018. https://www.nami.org/Blogs/NAMI -Blog/October-2018/Overcoming-Stigma.

Green, Carmen R., Karen O. Anderson, Tamara A. Baker, Lisa C. Campbell, Sheila Decker, Roger B. Fillingim, Donna A. Kaloukalani, et al. "The unequal burden of pain: Confronting racial and ethnic disparities in pain." *Pain Medicine* 4, no. 3 (2003): 277–94.

Green, Carmen R., S. Khady Ndao-Brumblay, Brady West, and Tamika Washington. "Differences in prescription opioid analgesic availability: Comparing minority and white pharmacies across Michigan." *The Journal of Pain* 6, no. 10 (2005): 689–99.

Greenberg, Alexandra J., Danielle Haney, Kelly D. Blake, Richard P. Moser, and Bradford W. Hesse. "Differences in access to and use of electronic personal health information between rural and urban residents in the United States." *The Journal of Rural Health* 34 (2018): s30–s38.

Greenfield, Brenna L., and Kamilla L. Venner. "Review of substance use disorder treatment research in Indian country: Future directions to strive toward health equity." *The American Journal of Drug and Alcohol Abuse* 38, no. 5 (2012): 483–92.

Greenhalgh, Trisha, Matthew Knight, Maria Buxton, and Laiba Husain. "Management of post-acute covid-19 in primary care." *BMJ* 370 (2020).

Greenhalgh, Trisha, Mustafa F. Ozbilgin, Barbara Prainsack, and Sara Shaw. "Moral entrepreneurship, the power-knowledge nexus, and the Cochrane 'crisis.'" *Journal of Evaluation in Clinical Practice* 25, no. 5 (2019): 717–25.

Grol-Prokopczyk, Hanna. "Sociodemographic disparities in chronic pain, based on 12-year longitudinal data." *Pain* 158, no. 2 (2017): 313.

Guerrero, Santiago, Andrés López-Cortés, Alberto Indacochea, Jennyfer M. García-Cárdenas, Ana Karina Zambrano, Alejandro Cabrera-Andrade, Patricia Guevara-Ramírez, Diana Abigail González, Paola E. Leone, and César Paz-y-Miño. "Analysis of racial/ethnic representation in select basic and applied cancer research studies." *Scientific Reports* 8, no. 1 (2018): 1–8.

Hacker, Karen, Jocelyn Chu, Carolyn Leung, Robert Marra, Alex Pirie, Mohamed Brahimi, Margaret English, Joshua Beckmann, Dolores Acevedo-Garcia, and Robert P. Marlin. "The impact of immigration and customs enforcement on immigrant health: Perceptions of immigrants in Everett, Massachusetts, USA." *Social Science & Medicine* 73, no. 4 (2011): 586–94.

Haider, Adil, Rachel R. Adler, Eric Schneider, Tarsicio Uribe Leitz, Anju Ranjit, Christina Ta, Adele Levine, et al. "Assessment of patient-centered approaches to collect sexual orientation and gender identity information in the emergency department: The EQUALITY study." *JAMA Network Open* 1, no. 8 (2018): e186506.

Haley, Jennifer M., Genevieve M. Kenney, Hamutal Bernstein, and Dulce Gonzalez. "One in five adults in immigrant families with children reported chilling effects on public benefit receipt in 2019." Urban Institute, Washington, DC, 2020.

Halfon, Neal, Efren Aguilar, Lisa Stanley, Emily Hotez, Eryn Block, and Magdalena Janus. "Measuring equity from the start: Disparities in the health development of US kindergartners: Study examines disparities in the health development of US kindergartners." *Health Affairs* 39, no. 10 (2020): 1702–09.

Halfon, Neal, Kandyce Larson, Michael Lu, Ericka Tullis, and Shirley Russ. "Lifecourse health development: Past, present and future." *Maternal and Child Health Journal* 18, no. 2 (2014): 344–65.

Hall, Joseph L., and Deven McGraw. "For telehealth to succeed, privacy and security risks must be identified and addressed." *Health Affairs* 33, no. 2 (2014): 216–21.

Hall, Michelle Flaum, and Scott E. Hall. "When treatment becomes trauma: Defining, preventing, and transforming medical trauma." *America Counseling Association* 73 (2013).

Han, Xuesong, K. Robin Yabroff, Elizabeth Ward, Otis W. Brawley, and Ahmedin Jemal. "Comparison of insurance status and diagnosis stage among patients with newly diagnosed cancer before vs after implementation of the Patient Protection and Affordable Care Act." *JAMA Oncology* 4, no. 12 (2018): 1713–20.

Hargraves, Ian G., Victor M. Montori, Juan P. Brito, Marleen Kunneman, Kevin Shaw, Christina LaVecchia, Michael Wilson, Laura Walker, and Bjorg Thorsteinsdottir. "Purposeful SDM: A problem-based approach to caring for patients with shared decision making." *Patient Education and Counseling* 102, no. 10 (2019): 1786–92.

Harris, Gardiner. "Talk doesn't pay, so psychiatry turns instead to drug therapy." *The New York Times*, March 5, 2011. https://www.nytimes.com/2011/03/06/health/policy/06doctors.html.

Harris, L. "The new national mental health crisis line wants to track your location." Disability Visibility Project, April 19, 2021. https://disabilityvisibilityproject.com/2021/04/19/the-new-national-mental-health-crisis-line-wants-to-track-your-location/.

Hartzler, Andrea L., Leah Tuzzio, Clarissa Hsu, and Edward H. Wagner. "Roles and functions of community health workers in primary care." *The Annals of Family Medicine* 16, no. 3 (2018): 240–45.

Harvey-Wingfield, A. *Flatlining: Race, work, and health care in the new economy.* Berkeley: University of California Press, 2019.

Hawn, Carleen. "Take two aspirin and tweet me in the morning: How Twitter, Facebook, and other social media are reshaping health care." *Health Affairs* 28, no. 2 (2009): 361–68.

Health Resources and Services Administration. "Health center program: Impact and growth." 2020. https://bphc.hrsa.gov/about/healthcenterprogram/index.html.

Health Resources and Services Administration. "National Health Center data." 2019. https://data.hrsa.gov/tools/data-reporting/program-data.

healthinjustice.org. "Home." https://www.healthinjustice.org/.

Henkelmann, Jens-R., Sanne de Best, Carla Deckers, Katarina Jensen, Mona Shahab, Bernet Elzinga, and Marc Molendijk. "Anxiety, depression and post-traumatic stress disorder in refugees resettling in high-income countries: Systematic review and meta-analysis." *BJPsych Open* 6, no. 4 (2020).

Herkert, Darby, Pavithra Vijayakumar, Jing Luo, Jeremy I. Schwartz, Tracy L. Rabin, Eunice DeFilippo, and Kasia J. Lipska. "Cost-related insulin underuse among patients with diabetes." *JAMA Internal Medicine* 179, no. 1 (2019): 112–14.

Herrera, Angelica P., Shedra Amy Snipes, Denae W. King, Isabel Torres-Vigil, Daniel S. Goldberg, and Armin D. Weinberg. "Disparate inclusion of older adults in clinical trials: Priorities and opportunities for policy and practice change." *American Journal of Public Health* 100, no. S1 (2010): S105–S112.

Hill, Holly A., Laurie D. Elam-Evans, David Yankey, James A. Singleton, and Yoonjae Kang. "Vaccination coverage among children aged 19–35 months—United States, 2016." *Morbidity and Mortality Weekly Report* 66, no. 43 (2017): 1171.

Himmelstein, K. E. W., and A. S. Venkataramani. "Economic vulnerability among US female health care workers: Potential impact of a $15-per-hour minimum wage." *American Journal of Public Health* 109 (2019): 198–205.

Hine, D.C. *Black women in white: Racial conflict and cooperation in the nursing profession, 1890-1950.* Bloomington, IN: Indiana University Press, 1989.

Hines, Anika L., Roxanne M. Andrews, Ernest Moy, Marguerite L. Barrett, and Rosanna M. Coffey. "Disparities in rates of inpatient mortality and adverse events: Race/ethnicity and language as independent contributors." *International Journal of Environmental Research and Public Health* 11, no. 12 (2014): 13017–34.

Hoffman, B. *Health care for some: Rights and rationing in the United States since 1930.* Chicago: University of Chicago Press, 2012.

Hoffman, Kelly M., Sophie Trawalter, Jordan R. Axt, and M. Norman Oliver. "Racial bias in pain assessment and treatment recommendations, and false beliefs about biological differences between blacks and whites." *Proceedings of the National Academy of Sciences* 113, no. 16 (2016): 4296–301.

Hoffman, Kelly M., Sophie Trawalter, Jordan R. Axt, and M. Norman Oliver. "Racial bias in pain assessment and treatment recommendations, and false beliefs about biological differences between Blacks and whites." *Proceedings of the National Academy of Sciences of the United States of America* 113, no. 16 (2016): 4296–301.

Hogarth, Rana A. *Medicalizing Blackness: Making racial difference in the Atlantic world, 1780-1840.* Raleigh: UNC Press Books, 2017.

Hollenbach, Andrew D., Kristen L. Eckstrand, and Alice Domurat Dreger, eds. *Implementing curricular and institutional climate changes to improve health care for individuals who are LGBT, gender nonconforming, or born with DSD: A resource for medical educators.* Washington, DC: Association of American Medical Colleges, 2014.

Horrigan, John. "Baltimore's digital divide: Gaps in internet connectivity and the impact on low-income city residents." The Abell Foundation, May 2020. https://abell.org/sites/default/files/files/2020_Abell_digital%20divide_full%20report_FINAL_web%20(dr).pdf.

Horwitz, Leora I., Carol Chang, Harmony N. Arcilla, and James R. Knickman. "Quantifying health systems' investment in social determinants of health, by sector, 2017–19." *Health Affairs* 39, no. 2 (2020): 192–98.

Howlader, N., A. M. Noone, M. Krapcho, N. Neyman, R. Aminou, W. Waldron, S. F. Altekruse, C. L. Kosary, J. Ruhl, Z. Tatalovich, H. Cho, A. Mariotto, M. P. Eisner,

D. R. Lewis, H. S. Chen, E. J. Feuer, K. A. Cronin, and B. K. Edwards (Eds.). "SEER cancer statistics review, 1975–2008." National Cancer Institute, Bethesda, MD, 2011. https://seer.cancer.gov/csr/1975_2008/.

Hsieh, Elaine. "Not just 'getting by': Factors influencing providers' choice of interpreters." *Journal of General Internal Medicine* 30, no. 1 (2015): 75–82.

Hsieh, Stephanie, Ann C. Klassen, Frank C. Curriero, Laura E. Caulfield, Lawrence J. Cheskin, Jaimie N. Davis, Michael I. Goran, Marc J. Weigensberg, and Donna Spruijt-Metz. "Built environment associations with adiposity parameters among overweight and obese Hispanic youth." *Preventive Medicine Reports* 2 (2015): 406–12.

Huang, Ya-Lin A., Emma L. Frazier, Stephanie L. Sansom, Paul G. Farnham, Ram K. Shrestha, Angela B. Hutchinson, Jennifer L. Fagan, Abigail H. Viall, and Jacek Skarbinski. "Nearly half of US adults living with HIV received federal disability benefits in 2009." *Health Affairs* 34, no. 10 (2015): 1657–65.

HUD User. "Assessing the accessibility of America's housing stock for physically disabled persons." https://www.huduser.gov/portal/pdredge/pdr_edge_research _101315.html.

Hughes, Cathy, and Nichola Kane. *Multidisciplinary care.* London: RCOG Press, 2008.

Hughes, M. Courtney, Tamara A. Baker, Hansol Kim, and Elise G. Valdes. "Health behaviors and related disparities of insured adults with a health care provider in the United States, 2015–2016." *Preventive Medicine* 120 (2019): 42–49.

Human Rights Campaign Foundation. "Healthcare equality index: Promoting equitable and inclusive care for lesbian, gay, bisexual, transgender and queer patients and their families." 2020. https://hrc-prod-requests.s3-us-west-2.amazonaws.com /resources/HEI-2020-FinalReport.pdf?mtime=20200830220806&focal=none.

Human Rights Watch. "Deported to danger: United States deportation policies expose Salvadorans to death and abuse." February 5, 2020. https://www.hrw.org/sites /default/files/report_pdf/elsalvador0220_web_0.pdf.

Hwang, Wei-Chin. "Acculturative family distancing: Theory, research, and clinical practice." *Psychotherapy: Theory, Research, Practice, Training* 43, no. 4 (2006): 397.

Infection Control Today. "ER visits for UTIs add almost $4 billion a year in unnecessary healthcare costs." May 6, 2013. https://www.infectioncontroltoday.com/view /er-visits-utis-add-almost-4-billion-year-unnecessary-healthcare-costs.

Institute of Medicine. 2011. *Relieving pain in America: A blueprint for transforming prevention, care, education, and research.* Washington, DC: The National Academies Press.

Interagency Pain Research Coordinating Committee. "National pain strategy: A comprehensive population health-level strategy for pain." US Department of Health and Human Services, National Institutes of Health 36 (2016).

International Organization for Migration. "Who is a migrant?" 2019. https://www .iom.int/who-is-a-migrant.

Isasi, Carmen R., Christina M. Parrinello, Guadalupe X. Ayala, Alan M. Delamater, Krista M. Perreira, Martha L. Daviglus, John P. Elder, et al. "Sex differences in cardiometabolic risk factors among Hispanic/Latino youth." *The Journal of Pediatrics* 176 (2016): 121–27.

Jacobs, Elizabeth A., Laura S. Sadowski, and Paul J. Rathouz. "The impact of an enhanced interpreter service intervention on hospital costs and patient satisfaction." *Journal of General Internal Medicine* 22, no. 2 (2007): 306–11.

Jacobs, Elizabeth A., Donald S. Shepard, Jose A. Suaya, and Esta-Lee Stone. "Overcoming language barriers in health care: Costs and benefits of interpreter services." *American Journal of Public Health* 94, no. 5 (2004): 866–69.

James, S. E., S. Herman, S. Rankin, M. Keisling, L. Mottet, and M. Anaf. "The report of the 2015 transgender survey." National Center for Transgender Equality, 2016. http://www.transequality.org/sites/default/files/docs/usts/USTS%20Full%20 Report%20-%20FINAL%201.6.17.pdf.

Janevic, Mary R., Sara J. McLaughlin, Alicia A. Heapy, Casey Thacker, and John D. Piette. "Racial and socioeconomic disparities in disabling chronic pain: Findings from the health and retirement study." *The Journal of Pain* 18, no. 12 (2017): 1459–67.

Jaschik, Scott. "Nursing textbook pulled over stereotypes." 2017. https://www.inside highered.com/news/2017/10/23/nursing-textbook-pulled-over-stereotypes.

Jefferson, Kevin, Tammie Quest, and Katherine A. Yeager. "Factors associated with black cancer patients' ability to obtain their opioid prescriptions at the pharmacy." *Journal of Palliative Medicine* 22, no. 9 (2019): 1143–48.

Jemal, Ahmedin, Chun Chieh Lin, Amy J. Davidoff, and Xuesong Han. "Changes in insurance coverage and stage at diagnosis among nonelderly patients with cancer after the Affordable Care Act." *Journal of Clinical Oncology* 35, no. 35 (2017): 3906–15.

Jemal, Ahmedin, Elizabeth M. Ward, Christopher J. Johnson, Kathleen A. Cronin, Jiemin Ma, A. Blythe Ryerson, Angela Mariotto, et al. "Annual report to the nation on the status of cancer, 1975–2014, featuring survival." *Journal of the National Cancer Institute* 109, no. 9 (2017): djx030.

Jibaja-Weiss, Maria L., Robert J. Volk, Thomas S. Granchi, Nancy E. Neff, Emily K. Robinson, Stephen J. Spann, Noriaki Aoki, Lois C. Friedman, and J. Robert Beck. "Entertainment education for breast cancer surgery decisions: A randomized trial among patients with low health literacy." *Patient Education and Counseling* 84, no. 1 (2011): 41–48.

Jimenez, Nathalia, Kristy Seidel, Lynn D. Martin, Frederick P. Rivara, and Anne M. Lynn. "Perioperative analgesic treatment in Latino and non-Latino pediatric patients." *Journal of Health Care for the Poor and Underserved* 21, no. 1 (2010): 229.

John-Baptiste, Ava, Gary Naglie, George Tomlinson, Shabbir M. H. Alibhai, Edward Etchells, Angela Cheung, Moira Kapral, et al. "The effect of English language proficiency on length of stay and in-hospital mortality." *Journal of General Internal Medicine* 19, no. 3 (2004): 221–28.

Johnson, Chris. "10 years later, firestorm over gay-only ENDA vote still informs movement." *Washington Blade*, November 6, 2017. https://www.washingtonblade .com/2017/11/06/10-years-later-firestorm-over-gay-only-enda-vote-still -remembered/.

Johnson, J. D., I. V. Asiodu, C. P. McKenzie, C. Tucker, K. P. Tully, K. Bryant, S. Verbiest, and A. M. Stuebe. "Racial and ethnic inequities in postpartum pain evaluation and management." *Obstetrics & Gynecology* 134 (2019): 1155–62.

Joy, Kevin. "'A seat at the table': Why U-M's medical school wants more students with disabilities." University of Michigan Office of Diversity, Equity and Inclusion, October 12, 2017. https://labblog.uofmhealth.org/med-u/a-seat-at-table-why-u-ms -medical-school-wants-more-students-disabilities.

Kaiser Commission on Medicaid and the Uninsured. "Emerging Medicaid account- able care organizations: The role of managed care." 2013. https://www.kff.org/wp -content/uploads/2013/01/8319.pdf.

Kangovi, Shreya, Nandita Mitra, David Grande, Judith A. Long, and David A. Asch. "Evidence-based community health worker program addresses unmet social needs and generates positive return on investment." *Health Affairs (Project Hope)* 39, no. 2 (2020): 207–13.

Kano, Miria, Nelson Sanchez, Irene Tamí-Maury, Benjamin Solder, Gordon Watt, and Shine Chang. "Addressing cancer disparities in SGM populations: Recommenda- tions for a national action plan to increase SGM health equity through researcher and provider training and education." *Journal of Cancer Education* 35, no. 1 (2020): 44–53.

Kantarjian, Hagop M., Tito Fojo, Michael Mathisen, and Leonard A. Zwelling. "Can- cer drugs in the United States: Justum Pretium—the just price." *Journal of Clinical Oncology* 31, no. 28 (2013): 3600.

Kanwal, Tehsin, Adeel Anjum, and Abid Khan. "Privacy preservation in e-health cloud: Taxonomy, privacy requirements, feasibility analysis, and opportunities." *Cluster Computing* 24, no. 1 (2021): 293–317.

Kaplan, Joshua. "Hospitals have left many COVID-19 patients who don't speak Eng- lish alone, confused and without proper care." *ProPublica* (2020).

Karliner, Leah S., Elizabeth A. Jacobs, Alice Hm Chen, and Sunita Mutha. "Do profes- sional interpreters improve clinical care for patients with limited English proficiency? A systematic review of the literature." *Health Services Research* 42, no. 2 (2007): 727–54.

Kaufman, B. G., R. Whitaker, G. Pink, and G. M. Holmes. "Half of rural residents at high risk of serious illness due to COVID-19, creating stress on rural hospitals." *The Journal of Rural Health* 36, no. 4 (2020): 584–90.

Keefe, Francis J., Laura Porter, Tamara Somers, Rebecca Shelby, and Anava V. Wren. "Psychosocial interventions for managing pain in older adults: Outcomes and clini- cal implications." *British Journal of Anaesthesia* 111, no. 1 (2013): 89–94.

Kelleher, Kelly J., Jennifer Cooper, Katherine Deans, Pam Carr, Richard J. Brilli, Steven Allen, and William Gardner. "Cost saving and quality of care in a pediatric accountable care organization." *Pediatrics* 135, no. 3 (2015): e582–e589.

Keller, Allen S., Barry Rosenfeld, Chau Trinh-Shevrin, Chris Meserve, Emily Sachs, Jonathan A. Leviss, Elizabeth Singer, et al. "Mental health of detained asylum seek- ers." *The Lancet* 362, no. 9397 (2003): 1721–23.

Keller, David, and Lisa J. Chamberlain. "Children and the Patient Protection and Af- fordable Care Act: Opportunities and challenges in an evolving system." *Academic Pediatrics* 14, no. 3 (2014): 225–33.

Kerr, Thomas, Sanjana Mitra, Mary Clare Kennedy, and Ryan McNeil. "Supervised injection facilities in Canada: Past, present, and future." *Harm Reduction Journal* 14, no. 1 (2017): 1–9.

Kessler, Ronald C., Greg J. Duncan, Lisa A. Gennetian, Lawrence F. Katz, Jeffrey R. Kling, Nancy A. Sampson, Lisa Sanbonmatsu, Alan M. Zaslavsky, and Jens Ludwig. "Associations of housing mobility interventions for children in high-poverty neighborhoods with subsequent mental disorders during adolescence." *JAMA* 311, no. 9 (2014): 937–47.

Khatri, Utsha G., Benjamin A. Howell, and Tyler N. A. Winkelman. "Medicaid expansion increased medications for opioid use disorder among adults referred by criminal justice agencies: Study examines receipt of medications for opioid use disorder among individuals people referred by criminal justice agencies and other sources before and after Medicaid expansion." *Health Affairs* 40, no. 4 (2021): 562–70.

Khoong, Elaine C., and Alicia Fernandez. "Language, culture and preventable readmissions: Pragmatic, intervention studies needed." *BMJ* (2019): 859–61.

Khosla, Natalia N., Sylvia P. Perry, Corinne A. Moss-Racusin, Sara E. Burke, and John F. Dovidio. "A comparison of clinicians' racial biases in the United States and France." *Social Science and Medicine* (2018).

Kiel, Joan M., and Laura M. Knoblauch. "HIPAA and FERPA: Competing or collaborating?" *Journal of Allied Health* 39, no. 4 (2010): 161E–165E.

Kim, Won. "Long-term English language learners' educational experiences in the context of high-stakes accountability." *Teachers College Record* 119, no. 9 (2017): 1–32.

Kiraly, Carmen, Melanie T. Turk, Melissa A. Kalarchian, and Cheryl Shaffer. "Applying ecological frameworks in obesity intervention studies in Hispanic/Latino youth: A systematic review." *Hispanic Health Care International* 15, no. 3 (2017): 130–42.

Koh, Howard K., Amy Bantham, Alan C. Geller, Mark A. Rukavina, Karen M. Emmons, Pamela Yatsko, and Robert Restuccia. "Anchor institutions: Best practices to address social needs and social determinants of health." *American Journal of Public Health* 110, no. (2020): e1–8.

Kok, Maryse C., Marjolein Dieleman, Miriam Taegtmeyer, Jacqueline E. W. Broerse, Sumit S. Kane, Hermen Ormel, Mandy M. Tijm, and Korrie A. M. De Koning. "Which intervention design factors influence performance of community health workers in low-and middle-income countries? A systematic review." *Health Policy and Planning* 30, no. 9 (2015): 1207–27.

Kong, Angela, Lisa M. Tussing-Humphreys, Angela M. Odoms-Young, Melinda R. Stolley, and Marian L. Fitzgibbon. "Systematic review of behavioural interventions with culturally adapted strategies to improve diet and weight outcomes in African American women." *Obesity Reviews* 15 (2014): 62–92.

Kozhimannil, Katy B., Ifeoma Muoto, Blair G. Darney, Aaron B. Caughey, and Jonathan M. Snowden. "Early elective delivery disparities between non-Hispanic black and white women after statewide policy implementation." *Women's Health Issues* 28, no. 3 (2018): 224–31.

Kravitz, Richard L., L. Jay Helms, Rahman Azari, Deirdre Antonius, and Joy Melnikow. "Comparing the use of physician time and health care resources among patients speaking English, Spanish, and Russian." *Medical Care* (2000): 728–38.

Krieger, Nancy. "Measures of racism, sexism, heterosexism, and gender binarism for health equity research: From structural injustice to embodied harm-An ecosocial analysis." *Annual Review of Public Health* 41 (2019): 37–62.

Kronsberg, Hal, Amie F. Bettencourt, Carol Vidal, and Rheanna E. Platt. "Education on the social determinants of mental health in child and adolescent psychiatry fellowships." *Academic Psychiatry* (2020): 1–5.

Kronsberg, Hal, and Amie Bettencourt. "Patterns of student treatment attendance and dropout in an urban school-based mental health program." *School Mental Health* 12, no. 3 (2020): 610–25.

Ku, Leighton, and Glenn Flores. "Pay now or pay later: Providing interpreter services in health care." *Health Affairs* 24, no. 2 (2005): 435–44.

Kwiatkowski, Kat, Kathryn Coe, John C. Bailar, and G. Marie Swanson. "Inclusion of minorities and women in cancer clinical trials, a decade later: Have we improved?" *Cancer* 119, no. 16 (2013): 2956–63.

Lambda Legal. "When health care isn't caring: Lambda Legal's survey of discrimination against LGBT people and people with HIV." *New York: Lambda Legal* (2010): 1–26.

Langmuir, Alexander D. "The surveillance of communicable diseases of national importance." *New England Journal of Medicine* 268, no. 4 (1963): 182–92.

Lara, Marielena, Lara Akinbami, Glenn Flores, and Hal Morgenstern. "Heterogeneity of childhood asthma among Hispanic children: Puerto Rican children bear a disproportionate burden." *Pediatrics* 117, no. 1 (2006): 43–53.

Larkey, Linda K., Julie A. Gonzalez, Lily E. Mar, and Namino Glantz. "Latina recruitment for cancer prevention education via community based participatory research strategies." *Contemporary Clinical Trials* 30, no. 1 (2009): 47–54.

Laviana, Aaron A., Amy N. Luckenbaugh, and Matthew J. Resnick. "Trends in the cost of cancer care: Beyond drugs." *Journal of Clinical Oncology* 38, no. 4 (2020): 316.

Lebrun-Harris, Lydie A., Judith A. Mendel Van Alstyne, and Alek Sripipatana. "Influenza vaccination among US pediatric patients receiving care from federally funded health centers." *Vaccine* 38, no. 39 (2020): 6120–26.

Lee, Anna, Kanan Shah, and Fumiko Chino. "Assessment of parking fees at National Cancer Institute–designated cancer treatment centers." *JAMA Oncology* 6, no. 8 (2020): 1295–97.

Lee, July, Janine Bruce, and Nancy Ewen Wang. "Opportunities for supporting Latino immigrants in emergency and ambulatory care settings." *Journal of Community Health* 46, no. 3 (2021): 494–501.

Lee, Rosalyn D., Xiangming Fang, and Feijun Luo. "The impact of parental incarceration on the physical and mental health of young adults." *Pediatrics* 131, no. 4 (2013): e1188–e1195.

LEP.gov. "Limited English proficiency." U.S. Department of Justice, 2021. https://www.lep.gov/.

Leslie, Mayri Sagady, and Amy Romano. "Appendix: Birth can safely take place at home and in birthing centers." *Journal of Perinatal Education* 16, no. 1 (2007): 81–88.

Lett, Lanair Amaad, H. Moses Murdock, Whitney U. Orji, Jaya Aysola, and Ronnie Sebro. "Trends in racial/ethnic representation among US medical students." *JAMA Network Open* 2, no. 9 (2019): e1910490.

Lett, Lanair Amaad, Whitney U. Orji, and Ronnie Sebro. "Declining racial and ethnic representation in clinical academic medicine: A longitudinal study of 16 US medical specialties." *PLOS One* 13, no. 11 (2018): e0207274.

Levit, Laura A., Erin Balogh, Sharyl J. Nass, and Patricia Ganz, eds. *Delivering high-quality cancer care: Charting a new course for a system in crisis.* Washington, DC: National Academies Press, 2013.

Lewis, Corinne, Yaphet Getachew, Melinda Abrams, and Michelle Doty. "Changes at community health centers, and how patients are benefiting." The Commonwealth Fund, August 20, 2019. https://www.commonwealthfund.org/publications/issue -briefs/2019/aug/changes-at-community-health-centers-how-patients-are-benefiting.

Linares-Orama, Nicolas, Katherine Miranda, and Annette Romero. "Identifying robust autism indicators for Latino children." *Puerto Rico Health Sciences Journal* 38, no. 2 (2019).

Lindberg, Nangel M., Victor J. Stevens, Sonia Vega-López, Tia L. Kauffman, Mariana Rosales Calderón, and María Antonieta Cervantes. "A weight-loss intervention program designed for Mexican–American women: Cultural adaptations and results." *Journal of Immigrant and Minority Health* 14, no. 6 (2012): 1030–39.

Lindrooth, Richard C., Marcelo C. Perraillon, Rose Y. Hardy, and Gregory J. Tung. "Understanding the relationship between Medicaid expansions and hospital closures." *Health Affairs* 37, no. 1 (2018): 111–20.

Linton, Julie M., Ricky Choi, and Fernando Mendoza. "Caring for children in immigrant families: Vulnerabilities, resilience, and opportunities." *Pediatric Clinics* 63, no. 1 (2016): 115–30.

Livingston, James D., Teresa Milne, Mei Lan Fang, and Erica Amari. "The effectiveness of interventions for reducing stigma related to substance use disorders: A systematic review." *Addiction* 107, no. 1 (2012): 39–50.

Long G. "I studied and practiced medicine without molestation: African American doctors in the first years of freedom." In Laurie B. Green, John Mckiernan-González, and Martin Summers (Eds.). *Precarious prescriptions: Contested histories of race and health in North America.* Minneapolis: University of Minnesota Press, 2014.

Lopez, William D., Daniel J. Kruger, Jorge Delva, Mikel Llanes, Charo Ledón, Adreanne Waller, Melanie Harner, et al. "Health implications of an immigration raid: Findings from a Latino community in the Midwestern United States." *Journal of Immigrant and Minority Health* 19, no. 3 (2017): 702–8.

Low, Daniel, Samantha W. Pollack, Zachary C. Liao, Ramoncita Maestas, Larry E. Kirven, Anne M. Eacker, and Leo S. Morales. "Racial/ethnic disparities in clinical grading in medical school." *Teaching and Learning in Medicine* 31, no. 5 (2019): 487–96.

Lu, Wendy. "Emily Barker wants accessibility to become the norm." *The Huffington Post.* https://www.huffpost.com/entry/emily-barker-accessibility-art-fashion-world _n_6021ff7bc5b6f38d06e68557.

Lucey, Catherine Reinis, and Aaron Saguil. "The consequences of structural racism on MCAT scores and medical school admissions." *Academic Medicine* 1 (2019).

Lynch, Julia. "Why framing inequality as a health problem may make it harder to fight." November 1, 2016. https://items.ssrc.org/why-framing-inequality-as-a-health-problem-may-make-it-harder-to-fight/?

Macías, Luis Fernando, and Bruce Anthony Collet. "Separated by removal: The impact of parental deportation on Latina/o children's postsecondary educational goals." *Diaspora, Indigenous, and Minority Education* 10, no. 3 (2016): 169–81.

Mackey, Katherine, Stephanie Veazie, Johanna Anderson, Donald Bourne, and Kim Peterson. "Barriers and facilitators to the use of medications for opioid use disorder: A rapid review." *Journal of General Internal Medicine* (2020): 1–10.

MacLean, Sarah A., Priscilla O. Agyeman, Joshua Walther, Elizabeth K. Singer, Kim A. Baranowski, and Craig L. Katz. "Mental health of children held at a United States immigration detention center." *Social Science & Medicine* 230 (2019): 303–08.

MacNell, Lillian, Sinikka Elliott, Annie Hardison-Moody, and Sarah Bowen. "Black and Latino urban food desert residents' perceptions of their food environment and factors that influence food shopping decisions." *Journal of Hunger & Environmental Nutrition* 12, no. 3 (2017): 375–93.

Makadon, Harvey J., Kenneth H. Mayer, Jennifer Potter, Hilary Goldhammer (Eds.). *Fenway guide to lesbian, gay, bisexual, and transgender health.* Second edition. Boston: The Fenway Institute, 2015.

Maldonado, Linda Tina. 2013. "Midwives' collaborative activism in two U.S. cities, 1970-1990." Publicly Accessible Penn Dissertations 896.

Mamtora, Pragati H., Zeev N. Kain, Robert S. Stevenson, Brenda Golianu, Jeannie Zuk, Jeffrey I. Gold, and Michelle A. Fortier. "An evaluation of preoperative anxiety in Spanish-speaking and Latino children in the United States." *Pediatric Anesthesia* 28, no. 8 (2018): 719–25.

Manion, Jen. *Female husbands: A trans history.* Cambridge: Cambridge University Press, 2020.

Marks, Amy K., Kida Ejesi, and Cynthia García Coll. "Understanding the US immigrant paradox in childhood and adolescence." *Child Development Perspectives* 8, no. 2 (2014): 59–64.

Marmot, Michael, and Richard Wilkinson (Eds.). *Social Determinants of Health.* Second edition. Oxford: Oxford University Press, 2005.

Marquisele, Mercedes. "Twitter/ @marquisele: * = health is a loaded af ideal and I agree with @DashaunLH's view that Black/fat/disabled/queer/trans bodies cannot be healthy because "health" exists in inherent opposition to these embodiments; it is an exclusionary construct. (5/x) May 11, 2021, 9:39 AM.

Marquisele, Mercedes. "Twitter/ @marquisele: The priority is to sever the link between healthfulness and inherent worth, between healthfulness and moral alignment, between the relentless pursuit of health and the right to be treated with respect. (4/x)." May 11, 2021, 9:36 AM.

Martinez, Omar, Elwin Wu, Theo Sandfort, Brian Dodge, Alex Carballo-Dieguez, Rogeiro Pinto, Scott Rhodes, Eva Moya, and Silvia Chavez-Baray. "Evaluating the impact of immigration policies on health status among undocumented immigrants: A systematic review." *Journal of Immigrant and Minority Health* 17, no. 3 (2015): 947–70.

Martos, Alexander J., Patrick A. Wilson, and Ilan H. Meyer. "Lesbian, gay, bisexual, and transgender (LGBT) health services in the United States: Origins, evolution, and contemporary landscape." *PloS One* 12, no. 7 (2017): e0180544.

Masten, Ann S., and J. Douglas Coatsworth. "The development of competence in favorable and unfavorable environments: Lessons from research on successful children." *American Psychologist* 53, no. 2 (1998): 205.

Matta, S., P. Chatterjee, and A. S. Venkataramani. "The income-based mortality gradient among US health care workers: Cohort study." *Journal of General Internal Medicine* (2020): 1–3.

Mattson, Jeremy. "Transportation, distance, and health care utilization for older adults in rural and small urban areas." *Transportation Research Record* 2265, no. 1 (2011): 192–99.

McCallister, Erika. *Guide to protecting the confidentiality of personally identifiable information*. Darby, PA: Diane Publishing, 2010.

McCarthy, Sean, Dylana Moore, W. Andrew Smedley, Brandon M. Crowley, Shannon W. Stephens, Russell L. Griffin, Lauren C. Tanner, and Jan O. Jansen. "Impact of rural hospital closures on health-care access." *Journal of Surgical Research* 258 (2021): 170–78.

McCurley, Jessica L., Margaret A. Crawford, and Linda C. Gallo. "Prevention of type 2 diabetes in US Hispanic youth: A systematic review of lifestyle interventions." *American Journal of Preventive Medicine* 53, no. 4 (2017): 519–32.

McElroy, Jane A., Jenna J. Wintemberg, and Kenneth A. Haller. "Advancing health care for lesbian, gay, bisexual, and transgender patients in Missouri." *Missouri Medicine* 112, no. 4 (2015): 262.

McHarry, Kirwan. "Trans bodies, trans selves: A resource for the transgender community by L. Erickson-Schroth." *Journal of Homosexuality* 65, no. 13 (2018): 1934–36.

McKinney, Jessica, Laura Keyser, Susan Clinton, and Carrie Pagliano. "ACOG committee opinion no. 736: Optimizing postpartum care." *Obstetrics & Gynecology* 132, no. 3 (2018): 784–85.

McLaughlin, Katie A., Karestan C. Koenen, Eric D. Hill, Maria Petukhova, Nancy A. Sampson, Alan M. Zaslavsky, and Ronald C. Kessler. "Trauma exposure and posttraumatic stress disorder in a national sample of adolescents." *Journal of the American Academy of Child & Adolescent Psychiatry* 52, no. 8 (2013): 815–30.

McMurry, Hannah S., Darren C. Tsang, Nicole Lin, Stephen N. Symes, Chuanhui Dong, and Teshamae S. Monteith. "Head injury and neuropsychiatric sequelae in asylum seekers." *Neurology* 95, no. 19 (2020): e2605–e2609.

Meghani, Salimah H., Rosemary C. Polomano, Raymond C. Tait, April H. Vallerand, Karen O. Anderson, and Rollin M. Gallagher. "Advancing a national agenda to eliminate disparities in pain care: Directions for health policy, education, practice, and research." *Pain Medicine* 13, no. 1 (2012): 5–28.

Mehta, Swapnil S., and Matthew L. Edwards. "Suffering in silence: Mental health stigma and physicians' licensing fears." *American Journal of Psychiatry Residents' Journal* (2018).

Merikangas, Kathleen Ries, Jian-ping He, Marcy Burstein, Joel Swendsen, Shelli Avenevoli, Brady Case, Katholiki Georgiades, Leanne Heaton, Sonja Swanson, and Mark Olfson. "Service utilization for lifetime mental disorders in US adolescents: Results of the National Comorbidity Survey–Adolescent Supplement (NCS-A)." *Journal of the American Academy of Child & Adolescent Psychiatry* 50, no. 1 (2011): 32–45.

Merikangas, Kathleen Ries, Jian-ping He, Marcy Burstein, Sonja A. Swanson, Shelli Avenevoli, Lihong Cui, Corina Benjet, Katholiki Georgiades, and Joel Swendsen. "Lifetime prevalence of mental disorders in US adolescents: Results from the National Comorbidity Survey Replication–Adolescent Supplement (NCS-A)." *Journal of the American Academy of Child & Adolescent Psychiatry* 49, no. 10 (2010): 980–89.

Metzl, Jonathan M., and Helena Hansen. "Structural competency: Theorizing a new medical engagement with stigma and inequality." *Social Science & Medicine* 103 (2014): 126–33.

Metzl, Jonathan M. *The protest psychosis: How schizophrenia became a black disease.* Boston: Beacon Press, 2010.

Metzl, Jonathan M., and Helena Hansen. "Structural competency: Theorizing a new medical engagement with stigma and inequality." *Social Science & Medicine* 103 (2014): 126–33.

Meyer, Jaimie P., Carlos Franco-Paredes, Parveen Parmar, Faiza Yasin, and Matthew Gartland. "COVID-19 and the coming epidemic in US immigration detention centres." *The Lancet Infectious Diseases* 20, no. 6 (2020): 646–48.

Miller, Kimberly D., Ann Goding Sauer, Ana P. Ortiz, Stacey A. Fedewa, Paulo S. Pinheiro, Guillermo Tortolero-Luna, Dinorah Martinez-Tyson, Ahmedin Jemal, and Rebecca L. Siegel. "Cancer statistics for hispanics/latinos, 2018." *A Cancer Journal for Clinicians* 68, no. 6 (2018): 425–45.

Miller, Lauren M., Michael A. Southam-Gerow, and Robert B. Allin. "Who stays in treatment? Child and family predictors of youth client retention in a public mental health agency." *Child & Youth Care Forum* 37, no. 4 (2008): 153–70.

Miller, Neil. *Out of the past: Gay and lesbian history from 1869 to the present.* New York: Vintage Books; 1995.

Mintz, Susannah B. *Unruly bodies: Life writing by women with disabilities.* Raleigh: University of North Carolina Press, 2007.

Miserandino, Christine. "The spoon theory." *But you dont look sick? Support for those with invisible illness or chronic illness* (blog). April 25, 2013. https://butyoudont looksick.com/articles/written-by-christine/the-spoon-theory/.

Mitchell, Shannon Gwin, Jennifer Willet, Laura B. Monico, Amy James, Danielle S. Rudes, Jill Viglioni, Robert P. Schwartz, Michael S. Gordon, and Peter D. Friedmann. "Community correctional agents' views of medication-assisted treatment: Examining their influence on treatment referrals and community supervision practices." *Substance Abuse* 37, no. 1 (2016): 127–33.

Mitra, Sophie, Michael Palmer, Hoolda Kim, Daniel Mont, and Nora Groce. "Extra costs of living with a disability: A review and agenda for research." *Disability and Health Journal* 10, no. 4 (2017): 475–84.

Moinester, Margot. "Beyond the border and into the heartland: Spatial patterning of US immigration detention." *Demography* 55, no. 3 (2018): 1147–93.

Mojica, Cynthia M., Deborah Parra-Medina, and Sally Vernon. "Peer reviewed: Interventions promoting colorectal cancer screening among Latino men: A systematic review." *Preventing Chronic Disease* 15 (2018).

Morabia, Alfredo. "Unveiling the Black Panther Party legacy to public health." *American journal of public health* 106, no. 10 (2016): 1732–33.

Moreno, A., and M. A. Grodin. "Torture and its neurological sequelae." *Spinal Cord* 40, no. 5 (2002): 213–23.

Morgan, Paul L., Marianne M. Hillemeier, George Farkas, and Steve Maczuga. "Racial/ethnic disparities in ADHD diagnosis by kindergarten entry." *Journal of Child Psychology and Psychiatry* 55, no. 8 (2014): 905–13.

Morris, Juliana E., and Daniel Palazuelos. "The health implications of deportation policy." *Journal of Health Care for the Poor and Underserved* 26, no. 2 (2015): 406–09.

Morrissey, Megan H. "The Downtown Welfare Advocate Center: A case study of a welfare rights organization." *Social Service Review* 64, no. 2 (1990): 189–207.

Mukherjee, Debraj, Thomas Kosztowski, Hasan A. Zaidi, George Jallo, Benjamin S. Carson, David C. Chang, and Alfredo Quiñones-Hinojosa. "Disparities in access to pediatric neurooncological surgery in the United States." *Pediatrics* 124, no. 4 (2009): e688–e696.

Mullan, Fitzhugh. "Social mission in health professions education: Beyond Flexner." *JAMA* 318, no. 2 (2017): 122–23.

Mullan, Fitzhugh, Candice Chen, Stephen Petterson, Gretchen Kolsky, and Michael Spagnola. "The social mission of medical education: Ranking the schools." *Annals of Internal Medicine* 152, no. 12 (2010): 804–11.

Murray, Genevra F., Hector P. Rodriguez, and Valerie A. Lewis. "Upstream with a small paddle: How ACOs are working against the current to meet patients' social needs." *Health Affairs* 39, no. 2 (2020): 199–206.

NAACP. "Criminal justice fact sheet." 2021. https://naacp.org/resources/criminal-justice-fact-sheet.

Nair, Aparna. "Public health campaigns and the 'threat' of disability." Wellcome Collection, September 8, 2020. https://wellcomecollection.org/articles/X1YhrRAAA Et_izkW.

National Academies of Sciences, Engineering, and Medicine. *A roadmap to reducing child poverty*. Washington, DC: The National Academies Press, 2019.

National Academies of Sciences, Engineering, and Medicine. "Integrating social care into the delivery of health care: Moving upstream to improve the nation's health." The National Academies Press, 2019.

National Academies of Sciences, Engineering and Medicine. *Medications for opioid use disorder save lives.* Washington, DC: The National Academies Press, 2019.

National Academies of Sciences, Engineering and Medicine. *Strategies for building confidence in the COVID-19 vaccines.* Washington, DC: The National Academies Press, 2021.

National Center for Health Statistics. "National health and nutrition examination survey." U.S. Department of Health and Human Services, February 25, 2019. https://www.cdc.gov/nchs/data/factsheets/factsheet_nhanes.pdf.

National Center for Injury Prevention and Control, Division of Violence Prevention. "The social-ecological model: A framework for prevention." U.S. Department of Health and Human Services, January 28, 2021. https://www.cdc.gov/violencepreven tion/about/social-ecologicalmodel.html.

National Harm Reduction Coalition. "Principles of harm reduction." https://harm reduction.org/about-us/principles-of-harm-reduction/.

National Immigration Law Center. "Health care," 2021. https://www.nilc.org/issues /health-care/.

National Public Radio, the Robert Wood Johnson Foundation, and Harvard T. H. "Discrimination in America: Experiences and views of LGBTQ Americans." November 2017. https://legacy.npr.org/documents/2017/nov/npr-discrimination-lgbtq -final.pdf.

National Research Council. *The growth of incarceration in the United States: Exploring causes and consequences.* Washington, DC: The National Academies Press, 2014.

National Research Council (US), Institute of Medicine (US). *Children's health, the nation's wealth: Assessing and improving child health.* Washington, DC: Institute of Medicine, 2004.

National Research Council (US) Panel on Race, Ethnicity, and Health in Later Life; N. B. Anderson, R. A. Bulatao, and B. Cohen (Eds.). *Critical perspectives on racial and ethnic differences in health in late life.* Washington, DC: National Academies Press, 2004.

Navarro, Ana M., Rema Raman, Lori J. McNicholas, and Oralia Loza. "Diffusion of cancer education information through a Latino community health advisor program." *Preventive Medicine* 45, no. 2-3 (2007): 135–38.

Negi, Nalini J., Patrice Forrester, Marilyn Calderon, Katherine Esser, and Danielle Parrish. "'We are at full capacity': Social care workers persisting through work-related stress in a new immigrant settlement context in the United States." *Health & Social Care in the Community* 27, no. 5 (2019): e793–e801.

Nelson, Alondra. *Body and soul: The Black Panther Party and the fight against medical racism.* Minneapolis: University of Minnesota Press, 2011.

Neta, Gila, Mindy Clyne, and David A. Chambers. "Dissemination and implementation research at the National Cancer Institute: A review of funded studies (2006–

2019) and opportunities to advance the field." *Cancer Epidemiology and Prevention Biomarkers* 30, no. 2 (2021): 260–67.

Neumann, Peter J., Jennifer A. Palmer, Eric Nadler, ChiHui Fang, and Peter Ubel. "Cancer therapy costs influence treatment: A national survey of oncologists." *Health Affairs* 29, no. 1 (2010): 196–202.

Newell, Alan F., Peter Gregor, Maggie Morgan, Graham Pullin, and Catriona Macaulay. "User-sensitive inclusive design." *Universal Access in the Information Society* 10, no. 3 (2011): 235–43.

Nguyen, Terry. "How young people are combating anti-Black racism in their ommigrant communities." Vox Media, June 22, 2020. https://www.vox.com/21295540 /second-generation-immigrants-black-lives-matter.

Noonan, Emily J., Susan Sawning, Ryan Combs, Laura A. Weingartner, Leslee J. Martin, V. Faye Jones, and Amy Holthouser. "Engaging the transgender community to improve medical education and prioritize healthcare initiatives." *Teaching and Learning in Medicine* 30, no. 2 (2018): 119–32.

Novak, Nicole L., Arline T. Geronimus, and Aresha M. Martinez-Cardoso. "Change in birth outcomes among infants born to Latina mothers after a major immigration raid." *International Journal of Epidemiology* 46, no. 3 (2017): 839–49.

Nsubuga, P., M. E. White, S. B. Thacker, et al. "Public health surveillance: A tool for targeting and monitoring interventions." In D. T. Jamison, J. G. Breman, A. R. Measham, et al. (Eds.). *Disease control priorities in developing countries.* Second edition. Washington, DC: The International Bank for Reconstruction and Development / The World Bank; 2006.

Nunez-Smith, Marcella, Maria M. Ciarleglio, Teresa Sandoval-Schaefer, Johanna Elumn, Laura Castillo-Page, Peter Peduzzi, and Elizabeth H. Bradley. "Institutional variation in the promotion of racial/ethnic minority faculty at US medical schools." *American Journal of Public Health* 102, no. 5 (2012): 852–58.

Nutt, A. E. "Long shadow cast by psychiatrist on transgender issues finally recedes at Johns Hopkins." *The Washington Post*, 2017. https://www.washingtonpost.com /national/health-science/long-shadow-cast-by-psychiatrist-on-transgender-issues -finally-recedes-at-johns-hopkins/2017/04/05/e851e56e-0d85-11e7-ab07-07d9f5 21f6b5_story.html.

Obedin-Maliver, Juno, Elizabeth S. Goldsmith, Leslie Stewart, William White, Eric Tran, Stephanie Brenman, Maggie Wells, David M. Fetterman, Gabriel Garcia, and Mitchell R. Lunn. "Lesbian, gay, bisexual, and transgender–related content in undergraduate medical education." *JAMA* 306, no. 9 (2011): 971–77.

Office of Inspector General. "DHS lacked technology needed to successfully account for separated migrant families." Homeland Security, November 25, 2019. https:// www.oig.dhs.gov/sites/default/files/assets/2019-11/OIG-20-06-Nov19.pdf.

Ogden, Cynthia L., Cheryl D. Fryar, Craig M. Hales, Margaret D. Carroll, Yutaka Aoki, and David S. Freedman. "Differences in obesity prevalence by demographics and urbanization in US children and adolescents, 2013–2016." *JAMA* 319, no. 23 (2018): 2410–18.

Ogden, Cynthia L., Margaret D. Carroll, Hannah G. Lawman, Cheryl D. Fryar, Deanna Kruszon-Moran, Brian K. Kit, and Katherine M. Flegal. "Trends in obesity prevalence among children and adolescents in the United States, 1988–1994 through 2013–2014." *JAMA* 315, no. 21 (2016): 2292–99.

Olsen, Lauren D. "The conscripted curriculum and the reproduction of racial inequalities in contemporary U.S. medical education." *Journal of Health and Social Behavior* 60, no. 1 (2019): 55–68.

Onik, Md Mehedi Hassan, Nasr Al-Zaben, Jinhong Yang, Nam-Yong Lee, and Chul-Soo Kim. "Risk identification of personally identifiable information from collective mobile app data." *2018 International Conference on Computing, Electronics & Communications Engineering (iCCECE)* (2018): 71–76.

Orom, Heather, Teresa Semalulu, and Willie Underwood. "The social and learning environments experienced by underrepresented minority medical students: A narrative review." *Academic Medicine* 88, no. 11 (2013): 1765–77.

Orrenius, Pia M., and Madeline Zavodny. "Do immigrants work in riskier jobs?" *Demography* 46, no. 3 (2009): 535–51.

Ostroff, Jamie S., Kristen E. Riley, Megan J. Shen, Thomas M. Atkinson, Timothy J. Williamson, and Heidi A. Hamann. "Lung cancer stigma and depression: Validation of the Lung Cancer Stigma Inventory." *Psycho-Oncology* 28, no. 5 (2019): 1011–17.

Oxford University Press. "Stigma." https://www.oxfordreference.com/view/10.1093/oi/authority.20111007171501221.

Papanicolas, Irene, Liana R. Woskie, and Ashish K. Jha. "Health care spending in the United States and other high-income countries." *JAMA* 319, no. 10 (2018): 1024–39.

Partridge, E., T. Dalzell, and T. Victor. *The concise new Partridge dictionary of slang and unconventional english.* New York: Routledge, 2015.

Patel, Manali I., Ana Maria Lopez, William Blackstock, Katherine Reeder-Hayes, E. Allyn Moushey, Jonathan Phillips, and William Tap. "Cancer disparities and health equity: A policy statement from the American Society of Clinical Oncology." *Journal of Clinical Oncology* 38, no. 29 (2020): 3439–48.

Patler C. "Blurring the borders of stigma: Socioeconomic reintegration among noncitizens following imprisonment." Presentation at UC Davis Hemispheric Institute on the Americas, University of California, Davis, 2018.

Patterson, Emmett, Margaret Hughes, Andrew Cray, and Hannah Hussey. "Disability justice is LGBT justice: A conversation with movement leaders." Center for American Progress. July 30, 2015. https://www.americanprogress.org/issues/lgbtq rights/news/2015/07/30/118531/disability-justice-is-lgbt-justice-a-conversation -with-movement leaders/.

Pavithra, V., and Jeyamala Chandrasekaran. "Developing security solutions for telemedicine applications: Medical image encryption and watermarking." In *Research Anthology on Telemedicine Efficacy, Adoption, and Impact on Healthcare Delivery*, pp. 612–31. Hershey, PA: IGI Global, 2021.

Pedraza, Franciso I., Vanessa Cruz Nichols, and Alana MW LeBrón. "Cautious citizenship: The deterring effect of immigration issue salience on health care use and bureaucratic interactions among Latino US citizens." *Journal of Health Politics, Policy and Law* 42, no. 5 (2017): 925–60.

Perez, Lilian G., Elva M. Arredondo, John P. Elder, Simón Barquera, Brian Nagle, and Christina K. Holub. "Evidence-based obesity treatment interventions for Latino adults in the US: A systematic review." *American Journal of Preventive Medicine* 44, no. 5 (2013): 550–60.

Pérez-Stable, Eliseo J. "Director's message: Sexual and gender minorities formally designated as a health disparity population for research purposes." National Institutes of Health, October 6, 2016. http://www.nimhd.nih.gov/about/directors-corner/message.html?utm_medium=email&utm_source=govdelivery.

Perfetto, Eleanor M., Laurie Burke, Elisabeth M. Oehrlein, and Robert S. Epstein. "Patient-focused drug development: A new direction for collaboration." *Medical Care* 53, no. 1 (2015): 9–17.

Perreira, Krista M., and Juan M. Pedroza. "Policies of exclusion: Implications for the health of immigrants and their children." *Annual Review of Public Health* 40 (2019): 147–66.

Perrin, James M., Genevieve M. Kenney, and Sara Rosenbaum. "Medicaid and child health equity." *The New England Journal of Medicine* 383, no. 27 (2020): 2595–98.

Perrin, James M., Greg Duncan, Angela Diaz, and Kelly Kelleher. "Principles and policies to strengthen child and adolescent health and well-being: Study describes National Academies of Sciences, Engineering, and Medicine reports on poverty, mental, emotional, and behavioral health, adolescence, and young family health and education." *Health Affairs* 39, no. 10 (2020): 1677–83.

Persky, Susan, Kimberly A. Kaphingst, Vincent C. Allen Jr., and Ibrahim Senay. "Effects of patient-provider race concordance and smoking status on lung cancer risk perception accuracy among African-Americans." *Annals of Behavioral Medicine* 45, no. 3 (2013): 308–17.

Petersen, Emily E., Nicole L. Davis, David Goodman, Shanna Cox, Carla Syverson, Kristi Seed, Carrie Shapiro-Mendoza, William M. Callaghan, and Wanda Barfield. "Racial/ethnic disparities in pregnancy-related deaths—United States, 2007–2016." *Morbidity and Mortality Weekly Report* 68, no. 35 (2019): 762–65.

Peterson, Ashley L. "Applying spoon theory to mental illness." Mental Health @ Home, January 28, 2019. https://mentalhealthathome.org/2019/01/28/spoon-theory-mental-illness/

Peterson, Cora, Mengyao Li, Likang Xu, Christina A. Mikosz, and Feijun Luo. "Assessment of annual cost of substance use disorder in US hospitals." *JAMA Network Open* 4, no. 3 (2021): e210242.

Petrou, P., G. Samoutis, and C. Lionis. "Single-payer or a multipayer health system: A systematic literature review." *Public Health* 163 (2018): 141–52.

Pew Research Center. "Modes of entry for the unauthorized migrant population." 2006. https://www.pewresearch.org/hispanic/2006/05/22/modes-of-entry-for-the-unauthorized-migrant-population/.

Phelan, J. C., and B. G. Link. "Is racism a fundamental cause of inequalities in health?" *Annual Review of Sociology* 41 (2015): 311–30.

Philbin, Morgan M., Morgan Flake, Mark L. Hatzenbuehler, and Jennifer S. Hirsch. "State-level immigration and immigrant-focused policies as drivers of Latino health disparities in the United States." *Social Science & Medicine* 199 (2018): 29–38.

Phillips, Christine B., and Joanne Travaglia. "Low levels of uptake of free interpreters by Australian doctors in private practice: Secondary analysis of national data." *Australian Health Review* 35, no. 4 (2011): 475–79.

Polite, Blase N., Jerome E. Seid, Laura A. Levit, M. Kelsey Kirkwood, Caroline Schenkel, Suanna S. Bruinooge, Stephen S. Grubbs, Deborah Y. Kamin, and Richard L. Schilsky. "A new look at the state of cancer care in America." *Journal of Oncology Practice* 14, no. 7 (2018): 397–99.

Polite, Blase N., Lucile L. Adams-Campbell, Otis W. Brawley, Nina Bickell, John M. Carethers, Christopher R. Flowers, Margaret Foti, et al. "Charting the future of cancer health disparities research: A position statement from the American Association for Cancer Research, the American Cancer Society, the American Society of Clinical Oncology, and the National Cancer Institute." *Cancer Research* 77, no. 17 (2017): 4548–55.

Potochnik, Stephanie, Jen-Hao Chen, and Krista Perreira. "Local-level immigration enforcement and food insecurity risk among Hispanic immigrant families with children: National-level evidence." *Journal of Immigrant and Minority Health* 19, no. 5 (2017): 1042–49.

Potochnik, Stephanie. "How states can reduce the dropout rate for undocumented immigrant youth: The effects of in-state resident tuition policies." *Social Science Research* 45 (2014): 18–32.

Pottie, K., A. Hadi, J. Chen, V. Welch, and Kamila Hawthorne. "Realist review to understand the efficacy of culturally appropriate diabetes education programmes." *Diabetic Medicine* 30, no. 9 (2013): 1017–25.

Powers, George M., Lex Frieden, and Vinh Nguyen. "Telemedicine: Access to health care for people with disabilities." *Houston Journal of Health Law & Policy* 17 (2017): 7.

Price-Wise, Gail. *An Intoxicating error: Mistranslation, medical malpractice, and prejudice.* BookBaby, 2015.

Pulrang, Andrew. "A simple fix for one of disabled people's most persistent, pointless injustices." *Forbes*, August 31, 2020. https://www.forbes.com/sites/andrew pulrang/2020/08/31/a-simple-fix-for-one-of-disabled-peoples-most-persistent -pointless-injustices/?sh=2a817d9b6b71.

Pumariega, Andres J., and Eugenio Rothe. "Leaving no children or families outside: The challenges of immigration." *The American Journal of Orthopsychiatry* 80, no. 4 (2010): 505–15.

Quadagno, J. *One nation, uninsured: Why the U.S. has no national health insurance.* Oxford, UK: Oxford University Press, 2005.

Quinn, Gwendolyn P., Julian A. Sanchez, Steven K. Sutton, Susan T. Vadaparampil, Giang T. Nguyen, B. Lee Green, Peter A. Kanetsky, and Matthew B. Schabath. "Cancer and lesbian, gay, bisexual, transgender/transsexual, and queer/questioning (LGBTQ) populations." *A cancer Journal for Clinicians* 65, no. 5 (2015): 384–400.

Rao, H., H. Mahadevappa, P. Pillay, M. Sessay, A. Abraham, and J. Luty. "A study of stigmatized attitudes towards people with mental health problems among health professionals." *Journal of Psychiatric and Mental Health Nursing* 16, no. 3 (2009): 279–84.

Rasanathan, K, Sharkey, A. "Global health promotion and the social determinants of health." In R. S. Zimmerman, R. J. DiClemente, and J. K. Andrus (Eds.). *Introduction to global health promotion.* San Francisco, CA: Jossey-Bass Public Health, 2016.

Ray, Victor. "A theory of racialized organizations." *American Sociological Review* 84, no. 1 (2019): 26–53.

Razali, Rina Azlin, and Norziana Jamil. "A quick review of security issues in telemedicine." *2020 8th International Conference on Information Technology and Multimedia (ICIMU)* (2020): 162–65.

Reid, M. Carrington, Christopher Eccleston, and Karl Pillemer. "Management of chronic pain in older adults." *BMJ* 350 (2015).

Reuland, Daniel S., Linda K. Ko, Alicia Fernandez, Laura C. Braswell, and Michael Pignone. "Testing a Spanish-language colorectal cancer screening decision aid in Latinos with limited English proficiency: Results from a pre-post trial and four month follow-up survey." *BMC Medical Informatics and Decision Making* 12, no. 1 (2012): 1–8.

Reyes-Gibby, Cielito C., Lu Ann Aday, Knox H. Todd, Charles S. Cleeland, and Karen O. Anderson. "Pain in aging community-dwelling adults in the United States: Non-Hispanic whites, non-Hispanic blacks, and Hispanics." *The Journal of Pain* 8, no. 1 (2007): 75–84.

Ripp, Kelsey, and Lundy Braun. "Race/ethnicity in medical education: An analysis of a question bank for step 1 of the United States medical licensing examination." *Teaching and Learning in Medicine* 29, no. 2 (2017): 115–22.

Roberts, Eric T., and Ateev Mehrotra. "Assessment of disparities in digital access among Medicare beneficiaries and implications for telemedicine." *JAMA Internal Medicine* 180, no. 10 (2020): 1386–89.

Rogers, N. "'Caution: The AMA may be dangerous to your health': The student health organizations (SHO) and American medicine, 1965-1970." *Radical History Review* 80 (2001): 5–34.

Rosenbaum, Sara, Jessica Sharac, Peter Shin, and Jennifer Tolbert. "Community health center financing: The role of Medicaid and Section 330 grant funding explained." Kaiser Family Foundation, March 26, 2019. https://www.kff.org /medicaid/issue-brief/community-health-center-financing-the-role-of-medicaid -and-section-330-grant-funding-explained/.

Ross, Casey. "Hospitals are using AI to predict the decline of Covid-19 patients— before knowing it works." *STAT*, April 24, 2020. https://www.statnews.com /2020/04/24/coronavirus-hospitals-use-ai-to-predict-patient-decline-before-know ing-it-works/#:~:text=Dozens%20of%20hospitals%20across,those%20with%20 the%20new%20disease.

Ross, Nancy, Robert Gilbert, Sara Torres, Kevin Dugas, Philip Jefferies, Sheila McDonald, Susan Savage, and Michael Ungar. "Adverse childhood experiences: Assessing the impact on physical and psychosocial health in adulthood and the mitigating role of resilience." *Child Abuse & Neglect* 103 (2020): 104440.

Rothe, Eugenio M. "Considering cultural diversity in the management of ADHD in Hispanic patients." *Journal of the National Medical Association* 97, no. 10 Suppl (2005): 17S.

Rousseau, Cécile, and Rochelle L. Frounfelker. "Mental health needs and services for migrants: An overview for primary care providers." *Journal of Travel Medicine* 26, no. 2 (2019): tay150.

Rubin, I. Leslie. "Social determinants of health." In I. Leslie Rubin, Joav Merrick, Donald E. Greydanus, and Dilip R. Patel (Eds.). *Health care for people with intellectual and developmental disabilities across the lifespan*, pp. 1919–32. Cham: Springer International Publishing, 2016.

Rubright, Jonathan D., Michael Jodoin, and Michael A. Barone. "Examining demographics, prior academic performance, and United States medical licensing examination scores." *Academic Medicine* 94, no. 3 (2019): 364–70.

Rumbaut, Rubén G., and Douglas S. Massey. "Immigration and language diversity in the United States." *Daedalus* 142, no. 3 (2013): 141–54.

Saadi, Altaf, and Lello Tesema. "Privatisation of immigration detention facilities." *The Lancet* 393, no. 10188 (2019): 2299.

Saadi, Altaf, Maria-Elena De Trinidad Young, Caitlin Patler, Jeremias Leonel Estrada, and Homer Venters. "Understanding US immigration detention: Reaffirming rights and addressing social-structural determinants of health." *Health and Human Rights* 22, no. 1 (2020): 187.

Saha, Somnath, Gretchen Guiton, Paul F. Wimmers, and LuAnn Wilkerson. "Student body racial and ethnic composition and diversity-related outcomes in US medical schools." *JAMA* 300, no. 10 (2008): 1135–45.

Saitz, Richard, Shannon C. Miller, David A. Fiellin, and Richard N. Rosenthal. "Recommended use of terminology in addiction medicine." *Journal of Addiction Medicine* 15, no. 1 (2021): 3–7.

Salahuddin, Meliha, Adriana Pérez, Nalini Ranjit, Steven H. Kelder, Sarah E. Barlow, Stephen J. Pont, Nancy F. Butte, and Deanna M. Hoelscher. "Predictors of severe obesity in low-income, predominantly Hispanic/Latino children: The Texas childhood obesity research demonstration study." *Preventing Chronic Disease* 14 (2017): E141.

Salinas Jr., Cristobal. "The complexity of the 'x' in Latinx: How Latinx/a/o students relate to, identify with, and understand the term Latinx." *Journal of Hispanic Higher Education* 19, no. 2 (2020): 149–68.

Saloner, Brendan, Emma E. McGinty, Leo Beletsky, Ricky Bluthenthal, Chris Beyrer, Michael Botticelli, and Susan G. Sherman. "A public health strategy for the opioid crisis." *Public Health Reports* 133, no. 1 suppl (2018): 24S–34S.

Sam, David L., and John W. Berry. "Acculturation: When individuals and groups of different cultural backgrounds meet." *Perspectives on Psychological Science* 5, no. 4 (2010): 472–81.

Santoro, Taylor N., and Jonathan D. Santoro. "Racial bias in the US opioid epidemic: A review of the history of systemic bias and implications for care." *Cureus* 10, no. 12 (2018): e3733.

Sarpel, Umut, Bruce C. Vladeck, Celia M. Divino, and Paul E. Klotman. "Fact and fiction: Debunking myths in the US healthcare system." *Annals of Surgery* 247, no. 4 (2008): 563–69.

Savas, Lara S., Sally W. Vernon, John S. Atkinson, and Maria E. Fernández. "Effect of acculturation and access to care on colorectal cancer screening in low-income Latinos." *Journal of Immigrant and Minority Health* 17, no. 3 (2015): 696–703.

Savitt T. "Abraham Flexner and the Black medical schools." *Journal of the National Medical Association* 98, no. 9 (2006): 1415–24.

Sawyer, Jeremy, and Anup Gampa. "Implicit and explicit racial attitudes changed during Black Lives Matter." *Personality & Social Psychology Bulletin* 44, no. 7 (2018): 1039–59.

Sawyer, Wendy, and Peter Wagner. "Mass incarceration: The whole pie 2020." https://www.prisonpolicy.org/reports/pie2020.html.

Sayers, William. "The etymology of queer." *ANQ: A Quarterly Journal of Short Articles, Notes and Reviews* 18, no. 2 (2005): 17–19.

Schenker, Yael, Eliseo J. Pérez-Stable, Dana Nickleach, and Leah S. Karliner. "Patterns of interpreter use for hospitalized patients with limited English proficiency." *Journal of General Internal Medicine* 26, no. 7 (2011): 712–17.

Schootman, Mario, Edward Kinman, and Dione Farria. "Rural-urban differences in ductal carcinoma in situ as a proxy for mammography use over time." *The Journal of Rural Health* 19, no. 4 (2003): 470–76.

Schütte, Stefanie, François Gemenne, Muhammad Zaman, Antoine Flahault, and Anneliese Depoux. "Connecting planetary health, climate change, and migration." *The Lancet Planetary Health* 2, no. 2 (2018): e58–e59.

Seattle Children's Hospital Foundation. "Seattle Children's Patient Navigator pilot and evaluation." March 13, 2013. https://www.phpda.org/projects/childrens-navigator-grant-and-clegg-evaluation-of-navigator-grant.

Sexual and Gender Minority Research Office. "Sexual and gender minority populations in NIH-supported research." August 28, 2019. https://grants.nih.gov/grants/guide/notice-files/NOT-OD-19-139.html.

Shanell Thompson. "Looking at race, poverty and disability." National Disability Institute, November 29, 2018. https://www.nationaldisabilityinstitute.org/blog/looking-at-race-poverty-and-disability/.

Shavers, Vickie L., Alexis Bakos, and Vanessa B. Sheppard. "Race, ethnicity, and pain among the US adult population." *Journal of Health Care for the Poor and Underserved* 21, no. 1 (2010): 177–220.

Sherry, Melissa, Jennifer L. Wolff, Jeromie Ballreich, Eva DuGoff, Karen Davis, and Gerard Anderson. "Bridging the silos of service delivery for high-need, high-cost individuals." *Population Health Management* 19, no. 6 (2016): 421–28.

Shi, Leiyu, Lydie A. Lebrun, Jinsheng Zhu, Arthur S. Hayashi, Ravi Sharma, Charles A. Daly, Alek Sripipatana, and Quyen Ngo-Metzger. "Clinical quality performance in US health centers." *Health Services Research* 47, no. 6 (2012): 2225–49.

Shin, Peter, Jessica Sharac, and Sara Rosenbaum. "Community health centers and Medicaid at 50: An enduring relationship essential for health system transformation." *Health Affairs* 34, no. 7 (2015): 1096–104.

Shinohara, Kristen, Cynthia L. Bennett, and Jacob O. Wobbrock. "How designing for people with and without disabilities shapes student design thinking." *Proceedings of the 18th International ACM SIGACCESS Conference on Computers and Accessibility* (2016): 229–37.

Shonkoff, Jack P., Andrew S. Garner, Benjamin S. Siegel, Mary I. Dobbins, Marian F. Earls, Laura McGuinn, John Pascoe, David L. Wood, Committee on Psychosocial Aspects of Child and Family Health, and Committee on Early Childhood, Adoption, and Dependent Care. "The lifelong effects of early childhood adversity and toxic stress." *Pediatrics* 129, no. 1 (2012): e232–e246.

Shor, Eran, David Roelfs, and Zoua M. Vang. "The 'Hispanic mortality paradox' revisited: Meta-analysis and meta-regression of life-course differentials in Latin American and Caribbean immigrants' mortality." *Social Science & Medicine* 186 (2017): 20–33.

Shpigelman, Carmit-Noa, Cheryl Zlotnick, and Rachel Brand. "Attitudes toward nursing students with disabilities: Promoting social inclusion." *Journal of Nursing Education* 55, no. 8 (2016): 441–49.

Siddall, Philip J., and Michael J. Cousins. "Persistent pain as a disease entity: Implications for clinical management." *Anesthesia and Analgesia* 99, no. 2 (August 2004): 510–20.

Siegel, Rebecca L., Kimberly D. Miller, Ann Goding Sauer, Stacey A. Fedewa, Lynn F. Butterly, Joseph C. Anderson, Andrea Cercek, Robert A. Smith, and Ahmedin Jemal. "Colorectal cancer statistics, 2020." *CA: A Cancer Journal for Clinicians* 70, no. 3 (2020): 145–64.

Siegel, Rebecca L., Stacey A. Fedewa, Kimberly D. Miller, Ann Goding-Sauer, Paulo S. Pinheiro, Dinorah Martinez-Tyson, and Ahmedin Jemal. "Cancer statistics for hispanics/latinos, 2015." *CA: A Cancer Journal for Clinicians* 65, no. 6 (2015): 457–80.

Singer, Margaret A., Manuela Gutierrez Velez, Scott D. Rhodes, and Julie M. Linton. "Discrimination against mixed-status families and its health impact on Latino children." *The Journal of Applied Research on Children: Informing Policy for Children at Risk* 10, no. 1 (2018).

Singh, Simone R., Gary J. Young, Shoou Yih Daniel Lee, Paula H. Song, and Jeffrey A. Alexander. "Analysis of hospital community benefit expenditures' alignment with community health needs: Evidence from a national investigation of tax-exempt hospitals." *American Journal of Public Health* 105, no. 5 (2015): 914–21.

Siotos, Charalampos, Paula M. Neira, Brandyn D. Lau, Jill P. Stone, James Page, Gedge D. Rosson, and Devin Coon. "Origins of gender affirmation surgery: The history of the first gender identity clinic in the United States at Johns Hopkins." *Annals of Plastic Surgery* 83, no. 2 (2019): 132–36.

Slagstad, Ketil. "The political nature of sex-transgender in the history of medicine." *The New England Journal of Medicine* 384, no. 11 (2021): 1070–74.

Smailhodzic, Edin, Wyanda Hooijsma, Albert Boonstra, and David J. Langley. "Social media use in healthcare: A systematic review of effects on patients and on their relationship with healthcare professionals." *BMC Health Services Research* 16, no. 1 (2016): 1–14.

Smedley, Brian D., Adrienne Y. Stith, and Alan R. Nelson. *Unequal treatment: Confronting racial and ethnic disparities in health care.* Washington, DC: National Academies Press, 2003.

Smith, D. B. *The power to heal: Civil rights, Medicare, and the struggle to transform America's health care system.* Nashville, TN: Vanderbilt University Press, 2016.

Smith, David P., and Benjamin S. Bradshaw. "Rethinking the Hispanic paradox: Death rates and life expectancy for US non-Hispanic White and Hispanic populations." *American Journal of Public Health* 96, no. 9 (2006): 1686–92.

Smith, S. L. *Sick and tired of being sick and tired: Black women's gealth activism in America, 1890-1950.* Philadelphia, PA: University of Pennsylvania Press, 1995.

Smith, Sonali M., Kerri Wachter, Howard A. Burris III, Richard L. Schilsky, Daniel J. George, Douglas E. Peterson, Melissa L. Johnson, et al. "Clinical cancer advances 2021: ASCO's report on progress against cancer." *Journal of Clinical Oncology* 39, no. 10 (2021): 1165–84.

Snyder, V. Nelly Salgado de, Deliana Garcia, Roxana Pineda, Jessica Calderon, Dania Diaz, Alondra Morales, and Brenda Perez. "Exploring why adult Mexican males do not get vaccinated: Implications for COVID-19 preventive actions." *Hispanic Journal of Behavioral Sciences* 42, no. 4 (2020): 515–27.

Sohler, Nancy Lynn, Lisa K. Fitzpatrick, Rebecca G. Lindsay, Kathryn Anastos, and Chinazo O. Cunningham. "Does patient–provider racial/ethnic concordance influence ratings of trust in people with HIV infection?" *AIDS and Behavior* 11, no. 6 (2007): 884–96.

Solar, O., and A. Irwin. "A conceptual framework for action on the social determinants of health." Social determinants of health discussion paper 2 (policy and practice). World Health Organization, 2010. https://www.who.int/sdhconference/resources/ConceptualframeworkforactiononSDH_eng.pdf.

Solomon, Marc. *Winning marriage: The inside story of how same-sex couples took on the politicians and pundits—and won.* Lebanon, NH: University Press of New England, 2015.

Spencer, Jennifer C., William A. Calo, and Noel T. Brewer. "Disparities and reverse disparities in HPV vaccination: A systematic review and meta-analysis." *Preventive Medicine* 123 (2019): 197–203.

Srivastava, A. Benjamin. "Impaired physicians: Obliterating the stigma." *American Journal of Psychiatry Residents' Journal* 13, no. 3 (2018): 4–6.

Stasio, B. J. "People with disabilities and the federal marriage penalties." https://publications.ici.umn.edu/impact/23-2/people-with-disabilities-and-the-federal-marriage-penalties.

Stearns, Elizabeth, and Elizabeth J. Glennie. "Opportunities to participate: Extracurricular activities' distribution across and academic correlates in high schools." *Social Science Research* 39, no. 2 (2010): 296–309.

Steel, Zachary, Tien Chey, Derrick Silove, Claire Marnane, Richard A. Bryant, and Mark Van Ommeren. "Association of torture and other potentially traumatic events with mental health outcomes among populations exposed to mass conflict and displacement: A systematic review and meta-analysis." *JAMA* 302, no. 5 (2009): 537–49.

Steinmetz, Katy. "The transgender tipping point." *Time* 183, no. 22 (2014): 38–46.

Stergiou-Kita, Mary, Cheryl Pritlove, and Bonnie Kirsh. "The 'Big C'—stigma, cancer, and workplace discrimination." *Journal of Cancer Survivorship* 10, no. 6 (2016): 1035–50.

Stille, Christopher, Renee M. Turchi, Richard Antonelli, Michael D. Cabana, Tina L. Cheng, Danielle Laraque, and James Perrin. "The family-centered medical home: Specific considerations for child health research and policy." *Academic Pediatrics* 10, no. 4 (2010): 211–17.

Stolbach, Bradley C., and Seeba Anam. "Racial and ethnic health disparities and trauma-informed care for children exposed to community violence." *Pediatric Annals* 46, no. 10 (2017): e377–e381.

Stop the Addiction Fatality Epidemic Project. "Naloxone Awareness Project state rules." 2020. https://www.safeproject.us/naloxone-awareness-project/state-rules/.

Stowe, James D., and Teresa M. Cooney. "Examining Rowe and Kahn's concept of successful aging: Importance of taking a life course perspective." *The Gerontologist* 55, no. 1 (2015): 43–50.

Stowell, Jeffrey R., Levi Filler, Marya S. Sabir, Albert T. Roh, and Murtaza Akhter. "Implications of language barrier on the diagnostic yield of computed tomography in pulmonary embolism." *The American Journal of Emergency Medicine* 36, no. 4 (2018): 677–79.

Streed Jr., Carl G., J. Seth Anderson, Chris Babits, and Michael A. Ferguson. "Changing medical practice, not patients-Putting an end to conversion therapy." *The New England Journal of Medicine* 381, no. 6 (2019): 500–02.

Streed Jr., Carl G., Mitchell R. Lunn, Jennifer Siegel, and Juno Obedin-Maliver. "Meeting the patient care, education, and research missions: Academic medical centers must comprehensively address sexual and gender minority health." *Academic Medicine: Journal of the Association of American Medical Colleges* (2020).

Streed, Carl G., Chris Grasso, Sari L. Reisner, and Kenneth H. Mayer. "Sexual orientation and gender identity data collection: Clinical and public health importance." *American Journal of Public Health* 110, no. 7 (2020): 991–93.

Streisel, S. E. "Intent to refer: Exploring bias toward specific medication-assisted treatments by community corrections employees." *Substance Use & Misuse* 53, no. 14 (2018): 2421–30.

Strings, Sabrina. *Fearing the black body: The racial origins of fat phobia.* New York: NYU Press, 2019.

Stubbe, Dorothy E. "Practicing cultural competence and cultural humility in the care of diverse patients." *Focus* 18, no. 1 (2020): 49–51.

Stubbs, Brendon, Pat Schofield, Tarik Binnekade, Sandhi Patchay, Amir Sepehry, and Laura Eggermont. "Pain is associated with recurrent falls in community-dwelling older adults: Evidence from a systematic review and meta-analysis." *Pain Medicine* 15, no. 7 (2014): 1115–28.

Suárez-Orozco, Carola, Hirokazu Yoshikawa, Robert Teranishi, and Marcelo Suárez-Orozco. "Growing up in the shadows: The developmental implications of unauthorized status." *Harvard Educational Review* 81, no. 3 (2011): 438–73.

Substance Abuse and Mental Health Services Administration. "2019 NSDUH detailed tables." U.S. Department of Health and Human Services, September 11, 2020. https://www.samhsa.gov/data/report/2019-nsduh-detailed-tables.

Suleman, Shazeen, Kent D. Garber, and Lainie Rutkow. "Xenophobia as a determinant of health: An integrative review." *Journal of Public Health Policy* 39, no. 4 (2018): 407–23.

Summers, Martin. "Diagnosing the ailments of Black citizenship: African American physicians and the politics of mental illness, 1895–1940." In Laurie B. Green, John Mckiernan-González, and Martin Summers (Eds.). *Precarious prescriptions: Contested histories of race and health in North America*. Minneapolis: University of Minnesota Press, 2014.

Surbone, Antonella. "A review of cultural attitudes about cancer." In *Global oncology in global perspectives on cancer: Incidence, care and clinical experience*, pp. 19–40. Santa Barbara, CA: Praeger Press, 2015.

Swartz, Jonas J., Jens Hainmueller, Duncan Lawrence, and Maria I. Rodriguez. "Expanding prenatal care to unauthorized immigrant women and the effects on infant health." *Obstetrics and Gynecology* 130, no. 5 (2017): 938.

Swietek, Karen E., Bradley N. Gaynes, George L. Jackson, Morris Weinberger, and Marisa Elena Domino. "Effect of the patient-centered medical home on racial disparities in quality of care." *Journal of General Internal Medicine* (2020): 1–10.

Taylor, David G. "The political economics of cancer drug discovery and pricing." *Drug Discovery Today* (2020).

Taylor, Janiece L. Walker, Claudia M. Campbell, Roland J. Thorpe Jr., Keith E. Whitfield, Manka Nkimbeng, and Sarah L. Szanton. "Pain, racial discrimination, and depressive symptoms among African American women." *Pain Management Nursing* 19, no. 1 (2018): 79–87.

Teicher, Martin H., and Jacqueline A. Samson. "Childhood maltreatment and psychopathology: A case for ecophenotypic variants as clinically and neurobiologically distinct subtypes." *American Journal of Psychiatry* 170, no. 10 (2013): 1114–33.

Terry, Jennifer. *An American obsession: Science, medicine, and homosexuality in modern society*. Chicago: University of Chicago Press, 1999.

Tervalon, Melanie, and Jann Murray-Garcia. "Cultural humility versus cultural competence: A critical distinction in defining physician training outcomes in multicultural education." *Journal of Health Care for the Poor and Underserved* 9, no. 2 (1998): 117–25.

Thomas, S. R., G. Pink, and K. Reiter. "Characteristics of communities served by rural hospitals predicted to be at high risk of financial distress in 2019." North Carolina Rural Health Research Program. Findings Brief. April 2019.

Thomas, Christopher R., and Charles E. Holzer III. "The continuing shortage of child and adolescent psychiatrists." *Journal of the American Academy of Child & Adolescent Psychiatry* 45, no. 9 (2006): 1023–31.

Thomas, Stephanie. "Adapt rides again in Phoenix." *Incitement, Incitement,* Spring 1987. https://adapt.org/wp-content/uploads/2017/04/incit03-2.pdf.

Tingey, Lauren, Francene Larzelere, Novalene Goklish, Summer Rosenstock, Larissa Jennings Mayo-Wilson, Elliott Pablo, Warren Goklish, et al. "Entrepreneurial, economic, and social well-being outcomes from an RCT of a youth entrepreneurship education intervention among Native American adolescents." *International Journal of Environmental Research and Public Health* 17, no. 7 (2020): 2383.

Torrey, Philip L. "Rethinking immigration's mandatory detention regime: Politics, profit, and the meaning of custody." *University of Michigan Journal of Law Reform* 48 (2014): 879.

Touloumakos, Anna K., and Alexia Barrable. "Adverse childhood experiences: the protective and therapeutic potential of nature." *Frontiers in Psychology* 11 (2020).

TRAC. "Record number of asylum cases in FY 2019." January 8, 2020. https://trac.syr.edu/immigration/reports/588/.

Trawalter, Sophie. "Black Americans are systematically under-treated for pain. Why?" Frank Batten School of Leadership and Public Policy, June 30, 2020. https://batten.virginia.edu/about/news/black-americans-are-systematically-under-treated-pain-why.

Treede, Rolf-Detlef, Winfried Rief, Antonia Barke, Qasim Aziz, Michael I. Bennett, Rafael Benoliel, Milton Cohen, et al. "A classification of chronic pain for ICD-11." *Pain* 156, no. 6 (2015): 1003.

Trent, M., D. G. Dooley, and J. Douge; Section on Adolescent Health, Council on Community Pediatrics, and Committee on Adolescence. "The impact of racism on child and adolescent health." *Pediatrics* 144, no. 2 (2019): e20191765.

Trent, Maria, Danielle G. Dooley, Jacqueline Dougé, Maria E. Trent, Robert M. Cavanaugh, Amy E. Lacroix, et al. "The impact of racism on child and adolescent health." *Pediatrics* 144, no. 2 (2019).

Tsai, Jennifer, and Ann Crawford-Roberts. "A call for critical race theory in medical education." *Academic Medicine* (2017).

Tsai, Jennifer, Laura Ucik, Nell Baldwin, Christopher Hasslinger, and Paul George. "Race matters? Examining and rethinking race portrayal in preclinical medical education." *Academic Medicine* (2016).

U.S. Census Bureau. "Detailed languages spoken at home and ability to speak English for the population 5 years and over: 2009-2013." October 2015. https://www.census.gov/data/tables/2013/demo/2009-2013-lang-tables.html.

U.S. Census Bureau. "QuickFacts: United States." 2019. https://www.census.gov/quickfacts/fact/table/US/RHI725219#qf-headnote-b.

244

*Bibliography*

U.S. Citizenship and Immigration Services. "Consideration of deferred action for childhood arrivals (DACA)." 2021. https://www.uscis.gov/humanitarian/humanitarian-parole/consideration-of-deferred-action-for-childhood-arrivals-daca.

U.S. Department of Justice. "Access to medical care for individuals with mobility disabilities." July 2010. https://www.ada.gov/medcare_mobility_ta/medcare_ta.htm.

UCLA Office of Information Technology. "Is COVID-19 a mass disabling event?" https://dcp.ucla.edu/covid-19-mass-disabling-event.

Ulloa, Jesus G., Omar Viramontes, Gery Ryan, Kenneth Wells, Melinda Maggard-Gibbons, and Gerardo Moreno. "Perceptual and structural facilitators and barriers to becoming a surgeon: A qualitative study of African-American and Latino surgeons." *Academic Medicine: Journal of the Association of American Medical Colleges* 93, no. 9 (2018): 1326.

Umberson, Debra. "Black deaths matter: Race, relationship loss, and effects on survivors." *Journal of Health and Social Behavior* 58, no. 4 (2017): 405–20.

Unger, Joseph M., Dawn L. Hershman, Cathee Till, Lori M. Minasian, Raymond U. Osarogiagbon, Mark E. Fleury, and Riha Vaidya. "'When offered to participate': A systematic review and meta-analysis of patient agreement to participate in cancer clinical trials." *Journal of the National Cancer Institute* 113, no. 3 (2021): 244–57.

UNHCR. "What is a refugee?" 2021. https://www.unhcr.org/en-us/what-is-a-refugee.html.

United Nations. "World migration report 2020." 2020. https://www.un.org/sites/un2.un.org/files/wmr_2020.pdf.

University of New Hampshire. "National survey of children's exposure to violence (NATSCEV I), final report." 2014. https://www.ojp.gov/pdffiles1/ojjdp/grants/248444.pdf.

Urquhart, Audrey, and Philippa Clarke. "US racial/ethnic disparities in childhood asthma emergent health care use: National Health Interview Survey, 2013–2015." *Journal of Asthma* 57, no. 5 (2020): 510–20.

Vargas, Edward D. "Immigration enforcement and mixed-status families: The effects of risk of deportation on Medicaid use." *Children and Youth Services Review* 57 (2015): 83–89.

Vargas, Edward D., and Maureen A. Pirog. "Mixed-status families and WIC uptake: The effects of risk of deportation on program use." *Social Science Quarterly* 97, no. 3 (2016): 555–72.

Varmus, Harold. "The new era in cancer research." *Science* 312, no. 5777 (2006): 1162–65.

Vaughn, Ivana A., Ellen L. Terry, Emily J. Bartley, Nancy Schaefer, and Roger B. Fillingim. "Racial-ethnic differences in osteoarthritis pain and disability: A meta-analysis." *The Journal of Pain* 20, no. 6 (2019): 629–44.

Vedam, Saraswathi, Kathrin Stoll, Marian MacDorman, Eugene Declercq, Renee Cramer, Melissa Cheyney, Timothy Fisher, Emma Butt, Y. Tony Yang, and Holly Powell Kennedy. "Mapping integration of midwives across the United States: Impact on access, equity, and outcomes." *PLoS One* 13, no. 2 (2018).

Velazquez Manana, Ana I., Ryan Leibrandt, and Narjust Duma. "Trainee and workforce diversity in hematology and oncology: Ten years later what has changed?" *Journal of Clinical Oncology* (2020): 11000.

Venters, Homer D., and Allen S. Keller. "The immigration detention health plan: An acute care model for a chronic care population." *Journal of Health Care for the Poor and Underserved* 20, no. 4 (2009): 951–57.

Venters, Homer D., Mary Foote, and Allen S. Keller. "Medical advocacy on behalf of detained immigrants." *Journal of Immigrant and Minority Health* 13, no. 3 (2011): 625–28.

Viale, Pamela Hallquist. "The American Society of Clinical Oncology reports on the state of cancer care in America: 2017." *Journal of the Advanced Practitioner in Oncology* 8, no. 5 (2017): 458.

Vidal-ALaball, Josep, Ruthy Acosta-Roja, Nuria Pastor Hernández, Unai Sanchez Luque, Danielle Morrison, Silvia Narejos Pérez, Jesús Perez-Llano, Angels Salvador Vèrges, and Francesc López Seguí. "Telemedicine in the face of the COVID-19 pandemic." *Atencion Primaria* 52, no. 6 (2020): 418–22.

Vokinger, Kerstin N., Thomas J. Hwang, Thomas Grischott, Sophie Reichert, Ariadna Tibau, Thomas Rosemann, and Aaron S. Kesselheim. "Prices and clinical benefit of cancer drugs in the USA and Europe: A cost–benefit analysis." *The Lancet Oncology* 21, no. 5 (2020): 664–70.

von Werthern, Martha, Katy Robjant, Zoe Chui, Rachel Schon, Livia Ottisova, Claire Mason, and Cornelius Katona. "The impact of immigration detention on mental health: A systematic review." *BMC Psychiatry* 18, no. 1 (2018): 1–19.

Walsemann, Katrina M., Annie Ro, and Gilbert C. Gee. "Trends in food insecurity among California residents from 2001 to 2011: Inequities at the intersection of immigration status and ethnicity." *Preventive Medicine* 105 (2017): 142–48.

Wang, Gary X., Heather R. Frank, Taruni S. Santanam, Erica Zeng, Madhulika Vulimiri, Mark McClellan, and Charlene A. Wong. "Pediatric accountable health communities: Insights on needed capabilities and potential solutions." *Healthcare* 8, no. 4 (2020): 100481.

Ward, T. J. *Black physicians in the Jim Crow South*. Fayetteville, AR: University of Arkansas Press, 2003.

Washington, H. "Profitable wonders: Antebellum medical experimentation with slaves and freedmen." In *Medical Apartheid: The dark history of medical experimentation on Black Americans from colonial times to the present*. New York: Doubleday, 2006.

Waxman, Matthew A., and M. Andrew Levitt. "Are diagnostic testing and admission rates higher in non-English-speaking versus English-speaking patients in the emergency department?" *Annals of emergency medicine* 36, no. 5 (2000): 456–61.

Wear, Delese, and Lois LaCivita Nixon. "The spirit catches you and you fall down: A Hmong child, her American doctors, and the collision of two cultures: [Commentary]." *Academic Medicine* 76, no. 6 (2001): 620.

Weaver, Garrett M., and W. James Gauderman. "Traffic-related pollutants: Exposure and health effects among Hispanic children." *American Journal of Epidemiology* 187, no. 1 (2018): 45–52.

Weeks, Elizabeth. "Medicalization of rural poverty: Challenges for access." *The Journal of Law, Medicine & Ethics* 46, no. 3 (2018): 651–57.

Weist, Mark D., Olga M. Acosta, and Eric A. Youngstrom. "Predictors of violence exposure among inner-city youth." *Journal of Clinical Child Psychology* 30, no. 2 (2001): 187–98.

White, Alexandre I. R. "Historical linkages: Epidemic threat, economic risk, and xenophobia." *The Lancet* 395, no. 10232 (2020): 1250–51.

White, K., J. S. Haas, and D. R. Williams. "Elucidating the role of place in health care disparities: The example of racial/ethnic residential segregation." *Health Services Research* 47, no. 3 (2012): 1278–99.

White, Kellee, Jennifer S. Haas, and David R. Williams. "Elucidating the role of place in health care disparities: Rhe example of racial/ethnic residential segregation." *Health Services Research* 47, no. 3 (2012): 1278–99.

Wijesekera, Thilan P., Margeum Kim, Edward Z. Moore, Olav Sorenson, and David A. Ross. "All other things being equal: Exploring racial and gender disparities in medical school honor society induction." *Academic Medicine* 94, no. 4 (2019): 562–69.

Wildeman, Christopher. "Parental imprisonment, the prison boom, and the concentration of childhood disadvantage." *Demography* 46, no. 2 (2009): 265–80.

Wiley, L. F., and G. W. Matthews. "Health care system transformation and integration: A call to action for public health." *The Journal of Law, Medicine & Ethics* 45, No. 1 Supplement (2017): 94–97.

Wilkie, Ross, Abdelouahid Tajar, and John McBeth. "The onset of widespread musculoskeletal pain is associated with a decrease in healthy ageing in older people: A population-based prospective study." *PLoS One* 8, no. 3 (2013): e59858.

Willen, Sarah S., Michael Knipper, César E. Abadía-Barrero, and Nadav Davidovitch. "Syndemic vulnerability and the right to health." *The Lancet* 389, no. 10072 (2017): 964–77.

Williams, Linda Faye. *Constraint of race: Legacies of white skin privilege in America.* University Park, PA: Penn State Press, 2010.

Williams, Walter W., Peng-Jun Lu, Alissa O'Halloran, David K. Kim, Lisa A. Grohskopf, Tamara Pilishvili, Tami H. Skoff, et al. "Surveillance of vaccination coverage among adult populations—United States, 2014." *Morbidity and Mortality Weekly Report: Surveillance Summaries* 65, no. 1 (2016): 1–36.

Wilson, Yolonda, Amina White, Akilah Jefferson, and Marion Danis. "Intersectionality in clinical medicine: The need for a conceptual framework." *The American Journal of Bioethics* 19, no. 2 (2019): 8–19.

Wingfield, Adia Harvey. *Flatlining: Race, work, and health care in the new economy.* Berkeley, CA: University of California Press, 2019.

Wong, Alice (Ed.). *Disability visibility: First-person stories from the twenty-first century.* New York: Vintage, 2020.

Wong, Tom, Sebastian Bonilla, and Anna Coleman. "Seeking asylum: Part 1." U.S. Immigration Policy Center, August 28, 2019. https://usipc.ucsd.edu/publications/usipc-seeking-asylum-part-1-final.pdf.

Wong, Warren. "How to honor patients' lived experience: Learning from community based organizations." July 18, 2017. http://www.ihi.org/communities/blogs/how -to-honor-patients-lived-experience-learning-from-community-based-organizations.

Wood, Evan, Thomas Kerr, J. Stoltz, Z. Qui, R. Zhang, J. S. G. Montaner, and M. W. Tyndall. "Prevalence and correlates of hepatitis C infection among users of North America's first medically supervised safer injection facility." *Public Health* 119, no. 12 (2005): 1111–15.

Woolf, Steven H., and Paula Braveman. "Where health disparities begin: The role of social and economic determinants—and why current policies may make matters worse." *Health Affairs* 30, no. 10 (2011): 1852–59.

World Health Organization. "WHO guidelines on ethical issues in public health surveillance." 2017. https://apps.who.int/iris/bitstream/handle/10665/255721 /9789241512657-eng.pdf.

Yeheskel, Ariel, and Shail Rawal. "Exploring the 'patient experience' of individuals with limited English proficiency: A scoping review." *Journal of Immigrant and Minority Health* 21, no. 4 (2019): 853–78.

Yoshikawa, Hirokazu, and Ariel Kalil. "The effects of parental undocumented status on the developmental contexts of young children in immigrant families." *Child Development Perspectives* 5, no. 4 (2011): 291–97.

Young, Daniel, and Elizabeth Edwards. "Telehealth and disability: Challenges and opportunities for care." National Health Law Program, May 6, 2020. https://healthlaw .org/telehealth-and-disability-challenges-and-opportunities-for-care/.

Yule, Kristen, Jessica Houston, and John Grych. "Resilience in children exposed to violence: A meta-analysis of protective factors across ecological contexts." *Clinical Child and Family Psychology Review* 22, no. 3 (2019): 406–31.

Zhang, Sarah. "The long history of discrimination in pain medicine." *The Atlantic*, 2017.

Zimmer, Zachary, and Anna Zajacova. "Persistent, consistent, and extensive: The trend of increasing pain prevalence in older Americans." *The Journals of Gerontology: Series B* 75, no. 2 (2020): 436–47.

# Index

Page references for figures are italicized

# About the Editor

**Zackary Berger**, MD, PhD, is a primary care physician and bioethicist at the Johns Hopkins School of Medicine and Johns Hopkins Berman Institute of Bioethics in Baltimore, Maryland. He has published widely in the scholarly literature and for the lay public on making healthcare a reflection of the health needs of ordinary people and communities.

# About the Contributors

**Inas Abuali**, MD, FACP, is a hematologist oncologist at Massachusetts General Hospital and instructor at Harvard Medical School.

**Dr. Tamara A. Baker**, PhD, is a professor in the Department of Psychiatry at the University of North Carolina at Chapel Hill in the School of Medicine. Her background in gerontology, psychology, and biobehavioral health has evolved into an active research agenda that focuses on understanding the behavioral and psychosocial predictors and outcomes of chronic pain and pain and symptom management among older adults from historically marginalized populations.

**Jennifer L. Barton**, MD, MCR, is the rheumatology section chief at the VA Portland Health Care System and associate professor of medicine, Oregon Health and Science University. Her research focuses on patient-clinician communication and the rheumatic diseases.

**Staja "Star" Q. Booker**, PhD, RN, is an assistant professor at the University of Florida. She is currently studying movement-evoked pain and functional performance in older adults with knee osteoarthritis and is passionate about resolving and philosophizing about pain disparities in older adults. As a registered nurse/nurse scientist, her work has impacted nurses' practice of pain assessment and management.

**Laura Calloway** is a PhD student studying computer security and public health at Indiana University Bloomington.

**Pooja Chandrashekar** is an MD/MBA student at Harvard Medical School and Harvard Business School.

**Briana Christophers** is an MD-PhD student training in cell and developmental biology at the Weill Cornell/Rockefeller/Sloan Kettering Tri-Institutional MD-PhD program in New York City. Her aim is to pursue an academic career as a physician-scientist in pediatrics, bringing social justice to the lab bench and hospital bedside.

**Don S. Dizon** is a medical oncologist in Providence and professor of medicine at Brown University. He specializes in the treatment of pelvic cancers and in the survivorship issues of people after a cancer diagnosis. He has a particular interest in disparities, especially as it relates to access and outcomes involving the LGBTQ+ community.

**Narjust Duma** is the associate director of the Cancer Care Equity Program at Dana-Farber Cancer Institute and a faculty member at Harvard Medical School. Her clinical practice focuses on the care of women with lung cancer. Duma's research team focuses on women with lung cancer, cancer health disparities, and social justice issues affecting medical education.

**Stefanie Gillson** is a child and adolescent fellow at the Yale Child Study Center. She graduated from general and public psychiatry residency at Yale University in 2021 where she was a chief resident of Diversity and Inclusion. She is an American Psychiatric Association SAMHSA minority fellow and an institute scholar at the Johns Hopkins Center for American Indian Health where she focuses on developing community-based initiatives to address mental health disparities among Indigenous populations through a historical and contemporary lens. She is a member of the Association of American Indian Physicians where she actively recruits Indigenous youth into the medical field.

**Danielle S. Jackson** is at the Department of Psychiatry, Rutgers-Robert Wood Johnson Medical School.

**Sachin Jain**, MD, MBA, is president and chief executive officer of SCAN Group and Health Plan.

**Mary Janevic** is an associate research scientist in Health Behavior/Health Education at the University of Michigan School of Public Health. Her research centers around promoting healthy aging, particularly in underserved populations, using community-engaged research methods. A major focus of her work is disparities in chronic pain and developing chronic pain self-management interventions for vulnerable populations. Related areas of interest are community health workers, mobile health solutions for chronic pain management, and the role of pets in coping with chronic pain.

**Ayana Jordan**, MD, PhD, is an addiction psychiatrist and the Barbara Wilson Associate Professor of Psychiatry in the Department of Psychiatry at NYU Grossman School of Medicine and Pillar Lead for the Community Engagement in the NYU Langone Institute for Excellence in Health Equity.

**David M. Keller**, MD, FAAP, is professor of pediatrics, University of Colorado, School of Medicine and vice chair, Clinical Strategy and Transformation| Department of Pediatrics, Children's Hospital Colorado.

**Hal Kronsberg**, MD, is assistant professor, Johns Hopkins School of Medicine Department of Psychiatry and Behavior Sciences, psychiatrist for Johns Hopkins Bayview Medical Center's Child Mobile Treatment Team and Expanded School-Based Mental Health Program, and program director, Johns Hopkins School of Medicine Child and Adolescent Psychiatry Fellowship.

**Riordan Ledgerwood**, MD, is a general pediatrician and assistant professor in the Department of Pediatrics, Uniformed Services University of the Health Sciences in Bethesda, Maryland.

**Maru Lozano** is a professional translator, workshop facilitator, and interpreter. She has acquired decades of successful results curating and sharing educational materials with low-literacy families for clients in the nonprofit, healthcare, and education sectors. Currently she serves as corporate communications translation manager at AltaMed.

**Max Jordan Nguemeni Tiako**, MD, MS, is a resident physician in internal medicine (primary care) at Brigham and Women's Hospital in Boston, Massachusetts.

**Edwin Nieblas-Bedolla**, MPH, is currently a medical student at the University of Washington School of Medicine. His academic interests include global neurosurgery, neuro-oncology, health disparities, immigrant health, and medical education.

**Shayla Partridge** is a family nurse practitioner student at Yale School of Nursing.

**Maria C. Mora Pinzon** is board certified in preventive medicine and public health and is an assistant Scientist with the Wisconsin Alzheimer's Institute and theCommunity Academic Aging Research Network at the University of Wisconsin–Madison.

**Arrianna Marie Planey** is an assistant professor in the Department of Health Policy and Management in the University of North Carolina Gillings School of Global Public Health and a fellow in the Cecil G. Sheps Center for Health Services Research. She is a health/medical geographer with expertise in measuring and conceptualizing health care access, health and healthcare equity, and spatial epidemiology. Her research and teaching focuses include the application of spatial analytic/statistical/epidemiologic methods to study interactions between health(care) policies, healthcare access and utilization and underlying, population-level health inequities, and identify points of intervention at structural- and system-levels.

**Rheanna Platt** is an assistant professor in the Department of Psychiatry and Behavioral Sciences at the Johns Hopkins University School of Medicine and a Child and Adolescent Psychiatrist with the Johns Hopkins Bayview Medical Center's Community Psychiatry Program.

**Dr. Altaf Saadi** is a general academic neurologist at Massachusetts General Hospital and instructor of neurology at Harvard Medical School. She is also the associate director of the Massachusetts General Asylum Clinic and medical expert for Physicians for Human Rights.

**Jennifer Siegel**, MD, is assistant professor of medicine at Boston University School of Medicine. She serves as medical director at the Center for Transgender Medicine and Surgery, as well as associate program director of the Internal Medicine Residency Program, both at Boston Medical Center.

**Nicholas Stienstra**, MD, is a practicing rheumatologist in Monterey, California, where he is also engaged in developing and promoting strategies to improve healthcare access and patient-centered high-quality care.

**Carl G. Streed Jr.**, MD, MPH, FACP, is assistant professor of medicine at Boston University School of Medicine and research lead in the Center for Transgender Medicine and Surgery at Boston Medical Center.

**Kimberly L. Sue** is a physician-anthropologist, author, and the medical director of the National Harm Reduction Coalition, a national advocacy and capacity-building organization that promotes the health and dignity of individuals and communities impacted by drug use and the racialized War on Drugs. She is a practicing board certified internal medicine physician and an assistant professor of medicine at Yale School of Medicine.

**Ben Wormser**, MD, MPH, is a general pediatrician and public health practitioner. He previously served as a General Academic Pediatrics Fellow at Johns Hopkins School of Medicine and now works in public health.